Raised on a ranch in Colorado, J.R. Daeschner won a Fulbright Scholarship to Latin America after university and gained firsthand experience of carnival, cholera and military coups. Between blackouts and water shortages, he also freelanced for the *New York Times*. He later worked on Fleet Street and Wall Street, with stints in Peru, Mexico and Brazil before settling in Britain. Now 34, he has lived in the UK for most of the past decade. His coverage of subjects ranging from male escorts and estuary English to the controversial World Economic Forum has been published on both sides of the Atlantic, from *The Times* to the *International Herald Tribune*. His humiliating shin-kicking debut was broadcast to the world by CNN.

D1099853

J.R. AND THE QUEEN OF BOGS.

TRUE BRITS

A TOUR OF TWENTY-FIRST-CENTURY BRITAIN
IN ALL ITS BOG-SNORKELLING, GURNING,
AND CHEESE-ROLLING GLORY

J.R. DAESCHNER

For Dominique and Nina

'There is no imbecility nor barbarity that human beings will not practise and even exalt, so long as it be sanctified by custom.'

Townie travel writer H.J. Massingham, on shin kicking

'It's very important to keep our traditions going in this country – our history. Once you've lost your history, you've lost your identity. You become like anybody, don't ya.'

West Country farmer David Hardwick, on cheese rolling

Contents

Calendar of Events

January

Mob Football, Haxey, North Lincolnshire (January 6th,
or 5th if 6th is a Sunday)

April

Hare Pie Scramble/Bottle Kicking, Hallaton, Leicester
(Easter Monday)

May

May Day in Padstow, Cornwall and Minehead, Somerset (May 1st)
Hot Pennies Tradition/Beating the Bounds, Oxford and London
(Ascension Day – 40 days after Easter – usually in May)
Cheese Rolling, Brockworth, Gloucestershire
(last Bank Holiday Monday in May)
Randwick Wap, Randwick, Gloucester
(first Sunday in May, and the following Saturday)
St Briavels Bread and Cheese Dole, St Briavels, Gloucestershire
(Whit Sunday – usually the last Bank Holiday weekend in May)

June

Shin Kicking and the Cotsworld Olimpicks, Chipping Campden,
Gloucestershire (the Friday after the last May Bank Holiday)

July

Swan Upping, Staines to Oxford (Mid-July)

August
Burry Man, South Queensferry, Scotland
(the second Friday after the first Thursday in August)
Bog Snorkelling, Llanwrtyd Wells, Powys (August Bank Holiday)

September
Horn Dance, Abbots Bromley, Staffordshire
(the Monday after the first Sunday following September 4th)

October
Quit Rents/Faggot Cutting, London
(usually, but not always, the second Wednesday in October)

November
Burning the Pope, Lewes, Sussex
(November 5th, or 4th if 5th is a Sunday)

December/January
Darkie Day, Padstow, Cornwall (Boxing Day and New Year's Day)

Regions Featured

London (Faggot Cutting, Sheriff Pricking and Coin Counting in the City)

Home Counties (Pope Burning in Lewes, East Sussex)
Nearest towns/cities: Brighton, Gatwick, Eastbourne

West Country (Darkie Day/May Day in Padstow, Cornwall)
(Cheese Rolling near Brockworth, Gloucestershire)
Nearest towns/cities for Darkie Day: Truro, Newquay, Wadebridge
Nearest towns/cities for Cheese Rolling: Gloucester, Cheltenham

The Cotswolds (Shin Kicking in Chipping Campden, Gloucestershire)
Nearest towns/cities: Stratford, Evesham, Birmingham

**M&S Oxford (Beating the Bounds and Hot Penny Throwing)

The Midlands (Horn Dancing in Abbots Bromley, Staffordshire)
Nearest towns/cities: Burton, Lichfield, Stafford, Uttoxeter

The Northwest/Lake District
(Gurning in Egremont, West Cumbria)
Nearest towns/cities: Carlisle, Keswick, Kendal,
Cockermouth, Barrow

The North/Northeast (Mob Football in Haxey,
North Lincolnshire)
Nearest towns/cities: Sheffield, Doncaster, Scunthorpe, Brigg

Other mob football games mentioned: Alnwick, Northumberland;
Ashbourne and Derby, Derbyshire; Corfe, Dorset; Columb Major,
Cornwall; Sedgefield, Co. Durham; Atherstone, Warwickshire;
Hallaton, Leicestershire; Jedburgh, Scotland; Kirkwall, Orkney
Islands

Scotland (Burry Man in South Queensferry,
next to the Forth Bridge)
Nearest towns/cities: Edinburgh, Glasgow

Wales (Bog Snorkelling in Llanwrtyd Wells, Powys)
Nearest towns/cities: Hay on Wye, Llandrindod, Cardiff, Newport

Northern Ireland (Pope Burning)
Ian Paisley and Orangemen in the Home Counties ('a little bit of
Ulster in London's backyard')

Ireland (Bog Snorkelling)
World Bog Snorkelling champ is from Dublin; main character in
True Brits is the Female Irish Bog Snorkelling champ from
Co. Kerry, who lives just 18 inches above bog level

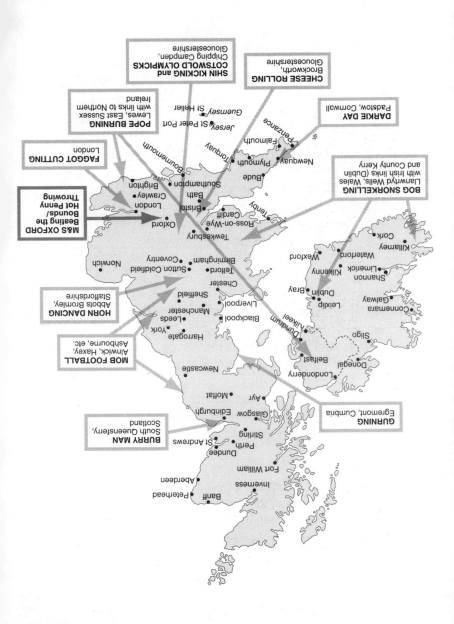

THE CHRISTIANS ARE BACK: The Revd Hugh Lee leads his flock through M&S for its annual blessing.

BEATING THE BOUNDS IN M&S

THANK YOU FOR YOUR CUSTOM

Special to Marks and Spencer

On any given day, the staff at Marks and Spencer has to deal with enquiries ranging from 'Excuse me, do you do Halibut and King Prawn Brochettes with Olive-Oil-and-Lemon-Juice-Dressed Linguini?' (*Yes, ma'am, but of course*) to 'Can I try on these underpants before buying them?' (*No, sir, definitely not*). Judging from the worried look on the assistant's face at the M&S in Oxford, my query falls nearer the strange-men-and-underpants end of the spectrum.

'Has the Beating of the Bounds procession passed through yet?'

'No, it hasn't,' she replies, her eyes saying, *Humour the mad American*.

Before she can call security, though, my salvation arrives in the form of a robed vicar flanked by fifty choristers and pensioners, all carrying big sticks and marching in from the rear, through the branded St. Michael products past the wine, juice and dairy sections, up the fruit aisle, and beyond the fresh flowers and greeting cards to congregate near the bikinis in the women's section, where a brass cross marks the carpet in front of the till. The customers in the queue don't know what to do: some smile; others pretend not to notice (*If I don't see it, it's not embarrassing*). Given the size of the silver cross borne by one of the choristers, and the fact that all the parishioners are armed with long bamboo rods, the bystanders could be forgiven for thinking that M&S has been invaded by a revivalist faction of jackboot Anglicans: *The Christians are back – and this time, no more Mr Nice Guy*. Indeed, the sight of them trooping through downtown Oxford this fine April morning has struck fear into the hearts of some wannabe sinners, such as the dreadlocked girl in combat trousers who ran down the street screaming 'Aaaaah! Run away from Jesus!'

In reality, the bespectacled vicar and his smiling flock are upholding an ancient tradition that was once common throughout Britain but now survives in only a handful of places. Every Ascension Day – that's forty days after Easter – the members of St Michael at the North Gate traipse through Oxford's shopping precinct in search of the hard-to-find crosses that define the boundaries of their parish. St Michael's annual recce was first recorded in 1428, but it may very well predate that. The church's Saxon tower – billed as the oldest building in Oxford – formed part of the original wall that defended the town against Viking invaders. Long before the era of reliable maps, let alone Ordnance Surveys, the priests would march the locals around the parish to make sure they knew their boundaries and, just as importantly, to keep those buggers from the parish next door from stealing their turf. Learning one's limits was so important, in fact, that in some places youngsters had the mental map beaten into them. Choirboys' heads or buttocks would be 'bumped' against the boundary stones – a custom practised to this day in parts of the West Country and Wales (reinforcing any number of unfortunate stereotypes). In London, the clerics of All Hallows by the Tower still travel by boat to the middle of the Thames, where they hold a choirboy upside down so that he can smack the water with his rod. Meanwhile, the congregation sings a special 'Beating Hymn' on the river bank, the futuristic bubble of the new City Hall in the distance. In genteel Oxford, though, the parishioners limit their thrashing to the boundary stones, shouting 'Mark! Mark! Mark!' in time with their blows. 'At one stage, we *beat* the choirboys as well as the stones, because that way they'd remember better,' laughs the Revd Hugh Lee. 'But that's no longer politically correct!'

However, Beating the Bounds does culminate in one decidedly non-PC custom: Hot Penny Throwing at Oxford University, an annual event that belies any guff about 'classless Britain'. Around noon, St Michael's parishioners finish their trek at Lincoln College, the church's patron, which hosts a special lunch for the occasion. Having checked their canes at the door, the boundary beaters file past the small quad into the college's oak-panelled hall. Surrounded by oil paintings of John Wesley and other Lincoln old boys (Dr Seuss and John le Carré have yet to find a place on the walls), the parishioners feast on pork pie, cheese and watercress salad, topped off with specially brewed 'ivy beer' and jam doughnuts. Outside, Lincoln's students kill time by offering mugs of the vine-steeped concoction to their visiting rivals from Brasenose next door. This boozy peace-offering supposedly harks back to the days of real Town vs. Gown violence, when Lincoln's porter refused to open the door to a Brasenose man being chased by a mob; the student subsequently met a sticky end.

In his memory, the narrow 'Needle's Eye' passageway between the two colleges is still opened once a year, on Ascension Day, so that the students from Brasenose can vicariously get their own back by watching their Lincoln counterparts pelt townie schoolkids with hot pennies. The uni students climb the forty-foot tower overlooking the quad and fling burning two-pence projectiles at children who have been bussed in from a local comprehensive especially for the occasion. Back in the bad old days, this type of sado-charity was widespread (see page 205). According to college lore, Lincoln's Hot Pennies tradition began after students got fed up with having to run the gauntlet of beggars outside. Instead, they decided to bring in the urchins to have some fun at their expense, gleefully watching as they burned their fingers trying to retrieve the coins. Nowadays, the kids avoid injury by wearing gloves, though occasionally stray pennies get trapped between cloth and skin. Still, the kiddies don't seem to mind being used for target practice – after all, they get a free lunch and a few pence out of it. Lincoln's students also have a high time – even the college chaplain joins in the fun – though a few of these sons and daughters of barristers, accountants and the odd shop clerk seem shaken by the experience, sensing that they've reverted to type. 'It just brings something out in you that . . . you hardly recognise,' confesses on bemused student.

At this stage, though, ivy beer and burning pennies are still eight stones away from Marks and Spencer, which is stop no. 21 on the boundary beaters' itinerary. In a town stuffed to its spires with guided tours, this must surely be the most unorthodox going, revealing parts of Oxford that you'd rather not see – bike sheds coated in bird droppings, back alleys reeking of rotting food – while providing unique perspectives on old landmarks, such as the Sheldonian Theatre, the Bodleian Library, the Town Hall and the college quads. Some of the boundary markers have been cut into the cornerstones of buildings, while others are simply scratched onto a wall each year with a piece of chalk. Many are hidden away in the unlikeliest places, including the back room of Bar Oz, next to a photo of a rugby scrum bearing the legend: AUSSIE BUMS. On each marker, the Revd Lee scribbles the year and the church's initials, S M N G, in the quadrants of the cross. Then he raises his voice and offers up a blessing tailored to the setting of that particular stone, praying for cyclists, lawyers and even politicians, proving that God's love truly knows no bounds. At that point, the parishioners step in and thrash the marker with their bamboo canes, crying *'Mahk! Mahk! Mahk!'* like demented seagulls. In their caning frenzy, overexcited beaters sometimes accidentally whack one of their companions on the head or, in Marks and Spencer, knock a hand off a mannequin.

The old boundary stone in M&S sits unmolested in a glass case next to the lifts, having been moved in 1976 to make way for the store. However, the metal-floor plaque still marks its original location. For a time this new brass cross was situated in the lingerie section, but a tactful reshuffle has saved the faithful of St Michael's from having to beat their sticks amid bras and knickers.

The Revd Lee traces the cross on the floor and says: 'Almighty God, bless all those who shop here and those who work here, as we mark this, our boundary stone, in the name of the Father and of the Son and of the Holy Spirit. Amen.'

With that, the canes clatter against the metal – putting the 'Marks' into Marks and Sparks – and the merry parishioners take the escalator to the staff canteen. After a customary break for tea and biscuits, and three cheers for their hosts, they file out of the store into the sunshine. The sign over the door thanks them for shopping at Marks and Spencer. But not so long ago, it read simply – and aptly enough: THANK YOU FOR YOUR CUSTOM.

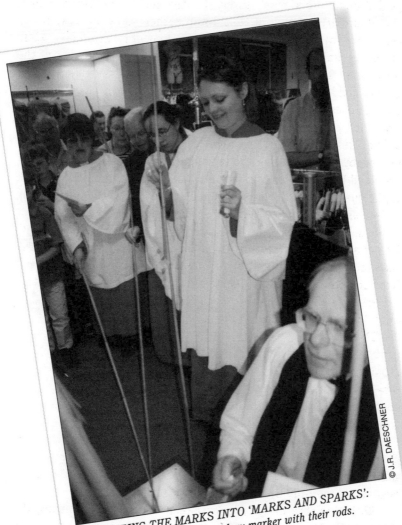

PUTTING THE MARKS INTO 'MARKS AND SPARKS':
Choristers tap the boundary marker with their rods.

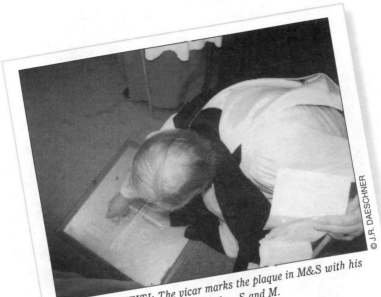

HOLY GRAFFITI: The vicar marks the plaque in M&S with his church's initials – S and M.

PENNIES FROM HELL: Kids from a local comprehensive await the hail of hot pennies.

A (PENNY) TOSSER: An Oxford student perfects his wrist action.

NO BURNT FINGERS: Nowadays, the schoolkids wear gloves to pick up the hot pennies.

© J.R. DAESCHNER

MAHK! MAHK! MAHK!: *The boundary beaters sour*
stone with their

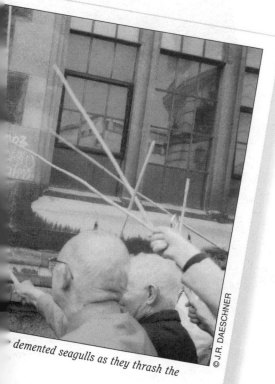

demented seagulls as they thrash the

INTRODUCTION

A RELUCTANT ANGLOPHILE

What in the world is shin kicking?!

As an American who'd lived in Britain for some time, I thought I knew a thing or two about the country. But I'd never come across this centuries-old 'sport', which had to be one of the most painful and infuriating ever invented. I had to find out more.

I soon discovered that Britain has hundreds of lunatic acts enshrined as traditions; strange-named events like gurning . . . the Burry Man . . . bog snorkelling . . . and Darkie Day. With so many events to choose from, I had to narrow the field. So I devised a test in the form of a simple fill-in-the-blank question:

'It's boring here, so to liven things up, why don't we _____?'

a) heckle the village idiot
b) cover ourselves in cockleburs
c) chase a cheese down a cliff
d) snorkel through a bog
e) burn the Pope in effigy

If the resulting sentence sounded unfathomably bizarre, then that was an event for me. However, eccentricity alone wasn't enough.

Coming from the Land of Wilful Wackiness, I have an inherent dislike of attention-seekers doing stupid things to get on TV. Call me a snob, but the events I wrote about had to have pedigree. It's one thing to do something stupid once, or even several times. But to do it year after year, *for centuries*, that's 24-carat, world-class, Olympic-gold stupidity – at least, on the face of it.

In fact, many practices that seem strange now were once perfectly acceptable forms of entertainment and, possibly, religious ritual. The World Gurning Championship, for example, supposedly dates from 1267 and originated with mocking the village idiot. By modern standards, that would be cruel and inhumane; in an age of bear baiting and cock fighting, though, encouraging the mentally deranged to make asses of themselves in public would have been must-see entertainment, a medieval version of reality TV.

So why do seemingly sane people continue these customs in the twenty-first century?

'It's tradition, innit?' they'd shrug before prancing around with reindeer antlers, or being crushed in a mob football match, or carpeted with prickly green burrs. That self-evident statement reflects an old-fashioned sense of duty: after all, the British take pride in keeping up standards, and the English in particular have a reputation to maintain as the most eccentric people on the planet. No surprise, then, that most of Britain's offbeat traditions are concentrated in England, with a smattering in Wales and Scotland. (On the whole, the Scots seem too sensible to waste time on not-for-profit idiosyncrasies, while unfortunately for many outsiders, Welsh culture as a whole is, well, a little *weird*.) In a society that traditionally valued Conformity right up there with God, King/Queen and Country, eccentrics have long been the pet rebels, the social upstarts, the colourful characters in an otherwise grey existence who were too rich, too ornery, or simply too crazy to care what the neighbours would think. Their antics have provided a vicarious outlet for people living in mortal fear of embarrassment. As long as they don't try to upset the established order – like those bolshie Nonconformists who set sail for the New World – eccentrics are quietly tolerated and even secretly admired. All this is changing, of course, as Warhol's Theory of Ephemeral Fame has been converted into a popular notion that everyone has a God-given right to fifteen minutes of celebrity. Nevertheless, the British still harbour affection for genuine rebels, preferably those without a cause.

A chartered-accountant-cum-bog-snorkeller came as close as anyone to explaining this national inclination toward eccentricity: 'We're always trying to prove we're not boring.' For being a bore is possibly the worst social crime a British person could commit, followed closely by being 'embarrassing' or 'awkward'. You can be a lousy parent, a womaniser, a drunk, even a certified lunatic, but God help you if you're boring. Bore-a-phobia has sent thousands of well-bred Englishmen on marvellous adventures, trekking through jungles, sailing around the world, slogging to the North Pole and scaling Mount Everest. George Mallory famously said he was climbing the highest point on Earth 'because it is there'. In a more loquacious moment, he explained that 'to refuse the adventure is to run the risk of drying up like a pea in its shell'.

In other words: 'I didn't want to be a bore.'

Seriously though – and I hope without boring you – Britain's offbeat events have survived into the twenty-first century because they reinforce a sense of identity, community and continuity, particularly in times of change. When every language in the world has its equivalent of 'Do you want fries with that?', people take an inordinate pride in the local idiosyncrasies that distinguish them from a thousand other places: they're proud to be peculiar. What's more, they're prepared to go to extremes to maintain their traditions, often despite repeated attempts to stop them. The Cooper's Hill Cheese Roll may stem from a pagan ritual first recorded in the fourth century AD, and survived cheese rationing during World War Two. However, in 1998, modern safety regulations forced the event to be cancelled after dozens of people were injured the previous year. Nevertheless, the locals held their own clandestine cheese roll. For them, it was a question of freedom and identity, of honouring their forebears. Their unlikely rebellion provides a perfect example of British Bloody-mindedness. As one said, 'If you can't get drunk and chase a cheese down a hill, what's the point of being British?'

But exactly. You can trek through Amazonia in search of a Stone Age tribe – *Look! They don't wear clothes!* – but, for my money, you haven't lived until you've seen an Englishman, a Paragon of Civilisation, hurl himself down a suicidal hill after a cheese, all in the name of tradition. Not for nothing did the great photographer Henri Cartier-Bresson declare England 'the most exotic place in the world'.

In writing *True Brits*, I've repeatedly interviewed gurners, Pope burners, horn dancers and madmen, catching them in action more than once to track their careers over the years. I've taken part in these events to give you a feel for, say, shin kicking, and – in the case of bog snorkelling – a taste of what they're really like.* At times, the madness seemed contagious, and I became, well . . . *unbalanced*, crossing the line from bemused outsider to crazed participant. My wife had nightmares of me chasing her with a giant cheese. I began worrying that the birth of our firstborn would clash with bog snorkelling (and our second with Scotland's Burry Man). Although I met countless characters and visited many beautiful parts of Britain, I also travelled to areas that could be the setting for *Ye Olde Deliverance.* The Catholic priest at Lewes – the Home Counties town that ritually torches the Pope every November the Fifth – warned me that the locals might burn me in effigy as an 'Enemy of Bonfire'. 'This man is looking for trouble, digging up Bonfire lore,' he said, introducing me to a parishioner. 'He may very well be the first American to be burnt.'

So here's what they can put on my epitaph . . .

As the great-grandson of German and Swedish sodbusters, I'm not your typical Yank in the UK: I'm not here to trace my ancestors, I don't care about the royals (even if they *are* more German than English), I didn't grow up playing 'Ring-a-ring-o' Roses' (I thought 'atishoo' was 'a tissue') and I don't go weak at the knees when I hear a posh accent (where I come from, if a man talked like that, he'd get beat up). Although I did think my travels would inevitably

*To see and hear these events, visit *www.truebrits.tv*.

take me to Britain at some point – on a stopover, you understand – I never expected to live here. In retrospect, my ignorance was impressive, even by American standards. Though I was somehow savvy enough to pronounce Leicester as 'Lester' rather than, well, 'Leicester', I can't honestly say I knew enough – or cared enough – to pinpoint London on a map of the UK.

I wound up in Britain purely by chance, mainly because – and here's a class signifier for you – that's where the work was. (I applied for the job in the first place only because I'd fallen for a girl who loved London. But that's another story . . .) Having written a book about Peru just after university (and earned the tabloid nickname *El Sacaronchas*, or 'the Hive-Inflictor', because of my embarrassing revelations about the Peruvian elite), I landed a job at the last British news group on Fleet Street. If I had any expectations – and this shows how little I knew – I expected the English to be more American than my countrymen, at least in terms of efficiency (my half-baked hypothesis being that we must have inherited our can-do way of being from someone). My only preconceptions – stiff upper lip and all that – had been influenced by expressions I'd learned in Spain and Latin America: *el corte inglés* was a catch-phrase for style, and *hora inglesa* meant 'on time' as opposed to *hora latina*.

However, after a few weeks of working with men and women who rolled into the office wearing any old drabbery and don't-give-a-damn hair, I began to question England's lingering reputation as a fashion capital (this was years before 'Cool Britannia'; also, I worked with journalists, a notoriously unkempt breed). Having experienced Tube delays, late reports and postponed meetings, I decided that *hora inglesa* could mean anything from 'on time' to 'some time that week'. What's more, England wasn't as 'civilised' as I'd imagined ('civilised' being code among Brits abroad for 'a place with gin and tonic'). I had survived a terrorist-plagued Third World country, where car bombs blew out the windows in my flat not once but twice, only to move to England, where whole blocks of London were regularly cordoned off for security alerts, and a massive car bomb blew a hole in the heart of the City.

On Fleet Street, I was the token Yank in that year's intake of mostly Oxbridge trainees. A clash of cultures was inevitable. Ever since I was five, I'd worked in one way or another – no violins, please – and I found the trademark Oxbridge blend of arrogance and ignorance, of book learning rather than street smarts, mystifying and, frankly, obnoxious. To be fair, many if not most of the British seem to feel the same way. Also, at least one of my colleagues turned out to be a good friend; and our Devon-born editor, the late George Short, was a Great British Character, the kind of self-deprecating raconteur that every foreigner hopes to meet when visiting England: Falstaff, Rumpole of the Bailey and the archetypal Fleet Street Hack, all rolled into one.

Looking back, I can now recognise the early signs of my long-lasting fascination with Britain: I liked the clear-eyed view of the US from this side of the Atlantic (like me, many Brits criticise America's faults but admire its virtues), as well as the sense of having the best of both worlds (importing much of the American lifestyle without the full-blown materialism, while also enjoying European perqs without having to suffer French intellectuals). I admired the lush countryside and the beauty of a clear summer's day in Britain (which almost makes up for the other 364 days a year), along with the endless creativity of a people who invented not only the English language but also the toaster.

Even in those early days, I managed to meet some 'ordinary' people who did extraordinarily strange things: trainspotters who invested their life savings in a house next to a railway junction so they could pursue their hobby 24/7; a doctor who ran a clinic dealing 100%-pure smack so junkies could shoot up safely on the NHS; and hookers who worked in an Amsterdam-style red-light district in a terraced row in Birmingham (where I first heard the term 'gobblejob'). Apart from these escapades, though, I ended up stuck in an office in London, marvelling at the antics and attitudes of my highly privileged colleagues, whose idea of a good time was getting drunk and setting fire to restaurant menus or getting drunk and bending car aerials. Unfortunately, I didn't get to know the other 99.99 per cent of the country very well. No surprise, then, that I couldn't wait to leave.

To my consternation, after a stint in New York, I found myself back in the UK – it's what I get for marrying a London-lover. Determined to make the best of it this time, I resolved to get to know that fabled place: the 'real' Britain (another resolution – to learn the rules of cricket – quickly fell by the wayside). And that's when I stumbled across shin kicking and its oddball counterparts . . .

Amazingly, no one had written about these events in any depth. Sure, there were a few books listing dates and locations, but they amounted to little more than catalogues of eccentricity. Hardly a day goes by without the British media featuring some silly pastime practised by funny foreigners. Strangely, they all but ignore the spectacularly daft traditions in the UK. Regional newspapers tend to overlook the events altogether – or take a macabre delight in casualties, covering them with full-colour, if-it-bleeds-it-leads sensationalism: CHEESE CHASE CHAOS. As for national TV and newspapers, when they do deign to report these events, they're usually at best patronising and at worst ignorant, the underlying tone being: *these Little Englanders, Weird Welshmen and Crazed Scots – these* little *people – are a national embarrassment.*

I, however, believe the opposite: with few exceptions, these people and their pastimes are nothing less than national treasures. They reflect everything that makes Britain great – and, at times, not so great. It's all here: race and religion, the monarchy and the aristocracy, beer and whisky, football and rugby, bluebloods and lumpenproles, North versus South, Town versus Country, Pagan versus Christian, the Old versus the New, the UK versus the EU, and England versus Scotland versus Wales . . . as well as nuclear waste and the conflict in Northern Ireland.

So, instead of blowing millions of pounds on the unlikely prospect of Britain hosting the Olympics, 'team GB' should invest in getting homegrown sports like gurning and shin kicking recognised as Olympian events. And rather than deriding cheese rolling and bog snorkelling as national embarrassments, people around the UK should celebrate them as a manifestation of their national identity.

To put it in touchy-feely terms, the British should embrace their Inner Bog Snorkeler.

Having now spent most of my adult life in the UK, I've become something I never thought I'd be: an Anglophile, albeit a reluctant one. Besides the aforementioned attributes, I've come to admire many other aspects of my adopted home: the fact that in a dispute, your opponent doesn't whip out a gun and try to shoot you first before suing you; the absence of venomous snakes, man-eating sharks, killer spiders and other deadly creepy-crawlies (when I was a toddler, a rattlesnake once took shelter under my toy box); the diehard hope that next time – *please God, next time* – England will win the World Cup or the Euro final or even that crucial friendly against Botswana (while the Scots, Welsh and Irish cheer the opposing side) . . . Why, I've even come to appreciate the reliably unreliable weather, which I'm convinced most Britons secretly cherish: after all, it gives them something to talk about.

In short, I like to think that I approach my subject with the same mix of affection and scepticism with which many Brits view the US. However, you may feel otherwise – that I'm a stupid Yank who over-generalises without understanding, an ugly American who's all mouth and no mind, with a chip on his shoulder and a gap between his ears – *Who does he think he is, anyway?*

Should any of my work cause offence, I'd like to take this opportunity to shift the bla— I mean, blame it on my childhood. After all, I *am* American.

So here it is: a portrait of twenty-first-century, turn-of-the-millennium Britain – in all its gurning, bog-snorkelling and even Pope-burning glory.

CHAPTER ONE

THE MOTHER OF ALL FOOTBALL MATCHES

SWAYING THE HOOD IN HAXEY

FIGHTING CHEEK TO CHEEK. *The Sway collapses on Blandie and a boggin.*

© J.R. DAESCHNER

PART ONE:
MUD, BLOOD AND BOOZE

'Savour the pain, boys! Savour the pain!'

That's easy for him to say. Blandie's lying near the top of the heap, and I'm down at the bottom, squashed by a dozen or more bodies. *Don't squeal like a pig.* I can't move, and I'm vaguely aware of groans emanating from the bald heads and buzz cuts around me. My ribs are creaking and my heart, liver and assorted viscera are being squeezed to the bursting point. My torso feels like a giblet bag crammed up the rear of a butchered turkey. The coroner will open me up and find nothing but a creamy pâté inside, human *foie gras* in a skin-and-bones bag. Still, at least I'm conscious – not like that kid they pulled out of the crush a couple of collapses ago. The Lord of the Hood – distinguished by his flowery top hat – jumped in to stop the ruckus, brandishing his wicker wand of office and bellowing: 'MAN DOON! MAN DOON!' The teenager was ripped out of the tangle of bodies and laid flat on the field, unconscious, his eyes fluttering and head and hands twitching. Either he was knocked out or he fainted from the lack of oxygen. 'I hate it when that happens,' an official frowned, without any irony.

But that kind of thing is bound to happen in the Haxey Hood, an organised riot that takes place every year on 6 January, supposedly since the 1200s. Take as many as 300 men, get them liquored up, stick them on a claggy field in the freezing cold and throw a leather tube into the mob. This being England, the goal of the game is a no-brainer: to get back to a pub for more drinking. The problem is, there are four favourite locals in a one-mile radius – three in Haxey and one in the rival village of Westwoodside, on the other side of the field. And if the game finishes too soon, it would spoil the fun. So, instead of heading straight for the nearest boozer, the competitors end up pushing in opposite directions, creating a slowly rotating human hurricane capable of trampling anyone or anything in its path, demolishing walls, tearing down hedges and bursting through people's front doors. This asphyxiating crush of humanity, this juggernaut of flesh and bone, has an absurdly genteel name: the Sway. It may look like the world's biggest scrum – in fact, it is an ancestor of rugby and football – but there are crucial differences. 'It's not a scroom because you're standin' up,' Blandie had explained in the pub. 'If you were bent over, you'd snap your neck.'

James Bland happened to be the first person I met in Haxey last year. We were crushed up against the bar in the pre-match pub-crawl – the pre-Sway Sway, so to speak. I didn't know it at the time, but I was standing next to a living legend, one of the hard nuts – or were they just nuts? – who stayed in the middle all day, their hands clamped to the Hood as they fought off rivals. James immediately stood out. Not because of his ginger mullet – short on top and wispy down the back – or his hooped earrings, but because of his goatee: a half-goatee, actually, one side of his face bare and the other carpeted with red whiskers. Not to be outdone, his friend had shaved a big H into the top of his head. They had groomed themselves especially for the occasion.

And they weren't the only ones. The two main officials, the Lord of the Hood and the Chief Boggin, wore black ties and red hunting jackets, as well as fetchingly floral top hats with tall pheasant feathers sticking out. The Fool had a blackened face with smears of colour on it, plus a bowler hat and a suit of rags, while the ten other boggins were dressed in scarlet sweatshirts with their jeans tucked into their socks in preparation for the mother of all football matches. For the time being, though, they were drinking and singing in boozers so crowded it was almost impossible to get to the bar.

Truth be told, I didn't think much of Haxey at first. Tucked in a misty corner of North Lincolnshire, right next to Yorkshire and Nottinghamshire, it was surrounded by towns and villages with names so miserable they must have been inflicted on purpose:

*Scun*thorpe, *Scroo*by, *Grim*sby, *Goole*. Maybe the Saxons thought that if they gave them ugly names, the Vikings wouldn't bother pillaging them. Haxey was a long, thin row of redbrick buildings that didn't seem to have any real beginning or end. The surrounding land – at least what you could see through the mist – was brutally flat: reclaimed marshland from the days when the area was an island, the Isle of Axholme. The Hood took place on what the locals called a hill, but Haxey Field looked pretty flat to me. The weather didn't help, either. Apart from the mist and patches of snow, the sky was an industrial, boiler-room grey. A half hour before the match, just as everyone was coming out of the pub for the Fool's Speech, a freezing drizzle completed the setting. The flat wasteland . . . the all-conquering mist and cold . . . the seemingly pointless strife: this was Sartre and Beckett territory, relocated to the North of England.

In fairness to Haxey, though, I was profoundly depressed at the time. For more years than I cared to count, I'd been sneaking away on weekends and spending precious holiday time in the backwaters of Britain, living a double life as a weekday wage-slave and a weekend shin kicker. Only my family and a few friends knew my secret. It wasn't the kind of thing you talked about in polite company; not in professional North London, at least. Once I'd gathered enough material, I quit the day job, remortgaged the flat and took a year off to finish my book. 'That's a brave move,' an ex-colleague said, 'especially for someone with a child.' The subtext was clear – by 'brave' he meant 'stupid' and possibly 'irresponsible'. More than a year later, I was facing ruin and ridicule. 'See that guy?' people would jeer. 'He bet his house on bog snorkelling!'

All that was the mental distortion, the hissing white noise warping my perceptions, when I first saw Haxey and the Hood. On the rare occasions that it is covered by the media, the Hood is hyped as being ultraviolent; but it isn't so much violent as . . . ultrasurreal – gloriously, profoundly absurd: a bizarre crush with no apparent reason for being. Dozens of men risk hypothermia to push and shove each other, arging and barging, hurling and burling, hubbing and bubbing in the mud and manure, making primal noises as they try to herd the slow-moving stampede across the field. The thing is, you can't even see the Hood, the object of all the grunting and shunting. In rugby and football, at least the ball is passed and kicked. Not so the Hood. A leather cylinder, it quickly disappears in the crush to resurface again only at the end. In fact, some years it has disappeared altogether – in the chaos of the Sway, the men didn't realise until it was too late that the Hood had actually been stolen.

Rather than a piece of leather, the men appear to be tussling over a boiling cauldron. Steam billows from the centre of the mob, the combined body heat vaporising in the cold. It takes nearly two hours for the writhing mass of humanity to cover 200 yards, mainly because it keeps keeling over in the mud. And when the Sway collapses, it takes a while for the officials to untangle the limbs and unpick the carnage. You'd get a similar effect if you shoved the men into a dumpster, lifted them fifty feet into the air, and then tipped them onto the ground. Spectators can get as close to the action as they dare – there are no sidelines or boundaries – and the wide-open field makes the spectacle look all the more surreal, like an urban commuter crush transplanted to the countryside, only without any obvious reason for the rough-and-tumble. The men are surrounded by acres of empty space; if they wanted to, they could stop and quietly disperse, without any need for crushing each other.

At one point, the players have to negotiate a muddy ledge onto a lower section of the field. The drop's only eight inches, but it might as well be eighty feet: there's no way the Sway can go down it without falling over. The mud around the ledge is unbelievably sticky, apparently a mix of earth, clay and superglue, so that the men's legs get locked in the mire while people are still pushing from the outside in both directions. Inevitably, the Sway collapses over the dividing line, bodies sprawled on both sides. After much negotiation, the boggins break the stalemate by hoisting the Hood – or rather, the men attached to the Hood – past the breaking point. Then it falls over again. A little guy is ripped out of the casualties and hauled off, his legs dragging in the mud. The boggins drop his limp body on the field. He's passed out, coated in mud except where his shirt's been pulled up, exposing the white, fish-belly skin of his stomach. An ambulance worker huddles over him, cocking his head to get some air into his lungs. Eventually, the guy's eyelids flutter to life, and he staggers to his feet like a discombobulated wino straight from the gutter. His hair is spiked and matted around his skull, his clothes are rumpled helter-skelter and his eyeballs are red and rolling in different directions. The right one even has a blotch of blood next to the pupil. *He's been squeezed until his eyes popped!* Rather than going home or to the hospital, though, he hangs around the sidelines, waiting for another chance to jump in the Sway. For Stephen Mitchell (initials: S&M), getting knocked down and out is all part of the fun.

'Oh, I got trampled on, yeah,' he tells me. 'Me 'ips aren't feelin' too clever at the minute. I'm bound to get a bollocking off me family because I need a hip replacement.'

'What?'

'The bones are crumblin'.' At thirty-four, he has chronic arthritis in both hips.

'So why on earth do you do this?'

He pauses, then grins wildly. 'It's the 'Ood – ya can't explain it. It's the 'Ood!'

What with the drinking and injuries, you'd expect the paramedics to frown on the Hood. However, the mustachioed man from the St John Ambulance takes the casualties in his stride. 'Mainly just sprains and strains, the odd bit of crushing. But, y'know' – he shrugs – 'it's brilliant. I think it's absolutely fantastic. It's Old England, isn't it? It's something that's been goin' on for years, something we should never get rid of.'

Over the next few hours, the swaying hundred-footed drunk, the bedraggled knot of humanity, stumbles through Haxey in the dark, steaming and heaving and careening off walls, windows and even a car. Halfway through, an old-timer shouts to the boggins to rescue him from the mob. Despite his wife's warnings, after downing two gallons of beer, he couldn't resist the pull of the Sway. 'I shouldn'ta been in it, lad,' he gasps. 'Aye, I'd an 'eart attack three months ago.'

By the time the Hood reaches the King's Arms on the other side of the village, I'm feeling revitalised by the mad rush I get when I see these events. Mud, blood and booze in Old England; maybe I'm not so crazy after all.

*

In case you ever doubted it, 'mob football' matches like Haxey's Hood prove that hooliganism was part of the beautiful game right from the very beginning. Of course, the British weren't the first people to realise that kicking or carrying a ball past a goal might be fun. But they were the first to organise and export the game via their empire, making the Victorian version of football a truly global sport, far removed from its gruesome origins. Various legends claim that the first football was actually the head of an executed criminal or conquered enemy. The noggin's nationality varies from Roman to Viking to Scottish, reflecting the home team's long history of fighting invaders. To the horror of Eng-er-land fans, football may even be a French import: the Normans may have brought it with them after 1066. Nevertheless, the English ended up making the game their own: watching a mob football game in the early 1800s, a shocked Frenchman gasped: 'If Englishmen call this playing, it would be impossible to say what they would call fighting.'

For centuries, football was a bloody, no-holds-barred 'sport' that often ended in riots, injuries and even deaths. The reformation of the game began at public schools such as Eton and Rugby, where the headmasters realised that sports were more productive than the other vices on offer: namely booze, gambling and sodomy. Rugby produced the first standardised rules of the game in 1846, allowing players to carry the ball – and kick each other in the shins, so long as they weren't holding each other. Other schools agreed to play by Rugby's rules, but Eton baulked about ball carrying. In 1863, football's Great Schism divided the kickers from the carriers, creating soccer and rugby. Overseas, the mania for rulemaking spawned different versions of the game in Australia, Canada and America, where Ivy Leaguers confusingly used the term 'football' to describe their ball-handling variation on rugby.

While these spin-offs have become global sports, mob football has survived as an intensely local event, concentrated in the backwaters of Britain and virtually unknown to the outside world. The UK still has at least eleven traditional mêlées, spread from England's West Country to the Orkney Islands north of Scotland.

Most games take place on Shrove Tuesday, traditionally the last day of fun and feasting before the forty days of Lent. In medieval times, 'Pancake Bells' would remind people to finish off forbidden food, particularly 'greasy pancakes' made with lots of eggs, and the men would get in one last game of football. In fact, the first record of football in England refers to Shrovetide matches in London around 1174. Although the tradition died out in the capital, many country versions of Shrovetide football reputedly date from the same era. Today, Pancake Bells still chime in several towns around the country, vying with more recent traditions such as pancake racing. However, London's élite Westminster School is the only place that actually combines pancakes and scrummage: at its annual Pancake Greaze, boys fight for a scrap of pancake thrown into the air.

Old Public Schoolboy Tony Blair likes to pose for pints with his constituents in the north-eastern town of Sedgefield, but it's hard to picture him joining in their annual Shrovetide football game, let alone the fights afterwards. A few years ago, a post-game quarrel turned into a street battle with the police, who used dogs and pepper spray to control the mob. In most games, though, the worst injuries tend to be broken bones, nosebleeds and black eyes galore, not to mention the 'biting and nipping' that supposedly takes place in the lawless ba' games of the Scottish Borders.

The projectiles vary from Haxey's Hood to distinctive spheres and casks of beer. Sedgefield's bruisers have been known to fight over an imported American baseball for novelty's sake, while Cornish 'hurlers' favour fist-sized wooden balls plated with silver. In the pretty market town of Ashbourne near the Derbyshire Dales, the players wrestle over painted and lacquered soccer balls packed with cork – to help them float in the river. Not far away, in Atherstone, Warwickshire, they use a 27-inch ball weighted with sand (the traditional ballast was beer). The games can last anywhere from less than an hour to more than eight, and the goals (if there are any) are often miles apart. One 'hurling' match boasts the biggest sports field in the world: the entire twenty-five square miles of the parish. Winners have to hurl a silver ball into a stone trough or carry it across the parish boundary. In other places, the men have to bang the ball against a goal situated inconveniently in the middle of the local river (resulting in drownings in the old days). Some games are literally free-for-alls, with every man for himself, while others are team brawls. Depending on the game, you can have Farmers versus Tradesmen, Townsmen against Countrymen, Up'ards fighting Down'ards, St Paul's versus St Michael's, or the widespread rivalry of Uppies versus Downies (or Doonies, as they say in Scotland).

As for rules, the old ban on murder still applies (in theory). Otherwise, pretty much anything goes. Some matches forbid vehicles, but elsewhere, cars and motorcycles have carried the ball to the goal and even smuggled it out of the country. Canny players will do anything to confuse their rivals, hiding the balls in toilets, prams, rubbish bags or special pockets sewn into their boilersuits. A father once hid a ball under a bucket, placing his little girl on top as a decoy until he could come back and score.

One of the quirkiest games takes place in the Dorset village of Corfe. The dark limestone known as Purbeck Marble hasn't been quarried on the Isle of Purbeck for years, but that doesn't stop the Ancient Order of Purbeck Marblers and Stonecutters from meeting every Shrove Tuesday, ostensibly to induct new members. Apprentices (if there are any) have to run a gauntlet of old boys and carry bread and a quart of beer to the town hall without spilling it. Afterwards, the Marblers kick a football around in a tradition that supposedly goes back 700 years. 'We could be responsible for all the football hooliganism in England!' says David Glassock, the group's steward.

Nowadays the play isn't too rough, though one man did break his leg the year before last. 'He didn't feel any pain – he'd 'ad a few gallons.' Provided they can still walk, the men proceed down Peppercorn Lane to Ower Quay, once Purbeck's main port. 'Basically, it's to keep the right of way open to Ower, but there's not a lotta point, seein's how a boat can't get in there anymore! It's all silted up!' Glassock laughs. Even so, every year, the woman in the cottage next to the quay receives a true peppercorn rent: one pound of peppercorns. 'She cooks for the *whole year* with them.'

In 1992, an overzealous policeman interrupted the proceedings by trying to confiscate the Marblers' football. 'Which 'appened to be mine at the time,' Glassock tells me. 'I told 'im to put it down before I 'ad to slap 'im!'

'So what happened?'

'Well, I don't think he'd ever been *talked* to like that before. So he got on the radio then. I think they told 'im to mind 'is own business.'

Likewise, the police know better than to intervene in the Hare Pie Scramble and Bottle Kicking in the picturesque village of Hallaton in Leicestershire. Every Easter Monday – the day the Easter Bunny dreads – the vicar throws handfuls of hare-meat pie to the crowds as a token rent for some land. Then young toughs fight over three 'bottles' – actually, small kegs of beer – kicking, throwing and running with them in what is one of the most dangerous mob football matches I've seen. Unlike the Haxey Hood, where the men back off when the Sway falls over, at Hallaton, they just keep piling on. A vicar attempted to stop the bone-breaking event in the 1700s. In protest, the locals broke his windows and daubed his walls with a warning: NO PIE, NO PARSON.

Appalled by such hooliganism, the upper classes tried to stamp out mob football in the 1800s even as public schools were reforming the game. In the castled town of Alnwick, however, the patron of the Shrovetide match was none other than the Duke of Northumberland, one of Britain's wealthiest and most powerful men. In 1828, he allowed the game to be played on his land rather than in the town's streets, thereby saving the free-for-all. The match still takes place on pastureland in front of Alnwick Castle, also the backdrop for another magical game – as Hogwarts in the *Harry Potter* films, it hosted the famous quidditch match.

Down in Derby, the authorities managed to stop 'dirty, unmanly and absurd play' by imposing martial law in 1846. The town's blood-and-guts match between rival parishes had been one of the most famous in the country – it's where the term 'local derby' comes from. Officials in nearby Ashbourne also called in the dragoons after a player drowned in the River Henmore in 1878. However, Ashbourne's game quickly resumed; half a century later, it had even come up in the world. The man who started the game in 1938 was none other than the Prince of Wales, the future King Edward the Abdicator, who gave locals all the justification they needed to rename their event Royal Shrovetide Football. Unfortunately, the prince made as much of a balls-up as a starter as he did as king: according to one apocryphal account, he ended up with a bloody nose after throwing the ball straight up into the air rather than away from his royal person.

Seventy-five years later, Edward's great-nephew fared somewhat better. Prince Charles graced the match with his presence in 2003, having postponed his visit the two previous years because of the foot-and-mouth crisis and Princess Margaret's death. Unlike his great-uncle, Charles allowed the players to carry him on their shoulders (before he quickly hopped off). 'We believe it's the first time that a royal has ever been picked up,' said a bearer of His Royal Backside. 'It's a big honour for us.' After praising 'Old England' and muttering 'God Save the Queen' in the rain, the 54-year-old heir to the throne threw the ball into the crowd. Although Prince Charles avoided a bloody nose, the exertion may have contributed to the royal hernia announced by Buckingham Palace a week later. No wonder he looked so worried the men were going to drop him.

Ignored by the royals, Haxey has to make do with local VIPs to start its annual brawl. Apart from its timing – on Old Twelfth Day, after Christmas – what makes Haxey's event unique is the Hood itself: a hefty leather cylinder about two feet long and three inches in diameter, stuffed with coiled rope and straw. Victorian folk collectors took one look at the Hood and decided it originally had a mystical purpose: like other mob football games, they argued, the match was an old pagan fertility ritual, possibly linked to animal or human sacrifice. And you didn't have to be a witch to find significance in the number of officials overseeing the event: thirteen.

However, Haxonians tell a more romantic tale, a legend of a damsel in distress that dates the game from the Age of Chivalry. The medieval lords of the manor were the de Mowbray family. Best known now for giving their name to the Leicestershire town of Melton Mowbray (famed for pork pies and Stilton cheese), the de

Mowbrays fought at the Battle of Hastings, forced King John to sign Magna Carta and eventually became the Dukes of Norfolk before losing everything for plotting against Richard II (landing Thomas de Mowbray a future role in Shakespeare's tragedy). Prior to the family's disgrace in 1399, the story goes, a Lady de Mowbray was galloping across a field outside Haxey on the Sixth of January when the wind blew off her hood. The thirteen peasants ploughing nearby gave chase, but the piece of red silk kept skittering away. Every time the men got bogged down in the mud, the lady would squeal with delight: 'It's boggined again!' Finally, the biggest man wrenched the hood from his rivals. However, he was too embarrassed to approach his social superior, so a bolder peasant presented the lady with the hood. 'You shall be a Lord,' she laughed, while declaring the shy man a Fool. As a reward, the Lord, the Fool and the 'plough boggins' each received a half-acre of land to play the game on every year in her honour. The field came to be called the Hoodlands, and to this day, the Lord of the Hood makes his wand of office from thirteen willow reeds, with one upside down in the middle to represent the Fool.

As much as I'd like it to be true, it's more likely that the locals cooked up the Lady de Mowbray Legend to explain why otherwise sane people would risk injury fighting over a scrap of leather in the dead of winter. Although Haxonians claim the event is ancient, the first known historical record of the Hood comes from 1815. Like football at Shrovetide, Haxey's Hood was probably part of the games on Plough Monday, the start of the ploughing season after the festive blowout of Christmas. To this day, Haxey remains a farming community at heart: it's one of the few places in the world where the medieval system of ridge-and-furrow 'strip farming' survives virtually unchanged. So when I heard 'Farmer's Boy', the de facto anthem of the Hood, the lyrics seemed particularly poignant. A crippled boy wanders 'across yon dreary moor' on a 'cold winter's night'. His father has died, so he has to scrape a living for his mother and four younger siblings. Knocking on a farmer's door, the shivering boy begs the man for work.

Though little I be no work I fear
If I can find employ
For to plough and to sow and to reap and to mow
And to be a farmer's boy
And to be a farmer's boy.

Maybe it was the beer, the men's voices or the fact that I come from sodbusting stock myself, but it seemed to me that 'Farmer's Boy' had to have been written by a local. (In fact, it's a traditional song found throughout England, and even in America.) What's more, the other two Hood songs seemed to reflect the secular trinity that made Britain what it is today: Land, Booze and Patriotism. 'John Barleycorn' is a paean to that most versatile of crops, depicting the murder, rebirth and transfiguration of 'poor Barleycorn' into a brew that will 'make a man become a fool, and a fool become an ass'. Paradoxically, the last song is a rallying cry for Englishmen to fight the Old Enemies by doing their patriotic duty – 'drinking old England dry':

For the French they invade us
And they say that they will try, will try
They say that they shall come and drink old England dry.

Give or take a few words, this could be England's national football anthem. In fact, professional football could learn a lot more than that from its amateur ancestors. If football is a proxy for war, then most modern battles are fought by mercenaries, country-hopping soldiers of fortune whose only loyalty is to the highest bidder. Ironically, many Premier League fans support their home teams based on their local affiliation, even though their star players often hail from overseas. International fixtures seem to be the few times when something other than money motivates professional foot-ballers. In contrast, the men of the Haxey Hood and other traditional football games play purely for hometown pride – and bragging rights. Come to think of it, they should have their own Mob Football League: the Ashbourne Up'ards and Down'ards versus the Kirkwall

Uppies and Doonies, the St Columb Hurlers competing against the Purbeck Marblers . . . and of course, the Hallaton Bottle-Kickers fighting the Haxey Hoods.

Now *that* would be football worth paying for.

PART TWO:
BACK TO THE HOOD

YOU ARE
NOW ENTERING
THE GRIM NORTH

They might as well put a sign up. Two hours north of London, the sun disappears, and mist envelops everything within a hundred feet. And to think it had started out as such a nice day. Snow had dusted the ground down south, but the sky was bright – a rarity for January. Sure enough, though, we hit a grim patch halfway into our trip.

I'm travelling to Haxey with Doc Rowe, Britain's top folk collector, who has been photographing, filming and recording singers, storytellers and obscure annual customs for the past four decades. Doc's been to Haxey every year since 1976, and his amiable mug, usually half-hidden behind a camera, has become as much of a fixture on Hood Day as the game itself. One year he nearly died after following the Sway for five hours in subzero temperatures. Returning to London, he collapsed in the street with a sickly-sweet taste in his mouth. It was only then that he found out he had hypothermia. Another year, someone pinched the Hood from the winning pub and held it to ransom; and in 1985, the Hood was actually stolen from the middle of the Sway: the players didn't realise until it was too late that they were fighting in the dark over nothing. 'I heard this *howl* of pain,' Doc recalls. 'It wasn't physical at all; it was emotional.' Everybody was wandering around in shock. Runners returned from the pubs to confirm that the culprit was nowhere to be found. 'Well, when they get 'im,' the Fool muttered, lighting a cigarette, 'I 'ope he likes 'ospital food.' (He never was caught.) And the locals still talk about the time a farmer sprayed liquid manure on the field in a vain attempt to keep the men off his land. It had snowed that year, so there were three layers clearly visible on the ground: white powder on top, brown mud on the bottom and a seam of bright yellow excrement running through the middle. Undeterred, the brave players ended up covered in liquefied chicken shit.

By the time we reach North Lincolnshire, the sky clears and the sun comes out to play. Over the past year, I've noticed that whenever I mention 'the Grim North' in mixed company, some Northern friends develop an involuntary twitch of the upper lip. I usually end up spluttering an explanation about how I don't mean to slur an entire region: every place has its good and bad spots. As far as I'm concerned, I'll add, fitting my other foot neatly in my mouth, the further you get from London, the friendlier the people – which manages to offend any Londoners in attendance.

Of course, some Northerners have argued that I haven't really been Up North at all.

'Lincolnshire?!' scoffed a friend from York. 'That's not The North!'

And so I braced myself for a tiresome round of 'More Northern Than Thou', a game that Northerners love to play with anyone from below Birmingham. No matter how far North you've been, it's never quite North enough. 'Manchester?' they'll snort. 'That's not The North! You wanna go to Newcastle – now *that's* The North!' From what I've been able to work out, the only parts of England that indisputably qualify as The North are those precious few feet near Hadrian's Wall. And even then, there's probably some deranged Northumbrian, the Troll of Hadrian's Wall, who spends his days heckling visitors as they pull up in the car park. 'That's not The Fookin North!' he'll shout, stomping up and down on the wall. 'Now this – *this* is The Fookin North!'

Having played the game before, I knew how to finish it quickly. I pointed out that the place where I'd been in Lincolnshire was roughly due east of Sheffield. Admittedly, the Capital of South Yorkshire isn't that far north on a map of the UK. But for proud Yorkshiremen, it presents a quandary: they can't bring themselves to admit that any part of Yorkshire might not be . . . More Northern Than Thou. So my friend had to concede that I had, in fact, been Up North.

'What part of Lincolnshire?' he grumbled.

'The area around Epworth.'

'Oh.' A pause. 'Well, that *is* the Grim North. Lincolnshire is the Land That Time Forgot. It's flat, and misty, and all they do is grow *cabbages* and things. What the *hell* were you doing there?'

Last year, I had wondered the same thing, but this time, with the sun out and the mist burned away, I can see that my first impressions were wrong. The home of the Hood looks much more welcoming than the rough stretch of redbrick houses I remembered. At the post office, the man behind the glass has some good news: the forecast for Hood Day is clear and sunny.

A woman in the queue is sceptical. 'It's not Monday yet,' she chuckles.

In the evening, Doc and I head over to Epworth. Every night from New Year's Eve to the Sixth of January, the men of the Hood tour the villages around Haxey, singing, collecting money and getting 'leathered', all in the name of charity. We catch up with them a couple of pubs into their trek. The Lord of the Hood and the Chief Boggin are decked out in their scarlet hunting jackets, the Fool is in his tatters and the rest of the boggins are wearing their scarlet sweatshirts.

Word soon gets round that I'm a Yank who's planning to brave the Sway, and the men go out of their way to give me helpful tips, while remaining deeply sceptical. One boggin in particular, Gary

Mann, makes no attempt to hide his doubts. 'He's too tall, really,' he frowns, sizing me up as we meet. 'Most people are small and stocky.'

Gary's actually the same height as I am – not an inch under six-foot-four. The problem with standing out from the crowd, he explains, is that 'everybody else is pushin' against your chest. You're gonna get a lot of push under your diaphragm, so ya lose your breath a lot. You've gotta control your breathin' and not panic.'

'Yeah, whatever ya do, don't panic,' another boggin agrees. 'When it falls over, it seems like an age, and ya may think you get to a point where ya need to panic, but people will help you.'

'The best advice somebody gave to me,' Gary cracks up, 'he said, "You'll fall over, you'll lose your breath, ten people'll be on top a ya – *but don't squeal like a pig*."'

I do my best to join in the laughter.

But seriously, my tutors continue, I need to keep my hands and arms tucked in tight against my chest, in a kind of standing foetal position – or an attitude of desperate prayer, in the same way that you might huddle in a doorway during an earthquake, praying the entire building doesn't collapse on you. If you stuck your arms out in the Sway, you'd risk having them wrenched out of their sockets when the whole thing falls over. Likewise, you should keep your legs together as you fall, without trying to catch yourself. 'Whatever you do, don't put your leg back and push against it,' Gary says, demonstrating with a shallow lunge. 'Honestly. I did that one year, and me leg went to the side, and this guy hit it, and it *went* – did me ligaments.'

That gets the other boggin talking about his injuries. Young and enthusiastic, James Chatwin is as small as Gary is tall; his friends call him Chat for short. Men like Chat face the opposite problem: they're constantly getting banged in the face. He mentions the upset of 2000, one of the few times in history that Haxey lost and the Hood went all the way over to the rival village of Westwoodside. 'That was the best 'Ood I've been in for a long time,' he recalls fondly. 'That's when I broke me ribs.'

Not for nothing, then, that when the boggins needed a substitute Fool, Chat was their first choice.

'The first thing you want to make sure of,' Gary's advising me over yet another pint, 'is that you tie your boots *really* tight.'

'Uhhh . . . I didn't bring boots. I brought wellies.'

He rears back and shakes his head in disbelief, nudging another boggin. ''Ere! He doesn't 'ave boots! He brought *wellies!*'

'Oh, those'll come right off.'

'What 'appens is, you're in there, and people are *stood* on your *feet*. Someone's always stood on your foot. Ya can go in with wellies, but you'll lose them in the mud.'

In setting my goals for the Sway, I had started out with fairly macho aspirations – *I'm gonna get my hands on that Hood,* I'd vowed, *or crack a rib trying*. A cracked rib would be painful, but it would heal. As a boggin puts it, with flawless logic, 'Ya break a rib, you're either gonna go in an ambulance or go to the pub. So ya might as well go to the pub.' But then the Chief Boggin, Ian Dawes, tells me how a broken collarbone ended his days in the Sway. Resplendent in his big flowered hat, he recalls how the mob had just moved off the field and onto the road when the whole thing fell on top of him. He was pinned on his side against the tarmac, and the falling bodies broke his clavicle, right where it connects to the sternum.

I wince. 'How painful was that?'

'Well, I passed out, and they dragged me out,' he shrugs. His collarbone has never healed properly, and the few times that he's ventured back into the Sway, the pressure has been unbearable.

I hadn't considered the possibility of permanently broken bones or crippling injuries. I don't tell the men this, but my sports career was cut short after I broke my hip when I was twelve. Two operations left me with a couple of pins in my hip and a foot-long scar. I hadn't finished growing at the time, and the surgeon warned me that if I broke the joint again, I could end up with a stunted leg or stuck in a wheelchair until I was old enough to have a hip replacement. Since then, I've become rather fond of using my legs. I find that walking is a much more convenient way of getting around than, say, crawling.

'It's a yoong man's game, innit?' Gary says to one of his colleagues.

'Oh, it is, it is. They bend better and mend better.'

'What's an old man?' I ask. 'I'm thirty-three.'

Gary leans in to break the bad news: 'You're totally fooked.'

The more horror stories I hear, the more scaled-back my ambitions become. Initially, I had planned to stay in the Sway the whole time on the field – even *I* wasn't stupid enough to risk getting crushed against the road in town. Then I decided merely to fight my way into the middle and make contact with the Hood before getting out. On second thoughts, though, I don't *really* need to touch the Hood at all, if I just get in the middle once, and even then, well . . . it goes on like this, until by the time I've finished, I'll be doing well to even set foot on the field, let alone take part in the scrum. 'Seven pounds is all it takes,' says Phil Coggon, the Lord of the Hood, referring to the pressure needed to snap a ligament like a rubber band. After each tale of woe, though, the boggins try to reassure me. 'We'll look after ya,' they say. 'You'll be all right.' As if that makes me the exception to the rule.

Ironically, the survival of Britain's mob football games has been threatened by crowd control concerns at modern soccer matches. Ever since ninety-six Liverpool fans were crushed to death in the Hillsborough tragedy of 1989, public events throughout the country have been forced to improve safety. In mob football, though, crushing is an essential part of the sport. 'They've got a big problem,' says one veteran of the Hood. 'They're worried that somebody's gonna break their leg, or whatever, and then try and *claim*. They're all paranoid about that.' As a result, the boggins try to discourage newcomers from taking part. Glory-seekers who endanger others to touch the Hood are told to 'Get the *fook* off.' The men wouldn't think any less of me if I backed out. But I can't. Half of Haxey seems to know that some stupid Yank is going to take part in the Sway. I just hope that for my sake, it won't be a case of pride going before a fall – particularly not a nasty one like Phil Scott's.

'Ask Phil what injuries 'e's 'ad,' Gary says, nodding towards a guy next to him, a Ray Winstone lookalike, only with a Northern accent. Phil, or Scottie, starts to laugh.

'Go on – tell 'im.'

'I, uh . . . snapped the top o' me tibia, snapped me cruciate ligament, tore me medial ligament' – both around the knee – 'and burst a blood vessel.' He grins. 'I didn't get off crutches 'til the . . . well . . . middle of April.'

'So was it worth it?'

'Yeah,' he beams. 'I wouldn'ta missed what I've done for the fookin' world, like. Now I do a fookin' sissy's job.' Last year, though, one of the boggins in the middle handed him the Hood. 'And I got on the fooking 'Ood, fooking 'ell, it were *absolutely* fooking – absolutely *marv*ellous, like.' His eyes are shining.

'It's an unbelievable feeling, isn't it – once you've got 'old of it,' Gary agrees. And then he repeats the wisdom I've been hearing over and over: 'The further in the middle, the safer you are. It's a big circle – if you're on the outside, the full circle falls on ya; you're in the middle, only 'alf the circle falls on ya.' Having imparted this Archimedean principle, he flashes a Eureka smile. 'It's all physics.'

Of course, he's right. Having twenty-five to fifty men fall on you must be much safer than being trampled by a hundred. That's still an awful lot of flesh and bone, though. A dozen men would weigh roughly a ton – much more than seven pounds of pressure. What's more, no matter how logical it may be, the Centre-Sway Strategy is deeply, *viscerally*, counterintuitive. Watching the human limb compactor grind across the field, your instincts scream at you to *get out of the way*. The last thing you think of is fighting through the crush so you can get mauled in the middle.

'We can get ya in the middle,' Gary says, 'but once you're in there, you've got ta really want it. Because there are dozens of guys who want nothing more than to get their 'ands on that Hood.' He fixes me with a solemn gaze, checking to see if I'm worthy to handle the Hood, their semi-sacred relic.

I make sure not to blink, but if I'm honest, my attitude is one of dreamy hopefulness rather than dead-eyed determination.

'There's no friends in there, either,' he continues, telling how men claw each other's hands to touch the hallowed Hood. 'People want it that bad, and you've got to want it more than them.'

Scottie nods wholeheartedly. 'It's a fookin' prized possession.'

*

The next night, on Hood Eve, the Fool has arranged to pick me up at the Mowbray Arms, named after the family that supposedly started the Hood. As it happens, James Bland is also inside. I recognise his ginger mullet immediately, but I'm surprised to see him wearing a full beard. 'I'll shave it tomorrow,' he explains. His drinking mate is Rick Gill, or Gillie, the beefy guy who shaved a big H into the top of his head last year.

At thirty-eight, James has been a mainstay of the Sway nearly half his life, having barged his way into the action after the infamous theft of the Hood in 1985. 'That was disgoostin',' he grimaces. Since then, the boggins have come to rely on locals like him to act as anchors, holding on to the Hood to make sure it doesn't disappear in the Sway. At the start of the match, once James snatches the tube from the air, he immediately yanks it down to gut level, gripping it with two wiry forearms and holding it close to his body. 'It should be well hidden from prying hands or anybody who wants to pinch it.' Ideally, he'll end up chin-to-chin and chest-to-chest with a veteran like Rick, while a couple of boggins guard the ends, 'stoppin' idiots from getting it': 'I just *loove* bein' there. It's not all *URRGHHHHUNNNGGGGHH!*' he grunts. 'There's so much craic in the middle of the Sway, it's fantastic. And I could just stay there all day, really.'

'Best place to be,' agrees Gillie.

To look at James, you can hardly believe that such a laidback, agreeable guy would stomp on someone's foot or elbow a man in the throat to get hold of the Hood. He's not one of these hard-muscled, raptor-headed types. A landscape gardener, he seems a peaceable sort, a family man who would avoid fighting unless he had to. You wouldn't expect him to fight dirty; but then again, there's no such thing as fighting dirty in the Sway. When it comes to the Hood, James is like a dog on a bone, albeit more of a terrier than a bulldog. 'I don't mind where it goes – I really don't – so long as I've got it when it goes up, and I've got it when it goes into the pub.'

Blandie and the other devotees talk about 'falling off' the Hood like other people might talk about falling off a cliff; it's understood that something terrible will happen if they do, so they stay glued to it at all times, even when the Hood is stuck in the mud.

And just as the players can fall off the Hood, occasionally the Hood can fall out of the Sway. As the mass of bodies swirls across the field, the men on the fringes spin off to try to direct it; occasionally, though, the nucleus will shoot out the side, unnoticed by the general argy-bargy. One time James and Rick found themselves lying on the ground in the dark, just the two of them holding the Hood, while the Sway went its way, the rest of the men completely unaware that they were fighting over nothing.

'Where are they 'eaded?' Blandie asked the Lord.

'They're off to Westwood.'

'Not without this they aren't!'

He held up the Hood, and the men promptly came back and crushed them. 'It was the worst thing I ever said.'

James assures me I'll have no trouble getting into the centre of the Sway. 'It's easy. All the lads that are round the outside, none of 'em like gettin' too near the middle. They all run away from it,' he says. But not him. 'The adrenaline's pumpin' already,' he smiles as he gets up to leave. 'I'm ready for it.'

And I'm sure I will be, too – after another night of drinking.

The morning of the Hood, I'm surprisingly calm – confident, even – resigned to my fate in the way condemned men must feel on the day of their execution. My landlady offers me her husband's size-13 gardening boots instead of my wellies. 'There's a hole in the top that goes right the way through,' she warns me. 'Your feet'll get wet.'

I reckon wet feet will be the least of my problems.

For the boggins, Hood Day starts with breakfast and triple brandies at the pub. The Lord and the Chief Boggin ceremonially blacken the face of the Fool, Dale Smith, adding smudges of red and green for good measure. Then they continue their tour of the pubs on the high street, with little boys harassing the Fool along the way. Every so often, Dale chases them, the tatters on his suit fluttering. When he catches up, he thumps them mercilessly with his weapon, a couple of balled-up socks tied to a stick. In the old days, this would have been an inflated pig's bladder, but modern health regulations have forced the men to improvise. One Fool used to stuff tennis balls inside the sock, Dale says, 'But they knocked some of the boys out.'

After multiple pints and shots, the boggins are singing with full-throated fervour, putting all their energy and emotion into the final renditions of 'Farmer's Boy', 'John Barleycorn' and 'Cannons'. The boozy choruses resound through the pubs, and everyone joins in. There's so much testosterone in the air, even the women's voices have dropped an octave. The pubs are crowded beyond belief, creating scenes that would trigger fights and arguments anywhere else. This good-natured crush is a kind of pre-Sway Sway, a taste of what we'll be going through out on the field. The boggins have their arms around each other's shoulders, swaying to the music, some with tears in their eyes. 'It's very. . . emotional,' one says. After the penultimate pub, a boggin shouts, 'What are we, lads?'

'Village people!'

At least, that's what I think I heard, but the man who wrote the book on the Hood sets me straight. '*Privileged* people,' Jeremy Cooper says, adding: 'We are, ya know.'

After each set of songs, the men bellow the rules of the Hood:

> Hoose agen Hoose!
> Toon agen Toon!
> If a man meets a man,
> Knock 'im doon!
> But don't 'urt 'im!

'Toon' is 'town' and 'Hoose' refers to the rival pubs, but it's the 'don't hurt him' bit that has special resonance with me. Aptly enough, it was probably tacked on by a former Anglican vicar, an outsider who kept the game going after many local men died in World War One. The Reverend Sheppard's support contrasted with the view of the Methodists, who helped stamp out traditional football matches around the country. In Haxey, they used to keep children in the chapel on Hood Day and pile furniture in the windows so the kiddies couldn't see the violent consequences of the demon drink.

As for me, I've downed two-and-a-half pints by the time we leave the last pub, having quickly switched from lager to Guinness because it somehow seems downright wrong to be drinking anything non-brown up here in the North. I'm hoping the alcohol will relax me when I fall – or possibly even act as a pre-emptive anaesthetic – though my Dutch courage begins to falter after a boggin asks me if I'm really going into the Sway.

'I'm gonna do my best,' I vow.

He makes the sign of the cross on my chest.

Once out the door, Dale tears down the street, but the boggins quickly collar him for the ritual Smoking of the Fool in front of the church. This used to involve tying the jester to a pole and swinging him over burning straw, but that died out, supposedly after one poor Fool fell into the fire. Nowadays, a wiser Fool stands on the stump of an old stone cross and welcomes the crowd while the men burn damp straw behind him. The aim is to generate as much smoke as possible. Only this year, the boggins have forgotten to wet the straw, so instead of smouldering, it actually catches fire. The Fool's doing his best to give his speech, pumping the Hood in the air, but he has to cut it short because orange flames start jumping up behind him, singeing the rags on his backside.

'As you can see, things are starting to *wamm* up,' he jokes in a solid Haxonian accent before leaping to safety. The crowd is cheering and the boggins are congratulating him, when out of nowhere, a funny little voice cuts through the noise, calmly informing him in a polite tone: 'Excuse me. You're on fire.'

The rags on Dale's back are blazing orange. He flops to the ground, and the men pound out the flames. Fortunately, this Fool is no fool – he wears fireproof overalls.

A big hurrah for the singed-but-unscathed Fool, and the action moves to 'yon hill' next to Haxey. With no mist clouding the ground this year, it's possible to detect the subtle bulge that qualifies the field as a hill – it isn't as flat as I remembered. The sky is mostly grey, with a few blue patches to prove the sun is still shining somewhere, and the temperature's a balmy zero degrees Celsius, contrary to grim forecasts of minus six. Still, I'm wearing a pair of overalls over my coat (extra padding).

The biggest surprise is the field itself. For the first time in years, it hasn't been ploughed beforehand, so instead of deep muddy furrows, it's an even surface with an overlay of dying grass and rushes.

Blandie – who shaved off the left side of his beard this morning – is surveying the pitch appreciatively. 'The ground's perfect,' he says, digging a toe into the turf.

'Nice an' firm,' his friend Rick agrees. 'Give it a while, though, with a hundred men on it, and it'll soften up.'

Although they reckon it's a small Hood today, it certainly looks big enough to me. Even though it's a Monday, several hundred men, women and children are loitering on the field, dodging the Running Hoods that are whizzing through the air. Unlike the one true Hood, these 12 'false' hoods are made of rolled-up sacking and can be run with rather than swayed. Most men in the Sway cut their teeth fighting over them as boys. Any kid who's fast enough to carry a sack hood off the field and into a pub wins one pound, but the boggins make sure that rarely happens. Despite their size, the men often put in full-body tackles, so the boys end up well and truly 'boggined'.

Just after three o'clock, an hour before sunset, it's time for the Sway to start. I huddle around Blandie with some other men, as Phil Coggon, the Lord of the Hood, reminds us that we're all taking part at our own risk. 'Don't worry,' someone scoffs. 'It's a mid-week Hood. We're all locals. We know what we're doin'.'

'HOOSE AGEN HOOSE! . . .' A local VIP crouches to throw the Hood.

The players crush together and jostle for position.

'. . . BUT DON'T 'URT 'IM!'

The Hood veers off to the side and sinks into a mass of men, drawing the rest of us in after it like a black hole. All space between bodies disappears and the air is sucked from my lungs. I've got my arms folded against my chest in crash-landing mode as the human gut compactor churns into motion. The grunting and shunting, the arging and barging start immediately, with some men chanting 'HAXEY! HAXEY!' and 'WESTWOOD! WESTWOOD!' while the rest of us make tortured-animal noises, groaning and straining and gurgling as if our torsos are clamped in vices, a single ratchet-turn from hearing our ribs go *Crrrrrrkkkk!!!*

Despite the gut-busting pressure from all sides, the sudden difficulty breathing, and the knowledge that sooner or later the clumsy hundred-footed beast is going to crash down on top of me – despite all that, and completely contrary to expectations – being in the Sway is . . . *fun*! It's . . . *exhilarating*! Whatever nervousness I felt beforehand is gone, squeezed out and absorbed by the comforting crush of bodies. Then again, maybe I'm just light-headed from a lack of oxygen. 'Ohhh – that feels good,' says one man, floating past as his innards are being compressed. 'Nice and warm.'

From in here, the scenes are even more surreal than they are on the outside. Gary Mann is standing a couple of crushed bodies away from me, chatting to a fellow boggin in the Sway.

'Yawright?'

'Fantastic day.'

'Couldn't be better.'

'Westwood's strong.'

'Where are all the 'Axey lads?'

'Must be in the pub.'

The surreal thing is, this everyday exchange of pleasantries isn't taking place in a pub or on the street. It happens as two men are being squashed to the point that their navels are nearly touching their backbones. Even so, they're laughing and joking: two sociable, smiling faces floating on a sea of heads in the Sway.

After all the scare stories, Gary has taken me under his wing, and for today at least, I don't think I'll ever have a better friend.

'Take small steps,' he advises me over the bald heads wedged in between us.

I'm doing the best I can, but with countless feet stomping my size-13s and kicking my heels, not to mention the slippery ground underfoot and the tug of war over my torso, I start to list and lean and finally keel over onto the men behind me.

'STEP *OOP*!! STEP *OOP*!!' a voice bellows in my ear. Whoever it is hooks me under my arms, either alone or with another guy, partly out of camaraderie but mostly for self-protection: if I fall over, the Sway will steamroll all of us. At first I don't know what he means – *Steps? What steps?* – but then I get the gist and jack-knife my legs as best I can. The stranger – I couldn't turn to look at him if I wanted to – props me up into a vertical position until I find my footing. The next time my feet start to go I rely on a tip I got from Blandie – I lift up and let the Sway carry me along, my entire body weight supported by the upper-body crush in a strange dance, a kind of Sway Ballet: Tippy-toe-tippy-toe – *lift!-lift!* Tippy-toe – *lift!* Tippy-toe – *lift!*

Inevitably, though, somebody stumbles, and the bodies start toppling like lead dominoes. If you're near the top, as Gary and I are initially, the collapse provides a welcome chance to flex your lungs. 'Oh good. We're going to have a lie down – just about . . . now,' he grins, relaxing into the heap for a quick rest before digging out the men beneath him. When you're buried down there, though, you get an entirely different perspective. After a few minutes, we fall over again, this time backwards. Gary lands on top of me, along with half of the Sway. The impact itself isn't that painful – the field has softened up nicely, and in any event, the poor guy under me has cushioned my fall – but it takes a while for the men who are still pushing on the outside of the Sway to realise that the nucleus has collapsed, so they keep bulldozing bodies on top of you. It's this terrible feeling of being pinned to the ground, bracing for unknown suffering as each fifteen-stone bag of gut and bones falls on you, that makes the Hood experience unique. In most other sports, injuries occur so quickly you don't have time to think about them, let alone avoid them – by the time you feel the pain, the injury has already happened. But in the slow-motion seconds between falling and being trampled in the Sway, you have eons to ponder your fate – before, during and after impact – and absolutely no way of avoiding it. This time, I'm lucky. The bodies stop dropping from the sky just as my hipbone starts to creak uncomfortably in its socket.

Back on my feet, I take a break to decompress my ribcage. By now, the Sway numbers at least a hundred men crammed into a motley circle some twenty feet across. A blond teenager is twitching on the ground, his head and hands spazzing. The Lord and some other men pick him up as he comes round.

'Wha – what 'appened?' the boy asks as he's being carted off.

'You was knocked out,' his friend says. 'Cold.'

'Was I?'

From his tone, it's clear he doesn't even know where he is. His friend could tell him he'd been abducted by aliens and he wouldn't argue. It takes him a while to come back to Earth, and when he does, he heads back into the Sway for more punishment.

Local lads or not, they're having a hard time finding their feet. The Sway keeps collapsing every few yards. The Lord marches in to chastise the men, waving his wicker wand and reminding them of the informal code of fair play: mainly that if you see a man down, you help him up, and you definitely don't crowd in to get your hands on the Hood while someone else is suffering at your feet. 'That 'Ood can be taken away any time if I say so,' Phil warns, 'and if you don't play by the rules, I'll stop the bastard!'

For the most part, the bruisers do as they're told, treating him with more respect than they might normally have for a man in a flowery hat. It's understood that Coggon and the Boggins are looking out for us, and whatever our pub preferences, we're all in this together. When you're down, the guy on top of you picks you up, and you grab hold of the man in front of you, and so on, until the boggins untangle the pile-up to dig out the three or four men sprawled every which way and stuck to the Hood. 'That's all we can pick up,' Gary explains over his shoulder. And when he says 'pick up' that's exactly what he means: the men at the centre can't pick themselves up because they've got their hands glued to the leather cylinder. So the boggins have to physically haul them up from the horizontal to the vertical before play can resume.

Blandie has manoeuvred his way into the middle, having fallen on top of the Hood when a rookie foolishly left it exposed. Gillie's down there, too, along with a couple of stalwarts, clinging to the Hood as if their – well, as if their very lives depended on it. From the way they're holding it, you'd think it's a vital organ to which they're surgically attached. Whatever it is, the Hood definitely has a mind of its own, an impish spirit intent on putting the manliest of men into some of the most embarrassing and awkward positions possible: Blandie and a boggin with their cheeks smooshed against each other in an unwanted kiss; Blandie bent in an A-frame over his fellow Swayers, his butt sticking straight up in the air; or Blandie lying right on top of Gillie, two men in the missionary position with a stiff phallic symbol between them.

'Get behind me, and I'll get you into the middle,' Gary promises. He points to the muddy jumble of limbs on the ground. 'The Hood's in there.'

I'll take his word for it. Forget about touching the Hood, I can't even see it, and even if I could see it, I couldn't touch it. So far, the closest I've been to the centre is the inner ring, just outside Blandie and the boys. The trick is to stand right next to the collapsed core and try to muscle in as it stands up – but once the Sway's up and running, you'd be crazy to try to reach over the top or finagle your fingers in between the crushed torsos; if you did, your arm would be contorted at such weird angles that when the Sway fell over again, you'd end up with multiple fractures.

'Have you been able to get your hands on the Hood today?'

'Just the one.' Gary shakes his head. 'That's not good enough.' He turns to start hoisting up bodies and snarls: 'If you've only got one hand on the Hood, then get the *fook* off! That's the rule!'

I get back into the Sway, and we're pushing in a swirl, chanting 'HAXEY! HAXEY!' while our opponents – whoever they are – shout 'WESTWOOD! WESTWOOD!' and those who can't make up their minds holler *'PUUUUSHHH! PUUUUUSSSHH!'* Suddenly, the Sway gets thrown into reverse, the lead dominoes start toppling, and I feel myself falling backwards in slow motion, unable to move my feet as the guys behind scuttle out of the way. My back hits the mud, and all I can see above me is a circle of grey sky ringed with shadowy heads. My legs are pinned down, exposing my feet and ankles: thirteen inches of foot perpendicular to the ground, just waiting to be compacted into countless fractures. My feet will be a size-8 by the time I get out. All it would take is one casualty to smash them flat and rip God knows what tendons in my ankle. *Seven pounds of pressure,* Phil said. Seven pounds and I'm hobbled for life. I wriggle like mad to rotate my foot before the coming crush, but my legs are trapped, as in a death scene out of a B-movie where a tree is falling, and the victim has plenty of time to see it and you think, *Get out of the way!* but they can't because they're pinned to the ground, and finally the tree comes thundering on top of them. Only in this case, it's not one tree but an entire forest of 200-pounders groaning through the air.

WhunnnarrggghhhHHUNNNHHHH!

The impact pushes my guts up into my throat, but fortunately my head and feet have been spared. *Whatever ya do – don't squeal like a pig.*

'Get 'em off me!' somebody's screaming.

'Savour the pain, boys!' Blandie shouts. 'We only get this once a year!'

The guy immediately on top of me has his own sage advice: 'Don't breathe!'

I couldn't if I wanted to. A thousand pounds of pressure are compacting my ribs, and I'm sinking under a dozen men. By the time they dig me out – *if* they dig me out – there's going to be an inch-deep outline of my body in the ground.

'In . . . your own . . . time . . . guys,' I gasp.

Ages later, the boggins come to the rescue, and I struggle to my feet, newly aware of the precise anatomical position of all two-dozen ribs. They're not cracked, or even bruised, just hideously compressed – like the folds of an accordion. The muscles around them feel oxidised and sore, as if I've just done a thousand sit-ups or, more accurately, had a dozen men sit on top of me. There's a certain . . . *resistance* when I breathe in as my lungs expand against my ribcage. My backside is covered in mud, the front of my shirt is soaked, and I've lost my wristwatch – but at least I still have the use of both wrists. After a few times pushing on the fringes of the Sway – at one point I get sucked in and spat out – I decide to walk away while I still can.

And before it gets dark. There's a very good reason why no sane contact sport is played in the dark: namely, you can't see. A couple of cars are shining their lights from the edge of the field, but their beams fall short of the Sway. In the gloaming, all you can make out are silhouettes and the dark spaces denoting mouths and eyes.

Unbelievably, after an hour, the Sway is still locked in a stalemate between Haxey and Westwoodside, stuck in a clumsy back-and-forth dance within twenty yards of where it all started. Whenever the Sway begins to swirl toward Haxey, the Westwood men form a wall to block it. Of the two sides, theirs is the 'uphill' task; the string of houses that makes up Westwood sits at the top of the slight incline. However, many Haxonians have stayed in the pubs, thinking that Westwood would be a walkover. Once they realise that their side is still stuck on the field, though, they venture out to break the deadlock. The Sway stumbles into a depression covered with thick, ankle-twisting grass, aiming for a hard-packed road that runs alongside the field.

With newfound traction, the Haxey men are able to make a panzer push straight into town – slap-bang into a portachippie, if they're not careful. It's parked right next to the road, a small white cubicle with swirly writing overhead: TRULY SCRUMPTIOUS. Normally I wouldn't associate that word with processed meat products, but it seems apt enough here: the Sway is about to put the 'scrum' into 'scrumptious'.

'Form a barrier,' Phil barks, and the boggins stand guard in front of the portachippie. The couple inside freeze. The jut-jawed man, a Burger Lothario, has dark hair, a black shirt and a gold chain twinkling in his chest hairs. He's ready to defend his burger van to the death, armed only with a pair of tongs for a sword and a hamburger bun for a shield. Fortunately, the boggins divert the onslaught, and the hustling and bustling continues on into town. The danger past, the man snaps back to business: 'Do you want cheese on that?'

The Sway bursts onto Haxey's main street. A dozen Westwood diehards make a last-ditch attempt to push it back toward their village, but the four-dozen men shoving in the opposite direction overwhelm them.

'We're all right now!' shouts one Haxey supporter.

Apart from the brick-and-glass gauntlet awaiting them, that is. The houses on the main street are built right up to the kerb, so the road is flanked by solid brick walls, with the occasional section of plate-glass or mullioned window providing yet another way for the men to be injured. Besides getting creamed against the brick wall, they could bleed to death by being pushed through the plate-glass. Throw in an additional stumbling block – the kerb itself – and the route could hardly be more dangerous, unless there were bear traps set out every few feet and rattlesnakes slithering on the ground. Whenever the Sway lurches toward a window, some brave soul – often the Fool – will jump in front of the glass and shout 'WHOA! WHOA! WHOA!' risking the Death of a Thousand Cuts while the people inside the building peek out nervously over his shoulders.

Trapped in the narrow channel, you can see why this steaming whirlpool of silhouettes is called the Sway: it sloshes from one side of the street to the other, zigzagging erratically, suddenly surging down the street and forcing the crowd to scatter. Massive clouds of steam billow from the centre, with men chanting 'DUKE! DUKE!' and 'KINGS! KINGS!' while women watch from the edge, doing their best fishwife impressions: *'GORRROONNNNNN!'*

The steaming Sway revs up and lurches across the street before bouncing back and beginning a long, painful scrape along the house fronts to the Duke William. Blandie's still in the middle, his mullet spiked with mud and sweat. His two brothers are in the crowd – one in a tuxedo, the other trying to keep the men from crashing through the Duke's window. By getting in the way, though, Blandie's brother forces the Sway to step around him; that's all it takes for the chaos to veer off course and miss the pub's entrance. The Duke's supporters rally for a second push up the incline, but the King's partisans have formed a wall in front, digging in their heels to repel the maul of men. The mob staggers backwards and collapses across the kerb, seemingly knocked out for the count while the boggins try to figure out how to lift Blandie and the men in the middle.

The Sway makes one last massive push up the street, steaming and grunting and shouting as all the King's men try to fight off the attackers. Spotting a gap, Blandie and the boys outflank their opponents and drive through to the entrance of the Duke, where the young landlord is fidgeting in the doorway. The Hood itself is nowhere to be seen. The landlord's too short to reach over the crowd, so he gets a lift. At first, he grabs the doorframe to lean out, but that's still not far enough, so he latches on to the fancy woodwork on the outside – a little more – until finally he's body-surfing on the mass of people crowding the doorway. The only parts of him in the pub are his feet.

'He's near enough now!'

'He's won it!'

'Right! Get it oop!'

Blandie and the men negotiate the handover. With one great guttural roar, they rip the Hood out of the tangle of arms, and the leather tube bobs into view above the swirl of heads. The bodysurfing landlord has both his arms outstretched, straining every . . . last . . . sinew – like man trying to touch God – until he clamps his hands on the Hood and pumps it in the air, shouting and thrashing while the crowd cheers. He's still fisting the air and shouting YES! YES! YES! maniacally as he's pulled back to safety inside the pub. The Sway surges through the door, steamrolling anyone in its path, and cans of free beer start flying across the bar.

The morning after, I awake to odd knocks and bruises, the kind you don't realise you have until you're putting on your socks, pushing against a door or sticking your hands in your pocket. There's a dent in my shin, a tender spot on a knuckle and bruises on my forearms where I shoved against the other men, not to mention the soreness around my ribs and the general aches from having spent the day picking up bodies.

Whatever my complaints, though, they can't be anything compared to Blandie's. Nevertheless, he's been up since 7 a.m., just like any normal workday. With the other half of his beard shaved off, he looks rejuvenated as he curls up on the settee, his wife working on the computer in the corner, and their dog conked out next to the fire. 'It were really good,' he smiles. 'I was well 'appy with it. I'm usually layin' in water and shiverin' by the time I get in the pub.' This year was relatively dry and mud-free. 'I come in and looked in the mirror – me face is clean! It looked like I 'adn't even been in it!'

This morning, though, he does have the marks to prove it. 'I've got a few bruises, but that's about all,' he shrugs. No big deal.

Then his wife prompts him to lift his shirt. On one bicep, there's a half-circle of purple splotches – fingerprints; on the back of his other arm, he has a big black-and-blue palm print. The thing is, the bruises weren't inflicted by his rivals, but by the boggins trying to help him. 'When they drag you up out of the Sway, they grip your arms like mad, so you've got fingermarks,' he grins, '*and* it feels like somebody's stamped in the middle a me chest – but apart from that, I'm all right. It was a good Hood.'

CHAPTER TWO

FEAR, FREEDOM AND THE FROMAGE FRAY

CHEESE ROLLING ON COOPER'S HILL

THE DIVING WEDGE: Steve Brain, Lance Townsend and Jason Kotwica hurtle downhill after a Double Gloucester.

THE UNLIKELIEST REBELS

For Iris Peasley and the other guardians of the event, there was never any question of cancelling it altogether. No one said as much; it was more of an unspoken conviction: *Who are we to stop it?* For that matter, who were the county council, or the media, or any other critics to stop a centuries-old tradition that was bigger than all of them put together?

Iris had lived on Cooper's Hill for all but three of her seventy-four years – so long, in fact, that she could remember every emcee from the past century. Even the cottage she and her husband lived in had links to the tradition, having been the home of Bill Brookes, master of ceremonies for more than fifty years starting in the late 1800s. Fox Brookes, the event was so important he was buried in his top hat; another emcee had his ashes spread on the hilltop. Iris's uncle had also served in the post, and her father had been chairman of the organising committee for many years. So many friends and family members had worked so hard to carry on the tradition that she would have felt deeply responsible – guilty, even – for letting them down. And in the past year, the organisers had lost not one but two members, including Iris's own sister. Feeling duty-bound and bloody-minded, the committee resolved, at the same meeting where they cancelled the public spectacle, to hold a clandestine race on the usual date – only this event would take place just after dawn, while most of their critics were sleeping.

So, at six a.m. on that chilly Bank Holiday Monday in May 1998, Iris, her husband, and a group of unlikely rebels trudged out to the hill to defy the handwritten, black-and-white sign planted in the middle of the slope: CHEESE ROLLING CANCELLED.

*

For sheer lunacy and danger, few events can rival cheese rolling. If you've never seen it, the ancient Gloucestershire tradition doesn't sound that daunting: a cheese is flung down a hill, and dozens of men chase it. Initially, I envisaged a wheel of cheese trundling down a long, grassy slope at a leisurely pace. Of course, some runners might take a tumble – that would explain the injuries every year – but they were probably reckless or just plain clumsy. In my naïveté, I even imagined that I might join in the fun.

Then I saw Cooper's Hill. From the bottom, the racecourse doesn't seem that dangerous; from the top, it looks suicidal. No matter how much you've heard about it, no matter how many times you've seen pictures of it, nothing can prepare you for the full jaw-dropping impact of seeing the slope in person. The first known photograph of the event, from 1911, assured readers: 'This gives no idea of the excessive steepness of the hill.' And even if you've seen this 'excessive steepness' once, it still comes as a shock when you visit again.

Cooper's Hill marks the midpoint between Gloucestershire's three contrasting regions: the Vale of Severn, the Forest of Dean and the Cotswolds. Like its hilly counterparts, it's more of a mound than a mountain, not even 900 feet above sea level. As you're driving on the motorway – or the Roman-built Ermine Way – Cooper's Hill stands out as the one with the maypole on top and a grass ramp shaved through the trees. A narrow lane leads you up the side of the hill to the cluster of cottages at the foot of the racecourse, while walkers on the Cotswold Way will stumble across it about halfway through their 100-mile trek. Standing on the summit, you can see for miles across the uneasy mix of town, country and motorway that makes up the Severn Vale: industrial Brockworth crowding the foot of the hill, the spires of Gloucester Cathedral a few miles away, Cheltenham huddled in the distance, the jagged Malverns to the north-west, and the Black Mountains looming just over the border in Wales.

When you look down, though, the ground suddenly disappears. Rather than a gradual incline, the hill drops away at a near seventy-degree angle, then quickly shifts to fifty degrees, then plunges again, then levels out, then falls one last time before abruptly flattening out – leaving runners only a few yards to stop before crashing into a cottage fence at the bottom. The 250-yard race-course is a short, sharp drop full of dips, bulges and any number of perils, seen or unseen: long, ankle-twisting grass; patches of slick, decomposing leaves; gravel outcrops lurking under the turf; tufted islands jutting up unexpectedly; eroded foot-traps masked by grass; not to mention big, fat Roman snails and the odd duck's nest. In short, the hill is a natural obstacle course containing just about every impediment Mother Nature could come up with, making it difficult to walk down, let alone run.

In fact, the runners don't dare start the race standing; instead, they sit at the starting line before flinging themselves off the ledge. There are three men's races and one for women each year. No one ever catches the cheese – it hurtles down at nearly seventy miles an hour. The winner is simply the first runner to hit the bottom of the hill.

'The trick is to try and stay on your feet,' advises reigning champ Steve Brain. But very few runners manage that feat. 'People literally fly through the air,' says Rob Seex, the current master of ceremonies. 'It just looks *insane*. You will be amazed that people aren't more seriously hurt than they are.'

To clear the casualties, paramedics rely on special rescue equipment, abseiling down the hillside to reach the fallen runners, then strapping them into stretchers and lowering them to the bottom. For several years, the only group that would perform this service was a team of potholing fanatics. Surprisingly, though, not even these hardcore cavers have ever chased the cheeses.

What's more, not even the organisers do it. Only a few inhabitants of Cooper's Hill (population: 39) have ever braved the event. Most of the organisers say they're too busy running things to actually take part in the race. The emcee claims his height and a back injury prevented him from competing. 'I'm six-foot-two, much too tall. You've got to be nice and short and five-foot wide.' But Iris Peasley's view may be closer to the truth. 'We're a bit chicken, I think,' she chuckles. 'We know the hill, and we know the dangers.' Like the others on the hill, she leaves cheese chasing to the youngsters from surrounding villages who have something to prove.

Every year, Jason Kotwica and his friends trudge up from Brockworth to run in the race. 'If you live locally, this is the main event in the whole year.' Despite his Polish surname – his grandfather came over during the War – the 22-year-old is Brockworth born and bred. A fence builder by trade, he sports a shaven head, a goatee and gold hoops in both ears. Like his fellow buccaneers, he's been chasing cheeses since he was in his mid-teens. He reckons it makes so-called extreme sports look tame. 'Oh, I've done bungee jumping,' he says dismissively. 'That's not *anything* compared to cheese rolling. When you do bungee jumping, you know it's all organised and safe, but when you run this, you could break your neck.'

To conquer their fear, most cheese chasers rely on Dutch courage. Like wine and cheese, drinking and cheese rolling have gone together for as long as anyone can remember. 'I don't think they get pissed up just for the sake of it,' one rescuer says. 'You *need* to have a few drinks to get yourself into a state where you'd actually throw yourself off the top.' For many runners, the anaesthetic of choice is locally made farmhouse scrumpy, although connoisseurs frown on chasing under the influence. 'I always feel that if they've had too much to drink, they'll never win a cheese,' Iris says. 'They might get to the bottom eventually, but they've got to have a certain amount of clarity in the mind to win one.' That said, drinking may help them stay in one piece. 'It does help if you're totally legless – you relax when you fall,' ventures another local.

Apart from an apocryphal story about a runner dropping dead centuries ago, cheese rolling has yet to produce a serious casualty, defined as a paralysing injury or, God forbid, a fatality. For the organisers, injuries are a sore point, so to speak. They accuse the media – particularly the local papers – of sensationalising the event by focusing on casualties. 'That's the only reason they report on this event, because they like to get as many as they can,' grumbles Tony Peasley, Iris's husband. 'They're so unremittingly negative about the cheese rolling.' In years when the body count is particularly high –

more than a dozen or so – the papers print close-ups of bloodstained competitors lying prostrate on the hill. For hardened veterans, though, gashed heads and broken bones are inevitable. 'That's the whole essence of the cheese rolling,' argues Tony. 'People know that there is an element of risk – there has to be. Otherwise, why roll cheeses down the hill and chase after them?'

Why indeed? For injuries, like alcohol, have always been part of cheese rolling. The first photos of the event capture an Edwardian casualty in progress: 'The leading competitor has pitched right over, and can be seen halfway down standing on his head,' the caption explains. In recent decades, the injuries have increased along with the speed. 'They didn't go so fast in the old days,' Iris maintains, recalling a couple of champions from the 1940s and 1950s who never fell down. 'It was much nicer to watch because there was more of an art to it. They just throw themselves like lemmings now.'

To prevent a tragedy, the cheese roll has the cave rescuers as well as the St John Ambulance on hand. The injuries on the hill range from grazed knees to suspected spinal trauma. Then there are the photogenic injuries like head cuts, which bleed a lot and make the hill look like a battle scene, yielding headlines such as CARNAGE ON COOPER'S HILL. The casualties increase during dry years, when the sun bakes the slope rock hard. In 1978, a runner was knocked unconscious for an hour, and a winner sprained his ankle and lost a front tooth: 'It snapped off clean,' the newspaper reported, alongside a photo of him posing with a gap-toothed grin, the very picture of a local yokel. To date, though, the worst wounds have been fractures. 'You get broken legs, broken arms, broken ribs, broken collarbones – I should think collarbones are fairly common,' the emcee says matter-of-factly, 'but a lot of injuries look worse than what they are.'

Still, some of the injuries are just as bad as they look. Surprisingly, cheese chasers aren't the only ones at risk. Bystanders have also been hurt – by out-of-control runners . . . and bouncing cheeses. Rob Seex does his best to make sure the VIPs who roll the eight-pound Double Gloucesters aim for a midpoint at the bottom of the hill, which, whether by coincidence or not, lies right next to the media's bullpen. 'This year there was a camera stand there, so I said aim for that,' the emcee smiles, 'but if the cheese hits a bump in the wrong place, it can take off and go well up in the sky.' Iris remembers dodging the cheeses as a child. 'Nowadays everybody gets a bit paranoid about the cheese, but in the old days, you didn't seem to worry about it – perhaps it was just that we were a bit thick; we didn't realise then that it would hurt!'

And then some. By the time they hit the bottom, the cheese wheels are spiralling unpredictably at top speed. 'That's gotta be a bit of a whack,' says Jason, whose mother was hit in the leg by a hurtling cheese. 'She had a humongous bruise and couldn't walk for a couple of weeks.' More recently, a spectator banged his head and fell a hundred feet down the slope after trying to dodge a wayward cheese. Fortunately, he didn't suffer the same fate as a fabled bystander from long ago. His epitaph declared:

> Here lies Billy, if you please
> Hit in the stomach with a cheese
> Cheese is wholesome fayre, they say
> It turned poor Billy into clay.

As crippling mishaps go, it would be hard to top Gareth Smedley's. When he was seven, his family went to watch the race on a hot Bank Holiday Monday in 1982. Rather than jostle with the crowds, they decided to watch from a field further down the slope. Just as the Cheese Roll began, though, a storm broke. The Smedleys and another family ran for cover under a tree. There was no bang or flash when the lightning hit. Gareth's mother, Barbara, woke to find herself lying in the wet field, dazed and unable to move. *A bomb's exploded!* she thought, but then she looked up and saw the races continuing as normal. That's when she realised: both families had been blown several feet from the tree, forming a ring of bodies around the trunk. None of them could get up – the electricity had contracted their muscles so violently their limbs were useless. Her husband had a singed spot on his leg, and little Gareth had a hole burnt in his T-shirt where he had been leaning against the tree. Someone alerted the medics, and the casualties were rushed off in an ambulance. All eight of them were released later that day, but it was a full week before they completely recovered. Barbara has been wary of Cooper's Hill ever since. 'I felt that we were jinxed from the cheese rolling.' If only Gareth would have listened.

At the age of seventeen, he decided to give cheese rolling a go. The timing of his debut didn't bode well – it happened to be the 10th anniversary of the Smedleys' first ill-fated experience on Cooper's Hill. Whereas old pros lean back at the start of the race, Gareth bolted headlong down the incline, leading the pack. But suddenly the hill flattened out, and he slipped, pitching him into a somersault that banged his head. Hurtling downhill, he did half a dozen side rolls, his right foot hitting the slope with every turn until his legs flopped beneath him like a messy pretzel. After a final back flip, he landed at the bottom, only yards from the finish line. Determined to win, he got on all fours and started crawling, but his right leg gave way. He tried to get up again but collapsed. He didn't feel any pain; it was as if his leg weren't there.

At least a dozen paramedics pounced on him. Despite his injuries and the blood streaking down his face, Gareth wasn't in agony; he was more concerned that the paramedics were cutting into his new jeans. His friends huddled round, not so much out of sympathy but curiosity: they wanted a glimpse of the gore – as did the cameras. If it bleeds, it leads, and Jason's blood-streaked visage, with a fat bandage on his head and a brace around his neck, provided the opening shot for the local TV news. As the medics lifted him into the ambulance, Gareth gave his mates two thumbs up, pumping his arms in the air. 'I'm sound as a pound,' he shouted.

Unfortunately, Gareth wasn't all right. At the hospital, X-rays confirmed just how serious his injuries were. Besides the gash on his scalp, which needed eight stitches, his thighbone – the longest and strongest bone in the human body – had snapped in half. After a five-and-a-half-hour operation to run an 18-inch pin through it, Gareth spent two weeks in hospital and another four months on crutches. He was in physiotherapy for the rest of the year. The doctors warned him that if he broke his thigh again, the pin would bend rather than break, shattering his femur into fragments.

A decade later, though, Gareth says the stark warning didn't scare him. In fact, he tells me that he and a friend ran down the slope the following year, after the official race. True to form, he broke his collarbone.

Gloucestershire is synonymous with cheese, so it's fitting that some of its more offbeat traditions focus on fromage.

The county's other cheese roll takes place at Randwick, a Cotswold village just fifteen minutes away from Cooper's Hill. The Randwick 'Wap' boasts two cheese-related events that used to count Laurie Lee as their patron; the *Cider with Rosie* author was a local from the Stroud Valley down below. On the first Sunday in May, a procession ushers a trio of Double Gloucesters into the church in garlanded wicker baskets for the Blessing of the Cheeses. Then, after the service, the sacred cylinders are bowled 'widdershins' around the building. The town crier explains why: 'They're rolled thrice anticlockwise so that the spirits of the dead can't see the cheese comin'.' One cheese is diced and devoured, while the other two are saved for the following Saturday, or Wap Day, when the mock mayor is borne through the village on a litter, then symbolically dunked in a shallow pool. After some speeches, the mayor, the Wap Queen, and their attendants roll the remaining Double Gloucesters down a footpath. Crucially, though, no one chases them.

There's no real danger at Gloucestershire's other dairy tradition, either, but it does share the helter-skelter spirit of Cooper's Hill. Every Whit Sunday, the villagers of St Briavel's in the Forest of Dean gather like pigeons outside their local church for the Bread and Cheese Dole. Two locals stand on a wall, flinging a hail of food into the air while men, women and children scramble below for the lucky morsels. In the old days, people used to fight over the stuff; some even pelted the vicar. Nowadays, most participants leave the cubes of bread and cheese to be gobbled up by dogs.

Like the Bread and Cheese Dole, the Cooper's Hill Cheese Roll may have been a medieval way of protecting locals' rights to common land. However, no one knows for sure. Whenever they're stumped by a tradition, academics have a standard, one-size-fits-all explanation. 'It's a ritual,' they'll say. This is code for 'We haven't got a clue', but sounds much more impressive. The most intriguing (and possibly farfetched) theory about cheese rolling is that it's a prehistoric sun ritual, or – to spice things up – a pagan fertility rite. Long ago, Europe's sun-worshipping pagans supposedly rolled blazing wheels down slopes during Midsummer celebrations to stoke the sun's fires and improve their crops. After briefly experimenting with maidens in burning wicker cages, the heathens of Cooper's Hill supposedly switched from rolling wheels of fire to . . . bowling discs of cheese.

As ridiculous as that sounds, there may be something to the legend (except for the virgin burning). The ancient Celts and their Druid priests worshipped the sun in the form of wheel motifs, stamping the symbols on everything from coins to cauldrons, and throwing them into sacred springs as votive offerings. The Dobunni, the tribe that lived on Cooper's Hill, ruled much of the West Country and worshipped the sun goddess Sul. When the Roman Empire's stormtroopers invaded in AD 43, some Dobunni resisted, while the ones around Cooper's Hill quickly capitulated. As a reward, the Romans allowed these turncoat Celts to more or less govern themselves, and the two sides settled into an apparently peaceful coexistence. The Celts stuck to their hilltops, while the Romans lived in the fertile valleys below, importing the fat edible 'Roman snails' that still occasionally trip up cheese chasers. (The immediate source of these sluggish delicacies may have been the sprawling Roman Dunroamin at the base of Cooper's Hill. The water trickling onto the ruins of the villa comes from an underground spring that also marks the finish line for the Cheese Roll.)

On the Continent, the Romanised Celts in south-west France had started rolling flaming wheels downhill to a river by the fourth century AD. A millennium later, a similar custom was recorded in England, at Winchcombe, only ten miles from Cooper's Hill. This unholy rolling took place on Midsummer's Eve, the red-letter date for ritual pyromania across Europe. The usual explanation is that 24 June marked the sun's peak; from then on, it slid across the horizon to its wintry nadir. By rolling fiery wheels down slopes, the Celts and their descendants may have been trying to revitalise the sun's life-giving power. Or so the story goes.

To prop up the theory that cheese rolling evolved from wheel rolling, I needed to find an event where the projectiles were used interchangeably. This missing link exists – just thirty miles from Cooper's Hill, at the Vale of the White Horse in Oxfordshire. The landmark is possibly 3,000 years old, and centuries ago, the locals used to clean the white figure every few years on Whit Monday (the same day as the Cooper's Hill Cheese Roll). As part of the festivities surrounding the Scouring of the White Horse, men would race down the steep gully to the springs at the bottom. Sometimes they would chase cheeses, other times wheels, but the prize was always cheese.

The Victorian novelist Thomas Hughes returned to his home village for this fair in 1857, shortly after penning his bestseller, *Tom Brown's Schooldays*. His obscure follow-up, entitled *The Scouring of the White Horse, or The Long Vacation Ramble of a London Clerk*, provides the earliest description of racing for cheese that I've been able to find. According to Hughes, the locals had been chasing missiles on the common land of the Vale since at least 1755. Unfortunately, the Scouring of the White Horse died out shortly after his visit.

As at the White Horse, cheese rolling was one of the main attractions at the Cooper's Hill Wake. In 1836, Gloucester's town crier provided the first record of the race, promising cheeses that were as 'hard as Pharoah's heart'. Other events included gurning through horses' collars, sack races, bobbing for apples and oranges, dancing competitions, a girls' race for a chemise, wrestling matches, and 'a bladder of snuff to be chatred for by hold wimming' (old women). For decades, the flat expanse at the top of the hill served as a fairground dotted with a maypole, gypsies' stalls, and contests of all kinds, including fistfights. 'After the wake was over, ruffianism commenced,' a local recalled in the late 1800s. 'The village feuds, grudges and personal quarrels were then settled. Sanguinary and prolonged fights followed.'

Cooper's Hill Wake survived until the 1930s, when the double whammy of Depression and War killed off many country traditions.

Even so, the locals made sure the main race continued. Cheese was rationed during the war (and for years afterwards), so they improvised with a wooden disc containing a morsel of the real thing inside. Winners didn't get to keep the titbit – or the dummy cheese, for that matter. As a teenager, Rose Hellerman was drafted into the ladies' race in 1942 during a particularly wet cheese roll. She ended up slip-sliding to the bottom in her mac, skirt and Wellington boots. 'I won the cheese, and then they had the next race, and I had the indignity of having to go all the way back up with the cheese!' she laughs. Nowadays, Rose runs a tearoom on the side of the hill, in the tiny bungalow where she was born seventy-three years ago. 'You see, you can't stop these customs – people *won't*,' she says. 'It's in my blood and it's in my son's blood. We've got to cling to our roots. *Heritage*, I suppose you'd call it.'

And that's why the tradition continues to this day.

For someone called 'Brainy', chasing a cheese down a grassy cliff doesn't seem the smartest thing to do. But Steve Brain is the King of Cooper's Hill. A bricklayer and former rugby player, Steve has the shaved scalp, pale eyes and a rough complexion that would mark him out as a hard man even if he's the nicest guy in the world. At thirty-two, he's won seventeen cheeses, putting him half a dozen fromages behind the all-time record set by his old rival, Stephen Gyde. The two Steves started running against each other in the late 1980s, and it was Brain who finally ended Gyde's winning streak. Ever since, he's been gunning for 'Gydie's' record of twenty-three cheeses. It's not for the love of cheese – he doesn't even like Double Gloucester; no, for Steve, who grew up with a view of the hill from his bedroom window, it's what the dairy discs stand for that counts.

The Cooper's Hill Cheese Roll has served as a rite of passage for the men of Brockworth for decades, if not centuries. 'No self-respecting young man in the village could face a young lady if he hadn't run down there,' one old-timer said. Steve's father and grandfather braved the slope at least once in their youth, as have many of his friends. So it was inevitable that he would do the same, partly out of respect for tradition, but mostly because he wanted to prove himself to his friends and family. Ever since he started running down Cooper's Hill, he's been winning races. When he was in his teens, Steve made his debut against Gyde, who was eight years older. Gyde went on to win the first race, but he sat out the last heat, leaving Steve to win his maiden cheese at just fifteen.

Nowadays, Steve regularly finishes the 250-yard race in just eleven seconds. Like any world-class athlete, he keeps videotapes of his performances and plays them back in slow motion to study his technique. At the top of the hill, the slope funnels into a bowl that wipes out most runners, so he tries to break out early to clear that bit. From then on, everything depends on the ground conditions. If it's been a dry spring, and the slope is rock hard, he has to take it slow. But if it's rained a lot, he can run fast because he can slow down when he needs to. For veterans, there are two ways to cut your speed as you're shooting down the hill: leaning back and skidding on your heels, or kicking out your legs and sliding on your backside until you can find your feet. For novices, of course, there is a third way to slow down: dropping and rolling.

Amazingly, after nearly two decades of cheese chasing, Brain has never had any serious injuries. He has gashed his head and twisted his ankle, but he's never broken any bones, though he did come close one time. 'I landed straight on my head, and my neck kind of . . . *clicked*. It was a bit stiff for a few days.' Lately, Steve has begun to think that he may start picking and choosing his cheese rolls. 'At the moment, when I run down the hill, I feel kind of invincible. If I hurt myself bad, I'll probably give it up, like, but I never 'ave – touch wood.' He grins and knocks on his noggin.

There for a while, though, it looked like the Cheese Roll itself was finished. Whereas it used to be just a local event, with crowds of 1,500 from surrounding towns and villages, in recent years, the tradition has attracted up to 4,000 from all over the world. Before the introduction of safety netting, spectators would often spill onto the racecourse. Many of the runners and onlookers had been drinking for a solid six hours beforehand, making collisions and trampling inevitable. In 1989, a cheese hit an eight-year-old girl, and a runner bowled over a boy. The following year, twenty-two people were injured, including a grandmother knocked out by a cheese. CHEESE CHASE CHAOS screamed the headline in the local paper. A concerned reader called for cheese rolling to be banned to ease the burden of treating the wounded on the NHS.

Still the body count rose. In 1994, a flying cheese broke a boy's leg. A year later, two runners had to be airlifted off the hill, and the St John Ambulance admitted that it had been unable to cope with the casualties for the first time in thirty years. The breaking point came in 1997, when the injuries totalled at least eighteen – and possibly twice that number – including seven spectators. One veteran, a cousin of Steve Brain, broke his left arm, having already broken his right arm a few years earlier, earning him a double fracture for his Double Gloucesters. During the race, two of the trophy cheeses were stolen, including one of Steve's, while the hillside rescuers complained that drunken yobs damaged their equipment and assaulted a paramedic. The local paper ran gory photos that made the bloodied competitors look like survivors of the Battle of Cooper's Hill. 'Greater Safety Needed' it declared in an editorial.

A few months before the next event, the county council began demanding insurance certificates, safety fencing, and consultations with Health and Safety officials – *about cheese rolling!* The hillside rescue team pulled out, fearing a repeat of the previous year's mayhem. Unable to find a replacement in time, the organisers were forced to do the unthinkable: with just five days to go before the Cheese Roll, the organisers announced that the event would be cancelled for the first time in living memory. The loss of a great British tradition made national headlines at a time when the English were already suffering from a national identity crisis. FEARS SCUPPER THE GREAT CHEESE ROLL, the *Daily Telegraph* declared, while *The Times* was even more final: CHEESE TRADITION ROLLS TO AN END.

Nevertheless, the mood on the hill that bank holiday morning in 1998 was relaxed and jubilant. Forget the bureaucrats, the journalists, the critics . . . Blow *them*! The people of Cooper's Hill were defying them all by forging ahead with their own clandestine Cheese Roll. They weren't doing it for outsiders or even themselves;

they were doing it for tradition's sake. Instead of thousands of people swarming over the hill, the spectators on this cool, overcast morning numbered no more than thirty. *This is how it must have started,* they said to each other, *as a small gathering of friends and families.* Rob Seex was there, decked out in his emcee's regalia, and the cheese was wrapped in its red and blue ribbons. However, a key component of the race was missing. They didn't have any runners. With no outsiders around to risk their necks, the locals were going to have to take the plunge.

After some hesitation, three men agreed to run, including Rose Hellerman's son. Peter Astman was as reliable as you'd expect a postman to be. When he wasn't making the rounds, he was usually helping out on one of the farms. His co-workers in Gloucester teased him about it all the time, nicknaming him Farmer. With his bristly beard and lean-muscled frame, he did look like a West Countryman out of central casting. (In fact, he once auditioned as an extra for the TV version of a Thomas Hardy novel.) Always willing to help out, here he was again, risking his neck to keep the tradition alive. 'We better make a show,' he told the others.

Peter also had his own reasons for taking part. Both his parents had run in the race when they were teenagers – his mother won it during the war years, having also been drafted in at the last minute. Although she didn't say as much, Peter couldn't help but feel that she had expected him to run at some point. He never had . . . until now. At the age of forty-four – well past his prime for this kind of lunacy – he realised that he would probably never get another chance to live up to his parents' legacy.

Those kinds of concerns didn't come into play for Peter's youngest competitor, the eight-year-old great-niece of Iris Peasley. Amelia Hardwick wanted to run down the slope simply because it looked fun. Her family owned a farm on the hill, and her father had been coming to the Cheese Roll ever since he was knee high to a grasshopper. Standing on the summit, Amelia informed her father that she was going to do her part for tradition. 'Hold my glasses,' she said, and with that, she took her place alongside the three middle-aged men on the hill.

Everyone agreed that instead of launching themselves from the top, the runners should start about halfway down. That way there was less chance of the cheese bouncing out of control and the chasers suffering serious bodily harm. After all, there were no ambulances on hand, and the hill hadn't been cleared, so it was even more treacherous than usual. A thick coat of scrub covered the ankle-twisting foot traps lurking underneath. What's more, the grassy cliff was saturated with dew, making it all but impossible for the runners to control their speed. Once they reached the bottom, they would have to stop quickly to avoid crashing into the wire fence.

Not for nothing, then, did Peter feel frightened.

'ONE TO BE STEADY!' the emcee hollered. 'TWO TO BE READY! . . . THREE TO PREPARE! . . . AND FOUR AWAY!'

The cheese hurtled downhill, and Peter started after it, slowly at first, running sideways to grip the turf. Before he knew it, though, little Amelia passed him, her ponytail bouncing behind her as she scampered down, her tiny trainers buried in the undergrowth. *She's goin' so fast!* The other men were well behind, struggling for balance on the slick, undulating slope. Peter also fell a couple of times, sliding on his backside until he found his feet again. Meanwhile, the little moppet in the red jumper dashed toward the finish, running so quickly that Peter wondered if he should let her win. But the answer that flashed through his mind was *No – I shall never do it again, and she'll have plenty of opportunity*.

Fence or no fence, he decided to go for it. And once he started going, he couldn't stop. Neither could Amelia. As she ran full-speed onto the flat bit at the bottom, she wiped out. Peter stayed on his feet, slip-sliding past her, only a few yards from the finish line. Pale and shaken, the little girl picked herself up and chased after him, closing the gap to three yards, then two . . .

But it was too late. Peter had won.

Afterwards, he and Amelia (the de facto women's champ) posed for their friends' cameras, holding the cheese overhead before it was cut up and distributed to everyone there. The photos later found their way into the local, national and even international media as proof of British Bloodymindedness.

On the afternoon of the secret Cheese Roll, Jason Kotwica and some friends from Brockworth also snuck up to the hill to stage their own event, using the only round cheese they could find . . . a Dutch Edam. But for the people of Cooper's Hill, theirs was the only truly authentic race. 'It was lovely,' Iris Peasley recalled. 'It was the best Cheese Roll ever.'

PART TWO:
A CHEESEMAN MEETS HIS DESTINY

Most runners risk their necks for the rush or the novelty of saying they've been there and done that, but this year one participant has made the pilgrimage to Cooper's Hill for reasons that have to do with his very identity. 'You'd think people with "cheese" in their name would have done it – but maybe I'm just mad,' laughs Simon Cheeseman.

That's right – this 27-year-old from West Sussex has travelled a hundred miles simply to live up to his name. Tramping up the hillside in the sporadic drizzle, Simon and his friend, Michael ('I'm the driver'), are goofing around between gasps about just how *kuh-raaaazy* they are to have come here.

Once they reach the top, though, they stop laughing.

'That is *quite* unbelievable,' Simon says, peering down the slippery ledge.

'The only thing I've seen that's worse is parachute jumping,' Michael agrees.

Cheeseman puts on his glasses to get a better look. Even with his specs, the bottom of the hill is just a misty green blur. Simon is 'partially sighted', meaning that the only part of an eye chart he can read is the top letter, the biggest one. You could argue that it's better to run blindly down Cooper's Hill – what you can't see can't hurt you. But in reality, his determination to run requires extraordinary courage – or foolishness, depending on your point of view. Whereas people with average eyesight can anticipate pitfalls, Simon sees them only at the last second, meaning that he has to react much more quickly. He's honed his reflexes by playing in England's Partially Sighted Five-a-Side football team. Even so, he's seriously wondering whether he can do this.

'It's starting to look a little bit better now.' After about five minutes of nervous laughter, Michael, at least, is becoming acclimatised to the hill.

'That's because you're not doin' it!'

However, Simon has made up his mind. Standing on the summit, the cold wind whipping around him, he sweeps his hand across the mist-laden Vale of Severn, sizing up an imaginary headline against the hills: CHEESEMAN WINS CHEESE ROLLING. Then he admits the more likely outcome: 'I'm gonna end up like cheese fondue.'

The next morning, the activity at the foot of the hill looks like the preparations for a pitched battle. A weekend of cold drizzle has left the slope exceedingly slippery, ensuring plenty of spills and tumbles, but also cushioning the runners' falls. About thirty medical workers, including a dentist, are readying themselves for the onslaught. Three ambulances crowd the small car park where the St John Ambulance has set up two orange medical tents. The one for serious wounds contains stretchers and resuscitation equipment with dials and tubes sticking out of it. Meanwhile, at the summit, the emergency rescue team practises hauling a neon orange stretcher down the bumpy hillside on ropes.

Hundreds of spectators are pressing against the orange safety fences running along the top and sides of the slope, while many more are still ascending the hill, forming long lines like ants climbing a mound. For the most part, the assembled families come from the hard-knock side of life, though there aren't as many lager louts as there used to be. As part of the safety measures introduced when the event was officially reinstated in 1999, the organisers now hold the Cheese Roll at noon rather than six p.m. to reduce the number of drunks and casualties. Up top, the Cheeseman is sharing a dainty bottle of French beer with Michael. They're as goofily exuberant as ever. Still, it's hard not to worry about the worst possible outcome: 'Er, broken arm . . . broken leg . . . crippled for life,' he says, squinting through his contacts.

'They've got the stretchers out for you,' laughs Michael, who's ostensibly here for moral support.

As Simon's personal high noon approaches, he swears he's not nervous. His palms are dry and his hands steady; he doesn't even have butterflies. 'I think it hits you when you go out on the ledge. It's probably not as scary as it looks. That's what I'm hoping – ask me later.' On cue, he and the other runners step out from behind the safety fence and file onto the last bit of level ground they'll see for the next few minutes. Simon sits in the middle of the ten-strong line-up. Though he doesn't know it, he's up against experienced cheese chasers, including Steve Brain, Jason Kotwica and Lance Townsend, who's run in the race for the past twenty years and vowed that he won't quit until he wins a cheese. These hardened veterans stare down the precipice without blinking, facing the breakneck descent like soldiers about to attack an old enemy. With his round chin, soft face and thinning hair, Cheeseman looks decidedly out of place amid the hard men of cheese rolling. Most of them have shaved heads, workingman's tans, and wotchyoulookinat faces. He's been sipping French beer from a tiny bottle, whereas most of them have been swigging hard cider from two-litre plastic containers. While he plays Partially Sighted Five-a-Side football, they play blood-and-guts rugby. Next to these hungry greyhounds, Simon is a well-fed pug.

Emcee Rob Seex, in his white coat and top hat, tells the men to slide down just below the rim for the start of the race. With his stick planted in the slope, and the red, white and blue ribbons on his hat fluttering in the breeze, Rob bellows the age-old orders: 'ONE TO BE STEADY! . . . TWO TO BE READY! . . . THREE TO PREPARE!' – the cheese bounces down the hill – 'AND FOUR AWAY!' – and the men go tumbling after.

Right from the start, the runners crash into each other as the hill funnels into a steep bowl – the Crucible of Pain, for lack of a better term. Picture ten men sprinting toward a midpoint a few yards away, tilt the racetrack at a 70-degree angle, and you'll get an idea of the chaos as they slam into each other, pushing and shoving in a vain attempt to stay on their feet. For anyone fast enough to beat the crush, there's another pitfall immediately afterwards: the far side of the bowl suddenly levels out, providing a perfect launch pad for inexperienced runners – it was this rim that sent Steve Brain somersaulting fifteen feet into the air one year.

Just a couple of seconds in, and the men are doing all kinds of freestyle gymnastics: the Sliding Wedge, the Cooper's Hill Head-Dive, the Fromage Freefall . . . Simon shrewdly opts for the Bottom Slide, using his butt like a sled on the muddy slope, desperately trying to avoid cracking a rib, breaking an arm or worse as he hears men smashing into each other all around him. Even so, he ends up losing control and does several rolls before plopping on his backside again.

You can't hear the men for the crowd's noise, but you can imagine their cries of pain punctuating every bounce, bump, cut and collision during their cartoonish descent. To fully appreciate this clumsy ballet of collisions, you'd need a slow-motion camera to see the exact moment when that skinheaded runner careened into and then leapt over the prostrate body of a fallen rival, or that superb Double Gloucester Somersault and Triple Side Roll before the runner miraculously bounced back onto his feet. Between watching the race and making sure the cheese doesn't hit you, it's easy to miss the finer moments of what has been termed the Fromage Fray.

Steve Brain keeps clear of the carnage and manages to stay on his feet all the way down for the first time in his career. Jason comes in a close second, despite having slammed into Lance, completed a somersault and landed on his neck. Simon slides in a respectable fourth after recovering from a Head Cheese Tumble and landing on his feet. Out-of-control runners crash into hay bales at the bottom or get tackled by 'catchers' recruited from the local rugby team. Jason is sprawled facedown in the grass, along with a couple of other casualties stunned by their self-inflicted injuries. The St John workers trot out in their spiffy green overalls to clear up the human wreckage. Amazingly, no one has been seriously injured. After a dramatic pause, Jason staggers to his feet. His neck is sore, but he plans to run again. Simon, too, is going back for more. 'It goes so fast, you don't have time to even think about it,' he enthuses.

This brief cycle of hilarity and horror repeats itself with every race: a few seconds of flopping down the hillside, followed by groaning at the bottom. His second time out, the Cheeseman gets the hang of it, taking off as soon as he can and watching for false starts. Again, Steve Brain leads the pack, bounding down the hill like a human springbok, each stride longer than the last, until he kicks out to slow down, performing a quick Quadruple Side Roll before bouncing back onto his feet and completing with a flying finish in twelve seconds. He wins by at least five yards, while the rest of the muddy runners stumble after him. Simon takes fourth again, having actually run some of the way this time. The last straggler crosses the finish line a full thirty seconds after starting.

But others are less fortunate. One runner splats to the ground after a bone-cracking collision. Ten spiffy green overalls surround him. You can hardly see the victim for the rescuers. He's conscious – that's a good sign – but they've had to put him in a neck brace – that can't be good. The medics stretcher him off to congratulatory clapping. Meanwhile, Jason Kotwica decides to sit out the last race because of his neck injury. Not so Simon, who's a shiny-eyed convert by now. 'It's good fun,' he insists.

The downhill heats for men and women are interspersed with comical uphill races for the kiddies. No matter how enthusiastically the children start scrambling up the slope, they soon slow to a painful crawl. They try to run, arms and legs pumping in slow motion, but gravity just won't let them. By the end, they're doubled over, effectively crawling up on all fours, pulling and pushing their way to the top.

For the ladies' race, only two teenagers volunteer. Sabrina Rimmer called Helen Thorp a chicken, so they've both ended up flinging themselves down the hill, with two overenthusiastic tots for company. The boys gallop past them, while the girls do unusual Cotswold Carpet Rolls down the incline. Helen hits the bottom first, while Sabrina stops ten yards from the finish, then picks herself up and tumbles the rest of the way.

At first glance, the girls don't look like the type to chase cheeses. Helen is a pretty, shorthaired blonde with sharp, saucy features and a stud in one nostril, while Sabrina is a pretty, long-haired brunette with wide eyes and a sensuous mouth. As it turns out, though, they're both card-carrying Ladettes, members of the equal-opportunity sisterhood whose motto is 'If Men Can Be Obnoxious, *Why Can't We?*' After recovering from the rough and tumble, Helen jumps around, sticking her finger in the air and whooping to her friends on the sidelines, 'Tonight we're goin' out on the piss!'

'I don't even like cheese,' she tells reporters, 'but it's a tradition, isn't it.' Her dad ran in the race, and Sabrina's sister won a cheese a couple of years ago. 'But I don't think I'll do it again,' Sabrina says, wincing from a back injury.

The photographers can't get enough of the photogenic fromagettes. They're lining Helen up against the hill as she cavorts for the cameras, posing with the cheese overhead. Hoisting the cheese soon gets her hot, however, and before you know it, she's stripped off her running jacket to reveal a short top underneath. For the snappers, this is a godsend – now, when Helen lifts the cheese, she also lifts her top, unveiling her flat alabaster belly with a ring through the navel. Her pale skin contrasts with her dirty jeans, which are fashionably low-slung on her hips, the band of her designer underwear peeking over the top. The Revelation of Helen's Belly is a windfall for the photographers, and their cameras kick into overdrive, a frenzy of clicks and whirrs as the girls frolic with the fromage. The men are begging them for poses that must – indeed, *need to* – appear in tomorrow's papers for a host of reasons mainly to do with the hang-ups of middle-aged news editors.

'Can you kiss the cheese for us?' a snapper leers, laying bare the sexual fantasies lurking behind every lens. The girls smile and pump the cheese overhead, they pucker up on either side to kiss it, and so on and so forth until the clicking reaches its climax, the men's lenses gradually lower, and both sides withdraw to recover from the exertion. An exhausted Helen hollers to the crowd, 'Does anybody have a fag?'

The last heat is packed out with thirty runners – every would-be hard man who's finally worked up the nerve to face the hill. Even the legendary Stephen Gyde has come out of semi-retirement. The threat of Steve Brain winning three cheeses in one year for the first time in his career seems to have helped the world record holder forget his age.

Gyde quickly cuts across the hillside and tries to slide in front of his rival. Their knees clash, but Steve stays on his feet, making a beeline downhill. Gyde recovers from his failed tackle and tries to chase Brain again, but before he can, another runner slides into him from behind, knocking his legs out from under him. Brainy sprints down the hill, dismounting with a neat somersault to complete his very first hat trick. As the reporters home in on him, the King of the Hill gives them insights into Zen-and-the-Art-of-Cheese-Chasing: 'Be cautious of the hill, respect it, but don't let it scare you.'

Gyde didn't even place, and he quickly disappears. For the Cheeseman, though, the third race was the charm. He beat all but two men to the bottom, sliding down most of the way but also running in fits and starts. He proudly claims his third-place prize – all of £3 – and earns a special mention over the loudspeaker because of his surname. He's so blissed out on adrenaline, he doesn't feel any pain. 'Ohh, that's a graze,' he says of the cut on his hand. 'No pain, no gain! He who dares, wins!'

Surprisingly, the St John diagnose all of today's injuries as 'minor' – including the possible spinal injury, the runner who was knocked unconscious, and the computer programmer who dislocated his shoulder for the second time in three years. The low body count delights the organisers but disappoints the media. 'No deaths!' a shutterbug says only half-jokingly.

An hour later, Simon is sitting on the terrace of Rose Hellerman's tearoom overlooking the vale. Having polished off some scones, the Cheeseman is already plotting his comeback, expounding on the different ways of conquering Cooper's Hill.

'Ohhh, he won't half have a big head tomorrow,' Rose says.

One of her friends chuckles. 'That'll be the bruises!'

PART THREE:
PRETENDERS TO THE THRONE

Despite his vow to return, Simon Cheeseman doesn't make it back to Cooper's Hill the following year. He's saving himself for the Partially Sighted Five-a-Side World Cup. 'Obviously, playing for my country, I can't really afford to get a broken leg.'

Jason Kotwica has also decided to stay on the sidelines after his injury last year turned out to be a broken collarbone, which wasn't diagnosed until three weeks after the race. However, nothing could keep Jason from sharing the excitement on Cooper's Hill. He's been up since 6.15, even though it's a Bank Holiday Monday. 'I tried lyin' in this morning, but it weren't 'appening. Couldn't sleep – like a schoolkid at Christmas!'

He and his crew have assembled at the top of the hill an hour before the race, cradling their bottles of cider and gazing nervously down the slope. The weekend showers have cleared, and the morning is sunny with white clouds coasting overhead. For the runners, though, a dark shadow has descended over the hilltop. These aren't the kind of men who readily admit to being scared, but when it comes to talking about the race, they openly confess their fears.

Next to Jason, Lance Townsend is smoking roll-ups in quick

succession, determined to win a race. 'No matter how many times you do it, it still frightens the life outta you.'

Lance has been putting himself through this heart-pumping, head-aching torture for the past twenty-one years without ever winning a cheese. I'd met him the previous year, after he lost out yet again to his old friend, Steve Brain. 'I've come in second and third more than anyone,' he moaned. 'Once I win one, I'll stop.' When I heard that, I imagined him as a wheelchair-bound competitor, rolling himself off the summit: *I said I won't stop 'til I win o-o-o-o-ne!* At thirty-five, Lance is already the senior citizen of the Cheese Roll; he's been running since Jason and his friends were babies. The stubble on his head is a mixture of blond and grey, and he has a tooth missing from his bottom row. The Townsends have never had much luck chasing cheeses. Lance's dad ran down the hill once but didn't even place, while his brother bashed his head on a rock and knocked himself out. When he was seventeen, Lance lost to Steve Brain in a just-for-fun race where their fathers bet 50p on them. You'd think Steve would let his old friend win once, just to see him smile – not his usual wry, down-in-the-mouth grin, but an ear-to-ear, 31-toothed smile of relief and elation. For Lance takes little pleasure in cheese rolling. Like a reverse Sisyphus, he's a slave to the hill: instead of pushing a boulder up the slope, he has to chase a cheese down it, repeating the ordeal for what seems like eternity.

But this year is different. 'This is the very last time,' he says determinedly.

'He says that every year, mind,' scoffs a young runner.

'No, I know I've said it every year, but I really do mean it. This is the last time. I'm thirty-five now, and I'm gettin' too old,' Lance insists, explaining that in all his years, he's never had any major mishaps: 'Dislocated shoulder, just a couple of sprained ankles. Nothing serious. Aches and pains and cuts and bruises like no tomorrow. I'll wake up the next day, I can't walk, I'm like an old man. You don't realise it until the next day how bad you are.'

A half hour before the race, the man they've all been waiting for finally appears. After last year's hat trick, the question this time is not 'Will Steve Brain win a cheese?' but 'How many cheeses will

Steve win?' If Lance has his way, it won't be more than two. The King of the Hill stakes out a place a few feet away, just outside the nervy vortex of Jason and his friends. Watching him lace up his rugby boots, Jason notices that the champ is sipping blackcurrant juice. 'That man runs down on a straight 'ead,' he whispers. 'Not me – I reckon it's definitely better to 'ave a drink beforehand – but like, Steve's got it to an art, 'asn't he? He seems to be the only bloke who can keep his feet – it's probably 'cause he 'asn't 'ad a drink!' He laughs, then turns reverent again. 'Last year, I only come a metre behind 'im. So he *can* be beaten. I'm only twenty-two – Steve's in 'is thirties. The year he retires, that'll be the year I win it, I reckon.'

And so the tradition continues . . . Just as Steve dethroned a man roughly a decade older than him to become King of the Hill, Jason and his fellow pretenders are waiting to take over his mantle. For now, though, the champ doesn't look too worried. Whereas his young rivals are sitting upright, nervously hugging their knees, Steve is lying back, sucking on a carton of fruit juice. Deep down, he's just as nervous as they are, but instead of guzzling cider and rabbiting on about past raccs and injuries, Steve shuts himself off, blocking out everything so he can concentrate on winning. He's working out the ground conditions, the best route down the hill and how fast he can go. This year, the slope is soft and wet, so he's decided to run flat out as far as he can. If he falls, chances are he won't hurt himself too badly – and anyway, by the time he wipes out, he should be far enough ahead to roll across the finish line.

You'd never guess all this is going through his head as he sprawls on the grass, squinting in the sunshine with his arms locked behind his head.

Jason watches admiringly. 'Pretty relaxed, there, aren't ya, Steve?'

'Catchin' some rays,' replies the King of the Hill.

I ask him if he's going to let Lance win this year.

He cocks his head to look over. 'No, he's gonna 'ave to earn it.'

Right from the start, Steve looks set for his second hat trick. Bounding down, he wins the first race by ten feet without losing his balance, delighting the crowd. Lance doesn't even place; still, he doggedly heads back up the hill.

Steve also clinches the second race, but twists his ankle along the way. True to form, Lance finishes third, having wiped out halfway down.

I catch him on the way back up the slope. 'Are you really going to run again?'

Lance sighs wearily. 'Probably.'

For the last race, Steve decides to go for broke. Ankle throbbing, he launches himself off the hilltop, running as fast as he can, pumped up on adrenaline and the full-on, heart-thumping thrill of tempting fate. He's not thinking – there's no time – just acting and reacting on pure animal instinct. All he does is watch his feet, constantly gauging his balance as the ground beneath him pitches and rolls. He doesn't look at the other runners; he senses them. Everything comes in flashes: the tangled arms and legs, the thuds and gasps behind him, the give-and-take of the turf, and finally, the oohs and aahs as he, Steve Brain, the King of the Hill, nears the finish . . .

Suddenly, his ankle buckles, catapulting him into a triple somersault. Still, he's far enough ahead to tumble across the line . . .

But then – out of nowhere – somebody sneaks past. He's not that fast, but . . . he's still on his feet! Steve tries to pick himself up and retake the lead. The other runner trips and tumbles – Steve sprints to the finish – but the other guy rolls across the line first!

Steve's usurper isn't Lance or any of the other veterans; he's a complete newcomer, a 26-year-old pub manager from Cheltenham named Craig Brown.

'I'M GONNA EAT THAT CHEESE!!!' he hollers, hoisting his trophy overhead and jumping around at the foot of the hill. 'I'm gonna put it on the bar in the pub, and everybody can sit there and eat it!'

Gracious in defeat, Steve shakes hands with Brown and poses next to the newcomer. 'I was hoping to win three this year, but fair play to Craig for stealing my hat trick,' he tells reporters. The champ hobbles home without seeking medical attention. All told, the St John reports only eleven minor injuries, but that doesn't include the dazed teenager found on a hay bale afterwards – he's rushed to hospital with a suspected concussion. 'The press didn't get that one,' an organiser says with satisfaction.

As predicted, Lance ran in all three races without winning a cheese. The spectators stream past him at the bottom of the hill, unaware that they're in the presence of a near-legend. He gazes up at his grassy nemesis. 'That's definitely the last time, that,' he vows, his hangdog face hanging even lower than usual. 'That's it. I'm gettin' too old for it. I only got a third this year. That's the least I've done, so I'm going to pack it in. That's it, I'm gone. Finished.' Like any junkie kicking a habit, he swears he'll be able to do without his annual adrenaline fix. 'In fact, I probably won't come up for the first two years, 'cause I know I'd wanna run. So I'll give it a rest, and then come up here when I'm gettin' older.'

And again I imagine him as an old man in a wheelchair, rolling himself off the summit: *I said I won't stop 'til I win o-o-o-o-ne!*

CHAPTER THREE

YE OLDE BLOODE SPORTE

SHIN KICKING AT CHIPPING CAMPDEN

HACKING FOR GOLD: *Two combatants square off in England's very own summer 'Olimpicks'.*

© J.R. DAESCHNER

PART ONE:
BACK FROM THE DEAD

Not many men live to dig their own grave, let alone climb out of it, but Ben Hopkins was planning to do just that in the summer of 1951. The Festival of Britain had revitalised the nation, boosting morale at a time when there were still shortages of food and housing six years after World War Two. In London, the organisers of the five-month extravaganza strained to look to the future, commissioning fantastical attractions called Skylon, the Dome of Discovery and the Outer Space Pavilion. However, in the old Cotswold town of Chipping Campden, the locals planned to celebrate their Britishness by doing what came naturally: reliving the past.

The festival's timing happened to mark nearly a century since the abolition of a little-known event that linked England with the ancient Olympian Games and the modern Olympics. England's very own 'Cotswold Olimpicks' had been held since at least 1612 on Dover's Hill outside Campden and survived until 1852, when rowdiness gave the authorities an excuse to shut it down. Ninety-nine years later, the people of Chipping Campden decided to revive their old-fashioned Olimpicks as their contribution to Britain's Festival. Instead of standard track-and-field events, these Olimpicks would feature tug-o'-war, sack races, morris dancing, greasy-pole climbing and 'throwing the sheaf' – hurling a hay bale with a pitchfork. It fell to Ben and a friend to re-enact the most infamous sport of them all: shin kicking, a brutal form of wrestling once common in England, Wales, and parts of America. Contestants would square off, lock arms and hack at each other's shins until one of them fell to the ground. In the old days, shin kickers wore metal toecaps on their boots, leaving losers – and winners – with permanently dented shinbones. Some were crippled for life, and a few even died from their injuries. As a result, the pastime itself died out by the early 1900s.

In the spirit of revival, the organisers decided to resurrect the sadistic sport, if only for show. Ben was roped in when his best friend, Joe Chamberlain, volunteered. 'We were young and silly,' he laughs. Both married and in their thirties, Ben and Joe could have been siblings, what with their hooded eyes and jutting jaws. In a photo from the time, they're standing side by side laughing, one in a pinstriped jacket and paisley tie, the other in a flat cap and overalls. Although Joe worked in town at the chemist's and Ben was a farmer, they lived next door to each other in Campden; the couples would nip into each other's houses for tea and conversation.

And shin kicking – even the pretend kind – was best done among friends. One overenthusiastic swing would be enough to infuriate anyone and turn a good-natured display into a grudge match. Ben and Joe tried to check their blows, kicking hard enough to make it look realistic, but pulling back just before impact. They also had padding sewn inside their trousers. 'Not *real* padding,' Ben emphasises. 'It was just a double thickness.'

'They Call It Sport, But We Say It's Plain Crazy!' a newspaper exclaimed, with a photo of Ben kicking wildly at Joe's bare shins (but missing by a country mile). Shin kickers of yore supposedly prepared by deadening their legs with hammers, so the friends pretended to do the same for reporters. However, their biggest stunt was yet to come. 'We dug our own graves on Dover's Hill,' Ben says proudly. While a marching band distracted the crowd, Ben and Joe, wearing neckerchiefs and old-fashioned shepherd's smocks, slipped into their shallow graves and were covered by coffin board and turf. After the band finished, two men disguised as poachers came up the hill carrying a jug of cider. 'I got a rabbit down 'ere!' one shouted and started digging frantically. To the crowd's surprise, they soon discovered the graves and lifted the shin kickers onto the ground. 'They lay us down, give us a drink of cider, and we started shin kickin'.'

The BBC was on hand to record the event in a black-and-white newsreel that opens with pastoral music and scenic shots of Campden and its Olimpicks. 'Among the villages of the Cotswolds was found renewed proof last week that the Festival is Britain's,' intones a tea-and-crumpets voice. 'At Chipping Campden, it was marked by seven days of celebrations, including a revival of the Cotswold Games.'

Cut to Ben and Joe, locked in combat, swiping at each other's legs. When one of them swings, the other jumps back. They kicked and feinted until they were tired, having decided the loser beforehand. 'It was *really* good,' Ben grins, 'and that was the beginning of all that.'

Strolling through Campden today, it's hard to imagine that this affluent, honey-gold town in the Cotswold Hills was once a virtual Mount Olympus of shin kicking. With its artists' studios, antiques shops and upmarket hotels and restaurants, Chipping Campden seems too well-heeled to have ever hosted a blood sport like shin kicking (the 'chipping' prefix is a reference to its former status as a market town rather than the damage inflicted by footfighting). For many visitors – Brits and foreigners alike – the Cotswolds in general and Campden in particular represent their dream of the English countryside made reality. Green fields and hedges surround the town, and its gently curved high street seems to have been hewn from a single block of grey-gold Cotswold stone. G.M. Trevelyan, a popular historian of the 1940s, called it 'the most beautiful village street now left in the island'. Much of this beauty dates from the era of the Golden Fleece, when England's wealth came off the back of Cotswold sheep. Campden's oldest mansion, built by a wool merchant in the fourteenth century, features a sundial, gargoyles, and a novel form of ventilation for the time (chimneys rather than holes punched in the roof). Further down stands a timber market hall, the Jacobean focal point amid the rows of Georgian and Regency-era houses, wood-beamed tearooms and pubs and coaching inns with arched carriageways leading off into courtyards. At the end of the mile-long high street, the large church towers over what little is left of Campden's seventeenth-century manor house, the exotic fantasy of Sir Baptist Hicks, one of the richest Britons of all time.

Still, not everyone has been bowled over by Campden and the Cotswolds. William Cobbett slated the area in his *Rural Rides* in 1826, calling it 'an ugly country' with 'less to please the eye than any other I have ever seen'. Maybe that was because back then, the buildings were whitewashed, covering up their golden stone. In any event, Cobbett has had plenty of company in critiquing the Cotswolds. A cleric visiting in 1836 declared Campden 'a dull, clean, disused market town'. More recently, Joanna Trollope, the *grande dame* of cottage-in-the-country fiction, dissed her native Gloucestershire in terms that made the Cotswolds sound like the Third World: 'Children in these honey-coloured villages go to school with no underclothes,' she claimed.

A famous Trollope's remarks about knickers were bound to have outsiders in stitches – 'Rural Idyll Caught With Its Pants Down,' sniggered the *Guardian* – but the residents of Britain's biggest 'Area of Outstanding Natural Beauty' were not amused. 'We just hope people do not take her comments too seriously,' a tourist official said. 'I have never seen anyone knickerless in the Cotswolds.'

To do that, he'd need to rent an X-rated video. Although the tourist office doesn't brag about it (I can't imagine why), Campden served as a film location for an adult version of *The Canterbury Tales*, directed by Pier Paolo Pasolini in 1971. The tacky spaghetti-sex flick featured a mostly English cast dubbed in Italian, including sex-farce stalwart Robin Asquith plus Tom Baker and his, um, sonic screwdriver before he took over as Dr Who. For the scenes in Campden, the crew transformed it into a medieval market town, with hay bales as fig leaves for the indecencies of twentieth-century development. Even so, keen-eyed viewers claim you can spot rogue TV antennas in Campden's high street. What with all the naked flesh on display during the rest of the film, though, these nitpickers are clearly missing the bigger picture.

Scoff if you will, but Campden's homespun Olimpicks provide a truer reflection of the ancient Olympian spirit than their more famous international counterparts. Some events may not have the glamour and suspense of, say, competitive walking or synchronised swimming, but what they lack in grandeur, they more than make up for in pedigree. Founded in 1612, the Cotswold Olimpicks represented the first attempt to revive the spirit of the Greek Olympian Games, predating their modern pretenders by nearly 300 years. For better or worse, the English were the main guardians of the Olympic flame between antiquity and the modern age.

Campden owes its Olimpick link to an outsider who transformed the area's rural pastimes into a fashionable spectacle sanctioned by the Crown. A country boy from Norfolk, Robert Dover studied law in London during the years when Shakespeare was writing *King Lear*, *Macbeth* and *The Tempest*. So when Dover returned to the country, settling in the Cotswolds, his head was full of Renaissance ideals, and, like any good Royalist (and closet Catholic), he hated Puritans.

Decades before they actually started killing each other, the Royalists and the Puritans fought a war of words over a seemingly unlikely subject – sports. The Puritans, gaining ground in Campden, feared the English were sports mad (even back then). However, royalists argued that games at country festivals were 'harmlesse mirth and jollitie', as Dover put it. So when the opportunity came to organise a sports extravaganza near his new home, he quickly took up the challenge. Not only would it be fun, it would peeve the Puritans.

The first poet to call the Games 'Olimpick' was Michael Drayton, a contemporary of Shakespeare who helped compile a flowery tribute to Dover called *Annalia Dubrensia*. Published in 1636, the book provides one of the earliest illustrations of shin kicking: two men in breeches grip each other's arms and hack at each other's tibias. The project attracted some well-known writers, such as Ben Jonson, but unfortunately, Shakespeare died before he could be pressed into singing Dover's praises.

With the start of the Civil War, bloody skirmishes replaced ritualised combat on Dover's Hill, and then the 'Cotswold Genius' passed away in 1652. After the restoration of the monarchy, though, his beloved games quickly bounced back. However, instead of his high-minded Olimpicks, they reverted to their hard-knock origins. Out went Dover's classical pretensions; in came knockdown, drag-out fights – between combatants *and* spectators. Local alehouses began sponsoring the event, and Dover's Olimpick spirit quickly drowned in Olympian amounts of spirits. Market towns like Campden had long looked down on the farmers in the valley, and teams of young bucks from the Wold – the hills around Campden – would spar against their rivals from the Vale of Evesham.

For over two centuries, the main attractions at Britain's home-grown Olimpicks and hundreds of other village fêtes were also the bloodiest. In theory, backswording, or cudgel 'play', was less brutal than shin kicking, known simply as wrestling throughout much of the West Country. Opponents whacked each other with sticks until one wound up with a 'broken head', verified by a trickle of blood at least an inch long on the scalp (an extension of the 'first blood' rule in duelling). A deft gamester could graze a scalp with surgical pre cision. However, backswording and shin kicking frequently degenerated into bloody spectacles, with participants maiming – and occasionally even killing – each other.

The first graphic account of shin kicking and backswording on Dover's Hill comes from William Somerville, a local justice of the peace. For him, Dover's Games were proof that England was going to pot. In his satiric poem, *Hobbinol* (1740), a farmer from the Vale fights a burly shin-kicking champ from the Wold. The rivals trade blows until:

> The sweat distils, and from their batter'd shins
> The clotted gore distains the beaten ground.

Afterwards, the losers from the Wold start a brawl, and:

> Like bombs the bottles fly
> Hissing in the air, their sharp-edged fragments drench'd
> In the warm spouting gore.

Although the Puritans had long since fallen from power, their reforming zeal was still a force through their spiritual heirs. In 1846, a young vicar fresh from Oxford took over the parish. George Drinkwater Bourne was shocked by the pandemonium on Dover's Hill, claiming that the Olympics had become 'the trysting place of all the lowest scum', attracting 30,000 outsiders, including railroad navvies and men from the mean streets of Birmingham. For him, the best way to stop Dover's Games was to kick them off their turf. At the same time, officials across the country were trying to shut down many other local festivities. Participants saw these traditions as high-spirited, old-fashioned fun, whereas opponents – often outsiders like Bourne – saw them as lawless, bacchanalian orgies of vice. And amid the mayhem on Dover's Hill, shin kicking and backswording were probably some of the tamer displays of violence.

West Country native Thomas Hughes, a fair-minded man of the law, wrote nostalgically about shin kicking and backswording in *Tom Brown's Schooldays* in 1857. 'Wrestling, as practised in the western counties, was, next to backswording, the way to fame for the youth of the Vale,' he recalled. However, he also acknowledged that rural feasts had deteriorated due to longer working hours and a lack of support by the gentry. In the end, he reckoned the change was good 'if it be that the time for the old "veast" has gone by; that it is no longer the healthy, sound expression of English country holidaymaking; that, in fact, we as a nation, have got beyond it, and are in a transition state, feeling for and soon likely to find some better substitute'.

In fact, just as England's first Olimpicks and other festivals were being shut down, a replacement of sorts was beginning barely sixty miles away, in the Shropshire village of Much Wenlock. These new games, started in 1850, were similar in spirit to Dover's early competition. The Wenlock Olympian Games included ancient and modern events such as racing and football. Their founder, Dr William Penny Brookes, hailed the 'harmless recreation' of 'Merrie England', and talked of the need to train 'a noble, manly race' to build the Empire and prevent the 'physical degeneracy' seen in France and America. The doctor's crusade quickly grew from its village roots to become the National Olympian Association. Penny Brookes was working on the most ambitious phase – an international event in Athens – when he came across a young Frenchman who had the same goal, as well as the connections to make it happen. Baron Pierre de Coubertin was that rarest of things: a Frenchman who admired Britain. The founder of the modern Olympics believed that 'since ancient Greece has passed away, the Anglo-Saxon race is the only one that fully appreciates the moral influence of physical culture', and the 27-year-old made a pilgrimage to see the wise man of Much Wenlock in 1890. Penny Brookes died four months before de Coubertin staged the first modern Olympics in 1896. However, he is still regarded as 'the father of the English Olympics', and Wenlock continues to host its games every July.

Meanwhile, Robert Dover's contribution has been all but forgotten. Britain's oldest Olimpicks were killed off in 1852 after the Reverend Bourne succeeded in enclosing Dover's Hill. The Olimpicks' organisers stayed defiant to the end. As the vicar won his legal victory in Parliament, they looked to the future: 'The celebrated and renowned Olimpic [sic] Games . . . are esteemed by all brave, true and free-spirited Britons,' their posters declared. 'The good old times will be revived.'

In the interim, though, good old sports like shin kicking and backswording also faced growing opposition. A small print tucked away in Campden's town hall commemorates a famous backsword match held at Dover's Games, possibly the same year they were shut down. The local champion, 'Nezzy' Plested, and a man called Spiers are locked in combat, wearing breeches and blousy shirts, with one hand bound to their thighs. The bout lasted a long time, possibly an hour and a half. In the end, Plested won the match but lost an eye; Spiers was 'incapacitated for further work' and died two weeks later. Fatal encounters like this triggered calls to ban the sports.

Nevertheless, shin kicking continued to be a crowd-puller. In the wrestling style that was popular at the time, competitors gripped their opponents' jackets by the collar and elbow while kicking and throwing each other. Collar and Elbow wrestling (still the national style in Ireland) was even exported to America. As a teenager,

George Washington was a champion, and at least two other presidents followed his example.

On the east coast of England, 'Collar and Elbow men' would batter each other in a now-extinct style known as Norfolk wrestling. (Incidentally, Norfolk was the birthplace of Cotswold Olimpicks founder Robert Dover.) A veteran gamester wrote a pamphlet on 'The Whole Art of Norfolk Wrestling' in the 1830s. In it, Charles Layton, nicknamed The Celebrated Game Chicken (roosters attack with their claws in cockfights), described the wrestlers' footwear as long socks and genie-style shoes with curled-up toes to help them hook each other's ankles. Officials would check combatants' legs and feet beforehand to prevent cheating, by the use of shin pads or shoes with nails in them.

In the West Country, the only place that frowned on shin kicking was Cornwall, home of what may be England's oldest wrestling style. Originally, Cornish combatants were allowed to use their feet and legs, but only to trip their opponents or hit them with their heels and insteps. Frontal toe-to-tibia attacks were forbidden, not least because wrestlers usually fought barelegged from the knees down. Trust their archrivals from the next county over to twist the rules to their advantage: by the early 1800s, the devious Devonians had taken to whacking their opponents in the shins while wearing heavy shoes and hobnail boots – sometimes even baking the soles to make them extra hard. If Cornish wrestling was brutal, the Devon style could be lethal. In 1840, a Devon wrestler threw his rival 'with so much violence, that his neck was dislocated and his back dreadfully injured, so that he now lies in a precarious state', a newspaper reported. On another occasion, a 22-year-old died from his wounds. Not surprisingly, Cornish wrestlers were somewhat . . . reluctant to fight the vicious Devonians. However, Cornwall won out in the long run: whereas Cornish wrestling has survived to this day, its Devonian pretender eventually died out.

Even so, shin kicking lived on in gory incarnations throughout the West Country *and* the rest of the country – as well as in America. Hobnailed boots and metal toecaps weren't enough for some fighting Welshmen; they wore thick shoes with nails sticking out of the sides.

In Lancashire, miners would grapple against each other stark naked, wearing only their clunky, metal-trimmed clogs. This may have been in imitation of the Greeks, who wrestled nude, or it simply may have seemed like a good idea at the time. One report tells of a clog fight near Manchester in 1843 between two young men, 'both in a state of nudity with the exception of each having on a pair of strong boots'. They kicked each other for forty-five minutes . . . all for one pound. Both wound up severely injured. The winner went on to kill another opponent and emigrate Down Under – though it's unclear whether this was his choice or Her Majesty's Pleasure.

Rather than Australia, the shin kicker might have been more at home in America. The most gruesome account of shin kicking comes from the US, where Welsh coalminers introduced shin kicking, or 'purring', to Pennsylvania. The New York *Sunday Mercury* described a 'purr' between two fighters called Grabby and McTevish in 1883:

> [Grabby] brought his left foot around and caught McTevish on the outside of the right calf. The flesh was laid open almost to the bone, and the blood spurted out in streams. McTevish never uttered a word. At the same instant that his own leg was cut he gave Grabby what is known as the sole scrape. Beginning at the instep and ending just below the knee, Grabby's left shin was scraped almost clear of skin . . .
>
> The first go or round occupied sixteen minutes. When the call of purr came again the purrers hobbled to the centre and took another hold. McTevish's legs, although bound up in plaster, were bleeding freely, and the exposed places looked like beefsteak. His opponent's shins had both been scraped clean of the flesh, and the blood was oozing out from between the strips of plaster.

Back in the Cotswolds, shin kicking – and backswording – continued long after Dover's Games came to an end. One famous venue was Cooper's Hill Wake: when the locals weren't chasing cheeses, they were kicking shins. The blood sports finally died out by the early 1900s. Travel writer H.J. Massingham collected several stories about the bad old days for his book, *Wold Without End*, in 1931. For instance, locals told him about an old stonebreaker in the Vale of Evesham whose shins looked like corrugated iron from his wounds back when Broadway fought Campden. The captain of the Campden team would 'thrape' the soft parts of his shins with a coal hammer at the aptly named Eight Bells pub; other men used wooden planks to deaden the nerves in their legs or vinegar as an astringent to keep the skin from splitting.

'They took it serious, y'see. Tough as hell – all of 'em were, in those days,' an Old Campdonian tells me. Shin kicking had all but disappeared by the time Fred Coldicott was born in 1910, but he remembers just-for-fun bouts as a boy. One kid in his gang was the nephew of the backswords champ who lost an eye and killed a man in the fatal bout held during the last years of Dover's Games. Wearing their flat caps, pullovers, long shorts and socks, the kids would play at leapfrog, tic-tac-toe . . . and shin kicking. 'Very often, you'd get one who'd cry – the weak-hearted ones. I don't think I ever come under that category,' laughs Fred, whose nickname was Tiger. 'We were ignorant little b's in those days. It was nothing to have a good stand-up fight. You'd run home with a bloody nose to your father, and he'd say, "Serves ya damn right, go back and give *'im* a nose bleed!" It was a funny old world.'

Outsiders came away with much the same impression. 'There is no imbecility nor barbarity that human beings will not practise and even exalt, so long as it be sanctified by custom,' Massingham wrote of shin kicking on Dover's Hill. 'Only a traditionalist or a good old Englander could regret the blessed silence and solitude that have come in the wake of the turbulent ways of men.'

PART TWO:
SHIN KICKING FOR THE CAMERAS

Basil Hart was just a boy when he saw shin kicking come back from the dead. He still remembers the shock of seeing Ben Hopkins and Joe Chamberlain jump out of their graves. 'It was incredible. As a child, naturally we thought they were diggin' up these folks! It was effective – it really was.'

So much so that Basil decided to recreate shin kicking's resurrection fifteen years later. Immediately after the Festival of Britain, locals had tried to convert Campden's one-off celebrations into an annual affair. However, a foot-and-mouth epidemic the following year and Queen Elizabeth's coronation in 1953 sapped momentum for a revival. More than a decade later, in 1964, a small group, including Joe Chamberlain, finally managed to organise a night of attractions for the eve of the Scuttlebrook Wake, Campden's village fair in June. Then, within two years, a newly founded Robert Dover's Games Society staged the first full-fledged revival of the Cotswold Olimpicks in over a century. Besides a bonfire procession and fireworks, the historic revival featured horse riding and motorcycle displays, tug-o'-war, greasy pole climbing . . . and shin kicking. Basil and a friend were the only volunteers to have their shins kicked in. 'Probably foolhardy,' he laughs. 'Everybody said we were mad doin' it.'

Like their role models years earlier, Basil and his friend chose to bring shin kicking back to life after being buried underground. For the display, they dressed in embroidered smocks, neckerchiefs and felt hats; Basil even wore Ben Hopkins's old shin-kicking corduroys – plus football shinpads, with an extra layer of padding to boot. 'The blows were fairly heavy still,' Basil remembers. 'There's no point in makin' it look soft.' Their play-acting was so convincing it upset some spectators. 'A nurse wrote a letter in the paper sayin' this should never be done, because she had seen damaged shins and what it can do to the rest of your life.' This only encouraged the shin kickers. 'We wrote back, and said well, of course, we been practisin' and we put skin-hardenin' stuff on our shins with vinegar, etcetera, to make it stay genuine,' he chuckles. They performed a couple more times in the 1960s, but Basil had problems finding a partner after his friend moved away, so shin kicking stopped.

However, Dover's Games continued, and gradually, the Cotswold Olimpicks began to receive international recognition. In the 1980s, the British Olympic Association formally recognised the games' place in Olympic history. An exhibition on Dover's Games featured at the Seoul Olympics, and British Olympians such as swimmer Sharron Davies began putting in appearances on Dover's Hill. Joe Chamberlain and Ben Hopkins were invited to kick shins on TV's *The Time of Your Life* as the host, Noel Edmonds, watched agog. It was the last time they displayed the sport: Joe died in 1994.

Although the Cotswold Olimpicks regularly attract hundreds of spectators and TV crews from as far away as Japan, the games continually battle against indifference within the UK. Shin kicking has all but died out, surviving as an anaemic re-enactment of its former gory glory. Basil last demonstrated the sport in 1992, when he was in his fifties, and a few years back, the organisers managed to scrape together enough shin kickers for a semi-finals *and* a final. Since that painful experience, though, the brutal tradition has all but disappeared by the time I arrive in Chipping Campden. 'It's just not done, really,' organiser Jane King tells me a week before the Olimpicks. 'Nobody does shin kicking anymore – it's just one of those quaint old English things we do when required, so to speak.'

It looks like the centuries-old sport has indeed died out.

Then, on the eve of the event, she manages to lure in some recruits, using a TV appearance as bait: two television crews – one from the BBC and the other from Central TV – have arranged to film some faux shin kicking on Dover's Hill a few hours before the Games.

Now, however, Jane's rookies have yet to appear. Perhaps they've come to their senses – they *did* seem a little dubious about the whole thing last night. 'How does it end? Like this?' one asked, punching a pretend opponent. Jane calmly suggested they get some last-minute advice from Basil. Maybe he talked them out of it.

Francis Burns looks worried. Pink-faced and roly-poly, the official Olimpick historian is on hand to lend some academic gravitas to the event. Francis earned his doctorate with a thesis on the Cotswold Olimpicks in 1960, and he has played a vital role in promoting them ever since. He quickly volunteers his son, Richard, a PE teacher from Birmingham, as a shin-kicking reserve.

Eventually, four other men arrive, sparing sixtysomething Francis from having to square off against his 26-year-old offspring. By pure coincidence, the display reflects the age-old rivalry between the Vale and the Wold: a farmer and a builder represent the Vale side, while the Wold's honour is being defended by an electrician – and a cake-maker from France named Jean-Michell Villain. Whereas he and his teammate, Adam Bennett, have slim builds and pale skin, their opponents from the Vale are tanned and burly bruisers: farmer Stuart Webb and builder Nigel Smith use their whole bodies when they work, not just their hands. Given that they're about the same size, they wisely decide not to fight each other; instead, they'll pick on the townie small fry. Stuart plays rugby, and no doubt Nigel has put in his fair share of tackles in his time. In contrast, Adam from Campden looks more like a cricketer, while Jean-Michell might be a mean competitor . . . in a cook-off.

The shin kickers put on white smock coats and stuff straw up the legs of their trousers like half-finished scarecrows, their shins bulging with the makeshift Popeye padding and tufts of straw sticking out around their ankles. Campden boy Adam tries to tidy up by tucking in the scratchy yellow stuff.

'Ow!' he yelps, holding up an injured finger.

Jean-Michell rushes to his aid and the two men stand squinting at Adam's boo-boo until the nimble-fingered cake-maker extracts the prickle.

Stuart watches bemusedly. 'You get thistles in hay, y'know.'

Adam and Jean-Michell are doomed.

The Central TV reporter is a middle-aged blonde with ruddy skin, high cheekbones and a jolly-hockey-sticks accent, a handsome woman who'd look most at home tramping across the countryside in a waxed jacket and wellies, surrounded by dogs – plenty of dogs. In that heigh-ho-have-a-go way of hers, she's decided to stage a minute-long shtick for the cameras. After stuffing plenty of straw up the legs of her tracksuit – so the camera can't miss it – she blocks out the scene for the other players: she'll do a short piece to camera while the shin kickers struggle behind her. Then she'll introduce Francis to talk a bit – but only a bit! – about the event's bone-breaking history. Suddenly, she'll join in the fun, and Richard Burns will step in to challenge her, pretending to kick shins until she takes a fall. Throughout this, the bystanders will cheer. As for the shin kickers themselves, well, they'll be slugging it out in the background, providing plenty of local-yokel colour.

At least, that's the plan . . .

Take 1: Cue shin kicking. Close up of the reporter's straw-stuffed legs, and pull back for her intro. Carefree hair blowing in the wind, she explains why she's here and turns to Francis for the hand-off. Unfortunately, he's so excited, he jumps the gun.

Cut.

The shin kickers have to be calmed down. Although they're trying to avoid serious injuries, inevitably they're exchanging some real bruise-inducing thuds.

Take 2: Close-up, intro, shin kickers . . . but Francis fluffs his lines.

Cut.

Before the reporter can start the next take, a muffled cellphone rings. 'Is that someone's mobile?' she asks imperiously. Half a dozen people guiltily frisk themselves. Turns out it's hers, hidden in her handbag on the sidelines. 'I don't *believe* it!' she huffs . . . and takes the call anyway.

Take 3: Same as before, with things going well until the reporter asks Francis what contestants wore during the games. 'They used to wear doububblble . . .'
Cut.

Take 4: They finally manage to make it past Francis to the shin kicking. A sucker for corn, the reporter cries 'To the death!' as she squares off against Richard. They swipe at each other's hay-padded shins for a while, then she turns and smiles to the camera: 'And don't forget – kick-off tonight is at 7.30!'

Kick . . . off – geddit? She's probably been working on that all afternoon.
'How long was that?' she asks the cameraman, lifting her head from the ground.
'Fifty-five seconds.'
She groans. 'We're a bit short.'
They need a full minute of airtime. She wants another take.
'No, no, no,' moans Adam, rubbing his battered legs. After ten minutes of stop-and-start kicking, he and the other men are worn out. They've been pushing and shoving, tugging at each other's lapels, and he and Jean-Michell have even been thrown to the ground. 'Surely they've got it by now.'
But they haven't, so Francis rallies the troops one last time . . .

Take 5: To pad the segment, the reporter has Francis coach her while she's shin kicking. This time, she decides to drop to the ground, smile at the camera and deliver her kick-off line before feigning unconsciousness.
Cut.

It's still 55 seconds.
'Shall we do it again?' she asks the cameraman.

He wisely decides against it, saving her from getting her head kicked in.

Two hours later, Jean-Michell Villain is plotting his revenge. He and Adam are standing behind the cutout castle that serves as the backdrop for the games, waiting for the Cotswold Olimpicks to begin. The relay events will pit their Campden team against the reigning champions – including their shin-kicking adversaries. Adam's encounter with Stuart has left him with a black spot on his ankle, while Jean-Michell has a bruise blooming below his knee. Nigel threw him several times during shin kicking. Now, the Frenchman is promising payback in the water-bucket race: 'We were supposed to be faking, but he didn't! He make me fly! But I will get him back with ze water. He will get wet.'

The team events take place on the second of two natural stages that make Dover's Hill the ideal venue for the Olimpicks. The hill lies on the cusp of the Cotswolds, providing a sweeping view of the Vale of Evesham below, with the Black Mountains of Wales in the distance. Against the vastness of this landscape, the tower blocks of Birmingham are little more than tiny rectangles in the middle distance. A broad tree-lined plateau tops the hill itself, giving way to a grassy slope that serves as a natural grandstand for spectators. The teams compete further down the hill, in front of the cutout castle, with its central arch and yellow shields depicting Robert Dover. From there, the hill rolls into the woods in the valley below. With the castle façade centrestage, the trees and valley in the background, and the sun setting stage left, Dover's Hill looks like an outdoor theatre, a co-production of Man and Mother Nature.

Unfortunately, the weather is typically atypical: the first days of June have been wet and chilly. Dramatic clouds cruise across the landscape, deciding the climatic fate of the humans below. On one side of the vale, farms bask in the sun's reddish-gold rays as a rainstorm works its way across the other side of the valley, enveloping towns in violet-grey mist. As the sun sets, you can see your breath against the cold wind. Nevertheless, at least 1,500 people have gathered on the hill. The expansive upper level is a fairground with kiddies' rides, morris dancing, marching bands, Punch and Judy, a dog show and a Chinese Boxing display, while the main events take place on the lower stage: relay races, a five-mile run, a backswords display and a Champion of the Hill contest, featuring four sports from the original Olimpicks: Putting the Shot, the Standing Jump, Throwing the Sledgehammer and Spurning the Bar (heaving an eight-foot telephone pole as far as you can).

Unlike their international counterparts, there's no inaugural extravaganza for these homegrown Olimpicks: no ageing pop stars, no iffy anthems and no choreographed conceptualist nightmares; just a boy leading a small procession up the hill, carrying the official Olympic flag. The reincarnation of Robert Dover (aka the local priest) and his sidekick ride behind the standard-bearer in their seventeenth-century finery. The Scuttlebrook Queen and a marching band follow on foot. Despite the undulating turf, the band members march with precision, their bagpipes wailing and white hats and red-and-black uniforms contrasting sharply with the lush greens around them. The procession passes through the castle's arch, and Father Brennan, mounted on his chestnut horse, takes the microphone: 'I, Robert Dover from yesteryear, declare my games open!' A cannon fires, and he and his escort ride off into the sunset.

The events that follow are so sublimely silly it's unlikely they would ever make it into the modern Olympics. Then again, you never know. There's a contest to push a wheelbarrow full of haybales across a seesaw; a sack race in neck-length plastic bags that make it all but impossible for contestants to catch themselves when they fall; a relay competition that forces team members to throw slippery objects to each other from precarious perches; and three-legged heats that end up as four- and five-legged scrums. The teams themselves are distinguished by coloured T-shirts rather than corporate logos, and instead of electronic scoreboards, the officials use a blackboard. Like the modern Games, however, cheating is common, though it doesn't involve anything as secretive as steroids. Instead, the rule breaking is so blatant it's comical. Rather than disqualify offenders, the emcee encourages the crowd to boo them, hollering '*Cheeeeeaaat!!!!!!*' as loudly as they can.

The final event provides the French Villain's chance for revenge. The course for the water-bucket race is a tarpaulin smeared with dishwashing liquid and surrounded by hay bales. Each team tries to fill a barrel with water by relaying buckets with holes in them across the slippery plastic sheeting. By the time it's finished, people are slip-sliding in a soapy mess, while others try to run on the bales. Before the judge can measure the liquid collected by Stuart and Nigel's team, though, *someone* tips over their barrel, handing victory to Adam and Jean-Michell's side. The event degenerates into an all-out water fight, and, in keeping with the cake-maker's vow, Nigel does indeed get wet.

As does everyone else. The rain that's been threatening to wash out the evening finally begins to fall, but the crowd stays put, patiently unfolding umbrellas to wait out the shower. Sure enough, after ten minutes, the drizzle stops, and the trophies are presented. Before the shin kicking can begin, though, two competitors sneak off to the car park. I don't catch up with them until hours later. 'I wasn't gonna do any more of that!' Adam laughs. Jean-Michell gives a different excuse – he had to take a shower.

Compared with the afternoon's tibia hacking, and the team events, the evening's backsword display proves disappointingly tame. Two middle-aged men in Cavalier gear enter the field carrying a wooden stick in each hand. The long staff is for bashing each other on the head, while the short one is for blocking blows. With a theatrical flourish, the men cast their plumed hats on the ground and cry 'God save our eyes!' – though surely 'God save our heads!' would be better.

The mock combatants form crosses with their cudgels and then begin a pretend swordfight, swatting at each other until one scores a blow on the other's skull.

'A palpable hit! Is Matthew all right?!?' Francis Burns, Master of Corn, tries to inject some suspense via the loudspeaker.

The crowd starts to boo.

'Kill 'im!' a man shouts.

Instead, both backsworders make a hasty exit, the loser holding his head. He has actually been bashed on the skull, though not hard enough to draw blood. The crowd will have to wait to see an authentic display of brutality.

Despite Adam and Jean-Michell's desertion – and Nigel's mysterious disappearance – the organisers somehow find three replacements for shin kicking, all fortified by drink. Richard Hemus, a student from Birmingham, has wandered onto the lower arena with a mate, and they've both started stuffing straw up their jeans. Before Francis can even explain the rules, such as they are, the two flyweights in sneakers are already going at it on the sidelines –

Thump! Thump! THWOCK! *Thump!*

They're laughing and hacking away like it's the best fun they've had in years. If there were points to be scored, they'd be racking 'em up left and right, landing direct hits on each other's shinbones, sending the straw flying. This is brutality verité – no fake falls, no feigned blows, no soft kicks. 'A bit realistic, that!' Francis mutters in amazement over the microphone.

Eventually, they calm down enough to don the white smock coats and square off in the grassy centrestage for the benefit of the crowd – and the cameras. Clamping their hands on each other's shoulders, they immediately launch into a vicious foot-fight of left and right hooks, kicking with the tips of their trainers and swiping with the sides of their feet. *Thump! Thump! THUMP!* Between shin-shots, they're also struggling to stay on their feet. The water race and the rain have turned the ground into a sodden mess. The flyweights twist their torsos for leverage, but, being the same size, they both end up flopping into the mud. As the last one to hit the ground, Richard is deemed the winner, meaning that he'll have the misfortune of more shin kicking.

Next up, in what can only be called the heavyweight class, are two bruisers, Stuart and a builder named Jim Groves. They play rugby against each other, and Jim even has a rugby grin – a hole where his upper teeth should be. Muscles bulging in the tight smock coats, Stuart and Jim grapple against each other in their own private scrum.

Thump! Thump!

The dumbstruck crowd can't decide whether to laugh or cheer.

Afterwards, Jim, the loser, is walking stiff-legged. 'It hurts more than rugby,' he reckons. 'It doesn't last as long, but it hurts more.'

No matter which worker had won, the clear loser in the final was always going to be Richard. In his slacker's uniform of sweatshirt, jeans and sideburns, he looks like one of those angst-ridden, slouch-hipped singers from *Top of the Pops* facing off against Stuart's burly, straw-stuffed Wurzel. When they put on the white smock coats, the contrast is even more ridiculous – a lab assistant fighting a slaughterhouse worker. Apart from being shorter and lighter than Stuart, Richard is at a clear disadvantage in terms of footwear. His trainers must feel like rubbery cushions compared with the clunky work boots his opponent is wearing. For some unfathomable reason – either the alcohol or the shock – Richard has decided to forgo any padding. Stuart, on the other hand, has tied thick pillows of hay into his khakis with baling string.

The final fight is as short as it is predictable. The Brummie flyweight does his best, swiping with all his might at the local favourite, but nearly every kick misses its target as Stuart holds him at arm's length. Richard's spindly legs are kicking so much, if Stuart weren't holding him by the lapels, he'd probably fall down due to his own exertions. After a few seconds of Richard's desperate flailing, Stuart scores a shin-cracking blow, followed by a swift left hook that scoops the ground out from under his puny rival. Richard hobbles away with a second-prize medal and a leg full of red welts that will be coming up all kinds of black and blue tomorrow. He smiles manfully: 'That guy can kick *hard*.' Stuart also has his share of injuries. 'My legs are absolutely bruised,' he admits, sipping bitter from his silver champion's cup. 'The left one feels a bit delicate at the moment – very delicate.'

When I tell Basil Hart the next day, at first he refuses to believe that shin kicking has been revived in all its bruise-inducing, dent-inflicting glory. He and his wife grin sceptically. 'They convinced *you* well!' he guffaws, wheezing with laughter at the foreigner who's been hoodwinked by the locals. 'It was stage-managed, I should think.'

Then I tell him how none of the shin kickers had practised beforehand – in fact, they didn't even know what shin kicking was until they actually did it – and once they found out, some vowed never to do it again.

'Well, perhaps they *were* that stupid!' Another wheeze of laughter. 'I can't believe they found anybody stupid enough! But I suppose if they'd had enough to drink, they wouldn't realise what they were doing.'

His wife chortles. 'They probably do this morning!'

PART THREE:

THE AGONY OF THE FEET

A year after his victory, Stuart Webb's shin-kicking title has proved a mixed blessing. He and Joe McDonagh, the landlord of his local, have demonstrated the sport on TV's *They Think it's All Over*, earning them an all-expenses-paid trip to London. Last week they did a photo shoot for a national newspaper, and the media enquiries have been coming in from as far away as Australia. 'The shin kicking's really taken off,' says one organiser. 'We've got the British Championship now – as seen on TV.'

Stuart has paid for his newfound fame in bumps and bruises. 'Everyone wanted to know what you had to do. So I had to keep demonstrating it. They don't wanna do it themselves, they just wanna get some other mug to do it,' he grins wryly. This year, he's going to stick to his winning formula: 'Hold 'em as far away as possible and kick hard.' However, he did have second thoughts about defending his title. 'I wasn't gonna do it, but I was told I had to. There weren't that many people entered in it last year, but this year,

I think there are quite a few. I think I know a few of them who want to kick me now.'

The local TV news is back again, with a different reporter dishing out the corny puns. The plummy, puffed-up man in the bow tie has decided against participating in the shin kicking, which is just as well, since he probably can't even see his shins. Instead, he opts for the usual light-hearted fakery for his news report. He rattles off his piece to camera, calling the contest 'strictly below the belt' (having nixed another turn of phrase, about contestants having 'the shins kicked out of them'). At the end, Stuart and Joe step in and pretend to nail him in the shins.

For the sake of authenticity, though, I've mustered up the stupidity to compete in the shin kicking. Last year, I'd chickened out after concluding that my flimsy rubber-soled shoes were no match for Stuart's heavy work boots. This time, I've come with my own shin-kicking footwear (unfortunately, without steel tips).

Trudging up to the games that evening, through the green fields speckled with sheep, towards the sun setting on the hilltop, I brace myself mentally. I've come up with what seems like a sure fire strategy: I'll go on the offensive with my strongest leg, kicking and sweeping with the right, so that I can defend my left shin and throw my opponent. As I pause to catch my breath halfway up the hill – *surely I'm not that out of shape!* – Campden glows honey-coloured below. My secret hope is that I'll get thrown, and thrown quickly; my main concern, aside from making a fool of myself, is that I might win. Victory has to be the worst possible outcome: you have to keep getting your shins kicked until somebody beats you. In shin kicking, the only real loser is the winner.

On the hill, Stuart is warming up with a few beers. He gives me some pointers: 'Get 'em off balance as quickly as possible. You wanna kick them first – and then, 'cause you've got hold of their shoulders, try to tip them over.' He pummels his opponents with both legs, delivering donkey kicks – left-right, left-right – until he can throw them off kilter. I tell him about my strategy of keeping one leg back and sweep-kicking with the other. 'Mmmm,' he muses sceptically. 'Although if they take away your other leg, you're gonna fall over. You gotta be careful. It's all about keeping your balance.'

Shin kicking's full-blooded revival means it gets its own ring this year, a roped-off area on the spacious plateau atop Dover's Hill, with the finals scheduled for the main stage below. Eight contestants have volunteered for the event, twice as many as last year. Apart from Stuart and me, there's Nigel Smith, his erstwhile partner from the previous year, and Joe the landlord, who's doubling as referee. Several wildcards from the audience have also decided to have a go, including an ageing heavy-metal fan with a black T-shirt, beer can in hand, and straggly hair flowing from the very top of his head. The survival of shin kicking will depend on a steady flow of volunteers like him, itinerant lunatics looking for new sadomasochistic pastimes.

The rules of shin kicking are simple: kickers who topple their opponents two out of three times go through to the next round. In the event that both men fall – often the case, thanks to the sheep droppings studding the grass – the last one to hit the ground wins. Competitors can pad their legs with as much straw as possible. The smartest wear tracksuits, so they can stuff hay *down* their legs rather than struggle to pack it *up* the narrow ankles of jeans or trousers. One guy must have a whole hay bale down there. Try as I may, I manage only half that amount.

In my hubristic stupidity, I've been hoping to square off against Stuart in the first round. That way I'll no doubt quickly lose, but still be able to say I fought the champ. Instead, I end up fighting a tall, spindly guy with puppy-dog eyes and an exotic surname. I met Eric Fabricius last night down at the Seagrave Arms, when he was quizzing Joe about shin-kicking techniques. Despite his fabulous pro-wrestling-style surname (his dad was a German POW who stayed in Britain), Fabricius isn't quite what I'm looking for in an opponent. At six-foot-three, he's an inch shorter than me, so I've probably got a longer reach; at 160 pounds, he's also a good deal lighter. What's more, he's injured, having cracked a rib after colliding with a competitor during the team events earlier.

I begin to worry that I might actually win.

I lock my hands on Eric's shoulders, the sleeves of the tight smock coat shrinking around my forearms. At Joe's cue, we start circling around the ring, grunting and growling, our feet a blur against the manure-studded grass. At first, my strategy pays off. I keep well away from his flailing feet, landing a couple of swift kicks to his right shin – *Thwock! Thwock!* – before throwing him to the ground.

During the next round, though, Eric quickly realises that if he waits for me to kick, he can hook me from behind and topple me.

Whump! My head hits the ground with a sharp blow to the base of my skull.

The few hundred spectators respond with stupefaction rather than any real enthusiasm. There isn't much cheering; just occasional gasps of astonishment.

Eric and I stagger to our feet for the final round.

'I don't know about you, mate, but I'm knackered,' he pants.

So, seeing how he's such a nice guy – and the hammer and tongs in my head are killing me – I let him win. At least that's what I'd like to think. Actually, I try my best to throw him – I'm battering away at his legs, scoring an impressive *THUMP* on his right shin – but all the while, he's standing there waiting, his left leg poised to knock my feet out from under me in a triumph of brains over brawn.

WHUMP! Before I know it, I'm flat on my back with another brain-shuddering impact. My only consolation as I crawl away is that he didn't manage to kick me even once, and I inflicted some serious damage, connecting several times. My overwhelming instinct to protect my shins has been, quite literally, my downfall.

I have good company in defeat. Stuart doesn't even make it to the semi-finals. A mystery contestant with a deadly kick and arms down to his knees quickly deposes the champ and becomes the hot favourite. It's obvious that we're all outclassed. Whereas the rest of us have been taking clumsy swings at each other, this guy stabs with precision strikes like a kung fu fighter. He's not even wearing padding! When he connects with his opponent's legs, he exhales sharply – *Doosh! Doosh!* As a general rule, any guy who goes *Doosh!* when he kicks is clearly in a league of his own.

Nigel Smith is the next unfortunate to face the Kung Fu Shin Kicker. Nigel has two big disadvantages – he's shorter and at least ten years older than his opponent – but he also has more weight to throw against him. The brawling builder manages to topple his adversary once, but the other guy evens the score as the fight turns nasty. For the final face-off, the men grapple with each other, kicking viciously and twisting for leverage until they both end up spinning over the rope and clocking a girl on the head. The Kung Fu Shin Kicker is declared the winner, having hit the ground last.

Amazingly, Eric also ends up as a finalist. Whereas the Kung Fu Shin Kicker has demolished all the tough competition (like the reigning champ), Eric has eliminated all the easy opponents (like me and Heavy Metal Dude). At least I can take some comfort from the fact that I lost to one of the finalists; mercifully, the less dangerous of the two.

The final is brutally anticlimactic. Poor Eric doesn't stand a chance.

Ooooo! The crowd gasps as the Kung Fu Shin Kicker's foot reverberates against Eric's shin like an axe chopping wood. *Doosh!* Eric tries to hook his leg, but the other guy flings him to the ground.

They lock arms again and the Kung Fu Kicker nails Eric once in the calf, then in the shin, before putting him out of his misery.

The new champion turns out to be more of a professional than anyone imagined. James Gabb, a law student who grew up in the area, already has black belts in kung fu *and* kickboxing, so he decided to try his luck at one of England's homegrown martial arts. He's been doing kung fu for twenty years and kickboxing for the past six, training every day, seven days a week. The new victor sums up his strategy with a fulsome grin: 'The guy was kicking me, so I kicked him back.' He turns somewhat sheepish when I ask why he didn't use any padding. 'I'm allergic to hay. I didn't want to come out in a rash!'

If only the others had known . . .

For his part, Eric seems remarkably upbeat, considering he has a cracked rib and battered legs. He grins with the alcoholic bliss of someone who's had seven bottles of lager, two double scotches and two-and-a-half Bacardi Breezers, lifting his trouser leg to show an angry red graze on his right tibia where the skin has been rubbed off. 'That scar – that's off you.'

'Sorry.'

'Oh, that's all right – it'll heal.' He points to a big welt on the same leg. 'You caught me up there, and then there's another one down there somewhere.' In contrast, the Kung Fu Shin Kicker focused on hooking his legs rather than pummelling them.

I feel perversely proud. 'So I can say I inflicted as much damage as the champ?'

'*Easily*.'

As the evening fades to darkness and the first lights glimmer in the vale below, the Olimpicks close with a bonfire, fireworks and a torchlight procession. Led by Robert Dover and the bagpipe marching band, hundreds of people carry torches down the narrow, mile-long road, strolling beneath leafy canopies, past drystone walls and thatched cottages. Spectators wander out of the pubs and houses to admire the Olimpick flames, a flickering trail from the ancient hill to the timeless heart of Campden. The stone buildings turn reddish gold, reverting to the sepia monochrome of old photos as the flames glint in the cottage windows. A paraffin haze fills the market place, and a final wail of bagpipes ends the procession, which is followed by a street party.

Suddenly, I'm accosted by Eric and two of his mates, who have appeared out of nowhere, pint glasses in hand.

'Look at it now! *Look* at what you did to me!' he exclaims, pulling up his trousers.

The graze on his thin, sinewy leg has ballooned into a ball the size of an orange on the front of his shin. By the light of my torch, it looks like he's grown a second calf muscle, only on the wrong side of his leg.

'That's what *you* did to me!'

It's then I remember that many shin-kicking matches of yore ended as punch-ups in local pubs. I apologise, bracing myself nonetheless.

Eric, however, laughs it off, taking another swig of anaesthetic before joining his friends for more carousing. 'See ya, mate!' he shouts, raising his pint.

Fortunately, he's a happy drunk.

CHAPTER FOUR

THE BURRY MAN HAS LANDED

SCAPEGOATING IN SOUTH QUEENSFERRY

THE REAL GREEN MAN: Covered in burrs, Scotland's John Nicols shows the Sassenachs how it's done.

© J.R. DAESCHNER

PART ONE:
A ROUGH JOB

It's Dress-Down Friday in Silicon Glen, and the alpha, beta and epsilon-grade workers of Agilent Technologies are hurrying toward the canteen. Dark-green plants flank the smoked-glass corridor, with grey tubing and metal grates running overhead. Clad in their button-downs and T-shirts, chinos and jeans, the foot soldiers of Scotland's future chatter about job cuts, technological break-throughs and their plans for the weekend. As they turn the corner, though, they encounter something so weird, so *alien*, that they can't help but do a double take. A man – or is it a mannequin? – stands propped up against the glass like a human starfish smothered in prickly green burrs. His mouth and eyes are nothing but dark, overgrown holes, and dozens of roses crown his head. His arms are spread wide – like his legs – and supported by two floral staves to keep them from sticking to his sides.

Confronted with this living relic, some of the twenty-first-century workers grin bemusedly, but most look away, rushing down the corridor without asking questions. They're too busy looking forward to the future – or at least lunch – to bother with the past. William Wallace is one thing, but a bug-infested plant man, well – it's not very *Braveheart*, is it? Not very jocko-macho. What with all the vegetation, the floral hat and the roses for nipples, the green alien in their midst could almost be (gulp) . . . *Englesh*.

In fact, the Burry Man of South Queensferry is as Scottish as the town's Forth Bridge, the Rampant Lion flag wrapped around his waist and the freehand shots of whisky he downs all day. Not that many people in Scotland know about him. Every August, Edinburgh's tourism machine gears up for the world's biggest arts extravaganza, the International Festival, accompanied by show-cases for films, books and jazz, as well as the infamous Fringe. Attendants at the Edinburgh and Lothians Tourist Board will helpfully direct you to an Irish drama in a public toilet, a play about Indian eunuchs or a musical starring a former Tory MP in fishnet stockings. Yet when you ask about a centuries-old Scottish tradition that ranks as one of the UK's most bizarre customs – putting so-called performance art to shame – the tourist office draws a blank.

'Barry Man,' says the chipper voice on the phone. 'How are you spelling that?'

'B-u-r-r-y.'

A burst of mystified typing.

'I don't have *anything* on that,' she says, then checks with her colleagues for confirmation. 'I'm afraid no one's heard of that.'

Compared with the English, the Scots seem altogether too sensible to indulge in not-for-profit traditions. But when they do come up with one, it's a real lulu. Just seven miles outside the capital, officially still part of the City of Edinburgh, the Burry Man stalks the shores of the Firth of Forth, the font of inspiration for Sir Walter Scott, Robert Louis Stevenson and local boy Iain Banks. If the Highlands are the romantic soul of Scotland, then the region around the Forth estuary represents its functional heart, encompassing the capital and its castle, medieval island ruins, the iconic Forth Bridges, as well as oil and gas pipelines and multinational technology firms. When the mist clears, you can even see the Highlands in the distance. All the major developments in Scottish history are distilled in this region, ranging from the Picts, the Romans and the Vikings through to Robert the Bruce and the English invasions, right up to the heights of Victorian engineering and the globalised twenty-first century.

For at least three centuries – and possibly much longer – the Burry Man has lumbered around South Queensferry, shocking adults and terrifying children. More than any other British custom I've come across, the origins of the ordeal are a complete mystery. The first record of the Burry Man dates the custom to at least 1746, putting its pedigree on a par with other symbols of Scottishness, like the kilt and the bagpipes (at least in their modern forms). Some say the Burry Man started out as a pagan fertility figure or possibly a local scapegoat, his burrs trapping evil spirits. One particularly farfetched story links his green bodysuit with the scales of a merman, while another reckons it was camouflage for a shipwreck survivor back in the days of Queen Margaret, the medieval saint who gave the town its name. However, the most widely cited theory is literally a fishy story: the Burry Man may have been a way to absorb bad luck and ensure a bumper herring catch. Two other ports, Fraserburgh and Buckie, reputedly had similar traditions. Then again, this theory may be nothing more than a red herring.

The truth is that nobody has a clue why an otherwise sane man (sadly, feminism has yet to produce a Burry Woman) would volunteer to be covered scalp to ankle in a scratchy, claustrophobic, bug-infested carpet of GM-sized burrs, then wade through town for eight hours at the hottest time of the year, with nothing but whisky to drink and no easy means of going to the toilet. Down in England, self-styled pagans and sissified morrissers love to dress up as the mythical Green Man, but the Burry Man is the real deal. The green burrs swarm over him like bees – along with the actual bumblebees that are attracted by the pollen in the plants stuck to his body. The burrs are seedpods with hooked spikes measuring up to an inch long. Completely dry, the Burry Man's outfit weighs as much as twelve kilos. When it's raining, the costume becomes even heavier as the burrs soak up the water – and evil spirits, liquid or otherwise. Stories abound of past Burry Men with nicknames like Tutti Frutti peeing and 'cacking' themselves and worse. More than once, veteran Burry Man Alan Reid, a former boxer who served for at least twenty-five years, finished the route doubled over and grabbing his back. After a full day of dehydration, his kidneys would simply give out.

Despite the suffering involved, serving as the local scapegoat is a great honour; most volunteers give it up only when they're close to giving up the ghost. One year, a last-minute replacement had to quit early – 'only' about six pubs from the finish – because he couldn't take the heat. His minders had to cut slits in the costume and cool him with ice. For most people, lasting as long as he did would have been admirable. By local standards, though, his performance was a failure, and he's never quite lived it down. More recently, a stand-in died tragically young (of a non-burry-related illness), before he could take over as full-time Burry Man. In a ritual that will no doubt bedevil future archaeologists, he was buried with a replica Burry Man hat and a can of Tennants lager . . . plus 50p for another in the Great Off-Licence in the Sky.

Mmmmm – grilled herring. The silvery fish glisten in the sunlight on the beach below. Like its name, the Firth of Forth seems to be a magical place where the fish virtually jump out of the water onto your plate, saving you the trouble of chasing them. I'm hungry after the eight-hour drive from London, and the salt air immediately puts me in the mood for seafood. A sign advises 'Please Don't Eat the Shellfish', but the North Sea is just the other side of the Forth Bridge. Surely, South Queensferry must be teeming with fresh, non-toxic seafood.

I'm staying at the Queensferry Arms, where the Burry Man traditionally gets dressed, but I decide to take a walk along the waterfront to the Hawes Inn at the base of the bridge. Sir Walter Scott, the clan chief of Scottishness, featured the inn in his favourite novel, *The Antiquary*, in 1816. By the time Robert Louis Stevenson came to frequent the place – he wrote part of *Kidnapped* in Room 13 – the Hawes was already a destination for literary pilgrims. 'Americans seek it already for the sake of *The Antiquary*, but you need not tell me,' he wrote, 'that is not all, there is some story, unrecorded or nor yet complete, which must express the meaning of that inn more fully.'

Actually, a dramatic story was staring Stevenson right in the face with the building of the Forth Rail Bridge, its trio of diamond-shaped centrepieces towering 370 feet above the water and spanning more than a mile. The cantilevered structure was the largest bridge on the planet when it opened in 1890. Of the 4,600 Scottish, English and Irish men who worked on it, 461 were injured and 57 killed. The casualty ward stood right next to the pub's garden. 'Many dead and injured men carried there would have escaped had it not been for the whisky of the Hawes Inn,' rued one official. Despite competition from the suspension Road Bridge built in the 1960s, the rust-red Forth Bridge still upstages its grey rival and ranks as one of Scotland's favourite national symbols. Viewed from South Queensferry, the two structures cut across the Forth at converging angles, framing the waterscape as a constant reminder of the old and new.

In the here and now, though, I'm so hungry I'm tempted to dice with death and try a Fried Mars Bar in the chippie-cum-convenience-store on the high street. I've never experienced this Scottish delicacy, partly for lack of opportunity, but mostly for fear of God. I chicken out, though, and decide to save myself for the Hawes Inn. It's not a long walk to the edge of town – maybe half a mile total – but by the time I reach the inn, I'm fantasising about food and drink. Then, just as I throw open the door, I spot the distinctive green lettering. It's enough to cause an Edvard Munch Moment, making you slap your hands upside your face and scream *NOOOOOOOOOOOO!*

A Vintage Inns menu. The chain has rebranded yet another historic drinking spot with an unrivalled location and literary pedigree. I know it's obligatory for travel writers to bemoan the demise of the Great British Pub. I wouldn't be doing my job if I didn't throw in some vintage rants about designer beers, crass commercialism and, while I'm at it, the iniquities of mobile phones. For the most part, though, I'm all for progress. Even I can remember that the Great British Pub wasn't always as great as people like to think. The staff in some pubs barely deigned to serve you. You practically had to beg them to accept your pounds sterling in exchange for victuals – provided, of course, that you hadn't arrived outside the strict two-hour time slots for lunch and dinner.

But Vintage and I have a history. In recent years, the company has turned two pubs that used to have outstanding food to match their surroundings into 'Vintage Inns': the Freemason's Arms, just around the corner from Keats's house in Hampstead, north London, and the Trout Inn near Oxford, next to the river where Lewis Carroll first told three sisters the adventures of *Alice in Wonderland*. In fairness to Vintage, it probably has raised the culinary standards in many places. However, standardisation can also kill off character. I'm standing next to the Firth of Forth, don't they have any local dishes?

'Local deshes?' asks the girl behind the bar.

'Like grilled herring – or any local seafood.'

'Oh noh.' She pauses, then adds brightly: 'Et's cooked here – yoo can't get more local than that!'

I opt for a pint while leafing through the programme for the Ferry Fair. In its modern incarnation, the weeklong celebration coincides with Burry Man Day in August and commemorates the arrival of Queen Margaret here shortly after 1066. Born in Hungary but raised in England, the Saxon princess had the key qualification for becoming a British saint: she was a foreigner. Her brother Edgar was the poor sap picked to take over from King Harold after he was killed at the Battle of Hastings. When it became apparent that William the Conqueror wasn't going home, Edgar and Margaret tried to sail to the Continent, but a storm forced them to Scotland, where they landed in Fife on the northern banks of the Forth.

Margaret probably knew the Scottish king, Malcolm Canmore (or 'Big Head'), from the days when they both lived at the English court. Since then, Malcolm III had won the Scottish throne by killing his father's killer, Macbeth, and – with a Shakespearean flourish – Macbeth's son. Years later, Malcolm took a liking to the refined young princess and made her his queen. As a sign of gratitude, she convinced him to found Dunfermline Abbey near the spot where she first set foot in Scotland. Despite the perilous river crossing, she regularly journeyed from Edinburgh Castle to the abbey (later the final resting place for Robert the Bruce) and the shrine of St Andrew. By 1164, 'the Queen's Ferry' was a crucial part of the pilgrimage trail, and settlements developed around both its southern and northern landings. Since 1930, South Queensferry has re-enacted the Queen's arrival by crowning a schoolgirl 'Queen Margaret' and honouring 'Prince Edgar' and other members of her retinue on the Saturday morning after Burry Man Day.

Tonight, though, the star attraction is a princess of pop: 'Absolut Britney'.

'That'll be absolutely *dire*,' the barmaid assures me. 'Look, I'm from here, I'm allowed to say that.'

It's attitudes like that that are threatening the fair's survival. Undeterred, I take the quickest way to the show – up a steep, wooded path beneath the bridge known as Jacob's Ladder. The wannabe Britney is doing a fine job singing. When she speaks, though, the illusion is shattered. Instead of a soft Southern drawl redolent of magnolias and mint juleps, her voice is pure Scottish burr: 'Thenk yoo! So hoo's a Bretney Spehrs fan, thehn?'

Following Scotney's performance (after all, 'Brit' is just a weasel word for 'English'), the entertainment shifts to the athletic field in front of the school for 'Smokey and the Ducks: The Deuks (*sic*) of Gizzard'. Smokey is a paunchy man with a droopy handlebar moustache and a red tartan deerstalker. His show, which he's fond of calling 'One Man and His Ducks', involves shouting and brandishing a cane at two hyperactive border collies as they frighten four ducks through an obstacle course.

And here's me thinking that Britain is a nation of animal lovers. Still, there's nothing like a bit of duck baiting to whet the appetite. I haven't eaten yet, so I head back to the hotel. Like the Hawes Inn, the Queensferry Arms has recently been taken over by outsiders: two Scots and an Englishwoman who used to run Montpelliers, a trendy burble of a restaurant in Edinburgh. In the past eight months, they've transformed the town's namesake pub along similar lines, with candles on the tables, an Italian coffee machine behind the bar and a sparkling red wine on tap called Latino. While collecting my key, I get talking to Peter Wilson, one of the new owners. He tells me how they want to turn it into a fully fledged 'bar' without that 'pubby feel' you find in typical Scottish boozers. 'You go into a bar in Milan or Madrid, and you can order a cappuccino and food, and there's a waiter walking around carrying a tray,' he says. This admiration of the Continent is reflected in their partnership's name: *Renaissance Ecosse Ltd*.

At first, it surprises me to hear a proud Scotsman hankering after Continental culture, especially one who probably looks more like the real Braveheart than Mel Gibson. I tend to associate francophilia with a certain type of Englishman (and American, for that matter): people whose pursuit of the finer things in life blinds them to the positive aspects of their own countries. But of course the Scots and the French go way back. In the thirteenth century, when William Wallace was on the run from Edward I – the self-styled Hammer of the Scots – he travelled to the Continent to try to get England's Old Enemy to intervene. It was the 'auld alliance' struck around the same time that eventually dragged Scotland into the catastrophic Battle of Flodden. Not long afterwards, Mary Queen of Scots was also briefly Queen of France, and her son, the first king to reign over both England and Scotland, adopted the French spelling of the family surname. The House of Stuart, right from old King James himself to both Charleses and James II, constantly looked to the Continent for tips on how to be better *bon viveurs* and waste more of England's riches. When they were finally kicked out of the country, their descendants, most famously Bonnie Prince Charlie, sought French support to try to retake the throne in the famous Jacobite rebellions. And way before all that, there was Queensferry's saintly namesake, Queen Margaret. The Hungarian-born Saxon princess devoted her life to civilising her illiterate Scottish husband and his rough retinue. She introduced Saxon as the language at court, replacing Gaelic (which, incidentally, is pronounced 'gallic' in Scotland), and Romanised the Celtic Church. She was later canonised as St Margaret for her services to Catholicism, although nowadays nationalists accuse her of undermining Scotland's native Celtic culture.

So there's a certain continuity in Peter's attempt to bring a Continental-style cultural renaissance to these shores. In terms of cuisine, he reckons the Queensferry Arms' restaurant is at least five menus away from perfection. 'We want to offer *good food* – not up-its-own-arse food, but *good food*,' he enthuses.

Despite Peter's assurances, the current menu sounds pretty arse-friendly to me, particularly the dish that apparently has Indian and Slovakian influences: two cultures thousands of miles apart brought together on one twelve-inch plate. His face falls when I tell him what drew me to the restaurant: the promise of haddock fried 'in a Queensferry Arms batter'. 'I'm not knocking it,' he says, recovering his composure, but from his point of view, there's nothing special about fish and chips.

Despite his lack of enthusiasm, Peter produces a fine plate of fish and chips. Even better is the view from the restaurant's wide bay windows: the old Forth Bridge illuminated a golden red in the darkness, with the water shining silver down below. As shallow and touristy as it may seem, what I'd really like is a dish that matches the vista, the culinary equivalent of one of those maps that says: 'You are here – not in India or Slovakia, but in Scotland – and not just in Scotland, but in South Queensferry, right on the banks of the Firth of Forth.' In the land of Adam Smith, you expect restaurateurs to focus on what they do best. Peter's ambitions to raise culinary standards are laudable, but with Edinburgh twenty minutes away, I could go there if I wanted homogenised cosmo-cuisine.

The next morning, I finally get what I want. The menu advertises a Traditional Scottish Breakfast, which has much in common with its Sassenach counterpart, except for two additions: a tattie scone – a wedge of potato pancake – and haggis. The Scottish mystery meat is tastefully presented, or at least as tastefully presented as chawed-up animal innards can be: rather than bursting out of an exploded sheep's stomach, it's served on its own, as a moulded spoonful with a sprinkling of parsley. Medium brown in colour, it has the liverish taste and consistency of pâté mixed with grain. Peter informs me that a famous poet once declared haggis the 'great chieftain o' the puddin' race'.

I know the quote, but I've never heard of 'Rabbie Bairns'.

For a second, even eager-to-please Peter can't conceal his shock. He gives me the same look as when I ordered fish and chips: *Stupid bloody Ya*— then regains his composure. It's only when he mentions 'Bairns Night', that I realise he's talking about Robert Burns, who's so well loved in Scotland that people refer to him on familiar terms, unlike other national poets like Billy Shakespeare or Johnny Goethe. Peter tells me that tourists go ga-ga over Burns Suppers, especially the Piping in the Haggis. They whip out their cameras as the men in kilts whip out their . . . daggers and plunge them into the bloated sheep's stomach, cramming handfuls of innards into their mouths.

Come to think of it, I have had haggis before – a long time ago, at a Burns Supper in Peru, of all places. Either I've suppressed the memory, or the shots of *Yohnnie Walkerrr* did the trick, but I vaguely recall the American ambassador in a kilt, the mix of Scottish reels and salsa on the dance floor and the puddles of bland purée served up for dinner. The mashed – or 'bashed' – foods were distinguishable only by their different colours: greyish-brown for haggis, greyish-orange for 'neeps' and greyish-white for 'tatties'. It looked like the stuff they serve in hospitals to people who can't chew, with straws instead of cutlery: when you're ninety-five and in a nursing home, every night must be Burns Night. Maybe the Scots lost their teeth prematurely from a diet of whisky and Fried Mars Bars. At the time, the manly, macho-jocko chest-thumping over what was essentially baby food struck me as being more exotic than the Latin American backdrop. I'm beginning to think that these contradictions – between roughness and refinement, tradition and modernisation, the romantic past and the pragmatic present – define Scotland. And I'm about to find out the hard way on Burry Man Day.

The Burry Man's head fills the screen, a chunk of ice melting on his shoulder. What used to be Young John Nicol's face is swarming with vegetation, except for two eyeholes and a tiny circle for his mouth. In close-up, the moist pink hole, its lips fringed with bristles, its teeth hidden in the bush, well . . . it looks obscene! Like an S&M fantasy for the garden-show crowd – *Shed of Pain: The Garden Gimp*.

Fortunately, folklorist Doc Rowe keeps the scene clean, interviewing the Burry Man on the Nicols' garden patio. 'Who are you in there?' he asks the Talking Bush.

'Oh, I'm the Burry Man,' John replies. He's drunk at least half a dozen freehand shots of whisky by now, and his answers seem to be coming from a very far-off place. 'Y'know, I've got, obviously, vegetation and plants that I'm thinking about a lot today.'

'You actually feel like a plant, then, do you?'

'Well, I think that's somethin' that . . . *definitely* there's a vegetation vibe goin' on.'

Watching the interview a year later in their sitting room, John and his parents are cackling at the TV screen. Contrary to his appearance in character, John doesn't take himself too seriously out of costume. The 28-year-old native son took over the role in 1999. 'I don't think there was, like, queues of applicants,' he deadpans. However, he didn't hesitate to accept the post. 'I don't actually know why! It's somethin' that I'm very, very proud of – it's an honour,' John adds, agreeing that 'the bizarre side of it' also appeals to him.

His mother's initial reaction to the Burry Man was less enthusiastic. Originally from Edinburgh, she hadn't seen the local bogeyman until 1973, when she was almost nine months pregnant with John. 'And I nearly died of shock! I couldn't *believe* how horrendous it was. I thought, My God! No *wonder* the kids scream!' She never imagined that her baby boy would one day become the Burry Man: 'No way.'

John still has a boyish face, with a thatch of dirty-blond hair and eyes that couldn't look mean if they tried. At six-foot-two, he carries an extra layer of padding, but it's just as well: on a hot Burry Man Day, he can shed half a stone in sweat.

The fixings for tomorrow's outfit are drying in the kitchen, thirty panels of burrs piled in a box with newspaper to keep them from sticking together. All told, they've probably picked around 11,000 burrs, and John and I are going to collect another carrier-bagful as soon as his best friend arrives. To my disappointment, though, gloves are a no-go, for the obvious reason that the burrs would latch on to them.

'Ya get in a bit of a mess,' John's dad cautions. 'They grow among nettles, which sting ya, and the bees like 'em as well, so you could possibly get stung.'

Great.

But no one's been stung this year, Old John assures me. 'They're full a bugs – beetles and things like that – so, ya chuck 'em down on the ground, and they just disperse.'

Moving swiftly outside to the patio, I ask John if he views the Burry Man as a kind of performance art. After all, he is a graphic artist, and he lists the Burry Man on his CV under 'Miscellaneous'.

'There's no relationship at all,' he concludes with a cockeyed squint in the sunlight. 'The Burry Man . . . it's just far more important. It's not really mine to subvert or to change it or to say it's performance art. I don't wanna sort of take the *pess* out of the Burry Man or belittle it in any way.'

He believes the tradition has something to do with 'gathering and collecting evil': 'I'm covered in stuff which is inherently sticky, I make myself as big as I can be (with limbs outstretched) and I essentially walk up and down every street, but – I don't know how important it is to me that I actually know the significance; it's important to me that the tradition keeps going. And I hope that it goes on forever.'

As with many customs down south, some latter-day pagans have tried to lay claim to the tradition, though none have actually come to the event. John wouldn't be opposed to neopagans tagging along. However, they might be taking their life into their own hands. 'We were the last people in the civilised world to burn witches, up here in Scotland,' Old John observes. At least ten women were locked up in Queensferry's Black Castle and Tolbooth as late as 1644. They were all executed, probably just outside town at a place called Ferrymuir. As proof of Queensferry's progress, though, the site is now home to a Burger King: instead of burning witches there, they flame-grill sandwiches.

Pagan tradition or not, John reckons the whisky given to him throughout the day represents payment for performing the ritual. 'It gets ya really pissed as well,' he laughs, before adding thoughtfully: 'The whisky's a really important part of the event as far as I'm concerned, because if I was sober through it, I think the discomfort would be a lot stronger, but the drunker I get, the more carefree I become.'

I ask how many shots he has during the day. He starts counting on his hands – 'I have a whisky here, a whisky there' – and soon runs out of fingers. All told, he makes at least seventeen stops for whisky.

'*Drams*,' Old John emphasises. 'A good shot. Not a hotel shot or a bar shot; you're talkin' about somebody at home givin' im a shot.'

As it happens, that tally is one short of the eighteen whiskies that Welsh poet Dylan Thomas drank before dropping dead. Altogether, the Burry Man probably downs an entire bottle of Scotch during the day. What's more, the burrs make it impossible to sip from a glass, so he has to drink the whisky through a straw. He might as well inject it into his brain with a hypodermic syringe.

'Whisky has a dehydrating effect,' his father adds. 'It stops you going to the toilet.' Which is the first thing John does at the end of the day. 'I go to the bathroom and stand and just have a pee for ten minutes. It's like – *Ahhhhh*, you *beauty*.'

'Do y'know, John *had* a pee last year,' Old John informs me.

Uhhh . . . no I didn't.

His son cracks up; there's no point being embarrassed. 'I actually needed ta pee for hours and hours last year.' About 2:30 in the afternoon, he finally told his father his predicament. 'And my dad cut me free, and I had a pee, and it was brelliant.' Somehow they managed to close the emergency flap in his costume, and John continued stalking the town. 'I was quite paranoid,' he laughs. 'I didn't know if I was actually tucked back in or not; if I was walkin' on the high street and wavin' about to the crowd.'

Ideally, John likes to take a good long soak in the bath after he's cut free from the burrs, but this year he'll have to make do with a shower because of a bust-up with the new owners of the Queensferry Arms. For nearly twenty years, the pub has hosted the dressing of the Burry Man in the morning and provided him with a bath at night. Last year, before *Renaissance Ecosse* took over, John donated his Burry Man Hat to the Queensferry Arms as a way of saying thanks. All the local landlords know that being entrusted with the rose-studded bowler hat for a year is a great honour and a sign of good luck; they proudly display the relic behind the bar until the Burry Man comes to reclaim it for the big day. Unfortunately, Peter and the partners of *Renaissance Ecosse* didn't know the importance of the tradition and the floral bowler hat. 'When the Queensferry Arms was renovated, they chucked it out,' Old John says, still riled. 'So we kind of fell out with the Queensferry Arms.' Eventually, the Nicols managed to find a replacement bowler, but a misunderstanding over the hotel's availability means that the Burry Man won't be getting dressed there this year.

'The Queensferry Arms used to be a *pub* that was full of rough diamonds,' Old John says, his voice brimming with nostalgia. 'It was a good pub. Y'know, ya got *good worthies* goin' in there. Okay, they were rough diamonds, and they did get drunk quite a lot. But now they've turned it from a boozer, in our speak, to – like a snobbish café-*bar*-bistro type of place. Pretty soon you won't be able to find a real pub.' His disgust is evident. Although the word 'rough' is often used in relation to Scotland – 'roughs' are even part of the national game – when John Senior talks about 'rough diamonds', you wonder just how rough they were.

Once John's friend George arrives, we head to some wasteland where there are plenty of burrs. While my eyes stray toward the green fields and flowers nearby, the Burry Man makes a beeline for a thick patch of burdock, a five-foot-high circle of stalks bristling with green-and-purple seedpods. Judging from the size of the burrs – as big as eyeballs, studded with spikes up to an inch long – I'm guessing this is Greater Burdock, as opposed to the Lesser variety. 'This is the biggest bunch I've seen,' John enthuses. 'These are massive. They're fantastic.' Still, it's not all happy hunting. He picks a withered brown weed and frowns. 'This is what happens when they use pesticides.'

The prickly pods covering the Burry Man are often called Nature's Velcro, and in fact it was burdock's cousin, the humble cocklebur, that inspired a Swiss engineer to create the space-age hook-and-loop material. The burrs' spikes have tiny hooks on their ends, enabling them to hitchhike on passing animals to spread their seeds. Whereas Velcro sticks only to itself, though, nature's original will stick to virtually anything that doesn't have a polished surface. The burrs make a satisfying pop when you pull them off the stalk, but they're deeply creepy to touch. The protective spikes shelter all sorts of beasties – black beetles, yellow spiders – both visible and invisible to the naked eye. The burrs themselves immediately latch on to your skin like dying insects grabbing their killers with one last reflexive impulse. If I weren't with the Burry Man, I'd probably be flicking my hand frantically and shouting *Get it off! Get it off!* Occasionally, the spikes may prick you, but for the most part, burr picking is merely unpleasant rather than painful – so long as you avoid the stinging nettles that grow among them, that is. I don't know how to recognise the jellyfish of the plant world, but they quickly identify me. By the end, my hands are covered in puffy welts and flecks of dead epidermis.

Carrier-bag full, we head back to the car. John and George have known each other since primary school. George reckons you could ask 100 people to be the Burry Man, and ninety-nine would tell you no, including himself; his best friend would be the only one to say yes: 'It's a very John thing to do.'

As a wee girl, Emma Loseby's first encounter with the Burry Man left her scarred for life. Her father was driving up the high street when he told her to look out of the window. 'All I can remember is seeing this big monster. I was *absolutely* terrified,' she recalls. Like many kids in South Queensferry, she used to have nightmares about the Burry Man. These days, though, Emma kisses him good morning: she's the Burry Man's girlfriend. In fact, this morning, she's even going to help with his costume. 'If I see him getting dressed, I know that it's him in there,' she assures me.

We're in the small back lounge of the Stag, characterised by its Gaelic-cum-Gallic interior: dark tartan carpet, corner view to the Forth Bridge and wall hangings to add a touch of class – namely, Paris street signs and prints by Picasso and Toulouse-Lautrec. John's standing in the middle of the room, legs spread on the square dance floor, flanked by a mirrored wall on one side and a track of disco lights overhead. He's wearing two layers of clothes, topped off with a long-sleeved shirt and baggy grey sweatpants, plus a pair of black Doc Martens shined especially for the occasion. The hot studio lights of a camera crew and a couple of photographers bear down on him, while the fireplace behind is blazing on full Bearskin Rug Ambience, even though it's August.

'You're quite shiny,' Emma tells him.

'I've got cream on my face.'

A scapegoat who moisturises: very New Burry Man.

Actually, John looks more like a big cuddly kid crossing his arms in bemusement as no fewer than seven people dress his six-foot-two-inch frame. They tilt the rectangular patches of burrs onto the Burry Man's body as if they were laying patches of turf for landscaping. This manscaping involves moulding the prickly sections to the contours of his calves, knees, thighs and, of course, his groin.

Emma switches into hostess mode, gesturing to a tartan tray laden with mugs of tea and a large bottle of single malt. 'Have you helped yourself to a whisky, everyone?' she asks the assembled journalists. It's just after 8 a.m.: too early for them to start drinking – at least, too early for them to be *seen* to start drinking – so they feign laughter. John's dad has already had a couple of warm-ups, and another old-timer takes Emma up on her offer, toasting Young John's good health. Whisky fumes soon fill the room.

As the green tide of burrs nears John's midsection, the jocular atmosphere turns serious. Emma and John's mother, Senga, get stuck in, so to speak, on his waistline, sewing his sweatpants to his shirt. This keeps the Burry Man's trousers from falling down and exposing him, while also preventing the spiky balls from slipping into his pants and inflicting untold damage on the family jewels. In their manner and appearance, the two most important women in John's life are strikingly similar. Both are full-bodied and blonde – Emma has a short bob while Senga wears her hair long – and they cluck and fuss over John like two mother hens. 'I tell him not to wear grey underwear in case he wets himself because that will show up at the end of the day,' Emma tells me.

The swell of weedpods reaches John's chest, and he obligingly stretches his arms. Two boys stand on either side of him, their heads serving as hand rests. It was right about now that John started to panic in his first year. Wearing long johns over his jeans in August, with a thick layer of burrs on top, he was already hot and uncomfortable by the time he had to extend his arms. *My shoulders are killin' me!* he realised. *And that's after five minutes – I've got to do this all day!*

As the burry tide threatens his face, John's friend, George, takes a break from sticking him and sidles up to me. 'So what do you make of all this then?'

'I can't believe he's so calm.'

'That's 'cause he needs to go somewhere!' he jokes, raising his voice for John's benefit. 'He has a place he needs to go!'

John smiles tightly, but he's not even going to acknowledge the problem. He's already been to the toilet about ten times this morning – 'just trying to squeeze the last drop out' – and references to calls of nature are particularly unwelcome. On Burry Man Day, the unspoken admonishment is 'Don't Mention the Wee'.

A Rampant Lion flag is wrapped around John's waist like a giant red-and-yellow cummerbund (with a border of burrs), and a helper pulls a black balaclava over his face.

'Bye, John.'

For a moment, he looks like a rogue Scot in the IRA.

'Ooh, I hate that bit!' Emma squirms, explaining that once the mask is on, the transformation is nearly complete. Then she stubs out her cigarette. 'I better get sewin'.' She and Senga start sealing him into his costume, stitching the skull-tight mask to the neck of his shirt. As the dressers start covering her boyfriend's face in burrs, Emma resumes her position as spectator, hiding in the corner and peeking over my shoulder.

'You can stand in front of me,' I offer.

'No, I'm fine here, thanks.'

The next time she peers out, John's face is lost in a prickly fuzz of green burrs topped off with a scalp full of flowers. He has two slots for his eyes, but no nose, and just a tiny inchhole for a mouth. 'Ooh, look at his wee lips!' Emma coos.

Then the dressers start adding floral accessories, festooning him with pink and yellow roses and covering up any gaps in his prickly armour. After a full hour, the Burry Man has been carpeted scalp to ankle, with only his hands exposed. He inches sideways down half a dozen stairs and through a tartan corridor to pose outside the pub's doorway.

'Hep hep hooray! It's the Burry Man's Day!'

A big white tour bus is stunned to a stop, its passengers gawping and pressing their cameras against the glass. The Burry Man is led through the streets like a convict, his arms and hands outstretched and a cowbell clanging as if to announce his impending execution. His stilted gait and green bodysuit also give him the appearance of a bogeyman, or a sci-fi alien from a B-movie, the kind who somehow manages to chase and catch his victims, even though he can't run or even bring his arms together. Maybe that's what he is: a Star(fish) Man, come to blow our minds. Lots of children lose it when they see him, shrieking in terror despite their parents' best efforts to get them to pose with the monster. The Burry Man carries two blue-and-white staves, topped off with frilly pink hydrangeas – the better to attract bees – and little Rampant Lion flags. In contrast, his attendants – John's dad and his uncle Alec – are smartly turned out in formal Argyll jackets and ties, with Black Watch tartan trews, or trousers. Old John is clean-shaven, but Alec has a moustache and a long grey ponytail. Their job is to support the Burry Man's arms and keep him from falling over. John also uses the wobble in their walk to gauge his own level of inebriation.

The Burry Man has his first whisky just after 9 a.m., sucking it down in two slurps before moving on. In the shadow of the Road Bridge, we have the option of whisky or Scotland's 'other national drink'. 'Would you like some Irn Bru?' a kindly woman asks, holding a container of garish orange liquid and glasses with what looks like an inch of water in them. It turns out that this is vodka; add a splash of Irn Bru, and you've got yourself a sweet, rust-coloured drink known known as a Girder. Not having grown up with Irn Bru, it's not my place to critique Scotland's answer to Coca-Cola. However, I'm fairly confident that the addition of vodka can only be an improvement. I'm told that whisky also makes a fine additive – but I'll take the locals' word for it.

Wisely, John sticks to the straight stuff, which appears on platters wherever he goes, as if by magic. Given that he's covered in noxious weeds and trailing seedpods, you might expect gardeners to greet him with shotguns; instead, they give the Weedman shots of whisky and drop coins in the collection boxes carried by half a dozen kids. One granny has even got dolled up for the occasion, wearing a mint-green trouser suit. She doesn't have a straw for the whisky, so she uses a baby spoon to feed it to the Burry Man, the liquid dribbling into his burrs. 'I'll help ya,' she says, taking a sip herself.

It's raining steadily now, in what's shaping up to be a typical August morning in Scotland, with temperatures so cold you can see your breath, and a thick sea fog, or *haar*, greying the distance. The clouds alternate between sprinkles and showers, making Edinburgh officially the wettest place in Britain today. Still, the Burry Man marches on, soaking up bad luck and precipitation.

The Burry Man's five- to six-mile route takes him from the cobbled high street, with its Victorian storefronts and split-level terraces, past the fifteenth-century Carmelite Friary and along the pebbledash housing that covers the hillside beneath the modern suspension Road Bridge. As cars fly overhead, on the other side of town trains trundle sedately across the Old Forth Bridge, their cargo containers so high in the sky they look like toys. The Burry Man heads toward the housing estate where Emma's parents live, and her cousin, in full Highland regalia, pipes in the procession, playing 'The Green Hills of Tyrol'. A reporter from Scottish TV is running alongside the Burry Man doing a piece to camera – something about 'Don't burry be happy' – holding a thistle in one hand and a little bottle of Bell's in the other. *Now if I did that . . .*

From Emma's, the trek turns into a long wet slog down monotonous rows of gritcast housing. Only a handful of followers accompany John on these desolate stretches, so he closes his eyes, letting his dad and uncle guide him, while listening out for friendly voices. 'If I turn a street corner, and all of a sudden there's a couple of friends there, it really spurs me on,' he says.

There's no such reception waiting for him at the Agilent Technologies plant. Here in South Queensferry, the American company produces the equipment used to test most of the world's mobile phones – a fitting reversal, given that the inventor of the telephone, Alexander Graham Bell, was a Scotsman transplanted to America. Agilent's dressed-down workers don't know what to make of the alien in their midst. 'Most of them come from the rest of Scotland, so they don't even know what the tradition's about, and they're puzzled,' explains John's uncle, who works at the plant. Either that, or his fellow employees are too worried about their jobs to care. At the height of the tech boom, the local outposts of IBM, Hewlett-Packard and other computer companies employed more than 50,000 workers, producing over 60 per cent of Scotland's exports and nearly a third of Europe's PCs. However, since the boom turned to bust, the land of Adam Smith has learned just how fickle foreign capital can be. More than 10,000 jobs have been axed, causing Scotland's doom-and-gloom media to rename the area 'Sili-gone Glen' and brand the plant closures as 'the twenty-first-century equivalent of The Clearances'. When mobile phone giant Motorola closed its outlet near Queensferry, a local paper ran a cartoon of a 'Buroo Man' covered in P45s. The Burry Man reference may have been a bit too exotic for newcomers, but for any Scots speaker, the message was clear: 'buroo' is slang for 'dole office'. Maybe that's why Agilent's workers are so reluctant to meet the Burry Man.

After ten minutes of virtual neglect in the futuristic corridor, John swings past the company crèche to shock the kiddies before heading to his parents' home on one of the estates built for Silicon Glen workers. Dozens of friends and family from as far away as Glasgow and Aberdeen have come to cheer him on. Senga has laid out a lunchtime buffet, but it's strictly whisky for John. As the guests mingle around him, he leans against the wooden patio fence, his friends taking turns to hold up his arms.

The whisky and conversation help compensate for the after-noon's mind-numbing trek through mazes of pebbledash housing. Members of the Ferry Queen's court traditionally decorate their homes for the week, and occasionally a colourful front-garden tableau will break up the grey monotony. One in particular features a trio of Highlanders guarding a cut-out wooden castle with the Scottish flag flying overhead. A couple of redcoated Englishmen lie dead or dying on the ground. For the most part, though, this stretch of the Burry Man's tour takes in unlovely sights such as a redbrick shopping arcade with a video rental place and a ScotMid convenience shop. The pubs that punctuate the day reflect a cross-section of boozers. Some are themed in keeping with their names, like the Stag and the Moorings, while others are nondescript drinking dens where the regulars are already knocking 'em back at 2 p.m., Burry Man Day or no. One place, described as 'a great wee pub', is a box of a room with wood panelling on the walls and tartan curtains in the windows. It's a kind of Andy Capp pub where the men send their womenfolk to the bar to fetch their drinks: 'There's a good pet!'

While the rest of us socialise, the Burry Man usually stands propped up against the wall, with even some locals wary of him. 'Are we allowed to talk to him?' they'll ask. However, John welcomes any comradeship, including my regular enquiries about his health. 'Keep talkin' to me. Please do. Because it helps me – I can just chat away to ya.' Hemmed in by whisky fumes and vegetation, he'll do anything to keep his mind off the dull ache in his hips and shoulders, the spikes jagging his skin and the uncomfortable ballooning of his bladder. In one dark, wood-panelled boozer, he ends up standing between the toilets marked 'Ladies' and 'Gentlemen', his staves blocking the doors: *If I can't go in, nobody else can either.*

Around three o'clock, the Burry Man and his followers descend into the old town for the final pub-crawl along the waterfront. As they turn on to the cobbled high street, I ask Old John whether they're going to set foot in the Queensferry Arms this year.

'Who knows?' he shrugs, swaying slightly. 'You could be a diplomat here, and go in and have a quiet word with them . . . and find out.'

I'm not entirely sure what he means, and I don't want to stumble into a local dispute without having clear guidance. The procession stops along the promenade so that the Burry Man can pose on the waterfront with the Old Forth Bridge in the background. Meanwhile, Old John takes me aside and explains that he and his family aren't ones to hold grudges.

'So what do you want me to do?'

'Well, why not be a bit diplomatic and say, "Look, there's been a bit of a misunderstanding. Would it be all right for the Burry Man to come in on the way back and bring you good luck?" Yeah, say that – "It's good luck to come into your pub." '

Now, I know how dangerous these shoot-the-messenger situations can be, but unfortunately, I have do-gooding deep in my bones. If I can do anything to help them meet midway, I have to try. I'm not so American as to expect a group hug, but they should be able to find some common ground: at least a ceasefire, if not a peace treaty.

So off I trot to the QFA. After some awkward blathering – I don't quite know how to put this – I level with Peter: would he mind if the Burry Man pays his traditional visit to the pub? After all, they say it brings good luck.

Keen to explain himself, Peter launches into a lengthy account of all the angry phone calls and the he-said/we-said arguments over the past several months. He takes me down to the banqueting-cum-conference room where the Burry Man used to get dressed. The Arrol Suite (named after the firm that built both bridges) represents the height of Scottish sophistication or a tartan nightmare, depending on your fondness for plaid. The dark criss-crossed pattern carpets the floor – except for the *de rigueur* disco square – and creeps up the walls. However, I'm too busy staring out of the windows to notice. The glass wall reveals a panoramic view of the Old Forth Bridge spanning the water. 'The view is stunning,' Peter says proudly, and I get the feeling it's the one thing he wouldn't change about the place.

According to him, the Nicols had demanded that he reserve the room for the Burry Man months in advance, clashing with his plans to renovate the entire hotel. He also claims that he and his partners had no idea what Burry Man Day involved when they took over. Crucially, none of the local staff told them the significance of the flowery hat on the bar. 'If I knew that hat was the Burry Man's,' he told John Senior, 'I wouldn't have it on top of the *bar*, in a smoke-filled room, I would have it put in a lovely case with a bit of information – more importantly, *history* – about what it was.'

Although he tries to make the right noises to me, every so often Peter lets slip with phrases that must infuriate the locals. For instance, he says he told the Ferry Fair organisers to write down their requests 'in clear English': 'We've got to develop this building before we worry about one wee thing out of the whole picture.' Of course, for natives, the final weekend of the Ferry Fair is a very *big* thing indeed. But Peter reckons 'it's just a general pess-up'; his sources have told him that 'the good local people won't be coming into town' because of all the boozing and brawling. What's more, during their argument on the phone, he says he told John Senior, 'Do you *really think* that when it comes to a half-a-million-pound investment, the Burry Man gettin' changed in here one day out of the year is a significant part of the handover?'

However, the biggest shock for the natives is yet to come. Peter tells me that *Renaissance Ecosse* plans to rebrand the landmark pub – by giving it a new name.

I don't know what to say. The Queensferry Arms is the only pub bearing the town's name – it even has Queensferry's coat of arms hanging outside, featuring St Margaret crossing the river in a boat. Getting rid of this unique link to the town – this history – not only seems foolish, but downright suicidal.

'How do you think that will go down with the locals?' I ask.

'I don't care. We don't care,' he emphasises. 'Because "The Queensferry Arms" is synonymous with a shithole of a pub.' He reckons that only one per cent of the town used to frequent the pub; the other 99 per cent stayed away. '*Good* locals' like the pub's next-door neighbours used to have to clean up broken glass and spattered blood after the street brawls every weekend. Not any more. Inside, he says, 'the staff used to sit on top of the bar and smoke cigarettes while they were servin' customers!' He's still horrified. 'The staff used to sit and watch television with the customers. The staff used to drink behind the bar. We stopped all of that.' These changes are all part of the *Renaissance Ecosse* philosophy: 'Ya stay local, you won't survive. The world's bigger.'

What the locals don't realise is that he and his partners have borrowed against their houses in Edinburgh to buy the Queensferry Arms. If the business fails, they could lose their homes. Peter says he told the Nicols, 'Please come and see me. I am not a bastard', but they never have – until today. 'Make it very clear,' he says, staring me straight in the eye. 'We have no *grudge* to bear. We welcome them in here.'

That's all I need to hear. I hurry back along the waterfront and find the Burry Man posing with a newlywed couple outside the Two Bridges: the bride in cream satin, the groom in grey formalwear, and the monster in green spikeballs.

'Have you made the peace?' Old John asks.

'It's sorted.'

At least, it should be. I know Peter said some harsh things, and the Nicols feel just as strongly, but if their Sassenach counterparts are anything to go by, the rival clans won't start arging or barging in their initial encounter. Immediately afterwards, they may stab each other in the back, but meeting face to face for the first time, their inherent grace and good manners – the qualities embodied by Queen Margaret – will win the day. I'll bet they end up chatting about the weather.

A couple more pubs, and the ragtag group heads down the high street towards the QFA, the bell clanging, the collection tins kachunking.

Old John motions to me. 'You're the mediator – you've gotta go in.'

But Peter and one of his partners, Eleanor, are already waiting in the doorway with whiskies on a platter. The Burry Man lumbers into the cool warmth of the café-bar, as out of place as a tartan carpet. Surrounded by flickering candles and blackshirted barmen, with American R&B in the air, he leans stiffly against the bar, steadying himself with his hands. Eleanor holds his whisky for him, stretching her arm as far as it will go and smiling tightly. In fact, it's tight smiles all around. If the Burry Man can smile underneath his mask, I'll bet he's smiling tightly.

Still, at least they're all smiling. To my relief, it seems to be going well. Maybe I'm not so bad at peacemaking after all. *Today South Queensferry, tomorrow Northern Ire—*

I don't see John or Peter. This can't be good. I hurry outside and find them face-to-face in the spitting rain, John in his tux and Black Watch tartan, Peter in his goatee and head-to-toe black.

The first thing I hear is Old John exclaiming: 'You're gonna change the name?! It's not gonna be the Queensferry Arms?!'

I don't believe it. They've only just met each other – I left them alone for barely five minutes – and they've jumped straight into the old argument! What happened to the climatic chitchat? And why on *earth* has Peter mentioned the name change!?

Senga notices the commotion and comes over.

Her husband is brandishing his whisky at the old-fashioned canopies over the doorways. 'This is the first pub I went into when I was old enough to drink,' John says. The fact that he was underage doesn't help his argument, but the sentimental attachment does explain why he was so keen to stop at his old watering hole.

The sprinkle turns to a drizzle, and Senga opens her umbrella; not even the rain is going to stop this argument. The translucent green fabric gives the combatants an unhealthy glow. John is bleary-eyed and slurring his Ss. After a dozen 'nips' of whisky, it looks like he wants to take a bite out of the man who's talking intensely, right up in his face. Peter's in full-blown dog-on-a-bone mode, gnawing on phrases like 'planneng permession' and 'lested building' and recounting how he told one of the Johns about the scheduling clash for the building work. 'And if you guys misinterpret that, I'm really sorry, but I spent a lot a time talking to John, and I'm *not* going to apologise. I said to him very clearly that *we* have borrowed money to buy this place, to refurbish it –'

'Well . . . but that's really your business,' John says.

'But that's the point!'

'No, it's not.'

'It *is* the point.' Peter's so wound up he's hitting high notes. 'The place has to be revamped very badly, and we will *not* be pressurised by people –'

'And what about the locals?' Senga interjects. 'Does that not bother ya? We've just spoken to *loads* of people along the road here, and they've said, "You're not goin' in there, are ya?"'

'We were not comin' here, until this man – this man –'

John's nodding at me.

Before I get sucked in the argument continues: one man

defending his dream, the other fighting for his memories, until John introduces 'fuckin'' into the debate – purely for emphasis – and realises his temper's rising. He breaks off and wanders into the pub.

'He's good,' Old John tells me. 'He's a businessman, and I'm just a – I don't know . . . when I came down here three months ago, that lady there –' he nods toward Eleanor – 'she thought I was a rude bastard. But – I'm not fuckin' rude.'

As we set off for the Stag, Senga calls me over, determined to have the last word about Peter. 'I still don't believe in what he said. He's probably talkin' sense, but he's talkin' ridiculous sense. I can see what he was sayin': it makes business sense not to have riff raff in his place. But if the *locals* are riff raff, then that's –'

The cheering interrupts her as the Burry Man returns to his new home. The stripping of the scapegoat is so quick it's anticlimactic. Around five o'clock, nine hours after the ordeal began, John takes a seat on the disco room floor, his back to the mirrored wall. Everybody crowds around to scrape off the burrs, including a little girl. The helpers make a few snips with the scissors and lift off the balaclava.

'Welcome home, John.'

The Burry Man has landed. Squinting from the sudden flood of light, he grins as if he's just stumbled out of bed to find a surprise birthday party waiting for him.

'It's good to be back.'

Somebody shouts 'Hep hep!' and the response roars back: 'Hooray!'

Balled-up clothes and clumps of burrs litter the dance floor. John's family gathers them into rubbish bags. They'll burn these discarded seedpods – saturated with evil and God knows what else – at a bonfire party in the next few weeks.

So would they consider returning to the QFA next year?

'No, no.' Old John shakes his head. 'This is the place. They would love to have it, but – this is the place. They told us to fuck off last year, this year, that's it.' He doesn't rule out another meeting, but he warns that he has a very low tolerance level for people like Peter.

'He's a businessman. As my old man used to say: he'll talk until the arse falls outta yer troosers.'

So . . . that went well, then.

Afterwards, Emma tells me that while her elders had been arguing outside, she had started her own spat with Eleanor at the bar. She says the pub's co-owner was very defensive, but that's hardly surprising, given that Emma's opening gambit was: 'I'm very disappointed to be in here . . .'

Propped up against the bar, Young John didn't want to be there either. After finishing with Eleanor, Emma asked him, 'Why are we here?'

The Burry Man sighed.

'JR – JR tried to make the peace.'

I try to protest my innocence, explaining that John's dad put me up to it, but she clearly doesn't believe me. Later, after multiple rounds of beer, whisky and tequila, I tell John the same thing: it wasn't my idea to get involved.

He shrugs and laughs. It's no use. The blame sticks.

I've been scapegoated by the scapegoat.

PART TWO:
THE BURRY MAN CHALLENGE

The following year on my return visit, I decide to stay at the Queensferry Arms for the sake of impartiality – and their fine Scottish breakfast. I'm counting on the potato scone and haggis to soak up the whisky as I take the Burry Man Challenge: matching John Nicol nip for nip until 'Firth of Forth' comes out sounding like 'Froth of Frith'.

'You won't make it to lunchtime,' he grins through his prickly mask.

His uncle's also doubtful. 'You'll be dancin' into a lamppost just like Gene Kelly.'

Only without the rain. Britain is set to hit 100-degrees Fahrenheit this weekend for the first time in history, but this morning is mercifully cool in South Queensferry, with the Forth Bridge invisible behind a thick curtain of *haar*. Nevertheless, John's burr-encrusted balaclava is already saturated with sweat at the start of his trek. He hasn't told anyone, but he has a bad feeling about today. During this week's heat wave, well-wishers have constantly been reminding him just how hot it's going to be. Inevitably, the warnings have begun to play on his mind.

When he first started out, John used to think that there might be a secret Burry Man motto passed down over generations, a quasi-mystical mantra to inspire him throughout the ordeal. As he waited nervously to make his debut, a former Burry Man put the final touches on his eyes and mouth. The other dressers had drifted away, leaving the two Burry Men, past and present, to confer in peace. *This is it,* John thought. *He's going to pass on the secret that will officially make me the Burry Man.*

Instead, the old boy looked him in the eye and said, 'Remember, John, if you can't do this, you let a lot of people down.'

And John thought: *You bastard.* How could that possibly be a useful thing to say? He was the first to admit that he didn't have a clue about what he had got himself into. He had no idea how difficult it would be – and nobody would be more disappointed than him if he didn't finish.

Unfortunately, today might be that day. John's enthusiasm and general popularity has led more people to offer him whiskies on his walk. The first unscheduled shot – the second nip of the morning – comes just fifteen minutes into his route. The new owner of the corner shop next to the Road Bridge is waiting for him with a quarter-bottle of firewater. John's father informs the Pakistani man that it's customary to have a drink with the Burry Man. The shopkeeper flinches, but duly returns with some glasses.

'He's a Muslim,' a local explains. 'He's not supposed to drink.'

'That's right. I didn't have a drink,' the owner smiles afterwards, holding an empty glass.

Ten minutes later, John and I have our third drink of the day, this one served by Betty Archibald, the elderly daughter of a deceased Burry Man. She warns him about the weather, adding some grandmotherly advice: 'Don't hurt yourself.'

I don't know about John, but I've never felt better, especially after our fourth shot at 9.35 a.m. 'I'm feeling *soooooo* friendly,' I scribble in my notebook.

En route to John's girlfriend's house, I ask the Nicols what they think of the rebranding of the Queensferry Arms. After a year of secrecy, the local paper this week had a front-page photo of Peter Wilson finally unveiling the new name for Queensferry's landmark pub: Orocco Pier, styled after iroko, the African hardwood they're using on the floors in the refurbished building. In keeping with their trendy moniker, they've adopted a modern motto, or 'strapline': 'dining | drinking | dreaming'.

'Yer arse!' John snorts. Even a man schooled in artspeak is unimpressed.

His father has gone so far as to look up 'iroko' on the Internet. According to his findings, the iroko is the tallest tree in the jungle. When Africans clear forests, they always cut it down last as a mark of respect. There's probably a metaphor in there about Westerners using an African tree for flooring while walking all over their own culture, but I'm too addled to find it.

'You're stayin' at the Queensferry Arms, aren't ya?' John Senior asks.

I nod warily.

'I think the only way we'll go in this year is if he invites us.'

Oh no. I'm not doing that again.

Young John has made several changes this year, most notably the deletion of Agilent Technologies from the itinerary. 'That for me was a really depressing part of the day. I didn't get a sense that people were all that bothered whether I was there or not.'

So instead we traipse through the gritcast housing estates at the top of town, drinking everything from Vagrant's Choice to supermarket-brand 'Scotch Whisky' and even a twelve-year-old single malt.

'Whisky fog 10.15 can still read handwriting,' I dutifully note.

Half an hour later, John stops to answer a call of nature among the flowers and shrubs outside the bowling club. 'There was too much water in those whiskies,' he slurs. Old John kneels in front of his son's crotch and asks if anyone has a knife – I feel woozy just thinking about it. Cut free, the Shrub Man does his business among the manicured greenery, one wrist bent and his legs akimbo. 'He's got a wee touch of Elvis in there,' his uncle jokes, swivelling his hips and singing a verse of 'Jailhouse Rock'.

A similar urge hits me not long after our seventh whisky:

'Noon: Need a pee,' I write.

'12.15: Upstairs on the left.'

The sun has begun burning holes through the firmament, or at least that's what I think I meant when I scrawled *'12.25 – sun off Alec's nose.'* Beyond Shot 10, my note taking deteriorates disgracefully.

1 p.m. – flag in the face

1.05 defecating dog

gran on tricycle zimmer

I'm sure they seemed noteworthy at the time.

Somewhere along the way, I'm introduced to a past Burry Man, who warns me to be careful how much I drink. Unlike John, he explains, I'm not sweating off the alcohol. In my hazy state, though, I can't decide if he's right. It seems to me that sweating could just as easily distil the whisky in your system. I have another shot to make sure.

By the time we stagger to the Nicols' house for lunch, we've had thirteen nips in four-and-a-half hours. That's five more whiskies than the Burry Man would normally have halfway through the day. Stupidly, I celebrate with a glass of champagne; by now, I'd drink lighter fluid if they offered it. John is slumped against the patio fence, propped up by me and another guy. After tenderly serving her son whisky, Senga notices that his lips have turned blue.

From that point, I vaguely remember helping to bundle the Burry Man into the kitchen and ripping off his balaclava while his mother stuffed ice into his costume and massaged his hair with water while holding a fan inches from his neck. In my concerned stupor, I squeezed his hand and counted out how many sips of glucose water he drank. I also insisted that someone remove the burry phallus that a joker had attached to his groin (instead, it wound up stuck to my trousers).

'Tell everyone I'm sorry . . . I'm sorry,' he kept mumbling, and Old John started making noises about calling it quits: it was simply too hot to continue.

Amazingly, though, the Burry Man made a recovery – or so I'm told. Seeing that I was in no condition to walk, John's de facto father-in-law bravely offered me a lift to the Moorings, the first pub on the route. I supposedly tried to enter the car on the driver's side before Ian reminded me that I was in the UK. I then knelt in the passenger's seat facing backwards, apparently reasoning that if people drive on the wrong side of the road here, they must also sit the wrong way round in their cars. Somehow, I made it to the Moorings, where I headed straight to the toilets and passed out, Elvis-style, in a cubicle. Over the next couple of hours, I occasionally emerged from my whisky abyss to marvel at how cool and soothing the floor tiles felt against my face, hoping that the toilet was in fact cleaner than the one in *Trainspotting*. I finally awoke around five o'clock. Outside, I stumbled into one of the Burry groupies, who directed me to the centre of town (the opposite of the direction I was headed). Just in time, I staggered into the Stag, to be greeted by John's girlfriend, Emma.

'This is proof positive: Americans cannot handle their liquor!' she shouted.

Which managed to irk me even in my muddled state. A professional to the last, I loaded my camera – strange how the body remembers what the brain's forgotten – and took a couple of snaps of John being cut out of his outfit at the end of the day. In my last moments of consciousness, I lurched back to the Queensferry Arms and collapsed again – this time in bed.

*

'It feels like I've died and been reborn,' John tells me the next morning. 'It was actually quite a scary thing that happened yesterday.' For someone who's had a near-death experience, though, he looks remarkably well, relaxing barefooted under the green-and-white marquee on his parents' patio and recounting how the ordeal has reminded him of the serious side to the ritual. 'You really have to *respect* the Burry Man. It's somethin' that ya can't take too lightly.'

Incredibly, while I was cheek-to-cheek with the floor tiles, John managed to hit all the main stops on the route in the afternoon and even continue boozing into the evening. However, the Burry Man didn't visit his old haunt, the Queensferry Arms, simply because no one was waiting for him there.

Peter Wilson says he was too busy running the hotel/bar/restaurant to wait for the Burry Man. 'The father of the Burry Man last year, he was *awful*,' he tells me, before heaping more fuel on the fire by comparing the Burry Man with the Orangemen who are holding marches in Glasgow and Edinburgh this weekend. 'Y'know, that horrible Orange Walk kinda attitude that they've got with the sashes . . . I know it's got historic value, but you go to Glasgow, you see it all the time, it's segregation, it's not a good feelin'.' When pressed, though, he admits that the Burry Man has nothing to do with sectarianism; he's referring to their 'smalltown mentality, that's all it is. Only *their* view is important.'

He takes a break from guarding the door during the Ferry Fair to give me a tour of the £300,000 refurbishment, explaining how they've finally received permission to knock out interior walls so that people will be able to see the Forth Bridge from the street and how they're planning to build a deck out back for summer parties next to the river. Instead of the patterned carpets and plush furnishings of a typical country hotel, the rooms have been given an urban makeover in the minimalist style: hardwood floors, pale grey walls, bare white beds, slate-like Italian tiling in the bathroom and, for decoration, a galvanized bucket next to the door holding a sheaf of twigs planted in pebbles. The beds' headboards are studded with tiny fibre-optic lamps that project balls of red, green and purple light onto the ceiling, a mini laser show. 'That's where the "dreaming" bit comes in,' Peter enthuses, referring to the hotel's new logo.

He's so excited, I don't have the heart to tell him that the fibre-optic display could also give you a bad case of the self-induced spins. What's more, as some trendsetters have already begun rebelling against modernism, I can't help but think that hardwood floors and fibre-optic light displays might be the swirly carpeting and flock wallpaper of the future: whereas all the best hotels in London will be refurbished in retro-Edwardian luxury, Britain's country hotels will be stuck with provincial minimalism. Until then, though, I reckon the owners of *Renaissance Ecosse* will manage to make a go of it with their combination of hard work, enthusiasm and chutzpah.

But without the Burry Man's blessing. John has no doubts about the prospects for Orocco Pier. 'It won't last,' he says. 'It won't.'

However, he plans to continue as the Burry Man for as long as possible, despite yesterday's scare. 'Oh, there's no change,' he says, squinting in the sunshine. 'There's no doubt in my mind. It's the continuing adventures of the Burry Man.'

CHAPTER FIVE

'IF WE JUST BUILT A BOG DEEP ENOUGH...'

BOG SNORKELLING IN LLANWRTYD WELLS

A LONG WAY FROM BONDI BEACH: An Aussie in a snorkel and a corset of cling film awaits his turn in the Welsh murk.

© J.R. DAESCHNER

IN THE BEGINNING WAS THE BOG

First came the Man versus Horse Marathon, and later the Real Ale Ramble – a hiking and drinking event – followed by its cycling spin-off, the Real Ale Wobble . . .

Every year, Gordon Green had dreamed up a new way of luring tourists to town – and Llanwrtyd Wells needed all the help it could get. Besides its unpronounceable name – the best that most foreigners could manage was 'Lan-something Wells' – the decaying Victorian spa town was located in the middle of Wales, which, to many outsiders, was synonymous with 'the middle of nowhere'.

As a hotel owner, the Englishman had a vested interest in boosting tourism. He was a big thinker in a little town, and plenty of locals – farmers and the like – criticised his newfangled ideas. However, newcomers such as Iris Shrigley admired him for fighting to keep the town on the map. Half English herself, Iris liked Gordon's open-mindedness and determination. As her husband put it: 'Gordon does, while other people think.'

But in the summer of 1986 the town's main tourist draw, the Man versus Horse Marathon, was in danger of being washed out. If it rained much more, the race would be off. Never mind the runners – or the horses, for that matter. They'd be all right, so long as they kept moving. The cars were the problem. Dozens of people would park on the sodden ground and then – *shlooooorrrrrp!* – before you knew it, they'd be stuck, mired down in the boggy farmland, never to resurface again. With only a few weeks to go, the organisers decided to hold a crisis meeting at Gordon's hotel one night in May.

Around midnight, long after the serious discussions had ended, Iris went to the bar to buy another round of drinks. She and Gordon started bemoaning the weather, and the town's resident impresario mentioned that he was casting around for fundraising ideas for a new community centre.

'Well, whatever you want to do, you can use our field,' she offered, 'but there are bogs – terrible bogs.' So terrible, in fact, that you could sink a foot-and-a-half in the ground if you weren't careful. You'd need to strap planks to your feet to walk across it. Maybe that's what they could do, she joked, bog skiing.

Laughing, Gordon launched into a boozy brainstorming session, until 'bog skiing' became something that would one day make Llanwrtyd famous.

'Bog . . . snorkelling – how will that sound?' he asked, just like an excited child, a big eureka grin on his face. '*Bog snorkelling!* That's *fabulous!*'

Within weeks, Llanwrtyd hosted the first World Bog Snorkelling Championships, featuring besnorkelled contestants swimming 400 feet through sick-making muck.

Years later, Iris is still bemused by her role in sporting history. 'It *is* silly,' she smiles. 'It's so silly that it was bound to catch on.'

Centuries from now, when bog snorkelling is revered as a Welsh tradition and an Olympic sport to rival synchronised swimming, the people of Wales will have a canny Lancashireman to thank. Llanwrtyd (pronounced 'hlan-OOR-tud') advertises its calendar of offbeat but environmentally friendly attractions as 'A Hatful of Green Events'. However, the 'Green' in its slogan could just as easily refer to the town's sixtysomething promoter extraordinaire. In his creativity, determination and quickness to cock a snook at authority, Gordon Green embodies the Best of British. Hunkered on his stool behind the hotel's half bar, the natural-born raconteur listens and nods while his regulars gossip and argue, his salt-and-pepper eyebrows forming two quizzical quotation marks – a kind of facial irony – beneath his white hair.

Gordon moved here with his wife, Diana, a native of the area, in 1975, escaping strikebound London for life in the country. After struggling for five years to make a go of the hotel, he hit on the idea of organising the Man versus Horse Marathon, which involved runners racing riders over twenty-two miles of up-and-down countryside. After that initial success, Gordon concocted a range of events, including a Roman mid-winter festival that began as an idea for a beer fest in January.

'Why don't you do a Saturnalia?' the local schoolmaster said.

'What the hell's a Saturnalia?'

'A Roman orgy at that time of year.'

With a pitch like that, Gordon immediately started researching its potential. The Romans used to brighten the darkest days of winter with feasting, drinking and orgies. Although the Welsh version includes togas, it stops short of wholesale sexual abandon. 'We do try to encourage it,' Gordon says, laughing one of his ripple-effect laughs. 'One of the things that the senators used to do was lie with their bare buttocks in the air, and the nubile girls used to nibble the grapes off them.' He laughs harder. 'We haven't re-enacted that yet, but I'd like to.' In the meantime, they can always nibble on other things. 'We do such delicacies as Roast Stuffed Testicles,' he says proudly. 'They're really tasty.'

However, the real test of authenticity came when Gordon decided to make absinthium, the Roman forerunner of absinthe. Many countries outlawed the green demon drink in the early 1900s due to its off-the-chart alcohol content – up to 75%, or 150-proof – and its killer ingredient: wormwood. Poisonous or not, Gordon was intent on brewing the real thing, even though the local doctor told him he needed a licence to buy the herb.

'Why?'

'Well, it makes you go blind.'

'So I was looking for some wormwood, you see,' he continues nonchalantly, as if it were just another routine task for a country hotelier, 'and we found somebody in the village growing this wormwood for home medicine. So we make absinthium wine.'

Llanwrtyd now has at least sixteen tourist events spanning the year. 'My wife won't let me organise anything else' – he laughs – 'she gets fed up! It's good for the town, and I . . . I get a buzz. But it's a lot of hard work.'

*

When you mention bog snorkelling to Gordon, you have to be specific; otherwise, he'll ask if you're talking about 'the swimming kind'.

Surely there can't be more than one kind of bog snorkelling!?

But sure enough, there is. The arguably more advanced version involves riding a bicycle around a bog while submerged in muck. 'I had it in mind for a long time,' he explains. 'I thought for many years that if we just built a bog deep enough, we could do mountain bike bog snorkelling.'

Given that the mountain bike version comes first in the Bog Snorkelling Calendar, I decided to give it a go before tackling the main event, mistakenly thinking it would be the easier of the two. Riding a bike around a bog didn't seem like much of a challenge compared with swimming facedown in slime. Unfortunately, my brain failed to grasp the full absurdity of the biking event. I thought the snorkels were a silly accessory; not a necessity. It was only after being told that I needed a snorkel that I understood the depths of Gordon's madness: bog bikers are submerged – *completely* – in the cold, dark bog. To keep them mired in the murk, they're also weighted with a diving belt and a backpack full of rocks. While they fight to keep their snorkel above the water line, they're struggling to pedal a bike around the bottom of a bog. Trouble is, they can't see where they're going, and the icy water makes it hard to breathe. In some countries, they'd call it torture; in Wales, it's 'event-led tourism'.

It's easy to dismiss bog snorkelling as a cynical ploy to sucker tourists into the backwaters of Wales, but the event also reflects Llanwrtyd's fight for survival, a textbook case of 'if-you-build-it-they-will-come' can-do. Instead of *Field of Dreams*, though, this picture would be called *Bog of Nightmares*. Very little remains of the original village, built around a church that may have been founded by St David, the patron saint of Wales. Nowadays, the town features sturdy Victorian houses gracing its handful of streets, with hulking green hills standing guard outside, decorated with sheep and pinewood forests. Quiet and unassuming, the shallow River Irfon runs through the middle of Llanwrtyd, seemingly incapable of having carved out the broad valley that bears its name. Ironically, water is the main constant in the town's history. As a Victorian spa, Llanwrtyd was renowned for the salubrious properties of its 'Stinking Well'; nowadays, the town is also famous for its smelly waters, which most bog snorkellers end up 'taking' involuntarily. In fact, Llanwrtyd owes its erstwhile spa status to a cheerful frog. Though the bath-loving Romans probably knew about them, the area's healing springs weren't documented until 1732. A local vicar, Theophilus Evans, had suffered for years from 'radicated scurvy' verging on leprosy. Willing to try any cure, the 38-year-old happened to hear about Llanwrtyd's sulphurous spring, and his nose quickly led him to the source. He later described his misgivings in third-person prose: 'As he was thus musing, a frog popped out of the bottom, looked cheerfully, and, as it were, invited him to taste the water; he then immediately concluded that the water could not have any poisonous quality, and took a moderate draught . . .' After drinking and bathing in the stuff for two months, the Reverend Evans declared himself 'perfectly whole', a claim that would have carried considerable weight in Wales: not only was he a man of God, he was also an esteemed author.

Fifteen years earlier, Evans had published a bestseller called *Drych y Prif Oesoedd* (*The Mirror of Past Ages*), a collection of legends dressed up as the true history of the Welsh people from the Tower of Babel to the murder of the last native Prince of Wales in 1282 (just ten miles from Llanwrtyd). According to Evans, Wales wasn't just a poor relation to England; it had its own venerable history, culture and language. Armed with a dodgy pedigree, the Welsh could look down their noses at the English for a change. After all, they were the true Britons, descended from the 'founder of Britain', Brutus of Troy; the English were mere usurpers, the hooligan offspring of Anglo-Saxon invaders. The Welsh were the guardians of the oldest language in Europe – and possibly the world – far superior to that mongrel mix of Germano-Scandi-French known as English. Stories by Evans and writers like him gave the Welsh an outsized national pride that has perplexed foreigners ever since. 'They are so well versed in the history of their descents, that you shall hear a poor woman derive her extraction from the first maid of honour to Nimrod's wife, or else she thinks she is a nobody,' observed an English traveller in 1749.

And if the Welsh had lapped up Evans' tales of ancient history, they were sure to swallow his claim of a water cure at Llanwrtyd. Healing springs were also discovered at nearby Llandrindod, where entrepreneurs were much quicker to capitalise on the spa craze. Even in the early days of do-it-yourself colonic irrigation, there were plenty of satisfied customers: one man drank twenty-three pints and passed excrement so hard it was practically petrified – even stomping on it with his shoes didn't dent it. Another patient came to the village to cure himself of violent stomach pains. After drinking the water, he defecated a tapeworm as thick as his thumbnail and *seven feet long*.

For its part, Llanwrtyd didn't become well known outside Wales until the arrival of the railways more than a century later. Suddenly, it became a boomtown, along with Llandrindod and two other spas in mountainous mid-Wales: Builth and Llangammarch. To promote them as health resorts, the railway company added 'Wells' to all of their names. However, demand quickly dried up in the early 1900s as doctors began to rely on scientific cures rather than natural remedies. With 'alternative' medicine now back in vogue, though, newspapers have long been predicting the revival of the Great British Spa. So far, it has yet to happen, although Llandrindod has re-opened its flagship spa as a museum and, for 10p, you can buy a shot of saline water in the restored pump room (which is probably more than you'd want; imagine downing a thimbleful of tears). By all accounts, the sulphur water in Llanwrtyd's pump house didn't taste much better.

In desperation, Llanwrtyd has tried to turn its decline into a selling point, proclaiming itself the 'Smallest Town in Britain'. But with a population of only 600 – compared to nearly 1,000 half a century ago – Llanwrtyd feels more like a village. Despite talk of restoring the spas back in 1982 for their 250th anniversary, the buildings remain closed, languishing next to the river. You can still smell the rotten-egg scent of sulphur water trickling in the gutter behind them. Even so, Llanwrtyd's heyday has been all but forgotten. The few tourists who do come to town tend to call it 'that place where they do bog snorkelling'. Even so, it's unlikely the locals will ever change the town's name to Llanwrtyd Bog.

It's the night before the Mountain Bike Bog Snorkelling championship, and I meet an English couple in Gordon's bar. They're both planning to take the plunge.

'C'mon, we'll go in our undies,' the guy says. 'You can't back out now.'

But God knows I want to.

During the night, I wake up repeatedly, imagining the worst – the bike will wipe out, and I'll drown with the weights in the fetid water. My only consolation is my height: *If it comes to it, I'm tall enough to cheat*.

The morning dawns windy and cool, the sun flirting from behind the clouds. The April chill in the air makes for ideal cycling weather – unless, of course, you happen to be cycling underwater. Outside the hotel, the English couple are sheepishly making their escape. The man mutters something about biking forty miles over hilly terrain to a place called Devil's Bridge. My only regret is that I don't have a bike to go with them.

Early in the afternoon, Gordon and I drive to the Waen Rhydd bog outside Llanwrtyd. We park about 150 yards from the snorkelling pond to keep the car from getting sucked in. The windswept plain of peatland is tinged with long, straw-coloured grass that contrasts with the verdant pastures surrounding it. Russet bracken and white sheep adorn the green hills in the distance. You'd never think a bog could be so beautiful; either that, or I'm just getting sentimental before drowning myself in a stinking sinkhole. As we carry the snorkelling gear to the site, tramping across the squelching bog, some sheep bleat suspiciously, gazing dumbfounded at this human folly, their ovine minds thinking, 'And they call *us* stupid.'

The course is little more than a water-filled pit measuring ten yards each way from the halfway marker – a fence pole. Some thirty spectators gather on the bank, including half a dozen photojournalists and several cyclists who have cruised over to watch their subaquatic counterparts suffer.

Gordon needs someone to test the waters, and bog snorkelling pioneer Dale Burrows agrees to brave the bog. The fourteen-year-old has the dubious honour of being the original guinea pig of mountain bike bog snorkelling. Dale ended up winning the junior championship his first time out with a time of 3:33, and he's come back this year to defend his title. Why does he do it?

'Cos it's *mad.*'

You have to wonder about Dale's own sanity. Donning a wetsuit that's several sizes too big, he wades into the water with the customised bog snorkelling mountain bike, which is rigged to make it as heavy as possible. Its wheels are lined with lead and its tyres filled with water – even the *de rigueur* water bottle has been loaded with lead shot. They've also attached a granny-style wire basket on the front. By the time that's filled with rocks, the bike weighs at least fifty pounds.

The Junior World Champion straps the snorkel to his head and mounts the bike. Hunched over the frame, his face stuck in the water, Dale looks . . . well, like someone who's about to snorkel through a bog on a bike. He starts off well enough, but as he pumps his legs, he quickly sinks from view, less than ten feet into the course.

The Junior World Champion has been swallowed by the bog!

Bobbing to the surface, he chokes and gasps, a very real fear of drowning in his eyes. He thrashes in the water, unable to touch bottom, retching and coughing, having inhaled a lungful of liquid bacteria.

This doesn't look at all good to Gordon; there's nothing like an accidental death to kill good publicity. 'What's the matter, Dale?'

The answer is dull-spirited and desperate. 'It sinks!'

Two other contestants, including the men's champion, Dave Atkinson, splash into the shivery bog to help Dale find the bike. After about five minutes of floating triangulation, they manage to dredge it up.

Dale clambers out of the water. 'It's *f-f-f-freezing* in there,' he shivers before stalking off to the changing tent, never to return.

Meanwhile, Atkinson, a 26-year-old journalist from Bath, is slowly acclimatising himself to the blood-chilling cold as a cloud starts to spit rain.

'Dave, c'mon!' a reporter shouts. 'We're gonna get wet!'

The defending champ emits a high-pitched giggle. It's not clear whether he's laughing at the joke or demonstrating the first signs of hypothermia. Wearing only a T-shirt, shorts and sneakers, the cyclist immerses himself in the murk, which Gordon reckons is 45 degrees Fahrenheit. Each level of submersion is demarcated by a breathless, high-pitched exclamation – *Ha-ah! Hoo! Haaa!* He finally takes a test run round the track, making the ordeal look deceptively easy. All you can see as he glides around are the snorkel and the top of his head. He huffs and puffs through the snorkel, his lungs seizing up on him in the gelid depths. The quick, sharp, rhythmic gasps would sound comical if they weren't so painfully desperate.

After the test lap, even Dave has to take a breather. His skin has turned a florid pink. However, he remains in the water as another cyclist attempts the course. In his sleek black wetsuit, the sinewy biker looks like a human greyhound. Wisely, he forgoes a test run and finishes in a solid 2:28:30.

Faced with his first serious challenge, the champ's ready to go again. Dave makes a strong start, but then he wobbles and falls over.

'Do you want another start?'

There's a tense pause. *Will he defend his title?*

'Yeah,' he says finally, with a determined gasp.

This time Dave coasts through the bog, barely stopping to round the halfway marker. *He must be changing gears down there!* He sails home in just 1:41 – nearly a minute ahead of Greyhound Guy but 27 seconds outside his own record last year.

In the meantime, I prepare for my own muddy debut. After half an hour next to the wind-chilled bog, my teeth are chattering – and I'm still wearing a sweater and jeans. With every single brain cell screaming against it, I strip down to my T-shirt and swimming trunks. Champion Dave kindly lends me his soggy sneakers (*lucky shoes*, I'm thinking).

'Do you do much mountain biking?' Gordon asks me.

'Uhhhh . . . no.'

'What about snorkelling?'

'Uhhhh . . . no.'

I'm behind even before I get started.

After several unsuccessful attempts, the guy in front of me has lost the bike. As I stand knee-deep in the freezing, foul water, with the wind whipping around me and whatever body heat I have left seeping from my legs, I sincerely hope the bike will be lost to the ages, swallowed by the bog, only to resurface again in a thousand years to mystify future archaeologists. I'm fantasising about feigning my disappointment – 'Y'know, I *really* wanted to freeze my butt off in that filthy bog, but *unfortunately* they lost the bike!' – when the spluttering idiot hauls up a wheel.

With no option but to take the plunge, I strap on the five-pound diving belt and lug on the rock-filled backpack weighing at least twenty-five pounds. Given the slippery mud underfoot, it's all I can do to stand, let alone mount a bike. I take the snorkel and mask from the guy who's just spent the past ten minutes spluttering in the muck. God knows *what* diseases he might have, but I'm not about to rinse the snorkel in the bog. The goggles are grimy, but it's probably just as well that I can't see the crowd's reaction as I face my Bog of Nightmares in my ridiculous get-up.

I decide to submerge myself in stages – dry land to ankle, ankle to thigh, thigh to navel and so on. I'm particularly wary of the make-or-break thigh-to-navel stage. As it turns out, though, the icy immersion of my groin isn't as bad as expected; or maybe it's just that the shock of the later stages numbs the brain. The instant my chest and head hit the water, I start to panic. The cold murk forces the air from my lungs, producing a strangled gurgle through the snorkel. Weighted down in the frigid gloom with a strange tube sticking out of my mouth, I inhale, involuntarily trying to vacuum in oxygen through every orifice in my face. Instead, I suck in water through my mouth *and* nose.

Always quick to see a promotional angle, Gordon announces that I'm American, making the event truly international. Underwater, I can vaguely hear the bystanders' good-natured laughter as they peer down at the poor Yank floundering in the bog on a bike. To be honest, I couldn't care less. I'm too worried about keeping my lungs from collapsing. All I'm thinking is *GET OUT OF THIS! GET OUT OF THIS! GET OUT OF THIS!* – an animal fear that my lungs will seize up before I make it even halfway. I can't get used to breathing through the snorkel, so I keep inhaling the foul water and spluttering. But I'm on my bike, and I'm going to do this if it kills me. (It's a toss-up whether I'll die of septicaemia or hypothermia.)

No matter how hard I try, I can't get any traction. I start to pedal-push through the murk, my head throbbing from the kind of headache you get when you eat ice cream too fast; only instead of having the ice cream *inside* my head, it feels like I've got my head in ice cream. And rather than New York Chunky Fudge, this is Llanwrtyd Septic Sludge.

After struggling along in a blind, brown panic for what seems like hours, I finally hit the halfway marker. I've never been so happy to crash into a pole in my life. Mounting the pedals again, I power away – *I might even place!* – but the front of the bike floats away from me, dumping me on my back at the bottom of the bog. Inevitably, the worst happens – I choke down a mouthful of liquid compost. Imagine the seepage from rotting vegetation, earthworm slime, sheep excrement, decaying animals and any other natural nasty you can think of – there might even be a bog body down here! – and ferment them all together to create a diarrhoea-brown cocktail called Funk of Mother Earth. *That's* what bog water tastes like. All told, I suck down half a pint of sick-making bacteria during my ordeal – and I consider myself lucky.

After involuntarily taking the waters, my farcical attempt to ride around the bog degenerates into a full-fledged fiasco. I end up doing some weird mix of snorkel-swim-cycling, bobbing above the mire to gulp for air, then blowing it out through the snorkel tube. With the crowd cheering me on – actually, I think they're trying to hurry me up – I struggle toward the finish line, spluttering and scuttling like a crazed swamp creature.

Staggering out of the mire, cold, mud-spattered and more than a little nauseous, I know I haven't done well. 'Are we timin' that in minutes or hours?' shouts a wise-guy official. It took me a full 3:36:31 to finish – more than twice as long as Dave.

I quickly realise why the other contestants have been reluctant to leave the water. With the arctic winds whipping round me, every muscle in my body is shivering with cold, and my skin has turned a furious fuchsia. The medical staff hand me a metallic wrap to protect against the buttock-twitching cold, and I change into my dry clothes in the tent that's been set up on the fringe.

The competition lasts an hour and a half, with only seven contestants. Dave retains his title, and I come in fourth – or *third runner-up*, as we losers like to say. I'm unbelievably proud of my consolation prize – a golden bog brush. I'd like to think the sponsors have given me the plastic trophy in recognition of my valour. In reality, I suspect they've done it out of pity.

PART TWO:
THE (BOG) WATER CURE

Julia Galvin was scared. Laid up in a hospital in Ireland, she was waiting to hear whether she would have to have life-threatening surgery. Ever since the car crash, her back had become worse, the sciatica sending crippling pains shooting down her legs. At best, she could hobble only a few feet on crutches, and of course, her weight didn't help. She had always been big – obese, even – but the weight was so much a part of her now that telling her to lose it was like asking a thin woman to make her arms just that little bit shorter. So, at the age of twenty-seven, Julia waited nervously to find out whether she would ever walk again, or – thinking the unthinkable – whether she would even survive the operation.

To keep her mind occupied, she read the *Guinness Book of Records*. Thirty-six pages in, she came across something that made her laugh, despite her grim state of mind, and Julia made a vow right there on her sickbed: 'If I ever get better and walk again, I'll do some bog snorkelling myself.'

Never mind that she couldn't swim, let alone snorkel.

With just two days to go, she received a reprieve. Fearing that an operation might cause a fatal blood clot, her doctor decided against it. Back in Victorian times, Julia would have been packed off to a spa like Llanwrtyd and ordered to drink gallons of saline and sulphur water and have hot baths in the smelly stuff. Fortunately, her spinal rehabilitation involved a water cure of a different kind: swimming . . . and bog snorkelling.

Fast forward a year, and Julia has made a pilgrimage to Llanwrtyd, the Home of Bog Snorkelling. 'This is my Mecca,' she says, straight-faced, sipping a Diet Coke in the bar where bog snorkelling was invented. A black T-shirt covers her roly-poly frame, and her auburn hair sports a patriotic green, white and gold braid. Thanks to her very own bog water cure, Julia can walk without crutches. 'And I'm also Bog Snorkelling Champion of Ireland – well, apart from the fact that nobody else entered. Which is very handy when you want to be a national champion.'

It's five months since my own Mountain Bike Bog Snorkelling debacle, and I've returned to Llanwrtyd to brave the bog again. I tried to meet up with Julia yesterday, but she was out practising. As a biology teacher from the land of bogs, she knows exactly what she's getting into. She lives on reclaimed peatland in County Kerry, in a house just eighteen inches above bog level. As a kid, she used to compete at 'bog leaping', or 'lepping', jumping over the water-filled holes left by the peatcutters. Now, though, bog holes are Irish swimming pools for Julia.

A little over a year after her eureka moment in the hospital, she is again waiting nervously – this time to fulfil her televisual destiny. 'Ever since I was very, very small, I always thought it was a natural progression for anyone to end up on television. I didn't think it would happen quite this way, though,' she laughs.

Three hours before the competition, Julia's strutting around, stripping off for countless photo shoots and revealing a form-fitting wetsuit that makes her look like the Michelin Man's aquatic sidekick. She's already taken a few practice laps, and she's got weeds and dirt on her face. Striking a pose, she flexes a pale, fleshy calf. 'Lovely legs, eh?' she laughs boisterously, shrugging off the unseasonable August chill. 'It's cold, but not Arctic cold. Gonads are the only things that get cold, and I don't have to worry about that, do I?'

Unfortunately, the school headmaster does. As the official timekeeper, he has waded into the septic swimming lane, a 200-foot-long trench of water about four feet wide, camouflaged by bulrushes and papery bog grass. Knee-deep in the muck, the principal stabs the water with a pitchfork to scoop out the dripping goop and rotting grass that's accumulated around the starting line. The motion stirs up the methane at the bottom of the bog, and the stinking gas bubbles to the surface and bursts.

Meanwhile, the photographers can't get enough of Julia. Flippers crossed, she's lolling on the grassy bank like a beached mermaid.

'I want to be the Queen of Bogs!' she says grandly.

What hath the bog wrought?

Some 300 curiosity-seekers have gathered for the competition, ranging from babes-in-arms to old farmers in cloth caps. At the starting line, Gordon announces the rules: contestants can't use conventional swimming strokes, women and juniors are allowed to rest for a minute at the halfway point, and all competitors must keep their heads underwater. 'You're allowed to look *occasionally* if you lose your bearings, and it's very easy to lose your bearings because you won't be able to see anything in the water.' Most onlookers chuckle, but some contestants are very serious, keeping their eyes on the £40 prize. 'Is the finish going *past* the post, or *touching* the post?' one queries. (For the record, it's touching the post.)

Julia is Contestant #3 and she chugs away steadily to finish in 3:30:07. 'It was not the greatest time in the world, but considering the size I am, I think I did very well,' she says. 'I don't think there'll be any open-top buses in Ireland for me yet, but I was very happy to have been able to do it.'

Most of the other snorkellers start out hard and fast on the first lap, then struggle on the way back to the finish line. The fastest ones keep their arms out straight and kick their flippers together, humping through the water like dolphins. The reigning champion, Craig Napper, lets me in on his secret technique. 'Keep nice and streamlined. Don't go too fast, and keep your arms out in front.' Oh – and try not to swallow the water: 'It's bad,' says the unassuming boyo with the squinting smile and straw-coloured hair. Craig won last year in 1:53, just nine seconds outside the world record set by another Welshman. He's hoping to finish in 1:40 or 1:45 this year, but he's feeling the pressure. Friends and family have come to see him defend his title. 'I'm a little bit nervous now. When you're world champion, people have got expectations of you.'

As the fourth greatest Mountain Bike Bog Snorkeller in the world, I know exactly what Craig means. Still nursing a hangover from last night, I suspect that immersion in sick-making bog water isn't going to do my stomach any favours. Still, I'm convinced that the swimming event could never compare to the mountain bike version. Surely the only thing you have to do in plain old bog snorkelling is jump in the water and kick. What's more, it's late August rather than early April. So for me, the water will seem blessedly warm, more like the Mediterranean than the Arctic. At least that's what I'm hoping. Most hardcore snorkellers have come well prepared, sporting polar wetsuits with fitted flippers and scuba goggles. All I've got is a T-shirt and swim trunks. Julia kindly offers to lend me her lucky snorkel, and I scrounge a pair of flippers from another swimmer. I realise I'm in trouble when the guy has to tell me how to put the flippers on.

I'm Number 28 out of fifty-one, and by the time I've figured out the complexities of attaching my flippers, it's my turn in the bog. So instead of doing the sensible thing and acclimatising myself to the water, I splash right in. After all, it's summer, right?

Hoo-oo-oo! Ha-aaah!

Immediately, that blind animal panic pounces on me, the gelid water squeezing the air from my lungs and forcing a gasp of anguish through the strange tube in my mouth. It's summer all right, but it's summer *in Wales*. The water's only a few degrees warmer – or rather, *less freezing* – than it was in April. In fact, the only discernible difference is the plethora of plant and animal life lurking in the murky depths. A friendly tadpole surfaces, then ducks underwater. Instead of swallowing the juices of dead creepy-crawlies, I'm going to be sucking the muck of *live* creepy-crawlies.

And then it hits me – I know how to swim, but I don't know how to snorkel, and a bog probably isn't the best place to learn. From the outside looking in, the course didn't look that bad. Sure, it's 200 feet, but that's only fifty feet longer than an Olympic-size swimming pool. Now that I'm chest-deep in effluent, though, my perspective is very different. From the starting point, the trench seems to stretch to the horizon. I'm in Wales, but the little white post at the end of the channel looks like it's somewhere over the border, forming a canal across Offa's Dyke right through England to the other side of the UK. And *that's* only halfway! I've got to swim across Britain *and back again*!

Nevertheless, I plunge in . . . and immediately sink. Frantic, I try to pull myself along the bottom, grabbing fistfuls of weeds and silty water, my flippers feeling five feet long as they dredge the bog, churning fitfully like paddlewheels stuck on a mud flat.

'He's not moving,' someone observes.

Technically, that isn't true. I'm definitely moving my arms; I'm just not getting anywhere. As for my legs, well, they're dead. Between mouthfuls of fetid water and methane gas, I manage to drag myself toward the halfway point. A few isolated cries urge me on, but a bored, embarrassed vacuum quickly absorbs them. I have two choices – I can make these poor people suffer with me while I struggle to finish the last length, or I can pull the plug right now.

And that's what I do. Instead of wasting five more minutes of their weekend – and filling my *other* lung with bog water – I put myself out of my misery. Clambering out of the slime like a weird, demented fish-man, I'm surrounded by an awkward silence, the killer of conversations everywhere, but multiplied by a factor of 300 so that it becomes a vast, noise-sucking void. Just in case I'm too stupid to feel embarrassed for myself, these kind folks have taken it upon themselves to feel ashamed for me. You might think boos would be worse, but being booed is at least an acknowledgement of your effort. What I'm feeling is the collective embarrassment of hundreds of people, all averting their eyes.

It falls to the kindly old man who helps fish me out to try to make me feel better. He insists that I keep my flippers on, making it even harder for me to flounder onto the bank. Not only have I failed at bog snorkelling; I can't even pull myself out of the bog!

'No wonder you had trouble,' he says. 'Those flippers are too long.'

Yeah, that's right – it's the flippers' fault!

Unfortunately, I never get a chance to use that excuse. The owner of the flippers comes up to me later and asks why I didn't finish. 'Those are a good pair of flippers, you know,' he says, as if my ineptitude were a slur on his equipment.

They certainly have worked for him – he ends up winning third.

Amid my humiliation, I'm vaguely aware that Craig Napper is also in trouble. The champ starts out beautifully, gliding down the first length, but his flipper comes off at the halfway mark, costing him precious seconds. He humps home in 1:56:55. The crowd groans – that's four seconds behind the fastest time so far – but Craig is unperturbed: 'I'm a little bit disappointed, but it's a laugh.'

His challenger is nowhere near as laidback. Peter Owen has placed third in the past two years, and this time he's determined to win, having slipped past the finish line in just 1:52:22. He's beaten Craig this time round, but he's still well outside the world record. Standing on the banks of the bog, Peter is quietly fretting as the snorkellers swim below. 'Well, there goes my timing. He's really strong,' he mutters to his girlfriend as a swimmer zips past their feet. An hour after his turn, and Peter's still in his wetsuit, ready to jump in again in the event of a swim-off.

Although Peter considers himself Welsh, he actually lives in England, near Bristol, 'on the wrong side of the water'. With his sharp nose, high forehead and proper accent, he definitely seems more of an Englishman than a Welshman. He'd never show it, but deep down, this 38-year-old is probably a roiling bundle of human emotion, hoping and praying that this year – please God, *this year* – he'll win. 'I'd always fancied doing a world championship and failed at everything else,' he jokes, adding that he's a chartered accountant by day. 'We're always trying to prove we're not boring.'

And with that, Peter comes as close as anyone to explaining why fifty-odd oddballs have risked septicaemia to snorkel through windswept slurry. Peter's father is on hand to encourage his son, insisting that he wasn't worried he'd lost his mind, 'but then, I'm a psychiatrist. It's a relatively mild form of derangement.'

Around five o'clock – three hours after we started – the fifty-first lunatic finishes the course. Barely forty people are left by now, mainly crazed contestants and their long-suffering friends and family. Craig Napper wins second, meaning that the world has a new Bog Snorkelling Champion – Peter Owen, or, as I like to think of him, Peat Bog Pete. Still in his wetsuit, he accepts his T-shirt, prize money and a small silver cup, visibly embarrassed by the cheering.

Julia doesn't win anything, but she takes the stage anyway, thanking the Welsh for their hospitality. The self-styled Irish champ ranks third slowest, after some guy who took 5:08:19 to complete the course. (Had I tried to finish, I'd probably still be out there.)

Meanwhile, Peat Bog Pete's doing a radio interview via cellphone, his silver cup stuck to his hand. 'I try to concentrate on a pure finning style without using my arms, to create a streamlined shape,' he's explaining in all seriousness.

After the professional snappers have finished, another photographer approaches Peter with a pocket camera. She's a very motherly woman with pewter hair, glasses, a blue fleece, and sensible trousers stuffed into her socks.

'Oh, you want one too?' he grins, feigning fatigue.

Without a word, she crouches to frame her boy holding his trophy overhead, the low-slung sun and the sloping hills in the background.

'Well done, son!' his father beams.

If mountain bike bog snorkelling had been a relatively private fiasco for me, bog snorkelling proper turned out to be a very public failure. Even a man who claimed he couldn't swim had completed the course – and in a decent time, too.

'You were the second one in a row to pull up,' a friend tells me later.

'Really?'

'Yeah – the other one was a twelve-year-old *girl*.'

I can't live with that kind of humiliation. No matter what level of success I achieve, I'll always feel I'm a loser with this wet, stinking albatross around my neck. My epitaph will read: 'J.R. Daeschner, Failed Bog Snorkeller.'

The more I ruminate on my defeat, the more convinced I become that I have to return next year to finish the race. Then I realise – in obsessing over my comeback, I've crossed a line, joining the crazed ranks of cheese chasers, shin kickers and bog snorkellers I've known, all of whom had their own reasons for taking part in madcap events. 'This is my Mecca,' Julia had said.

I've become one of them. I've lost my mind.

PART THREE:
THE WHORE OF BOGGY MONDE

The following year, the World Bog Snorkelling Championship has taken on a truly international dimension. Two weeks before the Welsh event, the sponsors organised a contest in Ireland, where a fifth of the country is covered in bogs. Julia Galvin defended her title against eight others but finished second last. 'I was a bit disappointed, to tell you the truth,' she says, the hush in her voice suggesting she was quite a bit more upset than that. 'But these guys are into things like underwater rugby. So I have to understand.' Then she brightens. 'But since I'm not champion, I've proclaimed myself president of the organisation.' In her new role, she has taken charge of half a dozen Professional Irishmen, the happy-go-lucky kind that are always drinking, cracking jokes and bursting into song for no apparent reason . . . other than the fact that they're Irish.

Back home, Julia has become a minor celebrity, featuring on national radio and a couple of TV shows. By now, she's honed her recovery to a 30-second saga in a soundbite, and this year she has a stuffed frog in her hair to give the photographers something new to focus on. She has even gone to the trouble of waxing her legs . . . and putting on make-up.

Given that she's about to wallow in muck, why bother?

She lets rip with a big laugh. 'That's 'cause I'm a media whore! Gotta look good for the world's cameras, y'know?'

This year, however, she's going to have competition. After more than a decade of hit-and-miss media coverage, bog snorkelling looks set to make its biggest splash ever: the *Sun*, the country's top-selling newspaper, is planning to photograph one of its topless Page Three Girls in the bog. Although you won't find it on the calendar, Britain is celebrating National Cleavage Week II, as declared by the *Sun*. As its name implies, the occasion is a sequel to the paper's first National Cleavage Week, which was inspired by the success of its original National Cleavage Day. For National Cleavage Week, the *Sun* has sent a couple of male journalists and Page Three Girls travelling around the country in a red double-decker to try to cajole young lovelies into shucking their blouses and plumping their bosoms. To their surprise, though, they haven't had to do much cajoling: they've had 'birds' flocking to them! In Blackpool, seventy women stood in line to flash their chests at the *Sun*'s four million readers. Why? For a shot at fame and fortune. 'And some are just exhibitionists,' the photographer shrugs.

Rather than a full-blown photo shoot, the *Sun*'s visit to Llanwrtyd Wells is merely a detour on its whistle-stop tour of Britain. Personally, I'm very excited about the prospect of meeting not only a Page Three Girl in the flesh, but also two *Sun* journalists, often reviled as the shock troops of Rupert Murdoch's media empire. Contrary to many 'right-thinking' caricatures, though, the men from the *Sun* are disappointingly normal. Okay, the photographer does have something of the freckled perv about him, what with the way his lips curl out and his nose flares, and he does call the Page Three Girl 'luv' a lot, but, for the most part, the men are far from the lugubrious sleazeballs of feminists' imaginations. In fact, they don't seem any sleazier than most journalists.

The emergence of the Page Three Girl from her makeshift changing room (the sponsor's ice cream van) causes a commotion, particularly – and predictably – among the male spectators. They've crowded around – don't fall in! – to watch her, uh, go to work. The *Sun* considers 'Delicious Danielle' to be a rising star. She 'wowed the nation' on the very first National Cleavage Day, after the tabloid discovered her while casting around for a stunner from the north-east to pose in front of the Angel of the North, the region's famous landmark. 'She was far more statuesque and blonde than the rusty old Angel of the North, so we cut the Angel out of the picture and used her big on the front page,' explains *Sun* reporter Charlie Yates, a veteran of National Cleavage Day and Cleavage Weeks I and II.

'It's *hell* out there,' he jokes. Danielle has also done well out of the Cleavage Calendar: after her big break, she's appeared twice on Page Three, doled out money for the National Lottery, and – so they say – landed a recording contract.

You know that Danielle's an up-and-comer at the *Sun* because she actually has a last name. I'm ashamed to admit I didn't even ask for her surname initially, because as far as I knew, Page Three pin-ups didn't have last names. The Page Three Girl is an object of male adoration, a goddess *du jour*, and goddesses don't have surnames. In the case of Danielle from Sunderland, her last name adds a delicious, softcore quality: Danielle May . . . *or May Not*. This ambivalence is reflected in her perfect Page Three smile, a naughty-but-nice cross between the girl next door and the slapper down the alley. Former Page Three photographer Beverley Goodway used to argue that the nudity was incidental; the eyes carry the picture. True, Danielle does have striking eyes – blue-green with golden starbursts around the pupils – but you can't really appreciate them in her nude photos. 'She's a pretty girl, and she's got a good personality. She's a *nice kid*,' says the photographer sent to Llanwrtyd, insisting that Page Three is about more than mere T&A. Sure enough, the Page Three website sums up Danielle as 'Shy' – not 'Flirty' or 'Tom Boy' – and 'Sporting' rather than a 'Party Girl' or 'Staying-in' type. She prefers 'Boffins' to 'Beefy' men, 'Cavemen' or 'Smoothies', and she's a 'Pussy Cat' instead of a 'Tiger' between the sheets. So by Page Three standards, she has personality to spare. 'That's half the battle,' the snapper adds. 'A lot of these girls are good-looking, but they have no personality. They wouldn't have come out here in a bog.'

Not so the girl with stars in her eyes. She has gamely agreed to travel hundreds of miles to pass the acidic bog test, ending up in some godforsaken part of Wales with an ice cream van for a changing room and all these weird Welshmen ogling her as she makes goo-goo eyes in the muck. For a glamour model, it's not . . . very . . . glamorous. But everybody has to start somewhere. And for Danielle, that somewhere is a bog hole.

Having tiptoed across the windswept plain, she surveys the

stinking mire with an incredulous look as loud as a neon sign: *I'm not gettin' into that!*

'Don't fancy hoppin' in there, luv,' the photographer jokes.

'How deep is that?'

'It's about four feet, isn't it,' Charlie assures her.

'So you'll have to unzip down to there,' the snapper smiles, measuring an imaginary water mark at her hips. 'Suits you, luv.'

The Sensation from Sunderland has distracted the crowd from the look-at-me antics of Julia Galvin, Superstar. 'You got nothin' on me, guhl!' the Irishwoman shouts, lifting her T-shirt to expose two black-clad medicine-ball breasts. For Julia, the Page Three Girl is just another Skinny Blonde, the bane of her life, though to be fair, Danielle's hair is actually light brown with platinum highlights, and 'skinny' doesn't do her justice.

Danielle's 36-28-34 figure is concealed by a fetching purple and black wetsuit that's unzipped to the waist, revealing perfectly bronzed skin, a beauty mark just below her right shoulder, and – to the crushing disappointment of the men crowding the bank – a string bikini top. With her wetsuit peeled halfway, she looks like a butterscotch tasty treat, the full glories of her Page Three figure kept tantalisingly under wraps. The silver bikini fabric shines like two mirrored disco balls.

Suddenly, all kinds of cameras appear in the crowd: massive network-news monstrosities, the kind that take two men and a mule to carry; camcorders with wing screens to monitor filming; cheap shutterbugs that are little more than boxes with film inside; and digital hand-jobs with telescopic phalluses to get right up into the soft give-and-take of all that buttery cleavage. The slack-jawed gapers on the bank have turned into would-be paparazzi, proffering their lenses to this Goddess of the Bog, shooting her from every peeping-tom angle imaginable except the front, where the *Sun* photographer is working. There are so many flashes from the bank that the *Sun* man has to keep asking them to stop, promising they'll be able to get their shots off later, and not just from behind.

The *Sun*'s snapper starts with a few preliminary poses next to the bog, his camera clicking and whirring. *Kzhkerr, kzhkerr –*

'All right, my luv – eyes this way.'

Kzhkerr, kzh –

'You're doin' very well.'

Kzhkerr-kzhkerr-kzhkerr –

'That's great. Flip that flipper up.'

One of the men watching all this flipper-flipping is staring at Danielle with cold, carnivore lust. He's the troglodyte with the tight pink tank top pulled over his paunch, complemented by grubby blue tennis shorts and striped ankle-length athletic socks. Sandpaper stubble covers his face, and pimples spot his half-tanned biceps. What kind of dark, fetid thoughts must be running through his mind as he sizes up Danielle like a lonely shepherd eyeing a sheep?

'How much do you pay these girls to come here and look like they're having a good time?' he asks the man from the *Sun*.

Either Charlie doesn't hear, or he doesn't want to hear.

Whatever they're paying her, it's probably beyond his budget.

For Danielle, the photo session gets progressively dirtier. The Page Three Girl starts out on the edge of the hole, with only her feet getting wet, but before you know it, the men from the *Sun* have coaxed her to get stuck in the bog itself.

'Aaagghhhh! It's 'orrible!' she cries.

The snapper takes photos of her in all kinds of poses: bulrushes in, bulrushes out, snorkel on, snorkel off.

The snorkel's obscuring her cleavage.

She moves it an inch or so to the left.

'Eyes this way. Big smile' – *Kzhkerr* – 'I think you're going to have to take the snorkel off.'

'Shall we get some mud?' Charlie suggests.

'*Nohhh*,' Danielle protests in an accent so northern it could be Nordic.

The snapper agrees. 'No, it's better without the mud.'

After all, this is a *serious* photo shoot. As if to prove the point, today's *Guardian* is on hand to lend gravitas to the event. For some mystifying reason, the men from the *Sun* are intent on snapping Danielle pretend-reading the broadsheet. In the take-no-prisoners politics of British journalism, this coupling is a bit disturbing – unnatural, even. It's the kind of bipolar convergence that could trigger chaos across the cosmos; the combination of a Page Three Girl and Respectable Journalism could set off a cataclysmic chain reaction that will cause the very earth to open up and swallow us whole, sucked down a Welsh bog hole.

Thankfully, though, it turns out that the *Sun*'s sudden affinity for the *Guardian* is nothing more than a good old-fashioned media stunt. Shortly after Britain's top-selling newspaper launched National Cleavage Week, a female columnist for the *Guardian* wrote an article pegged to the event, in which she wrote that 'nursing a child is erotic' amongst other statements that would make your average *Sun* reader's head spin. Well, that was all the *Sun* needed. With 'even the politically correct *Guardian*' – or 'the chattering classes' bible' – supporting its cleavage campaign, the *Sun* was quick to relay the news to its readers: 'The usually po-faced paper ran the headline: "Let's Hear It For Breasts",' the *Sun* crowed. 'We were stunned when the paper – read by social workers, outreach coordinators and pretentious media types – showed a rare flash of humour and backed our campaign.' The *Sun* is planning to end its quest for cleavage by parking its topless double-decker outside the *Guardian*'s offices in central London, with Danielle and five other Page Three Girls riding shotgun.

At this point, though, London's a long way away, and Danielle's up to her bottom in bog water, clinging to a copy of the *Guardian*.

'Cleavage *and* newspaper.' The photographer scrunches his arms together, and she mimics him, her bronzed disco balls bulging.

'It looks really nice in there – is it warm?'

'It's fookin' frehzin'.' So cold, in fact, that her skin is covered with butterscotch goosebumps. But Danielle's a pro. Even though she's freezing and feels things crawling on her feet, she's still giving those professional bedroom eyes, and, truth be told, she could entice more than a few men into joining her in the bog.

By now, the great big bubbly ball that is Julia Galvin, Superstar, is about to burst. For her, this dirty, stinking bog hole is *her* opportunity to be on TV and do all the things that society normally doesn't allow Big Chicks like her to do. Is nowhere safe from the Skinny Blondes of this world?

Armed with her Irish flag, stuffed leprechaun and the toy frog in her hair, Julia marches over to the bog on behalf of Big Chicks around the globe, intent on wresting back the media spotlight.

'Watch out for the frogs,' she says, trying to spook the bathing beauty.

Danielle ignores her, smiling obliviously to the camera.

'And the leeches,' adds a man who's miffed at being told to get out of the shot.

'*And* the skin weevils – they're worse than crabs,' Julia heckles boisterously. If they don't take a picture of her soon, she's going to do a bellyflop on Danielle. Charlie finally relents and invites her to take part. Julia slings on her snorkel and whips off her black shirt. With her medicine-ball body and hummocky white legs, Julia is everything that Danielle is not. As she splashes into the water, a male bystander mutters cruelly, 'That's raised the water level a bit.'

Julia's too excited to care. 'What do you want me to do?' she asks, fitting her mask over the stuffed frog in her hair. Whereas Danielle's afraid to dip below belly-button level, Julia's happy to wallow in the muck. 'Can you do me better than Page 29 of the Irish version of the *Sun*?' Ever the crowd-pleaser, she's soon hogging the slimelight, cracking jokes and sidelining Danielle.

The crowd also gets involved, smiling and cheering for their day in the *Sun*.

'Do you want me to jump in?!' Charlie yells to them.

He gets the answer he wants and wades into the bog in his jeans and *Sun* T-shirt. For a certain group of people – say, *Guardian* readers – the entire set-up epitomises the *Sun*. It's all here: the tabloid hack wallowing next to the blonde bimbo, urging the masses to cheer like monkeys. Typical *Sun*: so lowbrow it's below bog level.

Charlie's hoping to hoist Danielle in his arms like a bog mermaid, but Julia promptly tackles him, forcing him to dive for the bank, scrabbling for bulrushes, grass, moss, *anything* that will give him the traction he needs to shake off the enormous Irishwoman wrapped around his legs. Danielle doesn't know what to do, so she falls back on what she does best – smiling come-hitherly at the camera – all the while keeping half an eye on the crazy bog woman next to her.

Eventually, the mad Irishwoman is persuaded to let go of the nice man, and Danielle is allowed to get out of the bog.

Always one to nail down facts, I ask the *Sun*'s shutterbug why Danielle didn't go topless for the culmination of Cleavage Week.

He pauses and looks at me like I'm stupid.

'It's *cleavage*.'

But of course! The semantics of the tits and ass trade: the ABCs of T&A. Just as a girl who bares her breasts is a 'glamour model', two strips of cloth – or just two stick-on tassels – magically transform two naked mammaries into 'cleavage'.

After what Danielle's been through, I realise it's my duty – indeed, my obligation – to interview her. (Like Charlie said, 'It's *hell* out there.') As she squelches back to her ice-cream-van-cum-changing-room, her painted toenails picking their way through the sludge, Danielle explains how the *Sun* convinced a nice girl from north-east England to pose in the middle of a Welsh bog. 'I didn't say noh, but I didn't joomp at the chance. I joost agreed to do the job,' she laughs.

'What did you think bog snorkelling would involve?'

'I don't know?' she says with a lilt that sounds like a question. 'They didn't explain it, really, until I got here? And then when I seen it, I was like, *Oh my God*! You could feel things on your feet, 'orrible, it was frehzin', but I just had to grin and bear it.'

Without, alas, baring it.

Up until now, bog snorkelling has been a decidedly amateur event, but Ireland's reigning champion brings a new competitiveness to the sport. Shaven-headed Dubliner John Cantillon is a veteran of underwater rugby and hockey, as well as something called fin swimming. Suddenly, bog snorkelling isn't just a competition for white-collar vacationers and boyos from the valleys; this Irish guy has gills! John torpedoes through the water, snorkelling the 120-metre course in 1:39:13 – a new record! He's beaten the old one by five seconds, which might as well be five hours at these speeds.

Julia's been leading the chants: 'You'll ne-ver beat the Irish!' And it looks like no one will. The new world record holder comes across as one of the most pleasant people you could meet, especially with his kind eyes and top-o'-the-mornin' accent. Ask his time, for instance, and the youthful forty-year-old tells you: 'One turty-nine turteen.'

Cantillon's performance is all the more impressive, Julia says, because he was stung in the bog . . . near his groin.

Stung . . . near his groin?!? It's enough to cut my bog-snorkelling career short. I envision a bog-dwelling cousin of Bigfoot and the Loch Ness Monster. *'What did it?'*

'I don't know,' John says, unfazed. 'They say it's bog scorpions.'

Which explains his advice for the other contenders: 'Swim fast.'

Whereas most contestants are focusing on how quickly they'll finish the race, I'm worried whether I'll finish at all. My head's throbbing and my stomach's queasy after a night in the bar with a group of Irish and Australians, two of the hardest-drinking peoples in the world; they seem to think alcohol is a vital nutrient, the missing fifth food group. Of course, I may just be nervous about failing again. Having drawn the fifty-second slot out of more than sixty swimmers, I have plenty of time to worry.

When I first stepped onto the bog this afternoon, I was relieved to see that the course wasn't as long as I remembered it. But now, the moment I sit down on the bank and put on my flippers, the adrenal dread clears my amnesia. There it is: the little white pole at the end of the trench seems to lie somewhere off the east coast of England. In fact, it's probably a 50-foot column once you reach it; it just *looks* small from this distance.

Then there's the cold. My brand-new scuba suit, reassuringly stamped Scubapro, doesn't do anything against the frigid grip of the murk. As I lower myself into the water, my lungs immediately start to protest. I suddenly remember why I quit last time. Not only am I having to fight for breath just standing here, soon I'll be trying to swim *to England*. And as they say over there, *Stuff this for a month of Sundays.*

On the count of three, I hurl myself into the water. The moment

I break the surface, though, all my careful mental preparation vanishes, replaced by the familiar panicky fear, the mad drive to somehow, someway *GET OUT OF THIS!* I start kicking jerkily, but my flippers stop functioning, the weeds wrapping around them and pulling me down. My legs trailing behind me like lead pipes, I revert to flailing through the cold darkness, hands clawing at the stones, moss, peat, weeds and silt to pull myself through the water. My new wetsuit – the one so tight it felt shrink-wrapped – somehow starts to leak. Icy water gushes in around my arms and back. I might as well be naked. All I can remember is my goal: to finish.

I stop a couple of times, choking after trying to breathe underwater without my snorkel. As I gasp for air, a scoffer sneers: 'Impressive technique.'

Well, if it *is* a technique, it's the Help-Me-I'm-Drowning Stroke, a desperate, scum-sucking crawl for survival. I pop my face out of the water, peering through the mist-covered mask, only to find that my goal is so far away I can barely see it. Despite the dirty water in my ears, I can sense the crowd's vague disappointment. There's no cheering or booing; just a kind of muffled murmuring, a collective shaking of heads and clicking of tongues. Here's this big American, all six-feet-four-and-a-half-inches of him, with his beach tan and sleek wetsuit, the kind of guy who should have exploded off the blocks, and . . . the poor fool's drowning down there! Somebody throw him a lifejacket! Fetch the first aid – he's gonna need CPR!

Somehow, though, unbelievably, after what feels like hours of flailing, I float past the finish line. My time is risible – and believe me, plenty of people laugh about it. Three minutes and forty-four seconds?!? That's more than twice the new world record! And just three seconds short of Julia's time – and *she* has a back problem!

Technically, I too could claim to be injured, though my so-called injury would only lead to more wisecracks. As I crawl out of the primordial slime, calves and thighs aching, I notice a watery red stain mingling with the muck on my knee. A cut! No, this is more than a cut – this is a *wound*! I was *wounded* down there! Probably by the same thing that stung the world champion! If I have to live with such a pathetic finishing time, I should at least be allowed to feel a little macho.

In truth, my 'wound' was no doubt self-inflicted; I probably scraped my knee along the bottom. The woman from the first aid team informs me that yes, I am the only swimmer wimp enough to report an injury, with a cut that practically heals itself by the time I get back to the hotel.

But at least I've finished the race. And I've still got the scar to prove it – if you've got really good eyesight, or, even better, a magnifying glass.

The morning after, the bog-snorkelling burghers of Llanwrtyd awake to a shock: the *Sun* hasn't used any photos of the Page Three Girl in the bog. Instead of Danielle's coy cleavage, Britain's biggest newspaper has gone with the bare-breasted bounty of another girl: Abby, a leggy brunette from Blackpool who's wearing nothing but white pumps . . . and the grey pages of the *Guardian* over her groin.

Gordon shrugs off the news, having grown accustomed to letdowns over the years. 'What they should have done is put some weeds on her, but they didn't. It was all pretty-pretty shots,' he says.

Sun reporter Charlie Yates isn't sure why his bosses didn't run Danielle's photo. 'At the end of the day, there was probably too much chest in the paper.'

Now, for most people, this might come as a surprise: SUN IN 'TOO MUCH CHEST' SHOCKER! I, for one, thought the tabloid's editorial ethos was to put as many breasts as possible on its pages.

Whereas Danielle hasn't appeared anywhere, Julia has somehow managed to make it into the *Welsh Mirror*, the *Independent*, and the *Western Mail* – she's even on Page Two of the *Daily Star*, facing a topless lovely.

Over breakfast, the celebrity bog snorkeller explains her outlook on life. The crowds have gone, and her hammy jocularity has disappeared. Instead, her voice is hushed at times as she talks about media spin, celebrity and Skinny Blondes. *That's what sells papers*, she thought when she saw Danielle. 'But my game was to get in there, too!' she laughs. 'It's just finding the right spin.' Having grown up believing that TV was her birthright, Julia has found a measure of fame as a Big Chick snorkelling through muck. She's even managed to outshine the Skinny Blondes of this world, but this success hasn't sated her craving for more celebrity.

'It's not about fifteen minutes of fame, it's about *milking* it. Anyone can get fifteen minutes; prolonging the matter – *that's* the hard bit.' One trick is to come up with a new gimmick each year, like the tiny animal she wore on her head yesterday. 'This year, I'm still in the papers, and I shouldn't be there,' she admits. 'Y'know, I'm not champion of *anything* – now. I just had a frog in my hair.'

CHAPTER SIX

WHERE EVERYONE KNOWS THEIR PLACE

HORN DANCING IN ABBOTS BROMLEY

HOOFING IT: Tony Fowell (centre) puts the horn dancers through their paces.

© J.R. DAESCHNER

OLD WORLD, NEW WORLD

You're gettin' too old for this, Chick.

Tony Fowell wakes up the morning after, totally wrecked and soaked with sweat, thinking *Never again*. He's got a lump the size of a duck's egg on his shoulder and another bump on his elbow, but the main problem is his back. A lifetime of manual labour has ground down the cartilage in his backbone to the point that three of the discs have collapsed, pinching the nerves until it feels like somebody's rammed a red-hot poker down his spine. Bad backs run in the family, but just as importantly, so does stubbornness. Tony has always insisted on doing things his own way, even if he ends up hurting himself. Take yesterday, for instance. By the end of the twelve-hour ordeal, his body had gone into shock, shaking and shivering, hot to the touch but freezing inside. The pain – an excruciating ache – had spread from the base of his spine to his legs and shoulders. Now he sits rigid in his armchair, topping up the coproxamol with that Great British Cure-All – a cup of tea – and wondering about the future. For more than 450 years, the Fowells have passed the leadership from one generation to the next like working-class aristocrats, ideally from father to son, just as his dad did with him. But who will take over from him? His two boys don't seem to want the responsibility. And there's no way a woman could ever lead it, despite those stories of his great-grandmother filling in for her husband.

So Tony fights the pain and tries to keep moving, tipping himself out of his chair and onto his feet, shuffling like a sciatic patient much older than his forty-seven years – or, more accurately, like a sciatic patient who has just spent a day dancing with a pair of 25-pound reindeer antlers hoisted overhead.

*

Every Monday after the first Sunday following September the fourth, Tony Fowell and a dozen family and friends perform the Abbots Bromley Horn Dance, reputedly one of the oldest traditions in Britain – and Europe. In many parts of the world, wearing horns used to be the sign of a cuckold, but in Abbots Bromley, it's a great honour. Dressed in flat caps and short trousers, the men carry ancient antlers on their shoulders and traipse through the village and surrounding Staffordshire countryside, dancing, drinking and collecting money along the way.

Before you dismiss it as merely morris dancing with horns, you should know that most of the Abbots Bromley men are quick to distance themselves from the jingle-jangle ankle-slapping of their country counterparts. ('Morris dancers are kind of nancy boys,' one tells me.) Admittedly, though, the hard men of horn dancing do have traits in common with their more effete counterparts. Both traditions feature faux-archaic costumes designed to conjure up a romantic notion of Olde England. They also have several stock characters in common, like the Jester, the Hobby Horse and a gender-bending Maid Marian. However – and I can't stress how important this is – in the Horn Dance, there is no waving of hankies, jingling of bells or festooning of nipples (which, come to think of it, makes morris dancing sound more exciting than it is).

Although the first record of a Horn Dance-style hoedown comes from the late 1400s, many morris men believe it predates their own tradition, making it a possible forebear – maybe even a relic of the Pagan Fertility Dance that supposedly swept Stone Age Europe. As a result, Abbots Bromley is a kind of Mecca for morrissers – not to mention anorak folkies, born-again pagans and other world-class eccentrics. Stroking their goatees, they fold their arms across their potbellies and debate important questions such as whether other forms of entertainment should be allowed on the village green – or do they take away from the dance? Another favourite is trying to count the times the dancers repeat the various phases of the dance in an attempt to unlock the intricacies of the secret ritual. Elaborate diagrams have been drawn up with swirly arrows and complicated instructions. To the dancers, all this pseudo-scientific method smacks of madness. 'There is no set number of times to do any particular thing,' Tony shrugs. 'We just do it until I get bored with it.' Undeterred, Horn Dance devotees interpret this lack of design as proof that the magic of the supposedly pagan ritual is far bigger than the human beings taking part in it.

Not surprisingly, the true stars of the Abbots Bromley Horn Dance are the horns themselves. Weighing sixteen to twenty-five pounds and spanning up to three feet, the six antlers aren't just any old horns – they're a thousand years old. What's more, they don't come from native deer, but from a species of *reindeer* that died out in Britain during the Ice Age. No one knows how ancient reindeer antlers wound up in a tiny village in Staffordshire, but it seems most likely that they were imported from Scandinavia at a time when the Midlands was a war zone between the Saxons and the Vikings. Near Abbots Bromley, the River Trent provided a perfect invasion route for Danish longboats cruising down the Humber Estuary and straight into the heart of England. Abbots Bromley fell to the Danes for a time, and a later Saxon lord died fighting the Vikings in 1010. The horns date from around the same time. Unusually for an ancient tradition, there's actually scientific proof of this. A few decades ago, one of the smaller horns was repaired after centuries of wear and tear. A splinter of the bone was carbon-dated to around 1065 – the year before the Norman Conquest.

And Abbots Bromley is a place where the past is very much present. At first glance, there's nothing remarkable about the village: it's as pretty as countless others, with an ancient Butter Cross on the village green and a few half-timbered Tudor structures breaking up the long row of redbrick cottages on the high street. Most of the bricks were hand-cut from the local clay, the stuff that made Staffordshire one of the world's biggest ceramics centres – Abbots Bromley is less than thirty miles from the gritty towns known as The Potteries, where Josiah Wedgwood and others made their fortunes in the Industrial Revolution. Grim nicknames like 'the Black Country' still scare off tourists. However, Abbots Bromley's agricultural heritage protected it from industrial excesses. During the Middle Ages, the local serfs harvested the raw ingredients for the famous beer produced by their landlords: the abbots of Burton-upon-Trent. Now a sleepy commuter hamlet, Abbots Bromley is surrounded by rippling farmland, bosomy hills and thick woodlands. 'People who haven't been to Staffordshire before are always stunned,' claims Sir Charles Wolseley, a local blueblood. 'They say, "I've always thought it was factory chimneys and smoke and grime. It's really quite nice, isn't it?"'

Before she became Lady Bagot of Blithfield Hall, Nancy Spicer was just a girl from Wahroonga. When she was growing up outside Sydney in the twenties, England was still very much the Mother Country for well-to-do Australians like her. However, she never imagined she would end up marrying into an old English family – mentioned by Shakespeare – or saving an ancestral seat from destruction, or preserving one of Britain's oldest traditions.

Nancy met her husband on her maiden voyage to England just before the Second World War. When she turned eighteen, her mother decided that she should travel to England to meet her relatives – the Australian equivalent of coming out – and on the cruise, she met Caryl Bagot, a widower in his sixties who had been staying with relatives in Australia. Although he didn't tell Nancy at the time, when he saw her walking on board – a stunning brunette – he decided then and there that he would marry her. Chaperoned by her mother, Nancy and Caryl spent the next couple of years gallivanting between the UK and the Continent on a Grand Tour of Europe. It was only when they were separated by the war – and her parents – that Nancy realised she had fallen in love with Caryl. The age difference didn't matter to her. They married in Sydney in 1940 and lived in Australia for a couple of years before returning to London.

The fifth Lord Bagot died just after World War Two, and Caryl inherited the title at the age of nearly seventy. His predecessors had neglected the mansion to the point that it was uninhabitable except for three rooms. The roof leaked and was riddled with dry rot, there was no electricity, no heating except for open fires, and no bathrooms. Whenever it rained, the Bagots had to rush around, catching leaks with any containers on hand – hipbaths, buckets, basins and jugs. One winter, the upper gallery had flooded and frozen over, so the former lord had used it as a skating rink.

Lady Bagot also saw the Horn Dance during her first year at Blithfield. 'It was a misty day, the horn dancers walked across the park, and you heard the tinkle of the boy hitting the triangle. And they came up out of the valley of the River Blythe, you saw the tips of the antlers coming up out of the mist, and then they came on to the front lawn and danced there. It gave you quite a *shiver* – you felt that you'd *really* gone back in time – and actually, just after the War, they really looked . . . they had medieval faces.'

The Bagots can also trace their roots from the Middle Ages. According to family lore, Sir John Bagot was knighted when the king spent twelve days hunting in Bagots Park in the late 1300s (a Bagot also features in Shakespeare's *Richard II*). 'It's said that Richard gave the famous Bagot goats to the Bagots at that time,' Lady Bagot explains. These 'famous' animals had black-and-white coats and distinctive curved horns up to three feet long. A goat's head features on the family crest and on the Bagot Arms in Abbots Bromley, as well as the Goat's Head. The parish church at Blithfield must also be one of the few Christian sanctuaries where goats are elevated over sheep – in the stained-glass windows, on the tombs – there's even a helmet with goat horns sticking out of it, a replica of the one worn by a Bagot fighting at the Battle of Bosworth.

Legend has it that the Bagots' fate hinged on their eponymous breed: if the goats ever left Blithfield, so would the family. Lady Bagot is well aware of the caprine legend, though she and her husband never had children of their own. 'In the end, he thought it would be nice for me to have a child,' Lady Bagot recalls. When he was in his eighties, and Lady Bagot in her forties, the couple adopted a baby and named her Caryl Rosemary – Cara for short. 'Unhappily, he died before she was a year old.' Her adopted status also barred Cara from holding a title: she was simply 'Not the Hon.'. After Lord Bagot died, the rules of inheritance dictated that his peerage – and the estate – passed to a cousin, who sold off what was left of the land. Lady Bagot owned the house and gardens, but some heirlooms automatically belonged to the new lord, so she watched helplessly as they were removed and auctioned. After fifteen years of building up Blithfield by opening it to the paying public, she effectively had to start all over again. Without an estate for walks and picnics, it became harder to attract families; also, the novelty value of seeing how the other half lived had quickly worn off, particularly as it became possible to take cheap package holidays abroad. Lady Bagot closed Blithfield to the public in 1977.

Like many of her peers, she decided that the only way she could continue living at Blithfield would be to subdivide it into homes and sell them to the public. As a result, the new lords of Blithfield are the new rich: local business owners and professionals. Lady Bagot still owns the oldest part of the mansion, and she has ensured that the Horn Dance will continue at Blithfield, even after she's gone, by including the tradition in the terms of the lease. 'We certainly didn't want anyone to complain about them coming – not that I think they would.' Now in her seventies, she has also made preparations for the inevitable, entrusting Blithfield to one of her husband's great-nephews. In a neat completion of the circle, he's descended from the sister Caryl had been visiting in Australia before he met Nancy all those years ago. 'There's quite an Australian connection with Blithfield now,' she says with satisfaction.

The Bagots have spread across the world: to Ireland, America, Canada and even Eastern Europe. At Blithfield, though, the legendary link with the Bagot goats seems to have been proven true. After closing the hall to the public, Lady Bagot donated the last of her animals to the Rare Breeds Survival Trust. Although the breed has been brought back from near extinction, only about a hundred females survive. As for the Bagot lords, they're almost as rare as their caprine namesakes. 'It was always said that the Bagots loved their home so much they would never leave it,' Lady Bagot says wistfully. 'But I suppose in a way there aren't any Bagots here now.'

As befits a tradition straight from the 'mists of time', Horn Dance Day often dawns with a thick mist on the ground, enhancing the sense of mystery and timelessness surrounding St Nicholas Church.

Half a dozen regulars assemble inside early in the morning for a brief communion service, usually attended by a couple of disgruntled pagan outsiders who sit on the sidelines, their arms crossed in silent protest. Outside, more hangers-on wait impatiently for the Christian service to finish and the 'pagan' tradition to begin. A bearded accordionist peers through the church doors. 'I see the malicious lie hasn't ended yet,' he mutters.

The first horn dancers arrive as close to 7.30 a.m. as they can manage. Terry Bailey was roped in to the dance at the last minute twenty years ago, and he's been performing the role of jester ever since. He also acts as organiser, making sure the dancers keep to their schedule without lingering too long at the pubs along the way. Wearing T-shirts with their short trousers and stockings, he and another dancer begin removing the thousand-year-old antlers from the walls of the side chapel for their annual day in the sun. Over the centuries, the six horns have been painted various colours, and the dancers divide them into the 'whites' and the 'blues', even though the latter three are actually brown. The horns have crudely carved deer heads (probably dating from the 1500s) and vertical poles allowing the men to steady them on their shoulders.

The rest of the dancers straggle in over the next half hour, turning up in various states of undress while greeting friends and family around the church. The crowd numbers nearly 200, including a front-and-centre fringe of men and women who look as if they've just crawled out of the primordial slime, having spent the previous night sleeping rough or, to use the technical term, 'camping'. There's a woman in a full-length green velvet cloak, another sporting a black version with hair dyed to match, a born-again witch, or 'Wiccan', with what appears to be a string of three-toned ferrets hanging from her head, a man in a scraggly beard and a stained, billowy linen shirt with denim cut-offs and strappy leather sandals – a sixteenth-century-meets-1960s kind of look – and another guy who looks uncannily like James Brolin in *The Amityville Horror*, right after he stops washing his hair and starts terrorising his family. With him, it's a tough call, but most of the groupies are garden-variety pagans, like the guy in the black T-shirt with a Horned God and a pentagram on it. Add a smattering of journalists to the locals, witches and eccentrics, and you've got the makings of a typical Horn Dance Day crowd.

Inside, the reindeer antlers have been lined up in front of the altar, and the dancers take their places behind them for the Blessing of the Horns, a brief ceremony tacked on in recent decades to counteract the tradition's supposedly pagan magic. The previous vicar at St Nicholas repeatedly clashed with the Wiccans who gatecrashed the event, but Pastor Simon Davis is all smiles as the dancers take their place before him, removing their caps and bowing their heads. With his twinkly eyes, button nose and pink cheeks, he really does look like a younger, thinner version of Saint Nick, the church's jolly namesake. Simon doesn't get hung up on the custom's origins – which is just as well, judging from the surly stares he's getting from some of the pagans in the congregation, their hands clamped under their armpits. They're probably conjuring up spells as he speaks! Any longer, and they'd have him mopping his brow and tugging at his dog collar: *Ho-ho-ho – tough crowd!*

As the sun burns the mist from the ground, the dancers wander into the churchyard to resume mixing with family and friends they haven't seen since last Horn Dance Day. Except for the onlookers, the scene has the buzz of a village social. By now, most of the dancers have managed to put on their costumes, which are Victorian interpretations of Tudor wear, all in autumnal tones – copper caps, dusky rose and evergreen jackets with russet waistcoats peeking out from underneath, knee-length green breeches with a gold acorn and oak leaf pattern and long olive socks with black shoes, as well as some anachronistic accessories such as sunglasses. All told, there are six dancers, plus the Musician and two boys named after their percussion instruments – the Triangle and the Bow and Arrow – as well as three characters: the wooden Hobby Horse with its clackety jaw; Maid Marian, a stout, red-faced old man in a blue-and-gold frock topped with a crown; and Terry in his red-and-orange motley with a stuffed headpiece that curves to a jingle-bell tip in front of his forehead.

Despite his festive get-up, Terry's not a happy jester. It's a few minutes past eight o'clock, and the dancers should be on the road already. Doug Fowell, the oldest member of the troupe, strikes up 'The Wearing of the Green' on his button accordion. An Irish song seems like a strange choice for one of England's oldest traditions, but it's just the first of many foreign tunes played during the day. Besides old English standards like 'Cock o' the North', there's the Scottish favourite 'Roamin' in the Gloamin'' and even 'Yankee Doodle Dandy'. No matter the tune, when it comes out of a squeeze-box, it sounds jaunty and jovial, creating a rustic atmosphere and setting the tone for the day. This is dum-da-diddly-dum music, which explains why the people who are here love it, and why those who aren't don't.

The start is the hardest part of the day, nearly an hour of non-stop dancing first thing in the morning. With Tony in the lead, the men hoist the antlers on their shoulders and perform outside St Nicholas, next to the sandstone grooves in the church wall where Robin Hood and his men supposedly sharpened their arrows. Then they file out of the churchyard in a single line, quick-stepping to the centuries-old Butter Cross on the village green, where the timber beams once covered a dairy market but now serve as a bus shelter. Tony swerves out from the line, and the others break into two colour-coded groups that circle and serpentine. Sometimes the whites and the blues wind around in separate circles, and sometimes they head straight for each other but then twist away at the last moment to avoid a collision.

'Face!' Tony shouts, and the dancers form opposing lines, lilting in time with the music. The two sides promenade toward each other as if they're going to lock horns, but at the last minute, the Boy makes a rhythmic click with his bow and arrow, the Hobby Horse clacks its jaws, and the sides withdraw. This to-ing and fro-ing continues until Tony barks 'Through!' and they change sides, the whites going over and the blues ducking under, both teams twirling their horns in the sunlight as they reverse positions. After more facing and throughing, Tony hollers 'Off!' and they continue marching up the narrow high street, trailed by nearly 300 people, disrupting the rush-hour traffic for the commuters who have bought up much of the village. Most drivers watch with good humour, knowing there's nothing they can do but smile. However, a few are clearly annoyed about a traffic jam caused by men wearing caps and short trousers and prancing around with horns while an accordion dum-da-diddly-dees in the background. *Bloody ancient traditions! I'm ten minutes late for work!*

'You couldn't invent it, it's so ridiculous,' laughs a man from the *Guardian*, informing me that England has many events like this. 'They're taken very seriously – and thank God they are.' Having duly patronised the event, his work here is done. He soon leaves, as do most of the witches. The horns are safely out of the church, so they retire to their campsites for slap-up breakfasts of newt's eye and toe of frog.

The dancers, in contrast, are just getting started. Bounding with energy and jolly to a man, they're laughing and joking and needling each other as they parade through the village, stopping every ten yards or so to dance. On the outskirts, Daphne Hill is waiting for them at her farmhouse. For the past sixty years, she has been greeting the horn dancers with tea and biscuits. 'I started it during the War because the 'orn dancers were cold,' she says, 'and I've just done it every year since.'

Do the men ask her to arrange refreshment in advance?

'Oh, *no*.' She shakes her head. 'They never ask, no. Oh, no, no.'

After a short break at Mrs Hill's, the men head up the road for their first drink of the morning – a shot of whisky, just after nine o'clock. 'That sets 'em up for the day,' grins their host at Rose Bank Farm, a big-chinned man who has the honour of the first dance with the team this morning. Malcolm Breckons has no doubts that the dance works as a fertility ritual for both harvests and humans. 'Look at 'em all,' he laughs, pointing to the living evidence around him. 'All these kids 'ave got their birthdays around June. I've got two children – one's born the fourth of June, the other one's the tenth, nine months to the day.' Another farm owner also vouches for the dance's conceptive powers. 'I came here, and we had a baby the first year, and we had a baby the second year. We gave up after that!'

Then he'd better keep the jester away from his wife. The oddly coloured balloon carried by the fool is actually an inflated pig's bladder. The veined membrane starts out pink and slimy in the morning and ends the day brown, leathery and semi-deflated. During the dance, the jester scampers around, playfully thwacking women with his piece of pig on a stick. 'If a woman gets it with this,' Terry says, raising the pig's bladder, 'she'll get pregnant.' To paraphrase an old saying: continental people have sex, the English have inflated pigs' bladders.

The rest of the morning is spent dancing . . . and drinking. Not in a ten-pints-and-a-kebab kind of way, but in an atmosphere of pace-yourself conviviality. The dancers 'rest' every half hour or so, absorbing the alcohol with platters of sausages and sandwiches. This abundance of alcohol is perfectly understandable, given that Abbots Bromley is only 11 miles from the Brewing Capital of Britain. Burton-upon-Trent is also the home of Marmite, made from a beery byproduct. 'Depending on the direction of the wind, you smell hops or Marmite – or sometimes the two mixed together,' says a photographer who recently moved to Burton. 'What's really bad is when you're hung over, and you open the window. They tell me I'll get used to it – but it's disgusting.'

Throughout the day, the mood of the Horn Dance alternates between a cosy family reunion attended by only a few dozen people and a public spectacle watched by hundreds. Along the way, there are glimpses of an England more often imagined than seen, like the first major dance of the morning, when the horns duel on the village green with the timber Butter Cross and black-and-white Goats Head Inn in the background. The dancers reckon they cover fifteen to thirty miles during the day on foot and by van. When they're not dancing, the men casually leave the horns lying on the grass, concrete or tarmac – whatever's convenient. The dancers reckon that if they've lasted a thousand years, they can withstand any minor wear and tear.

Around midday, the men cross the reservoir to pay their respects – and fill their coin boxes – at Blithfield Hall. The mansion's grounds have been converted into a small car park for the occasion, and the walled ditch, or ha-ha, that prevents the estate's sheep and cattle from straying onto the lawn in front of the hall also serves to keep the members of the public in their place. The great unwashed stand in the grassy ditch, next to their cars, gazing up at the raised lawn where a smattering of well-heeled onlookers stand. Entry to the lawn is strictly guarded by a couple of locals empowered to separate the sheep from the goats: only at Blithfield, the goats are the chosen few. Lady Bagot and her neighbours have invited guests to see the dance, and they stand in separate clusters, without intermingling.

The dancers march in through the hall's grandiose arched gate, over a gravel path and onto the lawn, forming two facing rows as they begin their performance, with Doug Fowell playing 'Lady Bagot's Tune' for her ladyship's pleasure. A wide stretch of grass separates the dancers from their patrons. With its feudal overtones and imagery of the hunt, the tradition seems tailor-made for the fairytale setting of a country mansion. Technically, of course, it shouldn't work at all. The scene is a confusion of clashing styles and periods. The hall's pseudo-Gothic façade, with its stone-coloured cladding, pointed spires and arched windows, is a Georgian fabrication of a medieval palace, while the dancers' costumes are modern approximations of what late Victorians thought Tudor outfits looked like. As for the current incarnation of the dance, well, who knows when that dates from? But somehow, all these contradictory parts come together to create a uniform whole, with the horn dancers weaving their magic for the gentry, and the hoi polloi down below, peering through their binoculars and telescopic lenses. A place for everything, and everything in its place – or should that be 'everyone'?

After the dance, Tony Fowell and Lady Bagot leave their respective sides and meet in the middle ground. The lord of the dance and the lady of the manor come together for their annual chat, Tony removing his cap and leaning over to address the stooped dowager in a brief encounter that has more symbolism than substance to it – they talk about the weather, the costumes, the dancers and so on. But the meeting bridges the gap between the performers and the spectators, the commoners and the gentry. As the dancers line up along the edge of the ha-ha, their horns at their feet, the partygoers follow Lady Bagot's lead and tentatively approach them.

The men perform one more time before filing out through the gate and proceeding to the side of the hall, where women serve them sandwiches and drinks through a kitchen window. The men and their families sprawl on the forecourt, some sitting on benches, others on the pavement. More than a little embarrassed, I have to step over them to get into the house.

'You're goin' in *there*?' Terry Bailey asks in amazement, unable to believe that mere mortals could cross Blithfield's threshold.

I can hardly believe it myself; with my worn boots and coat, I'm not dressed for a garden party. Every other year, Lady Bagot throws a party for 120 friends and dignitaries such as the former Archbishop of Birmingham. This year, she's putting on a small buffet to thank a handful of foreign Bagots for their (financial) support of Blithfield and the Horn Dance. Like the dancers outside, her guests are treated to finger food. Inside, though, the sandwiches are roast beef and horseradish rather than ham and cheese, the drink is wine instead of beer, and there's an additional selection of mushroom-and-asparagus quiche, profiteroles, meringue puffs laced with butter-cream and tiny scones filled with strawberries and cream.

Lady Bagot's guests are a couple of local women, plus a Bagot from the Irish branch of the family and a Daughter of the American Revolution named Virginia, who's actually from Oklahoma. Where I come from, DARs are WASP queens, an exotic breed you know of, but never expect to meet. To be a member, you have to prove – with documentation – that you're the lineal, blood descendant of someone who helped the colonies in the War of Independence. Virginia has her pedigree chart with her, which may be the done thing in case anyone does a spot check on her ancestry.

After lunch, Lady Bagot takes us on a tour of her section of the house, including the upstairs apartment where she and her husband made do while they renovated Blithfield. One room features the two gold-trimmed velvet chairs where she and her husband sat for eight hours during Queen Elizabeth's Coronation. Lady Bagot and the other members of the aristocracy quickly had to brush up on court protocol for the occasion. For instance, the train of a duchess's gown was much longer than that of a baronet's wife like herself. On the big day, the weather had been wet and miserable, she says. 'It was so cold we all had to wrap our gowns around us.'

'I know,' one of the locals pipes up. 'I slept in Hyde Park. Just opposite the Dorchester.' Despite the potential for embarrassment on both sides – after all, one Lady was wrapped in a gown and jewels while the other was wrapped in God-knows-what and sleeping rough – the two women natter on about what a glorious event it was, reminiscing about their common experience, as seen from very different perspectives.

Meanwhile, Virginia has been dutifully crosschecking her pedigree chart and providing a running reaction to Lady Bagot's commentary. At one point, she manages to slip in a confession. 'This isn't something I like to go around saying,' she claims, lowering her voice to a hush. 'But I'm a member of the *DAR*? – the Daughters of the American *Revolution*?' It's unclear whether her reluctance is born of humility or fear that she'll be attacked by an SOB, or Son of Britain. Lady Bagot mentions how she has managed to buy back bits of the Bagot estate, most importantly the portraits, while distant relatives have donated other items. 'I suppose the Bagots are very pleased to have a place to focus on,' she concludes modestly.

'Hear, hear!' Virginia exclaims, reaching way back in her race memory to express her enthusiasm. 'The Bagots of America are very thankful for all your efforts.'

Maybe it's the wine, but most likely Virginia is simply intoxicated by her surroundings. She has tasted the fruit of her family tree and found it to be very good indeed. Her reflex smile is on full beam. And who can blame her? Imagine being able to trace your ancestors back a thousand years and finding not just a dry list of marrying and burying, but stories and books about their lives and exploits – there's a Bagot in Shakespeare, for heaven's sake! And instead of featureless graves, think what it would be like to see your family features etched in brass and marble, at your family's ancestral mansion, with a living aristocrat still in residence! And to top it all off, you find that this ancestral seat is the site of a tradition that may date from pagan times. So you can understand why Virginia is thrilled to be at Blithfield.

Or maybe not. At the very least, she and her husband are good company. After Lady Bagot finishes in the house, the tour shifts to the small thirteenth-century church behind the hall. The parish church is also the Bagots' private burial ground.

While we're sitting in the sanctuary, surrounded by dead Bagots, our guide casually explains that the pews date from the 1400s.

'The *1400s*?' Virginia's husband says. 'Oh, my *goodness*!'

Truly, it takes an American to appreciate England's history.

By the time I catch up with the horn dancers, it's nearly three o'clock, and they still can't get over the fact that a commoner like me could have lunch with Lady Bagot.

'You went into the Big House, didn't ya!' says Mick the musician.

'While we were eatin' sandwiches, you were feastin' on game and pheasant!'

'Yeah – you were hobnobbin' with the high and mighty!'

The horn dancers are on the last stretch to Abbots Bromley. Once again, the event has reverted from a family reunion to a boisterous public performance. Throngs line Bagot Street as the dancers begin their triumphant pub-crawl at the Bagot Arms. They're running behind schedule, but for once, Terry Bailey doesn't seem to mind. 'It's great bein' the centre of attention. It's like bein' a film star. If people have come here to see us, we can't just dance once and that's it. We have to entertain them.'

So much so that it takes two hours to process to the village green, partly because there's another pub en route. One of the Fowells is drinking behind the Royal Oak. 'How're we doin' on time?' he asks another dancer.

'You're late.'

'Oh well. After a thousand years, three-quarters of an hour – that's nothing.'

Terry somehow manages to reassemble the group, and around 6 p.m., they make it back to the village green, dancing for the crowds at the Goat's Head pub. A handful of stalls have been set up around the Butter Cross, some selling food and bric-a-brac, others flogging crafts and postcards of the event, such as the Wiccans pushing BORN AGAIN PAGAN badges. The dancers stop for tea, sandwiches and more beer at the Crown just across the way. Then it's a long slog up the hill behind the village and back down again, with several dozen hangers-on following them, including a drama teacher who has rushed from Nottinghamshire to catch the end of the dance. A hardcore folkie, Corinne Male blames the upper classes for the Horn Dance's relative obscurity, claiming that they denigrate working-class customs while glorifying their own pastimes, such as foxhunting. 'The Irish are bloody proud of their traditions, the Scottish are bloody proud of their traditions, but the English only poke fun at theirs. We're meant to feel ashamed of ours,' she says indignantly.

Undeterred, she proudly tramps through the steady drizzle that's started to fall. The dancers stop to dance in the rain before driving on, marching across a football pitch and back down into the village. 'The dance goes on, regardless,' Tony says. 'It doesn't matter what the weather's doin'.' Fortunately, the rain clears up by the time we reach the Coach and Horses, the penultimate stop of the day.

The men must be getting tired – they're letting in the women . . . and me. Terry Bailey asks if I'd like to join in, giving me the honour (I think) of carrying the heaviest horns, with a male Fowell leading on my right and a female cousin dancing to my left. I've got broad shoulders, but the Great Horns are too wide for me. Before I was invited to join the dance, a Wiccan priest had told me about his experience: 'It was amazing. I wasn't following the person in front of me; I was following this path of *energy*.'

I'm not asking for anything as fancy as a path of energy; I'd be happy with just some white footprints on the pavement marking out the steps. This close to the finish, the dancers are burning up their reserves, clowning around and pushing each other to the limit. Our leader enjoys spinning in tight circles so that the tips of our antlers are almost touching, then shouting 'Through!' as often as he can. As a result, the whites and blues are constantly lifting and spinning to switch sides, with the accordion pumping dum-da-diddly-dum-da-dee in a game of Musical Horns. As a left-footed novice, I'm the one who always gets caught out. Just when I'm getting comfortable, locked into a groove by the weight of the horns, the leader will bark an order. I keep lifting the horns at the wrong moment and missing the cue to circle.

Not a moment too soon, I get to hand the horns back to the professionals for the triumphant return to the heart of Abbots Bromley. It's nearly eight o'clock, and there's a chill in the air after the rain. The mottled grey clouds are barely visible as dusk turns to darkness. The horn dancers march down the road, with Tony and his cousin taking turns leading, ribbing each other as they call out steps. A hundred hangers-on follow them from the Coach and Horses on the edge of the hamlet, strolling past illuminated street lamps to the Crown on the village green, where the war memorial and the church tower are also lit up. Assorted morris and clog dancing groups have kept the crowds occupied for the past hour or so, while the horn dancers made their way round the back of the village. But now, just before eight o'clock, the Horn Dance returns to centre stage in front of the pub for the last performance of the evening.

For Tony, the atmosphere is electric. Maybe it's the relief of knowing it's the last dance of the day – *soon I'm going to hang this damn horn up* – or something to do with the ley lines the pagans talk about . . . or simply the giddy cocktail of alcohol and fatigue finally taking effect. But for him there's something special about the night-time dancing in the heart of the village, the duelling horns surrounded by hundreds of spectators, with the timber-framed Butter Cross and the Goat's Head pub behind them, and the church tower glowing in the background. Their dancing done, the men march off the green and through the gate of the churchyard, with Doug Fowell ending the day as he began it, pumping out whatever tune pops into his head: 'The Battle Hymn of the Republic' or 'It's a Long Way to Tipperary'. Modern church muzak accompanies them as they line up at the altar where they started out more than twelve hours ago. Pastor Davis briefly thanks God for protecting the horns and the dancers, and the men return the ancient antlers to their mounts in the side chapel. The horns cast tangled shadows across the weathered stone. 'Those horns are older than the walls they're being hung on,' whispers one admirer.

The vicar invites the hundreds of spectators to stay for a short follow-up service, but barely two dozen do. Most of the horn dancers scatter, going home to shower and change before spending some of their hard-earned collection money in the Crown. In the meantime, I decide to get a head start on them. Some Horn Dance groupies are hanging out at the Royal Oak. One couple I met earlier have been coming to Abbots Bromley for years. They're both witches, you see, with their own coven in south London. They saw me dancing, and they can barely contain their envy. '*Now* they let loads of people dance with the horns,' the man informs me, 'but when I danced in it, after eight years of coming here, it was a great honour. You had to practically be born in the village before they'd let you touch the horns.'

That's what he gets for drinking bitter: you are what you drink. When I first talked to him in the afternoon, he'd been savouring the brown stuff. 'That's the first decent beer I've had . . . well, in a long time,' he declared. Not yet knowing how to recognise a Real Beer Bore, I had confessed that I actually prefer lager. His disdain was absolute; he urged me to sample the beer at the Oak, and now that I'm here, the Abbot Ale seems the natural choice, even if it doesn't come from Abbots Bromley. To my philistine tastes, the beer is smooth but dull. That said, it's no duller than his company.

I try to escape, but on the way out, I bump into Malcolm Breckons, the amiable man who served the horn dancers their first shot of the day. He insists that I go back inside to join him and his friends for a pint. I order another Abbot Ale.

'Do you like that?' he asks incredulously, unable to believe that anyone would drink it of their own free will.

'It's all right,' I fib, explaining how I try to sample the beer wherever I am, and how, being so close to the brewing capital of Britain, I feel duty bound to drink real ale.

'That tastes like *shit*,' he says after listening to my spiel. 'Get yourself a lager.'

And seeing how he's a local, I don't feel too bad ordering one.

A couple of pints later, I make it back to the Crown, where the horn dancers and their kin have crowded into the small front section of the pub. They're decked out in their Friday best for the annual Monday night celebration, the men in matching shirts and trousers, the women in name-brand country clubbing gear. Tony looks exhausted, sitting stiff-backed in the corner, and he makes an early exit to begin his recuperation. However, the rest of the men are shiny-eyed and full of energy. You'd never guess they've just spent twelve hours slogging around the countryside with horns on their backs. Maybe it's the special brew on tap – Horny Ale. The back of the room has turned into an impromptu family reunion for the Fowells; up front, some Horn Dance groupies watch longingly, ready to whip out their melodeons at the slightest hint of a singalong. A folk-music session would seem the perfect ending for one of England's oldest traditions, but the dancers have shed their Olde English costumes, and now they're singing a different kind of folk music, as interpreted by a mustachioed crooner in the corner: 'Crazy', 'Delilah' and 'Ferry 'Cross the Mersey'.

PART TWO:
THE NEW POOR AND NOBLE PROLES

Jeannie Wolseley always feared she would end up a bag lady. As plain Jeannie May in 1950s Ohio, folks had told her she was a handful. By the time she was twenty, she had fled Small Town America, married and moved to Miami. Two decades later, as her marriage headed toward divorce, Jeannie found a new passion: Britain. While researching a book about American heiresses who bailed out the

British aristocracy in the nineteenth century, she became fascinated by one story in particular: that of Anna Murphy, the daughter of an Irish immigrant who made his fortune during the California Gold Rush. As a status-conscious Catholic – confirmed by the Pope himself – Anna ventured all the way to the Old World to find her Mr Right – a Catholic Sir. The ninth baronet Wolseley seemed ideal, the scion of one of the oldest landed families in the kingdom, based at Wolseley Hall near Abbots Bromley. In 1883, Anna and Sir Charles married. But before the baronet could get his hands on her dowry, he made it clear he was only after her money. They stayed together long enough to produce an heir, but Lady Wolseley soon ditched her penniless husband and spent most of her life travelling the globe.

To Jeannie's delight, the great-grandson of this union was the current baronet, also named Sir Charles. When they met, the attraction was mutual. She was a sassy American with a passion for history, and he was a handsome aristo from a family that predated the Norman Conquest. Within months, they had fallen in love.

There was only one problem: Sir Charles was married with four children. His affair with Jeannie became public when he filed for divorce in 1984. Despite the tabloid attacks, the couple stayed together, Sir Charles married his new Lady, and they lived in the Home Counties before returning to his ancestral home in Staffordshire.

After visiting England's National Rose Collection in 1986, Jeannie got to thinking. 'We've got a bigger walled garden than that.' And so a multimillion-pound dream was born. A chartered surveyor, Sir Charles had years of expertise managing rural estates. Building a vast garden on his own land seemed the natural culmination of his career, and for him and his new wife, the sixty-acre paradise would symbolise their marriage of English pragmatism and American vision. It would be their own Arcadia in a cultural wasteland, offering combined tickets to their garden park and Shugborough, the home of their neighbour, Patrick, aka Lord Lichfield, the Queen's cousin.

Within a few years, though, the Wolseleys were bankrupt. After spending £1.73 million on the park, they realised they were being charged interest at 30% a year – *compounded*. The bank cut them off, and the park opened, unfinished, in 1990, just as the country was sliding into recession. However, they now admit that the most basic reason their dream went down the pan was because they waited until the end to build toilets in Wolseley Park. In their rush to venerate Nature, they forgot to heed nature's call. Like civilisation itself, public attractions depend on the humble toilet.

As their debts ballooned to £4.6 million, the Wolseleys hoped to avoid bankruptcy by selling the huge gravel quarry on their land for £10 million. According to them, though, the sale turned into a saga of corporate skulduggery, and they ended up selling for a knockdown price – an estimated £2 million. The Wolseleys promptly sued the buyer, but a court ruled in the company's favour. After seven years of hoping that they might pull through, the Wolseleys were ruined. It seemed that Jeannie's worst bag lady nightmare was about to come true. Sir Charles became a nobleman on the dole, and Jeannie was reduced to wearing second-hand designer gear donated by friends. Instead of saving an English dynasty like the American heiresses of old, she had inadvertently helped destroy it. And here's the kicker: unlike Lady Bagot and other landed families, the Wolseleys had no need to open their estate to the public. They could have lived very comfortably off their land without ever having catered to the lower classes.

More than a decade later, the Wolseleys are still hoping to wake from the nightmare. It's only because of a quirk in the law that Jeannie and Sir Charles have been able to stay in their Georgian home on the edge of the estate, and they will most likely be the last Wolseleys to live there. By six o'clock in the evening, they're well into cocktail hour, smoking and knocking back gin and tonics in their grand sitting room. At their feet, a terrier and two black Labs vie for affection, while overhead, Sir Charles's oily ancestors frown down at them. The Wolseleys are known for their large noses, and Sir Charles's is a fine example – a long, sloping ridge that keeps on going until gravity forces it south. When it comes to discussing his current difficulties, he literally keeps his head down, tucking his chin against his chest as his wife does most of the talking.

The last chatelaine of Wolseley Park remains very much a brass-tacks gal from the Midwest, despite the transatlantic lift in her vowels. At times, her voice alternates between bitterness and sarcasm. Describing the ruinous state of the garden now, she tells me that the locals are indeed benefiting from their benevolence. 'They fish, they walk the dog, and they . . . steal plants and set fire to the buildings,' she deadpans. Her candour also comes as a surprise. Explaining that her high-necked dress comes from Atlanta, she adds: 'The underwear's Miami.'

Which is certainly more than I wanted to know. I first saw the Wolseleys a few years ago, in a documentary on the aristocracy. For me, the bankrupt baronet triggered conflicting emotions. The democrat in me thought that after a thousand years of living off others' accomplishments, it was about time the Wolseleys started earning their keep. But that hardhearted assessment was softened by my own experience of failed dreams and financial ruin. My parents nearly went bankrupt when I was a boy – after building a small theme park, incidentally – and I could imagine the guilt that Sir Charles must feel. If he managed to stay in his home, he would live out his days with the portraits of his more capable forebears bullying him from the walls; if they could talk, they'd be saying something like 'Thou shmuck.'

It's a shame he didn't heed his family motto: *Homo homini lupus* – 'Man is a Wolf to Man.' 'I used to think it was a crappy motto,' Jeannie says. 'I mean, it's rather cynical. But now I've come to think it's pretty appropriate.'

'Talk about "Man being a wolf to man",' she continues, reciting the litany of alleged indignities, dirty dealings and Machiavellian manoeuvres that she and her husband have suffered. 'Being on the dole – try that,' she says. 'Try living on £160 for two weeks.'

'£147.'

'Yeah, they cut it down, didn't they.'

Charles tries to lift her spirits. 'There are a lot of benefits from being bankrupt as well, I can tell you,' he says. 'You don't pay tax –'

'And we've made a fine art out of shopping in charity shops,' Jeannie says, without any apparent embarrassment.

'There's great satisfaction to be gained from it, I tell you. You get far more pleasure by finding something you really like in a charity shop for £2.50 than you ever do by going into Gieves & Hawkes in Savile Row and buying some –'

'– He used to have all his stuff made there, but . . .'

'You get far more satisfaction from finding something like this handkerchief for fifty pence.' He proudly produces a gaudy cloth that's big enough to be a woman's headscarf. 'I came back very pleased with myself after that,' he smiles.

However, Jeannie can top that. 'Since 1990, I have not bought a new article of clothing,' she declares. 'It's almost *embarrassing* –'

'She gets care parcels from America. Some are the size of this room almost –'

'– I really am like the Imelda Marcos of Staffordshire. I must have, conservatively, a hundred pairs of shoes, none of which I've bought. We're talkin' Valentino, Ferragamo –'

'It's sort of a loaves and fishes kind of situation.'

'I have to be careful, in the sense that people just don't understand how it's worked for us,' Jeannie says, struggling for words. 'In a way – in a really sort of sick way – I wouldn't have missed it for the world, in that it's very easy to trust God when everything's going your way. But you try trusting Him when, uh –'

'– when you're in the shit.'

'But it's just been *absolutely* astonishing.'

'We've wanted for nothing.'

'It's been almost embarrassing at times.'

Roughly two G&Ts and three glasses of wine into the evening, Jeannie tells me about the family's history, and how one past Wolseley was fond of urinating in public.

'I shall go and follow his example,' Sir Charles declares, rising to his feet.

At first, I think he's joking; then he turns on his heel and disappears outside.

'Charles doesn't believe in flushing water down the toilet,' Jeannie says.

Which may explain the lack of toilets in their garden park.

While Sir Charles is apparently leaving his mark on territory that's no longer his, I opt for the indoor facilities. Afterwards, he tells me he doesn't blame Jeannie for his downfall; he went into the venture of his own free will. He seems somewhat bemused by the loss of his estate. 'It all sort of happened gradually . . . I got accustomed to the idea,' he says, adding quickly: 'As they say, the fat lady hasn't sung yet.'

The Wolseleys are still hoping to win back their estate 'one way or another'. 'We haven't been here a thousand years for nothing!' he says determinedly. 'And if I've been screwed, I'll screw back as best I can – even if it's up against the big boys. I know it's peanuts to *them*, but, y'know, the small guy can win.'

And with that, Sir Charles sums up just how far Britain's aristocracy has fallen: a former lord of the manor is just a little guy battling the 'big boys' of trade and industry.

'It's very sad for his son,' Jeannie says.

'He's marvellous.'

'He's been very good about his inheritance being lost, but we feel terrible about it. Because . . . you want to pass it on –'

'Well, that's what I was saying – the fat lady hasn't sung yet.'

'No, the fat lady's stood up, cleared her throat, and taken a deep breath – but she hasn't started to sing.'

It's the Sunday before the Horn Dance, and Cara Bagot is going to church. While her fellow parishioners have to drive to St Leonard's, for her, it's a short walk. The parish church stands right behind Blithfield Hall, having served for centuries as the Bagots' de facto private chapel, even though it was officially a public house of God. Lady Bagot is resting up for tomorrow, leaving her daughter to keep up a Bagot tradition all on her lonesome: sitting in the family pew in the chancel, near the altar and tombs, cut off from the congregation *and* the vicar by one of the few rood screens to survive England's Civil War.

Now, the first time I saw this crude class division – something I thought had died out *ages* ago – alive and well and passing without mention in the heart of twenty-first-century England – well . . . I couldn't believe my eyes. Not for the first time, I thought I'd strayed into the Middle Ages after leaving the motorway. And I wasn't the first foreigner to lose his bearings. An American Bagot told me he once asked the lady of the manor why she sat in the chancel rather than out in the nave.

'Because these are our *seats*,' Lady Bagot replied.

Despite their privileged seating, Lady Bagot and her daughter mix easily with the commoners. The church's two-dozen regulars are friendly folk from the surrounding farms, making St Leonard's a country church in a very old-fashioned, even feudal, sense of the term. After all, the lord and lady's patronage remained firmly in place well into the twentieth century, when Lady Bagot and her husband finally sold the right to appoint the parish priest to the Bishop of Lichfield.

Unfailingly polite, Cara has invited me to join her in the VIP part of the church. 'Otherwise, I'd have to sit up here in lowly state,' she whispers, obviously uncomfortable with her adopted duty. 'I think the people would like us to sit out there, but ma-mah's always been very insistent that *the Bagots have always sat here*.'

It's definitely a mixed blessing. The full-length seats may be more comfortable – the commoners' pews jab you in the back – but at least the nave has heating. Even now, in early September, there's a dank chill inside the chancel and a patch of moss thriving on the wall. In winter, it must be all one can do to keep one's stiff upper lip from quivering. 'They probably sit out there and laugh at us!' Cara jokes as the Reverend Davis welcomes the congregation.

From where we're sitting, the pastor actually has his back to us. To make sure we're still with him, he turns from the pulpit every once in a while to smile at us through the screen, Kris Kringle in robes, twinkling through the woodwork. After we sing a hymn and ask God to save the Queen, Davis begins his sermon. For his text, he's chosen a passage from the Bible that reminds you just how revolutionary Christianity once was. Given the audience, it also seems shockingly controversial. In a letter to his fellow believers, James, the half-brother of Jesus, admonishes them to treat each other equally. He starts off with an example: say two men come to your service, one wearing fancy clothes and expensive jewellery, and the other dressed shabbily. 'If you give special attention and a good seat to the rich person, well, doesn't this discrimination show that you are guided by wrong motives?' he asks.

And then Simon – I mean, James – really lets rip with the question and exclamation marks: 'Hasn't God chosen the poor in this world to be rich in faith? Aren't they the ones who will inherit the Kingdom he promised to those who love Him? And yet, you insult the poor man!' He goes on like this, and finally declares: 'If you pay special attention to the rich, you are committing a sin.'

In other words, the Reverend Davis explains, God doesn't make distinctions between the rich and the poor; it's man who creates the barriers. 'The worst case I've seen of this was in a church,' he says.

Cara turns to me with an embarrassed frown, no doubt worried he's going to single her out. With a searing rhetorical flourish, the vicar's going to point through the rood screen and shout: 'The worst case I've seen of this – has been right here – IN THIS VERY CHURCH!'

But, of course, he doesn't. Instead, he conveniently focuses on Somewhere Else – an old church in Somerset. One side had self-contained box pews eight feet high, some with their own fireplaces. Centuries ago, landed families could lock themselves away during church while the poor shivered on rough-hewn slabs outside in the nave. As the Reverend Davis stresses the importance of treating everyone equally, Cara sits cut off from the rest of the congregation, with only her adopted ancestors and me for company: the living and the dead. The tiny chancel has been stuffed to the rafters with memorials to the Bagots' glories – raised tombs, engraved images, sculpted effigies and marble slabs, dating from 1499 to a couple of decades ago, including a plaque marking where Cara's father used to sit. Before the service, she told me that the family used to fund the upkeep of the church. Then she echoed a wistful refrain that I'd first heard from her mother: 'Unfortunately, the Bagots are no more.'

The sermon ends with the vicar exhorting his audience to

disregard rank and riches. 'If you meet the binman, the *dustbin*man, treat him as if he were Prince Charles. And if you meet Prince Charles, treat him as if he were the dustbinman,' he declares.

In his own mild, button-nosed manner, this country vicar sounds hell-bent on levelling class barriers. During the prayers for the sick and the elderly, he refers to the church's patroness as 'Nancy Bagot' – not 'Lady Bagot'. Even more surprisingly, he doesn't put her at the top of the list; she's third or fourth down.

Cara must be seething. *So much for his invite to the Horn Dance soiree!* Why, back in the days when the Bagots were still running the place, they might have cut off his salary and kicked him out of the parish. 'Nancy Bagot' indeed!

But Cara wears her status very lightly. She doesn't seem at all peeved by the vaguely revolutionary content of the sermon. Either that, or she's simply chosen to ignore it, focusing on another aspect instead. Shaking the pastor's hand, she jokes about one of his other remarks; how people clam up at parties when they find out he's a vicar. 'I shall be very careful how I introduce you tomorrow, Simon,' she says, making a point of reminding him to bring his wife to tomorrow's garden party.

When I catch up with the vicar later, he's relaxing at the parsonage in Abbots Bromley. His blue shirt and dog collar say 'vicar on call', but his shorts and sandals say 'preacher-man off-duty'. He's shocked – *shocked* – to think that I could have misinterpreted his sermon as a call to storm the chancel and demand equal seating. 'Aw, *gosh, no!*' he says. 'The whole point of the sermon was, "Who cares where ya sit?" It doesn't matter two hoots, does it, really?' As for the reference to 'Nancy Bagot', he smiles – 'Well, if God isn't on first-name terms with her, then who is?'

Admittedly, Cara didn't seem at all offended by any of his remarks. 'Well, she wouldn't,' he grins and shrugs. 'When you know your congregation . . .'

And so, having fudged the issue in time-honoured Anglican fashion, everything stays the same: *As it was and ever shall be, world without end, Amen.*

*

However, this year there is change afoot in the Horn Dance. Tony Fowell is planning to hand over the horns to his eldest son and let him lead a few dances. 'I'll find some quieter places, and just let him loose, basically,' he says.

And then all hell will break loose. As the future leader of a quaint folk custom, you couldn't imagine a more unlikely character. Mark Fowell is a former punk rocker best known by the rest of the troupe for dancing with dreadlocks – and one year a multicoloured mohican. Hard living has left him much older than his thirty-odd years. He has the kind of malnourished look that would move many mothers to take him home and get some good food in his belly – *if* they weren't scared off by his tattoos, metal faceware and surly countenance. At most of the stops, he tends to collect his drink and slope off with a cousin to sit and smoke. He greets me with a sceptical squint, head cocked to one side, his earrings and eyebrow spike glinting in the sun. A medley of whorls and swirls sprawl across his thin frame – 14, at last count – a fox on one bicep, a snakeskin on the other, an eagle on his forearm, a pitbull on his chest, a fire-breathing skull on his shoulder, a naked girl in an inky mist on his wrist, and, most appropriately for today, a Horn Dance deer head on his right calf. All told, the bespoke scars would cost about £500, but Mark gets them free for serving as a guinea-pig canvas for a mate who's a tattooist (his friend is also a taxidermist, which will no doubt come in handy in the future). For now, though, the future of the Horn Dance rests on the narrow, tattooed shoulders of this spike-browed former punk turned occasional folk dancer.

And Mark seems to have his doubts about prancing around in short trousers. Although he pays lip service to the tradition, he's also blunt about his motivation. 'If truth be known, a lot of us just do it for the free beer,' he grins, explaining that he's currently out of work. When it comes to the task at hand, he puts on an undaunted façade. He has taken over for his dad a few times before. 'It's not all that bad, really. It's not too 'ard.'

Still, when the time comes to take over, he seems less sure of himself. Terry Bailey comes up while he's drinking on the sidelines of a redbrick Victorian farm.

'You want to lead it?' the jester says, telling him more than asking.

Mark looks at him like he's joking.

'Wot? Me?'

'Yeah! You want to lead it?' more insistently.

Whether he wants it or not, the leadership is thrust upon him, and Mark puts the men through their paces. 'The problem is, he's still young and full of energy,' Tony says in praise of his son. 'Whereas I usually make 'em dance for five minutes and stop, he makes 'em go for five minutes, and then he really starts to dance.'

Strangely, some dancers don't even know Mark's name, even though they're his relatives. That can't bode well for his leadership potential. Throughout the day, he does command the crowd's attention – but for all the wrong reasons. Waggish onlookers refer to him as 'the one with the trainers' or, even more damningly, 'the one with the Walkman' – *guess he must not like the music!* Actually, the black cord in his ear is connected to a mobile phone. That's why he mumbles to himself while to-ing and fro-ing. 'I can just talk while I'm dancin'. It doesn't look so obvious.' At least not as obvious as it could. If it weren't for the earpiece, he'd have to whip out his mobile every few minutes to tell his friends where he is: *I'm dancing at Blithfield for a bunch of toffs! Yeah, I know – but the beer's free!*

Lady Bagot is throwing her garden party for the country gentry: grey hairs all around, with more floral prints on display than there are flowers in the natural world, plus every tweed known to man and a few rogue specimens of polyester. They're all assembled on the lawn of Blithfield Hall to watch the Horn Dance on a warm day that's more like late summer than early autumn.

Afterwards, the dancers stand at attention along the edge of the ha-ha with their horns at their feet. Lady Bagot works her way down the line, making polite conversation worthy of the queen herself, but the niceties elude her when she comes to one dancer.

'This is Mark, my oldest son,' Tony says proudly.

'Oh, hello,' the lady says, shaking his hand.

That spike – those earrings!

She turns to Tony. 'Do you have any more family here?'

Lady Bagot's not the only one lost for words. After last night's sesh, the Wolseleys are looking a little delicate. I said hello to them when they arrived, but they seemed somewhat embarrassed – or maybe they were simply trying to keep the gravel from grinding too loudly underfoot.

Ever the impeccable hostess, Cara Bagot approaches the Wolseleys and a couple of plummy acquaintances.

'Would you like to come talk to the horn dancers?'

They're hardly going to say no, so Sir Charles, Jeannie and their friends trudge over to the line-up. 'What do you ask a horn dancer?' one of the men wonders.

But of course – the old fallback. '*Boiling* hot,' he suggests to a dancer.

'It must be the hottest day you've had in years,' Sir Charles adds.

Later, at lunch, one of the dancers reflects on his impressions of the gentry. 'I'm always surprised how little they know,' he muses, chewing a white-bread sandwich outside the hall. 'You get better questions from the common people.'

As the dancers head into the village, a female Fowell is roped into donning a costume to replace one of the men. 'But I'm not takin' my lippy off,' she jokes, tucking her hair under her cap. Lynne Roper is one of musician Doug Fowell's six daughters. The oldest member of the group, Doug has had a brush with skin cancer in recent years, and the dark-brown patch of skin on his right hand seems to flare up during Horn Dance Day – hardly surprising, considering that the melodeon strap constantly rubs against it. Although he flags toward the end of the day, Doug stubbornly plays on, just as he's done for more than fifty of the past 65 years he's been in the dance. In any event, the eldest Fowell looks a lot younger than his seventy-three years. Earlier, somebody told him that his brother was doing a good job in the dance.

'Brother? I haven't got a brother,' Doug replied.

Then he realised – the man meant Tony, his nephew, who is twenty years his junior. 'But don't tell Tony that!' he laughs.

Meanwhile, his daughter tells me outside the Crown that she's 'well chuffed' to have the rare opportunity to carry the horns. 'The lads know how much this day means to us, and we've always regretted, sort of, not being a boy to be able to do it – officially, so to speak. I've heard a lot of comments from people saying, "My God, it's a woman!"' She and her sisters are careful not to upset the way things are. 'I am big into tradition, and I do honestly believe that if it is a man's thing, then it should be left a man's thing.'

Inside the Crown, the men are finishing their tea, and Tony is having a smoke. The pain has kicked in, spreading from the base of his spine to his legs and shoulders.

I ask why he's not taking any medication.

He smiles. 'If I 'ave painkillers, I can't drink, can I?'

One of his cousins comes up and tells him that Mark's been in the toilet for a half hour; they're worried about him.

'He's pissed,' Tony mutters, struggling to his feet like an old man with rusted-out joints. Just as he manages to stand, his son appears, unsteady and dishevelled.

'Take it easy on the ale,' Tony says.

'What?' A sullen, red-eyed stupor.

His father mumbles a reprimand.

'You call this pissed?' Mark protests, defiantly doing up his waistcoat.

He misses a button.

The dancers set off on their final foray. At the Coach and Horses, Tony reckons his son will stay inside until the other dancers drag him out. And that's just what they have to do. This time it's Terry who tells him that Mark has locked himself in the toilet.

As someone else goes to check on his son, Tony tells me he doesn't think either of his boys has what it takes to be leader of the Horn Dance. 'Whatever *it* is.'

I point out that people probably said the same about him; he was a hellraiser, too, in his day. Tony nods, but he's already discounted it. When he was Mark's age, he was married with a son and he had spent four years in the army. So at least some sense of responsibility had been knocked into him.

Most years, by this time in the evening, Tony starts thinking about hanging up the Great Horns for good, but there's no chance of retirement yet. 'That's one of the reasons I keep pushin' it back,' he sighs. 'No one wants to take over. No one wants the responsibility.' Weary and hurting, he braces himself for the triumphant return to the church – *soon I'm going to hang this damn horn up* – knowing full well that he'll be back next year unless he can find someone else to shoulder the burden. And even if his sons don't follow in his footsteps, he knows that the family legacy will continue one way or another. Maybe his younger brother will take over – or his cousin, who has a son, who has a baby boy of his own.

'There's enough of us,' he says. 'It will always go to a Fowell, regardless.'

CHAPTER SEVEN

THE OOGLY TRUTH ABOUT ENGLAND

GURNIN' IN EGREMONT

THE COUPLE THAT GURNS TOGETHER: The Woods prove that the longer people live together, the more they look alike.

BUTTOCKING, ROUGH BITCHES AND THE BIG FACE-OFF

Newsflash – the World's Ugliest Man works in a nuclear power plant, and the World's Ugliest Woman is . . . an Avon lady.

That's what they say in Egremont, and they should know. Every year, supposedly since 1267, this hard-luck town outside the Lake District has hosted the World Gurning Championships, where men, women and children compete to pull the ugliest face. But don't think the naturally ugly, or 'oogly', have an unfair advantage. Contestants are judged on their before-and-after transformations. 'Say you're oogly in the first place, and ya pull a gurn, an' you don't look much different,' explains champion Peter Jackman. 'Well, just because you're oogly doesn't mean to say that ya win it. Because gurnin' means the Art of Pullin' Faces, not oogliness.' Unfortunately, that distinction is lost on some contestants. 'There's one lady in particular. She was ugly to start with, and she didn't look any different when she gurned,' chuckles organiser Alan Clements. 'Then you get fellows like Peter. He's a good-lookin' guy, but he can make himself into a monster – that's what you're lookin' for.'

Gold-medal gurners train like Olympic champions, experimenting with different faces until they hit on a suitably ugly mug. Most give their faces a nickname. All-time champ Gordon Mattinson called his Quasimodo, while the late Ron Looney named his Popeye – though surely his own last name would have worked just as well. An Australian stands out for having one of the weirdest gurns in recent memory. 'He used his eyes – that's never been done before,' Clements recalls. 'He could actually turn one one way and one the other way.' However, the Aussie's odd eyeballs weren't enough to convince gurning aficionados: 'He was movin' his eyes and showin' his teeth, basically. He didn't do a lot with his face.' In general, amateurs rarely make it to the final round. 'They don't really know what gurnin's about,' says Jackman. 'They've gotta try and learn and look up the rules of gurnin'.' Try as they might, though, first-timers are unlikely to find any regulations for the essentially free-style event. 'Somebody asked me, "Do you think gurnin's a sport?" ' another finalist recalls. 'I said, "It's the oogliest sport in the world. Where else in the world is there an oogly sport like this?" '

As the de facto World Gurning Capital, Egremont is as fitting a place as any for a celebration of ugliness. Although its centre is pretty enough, with castle ruins, Victorian churches and the occasional sandstone building, once you stray from Main Street, you find petrol stations, industrial estates and long rows of gritcast housing. You'd never guess that this former mining town is only a few miles from some of the most scenic sights in England. Stranded on the coast of West Cumbria amid sloping hills and farmland, Egremont is locked out of the Lake District by the mountains that form a natural amphitheatre around that famously beautiful region. Instead, the steaming towers of Sellafield – the site of the world's first nuclear accident – blight the views around Egremont, while the Irish Sea lies just out of reach, depriving the town of seafront sunsets. The name of a nearby hamlet, Nethertown, could just as easily apply to Egremont itself.

In fact, West Cumbria is something of a nether land, a remote, put-upon corner of Northern England stuck between Wales and Scotland. A succession of unsightly industries has marred the area over the years, from coal and iron ore mines to chemical factories and nuclear reactors. 'This area has always been known as a doomp,' says local historian Alan Read. 'It's far from the southern part of the country where the Old Boys are, and they're not interested in north-west England.' The few tourists who do visit are easy to spot; they're the ones who don't have tattoos. In addition to *de rigueur* gold earrings, many Egremont men – and women – have sprawling blue-green scars that look like they've been there since birth. You wonder if the hospital gives mothers a choice for their newborns: 'Would you like the skull and crossbones on your baby's forearm or the dripping dagger inscribed with 𝕸𝖔𝖙𝖍𝖊𝖗?'

However, none of this should be seen as a slur against Egremothians themselves. Like most West Cumbrians, they're some of the friendliest people you could meet. If you show the slightest interest in Egremont, the locals will go out of their way to tell you all they can, with an enthusiasm that would be unheard of in the tourist-jaded towns of the Lake District. Ask a stranger about the castle, and he'll give you an impromptu tour. Ask about the Florence Mine, and the attendant will fetch the owner to help you. Ask Hartley's ice cream store about their unusual flavours (*Christmas Pudding ice cream?*), and the owner will stop to explain the origin of every one of them. Mention that you attended the gurning championships, the highlight of Egremont's Crab Fair, and they'll eagerly seek your reaction – did you really, *really* like it? Honestly?

Known colloquially as 't'Crab', the age-old festival ranks as the town's big day. 'You have the Seven Wonders of the World – you have Christmases, Easters – but for Egremont, it's Crab Fair Day,' says gurning champ Peter Jackman. Sure enough, the local newspaper reckons the fair is one of '100 Reasons to be Proud of West Cumbria', although it ranks well behind the region's natural attractions, its strong links with America (number 8), Egremont Castle (12), locally made Kangol hats (13) and native son William Wordsworth (34). Bizarrely, even the notorious nuclear plant outranks the Crab Fair by one spot at number 44. 'Only stupid people do gurning,' a local mother explains. 'When you go on holiday, you don't say "I'm from Egremont." You say you're from Cumbria. Otherwise, people say "Oh, that's that place where they pull them faces!" It's embarrassin'.'

Gurning is billed as a bit of fun today, but sensitive souls might frown on its origins. As far as anyone knows, the contest began centuries ago as a mockery of the village idiot. 'They used to put a horse collar around his neck and let him gurn and then treat him to a pint or two,' the town historian says. 'In those days, the poor lad who was the village idiot, the mickey was always taken out of him – in all places. But in Egremont, it seems to have continued and become a competition finally: who could pull the – well, I don't know what you would call it – the worst face or the best face.'

The Crab Fair itself supposedly dates from an annual festival started in 1267. Given its name – and the fact that the Irish Sea is just next door – you might think the Crab Fair has something to do with crabs. In actuality, it gets its name from crab apples (though these too are strangely absent from the event). In the Middle Ages, peasants would pay their debts during the harvest festival, topping up their dues with wild fruit. Tradition has it that the Lord of Egremont would then return some of this bounty to them by throwing crab apples at the serfs' children. Now, having the lord of the manor pelt your kids with sour green apples might seem like the final insult after a lifetime of exploitation. In the hand-to-mouth Middle Ages, though, the serfs would have happily eaten any scrap of food thrown at them. Even more importantly, it must have been fun for the lord, watching his littlest subjects fight for food. So everybody had a good time.

Come to think of it, modern do-gooders could learn a lesson from the old sado-charities of yore: to get the rich to give, you have to make it *fun*. Take the Hot Pennies tradition that used to be popular throughout Britain. In Beaumaris, Wales, the big-hearted English gentry would throw steaming pennies into the street on Boxing Day to see Welsh waifs fight for the money . . . and burn their little fingers. In those days, it truly was better to give than receive. Surprisingly, several places in England still re-enact this custom, most notably at Oxford University. Famous alumni of Oxford's Lincoln College include John Wesley and Dr Seuss, though it's unclear whether the preacher or the writer ever took part in hurling Hot Pennies. On Ascension Day – that's forty days after Easter – students stand on the roof of the college and pelt hot pennies at townie school kids. Nowadays, though, the children come prepared – they wear gloves.

As for Egremont's Crab Fair, the legend lives on in the form of the Parade of the Apple Cart, in which bystanders are bombarded with fruit. However, that's just a warm-up for the main attraction. During the World Gurning Championships, contestants stick their faces through a leather horse collar or 'braffin' and pull a face for up to a minute. Besides being able to claim he's the Ugliest Man in the World, the winner gets a silver mug, a trophy and a cash prize. 'It's just a hundred pound,' Alan Clements says. 'We're makin' money for charity. We're not out to make people rich.'

Like Alan, most locals describe gurning in jocular terms, but Peter Jackman talks about it with the passion of a man who's found his calling in life. Normally all jokes and smiles, he turns dead serious when discussing the 'Art of Pullin' Faces'. 'I do think that I was put here to gurn,' he says earnestly. 'I am an Egremont person. I've got love and heart in gurnin'. There's nothing else that I want to do – or even dream of.'

For all his enthusiasm, the 42-year-old Sellafield worker discovered his knack for unattractiveness late in life. His nephew started him on the road to gurning greatness on Crab Fair Day in 1992, when Peter entered on the spur of the moment and came in third. What began as a whim quickly turned into a passion. Within three years, he won the championship. Since then, gurning has turned Peter into a local celebrity, with a couple of national TV appearances to boot. A local pub has even served a special Crab Fair brew with a picture of him gurning on the tap.

When's he's not gurning, Peter looks like a middle-aged elf, what with his bald, high-domed head, grey-flecked goatee and low-slung beer belly. 'I've always been a good-lookin' baby,' he laughs, but then he transmogrifies from a good-natured gnome into a snarling gargoyle. Whereas other gurners go for the Village Idiot Look – all crossed eyes and goofy grins – Peter strives for a more sinister visage: the deranged psychopath. Grunting and growling, he rolls his eyes back in his head like a demonic doll and shoves his dentures under his lips to form a U-shaped crater around his nose. Like any great artist, Peter spent years experimenting before hitting on his winning face. The two other gurns in his repertoire include one inspired by Stan Laurel, the dopey half of Laurel and Hardy, who hailed from nearby Ulverston. 'I used to smile, take me teeth out and play with the top o' me head like Stan used to do.' However, comedy soon gave way to terror: 'Y'know the alien in *Predator*? That was one o' me early names – Predator. I used to try an' feel ugly an' look ugly as the alien in *Predator*.'

His breakthrough came late one night while watching clips from old Dracula movies, or 'fillums', on TV. 'It was a fillum called *The Face at the Window*,' he says. 'It's the very first Dracula fillum that Bela Lugosi was in. He just kinda like walked to the window, lookin' through to see 'is victim – and that face resembles me – bald 'ead, biggish ears and white eyes. When I saw that, I thought, yes, I've gotta have that look. That's my gurnin' face – Bela Lugosi.' (For the record, Lugosi didn't appear in *The Face at the Window*, a 1939 film about a killer wolf-man. But hey – it's a good story.)

Aptly enough, the World Gurning Championships take place on land once owned by a madman. During the Victorian era, the owner was locked up by the indelicately titled 'Masters of Lunacy'. After his death, the local council acquired the Main Street property to build a town hall and an auditorium. A few years ago, the Victorian market hall hosted a mix-up that would have tested even the Masters of Lunacy. The Great Gurning Fiasco involved an actor, a strongman, and two Peters. The trouble began when the organisers invited John Evans, International Head Balancer and Strongman, to help judge the gurning. Evans had entertained the Crab Fair that afternoon by balancing dishwashers, beer barrels, and even a 352-pound Mini Cooper car on his head. 'But let's face it,' a local tells me, 'you don't 'ave to be very smart to balance things on your 'ead.'

Unfortunately, Evans and his sidekick got the contestants mixed up. Instead of marking Peter Jackman as the winner – as the other judges did – they mistakenly wrote down the number of another Peter who was from out of town. When the interloper was declared the winner, the audience started booing and throwing beer bottles. The disputed winner was just as surprised.

'This guy from Manchester was actually leavin' the hall at the time. He wasn't able to gurn, and we'd announced him as the winner,' groans Alan Clements. 'The worst thing possible happened after that – this guy's an actor. And he had an agent. So his agent told the media, and they got it on the front pages of the tabloids.' By the time the organisers corrected the error, there were red faces all around. 'Things Turn Ugly After Face-Off in World Gurning Contest' joked one national newspaper. 'Officials Grimace After Gurning Error' another cracked.

The confusion also caused hard feelings among the contestants. 'They didn't do themselves any favours,' grumbled Gordon Mattinson, who finished in second place behind Jackman. 'It was a helluva mix-up.'

As the World's Ugliest Woman, Anne Woods is not your average Avon Lady. Winner of nearly two dozen championship titles, she's a before-and-after testimonial for cosmetics. At rest, her face has a certain sweetness etched with the wrinkles from a lifetime of smoking. When she gurns, though, this diminutive, grey-headed granny transforms herself into her customers' worst nightmare – a crater-faced hag. 'She shows 'em what could happen if they don't buy make-up,' her husband jokes. Unlike the Avon Ladies of popular imagination, Anne doesn't go for coiffed hair, colour-coordinated suits or even make-up. Instead, she favours the casual look – T-shirt, jeans and trainers.

Anne claims her customers aren't put off by the prospect of buying make-up from the World's Ugliest Woman. However, she was initially worried that Avon might disapprove. When she confessed her ugly secret, though, her superiors didn't bat a mascara-lashed eye. 'They were pleased – I think. They just said we could go ahead with what we were doin'.' Fortunately, they didn't ask Anne to wear make-up while she gurns. 'By the time you were finished, the lipstick would be all over the place,' she says, marking a messy crescent across her forehead.

Anne got into the gurning game back in 1977 when her sons entered her into the contest as a joke. Despite her nerves, she won the first time out. 'It was great,' she recalls, sitting surrounded by trophies in her living room. 'It was a real surprise.'

Not as big a surprise as it was for her husband, a burly former oilrig worker. Alex Woods found out about her victory the hard way. 'This bloke come up and said, "Your wife's just won the gurnin'." Well, I thought he was takin' the piss. So I lifted him up the wall,' he says, raising a big, meaty fist to demonstrate. 'And when I found out she *had* won, I had to say "Sorry, fella." He's never spoken to me since!' Alex guffaws. 'Well, if someone comes up to you and says, "Your wife's just won the world championship for the Oogliest Woman in the World", you don't take it as a bit of fun, do ya?'

These days, Anne hardly gets nervous at all, except about outsiders, such as the Londoner who came up one year. 'I thought, "She's got to be oogly, if she's comin' all the way from London."' But nobody's uglier than Anne when she gurns. Dentures out, she crumples her face so completely that her upper jaw disappears, concealed by her button-flap lower lip. Unlike most champion gurners, she doesn't have a nickname for her gurn. 'I think she took it off a donkey walkin' up and down the road,' Alex jeers. More than twenty years after his wife's debut, he has also been bitten by the ugly bug. Like Anne, Alex removes his teeth to gurn, but he has an added advantage – a broken nose from a fight when he was in his twenties. Thanks to a flying barstool, Alex can twist his proboscis to touch the middle of his cheek, tucking it under his lip so that it lies flat against his face when he gurns. He won third in his first year, and he hopes to win the main title someday . . . by a nose.

Even so, he'll have a long way to go to catch Anne. Her winning streak has been interrupted only once, by rival Pauline Hoyles, an eccentric with gypsy heritage who lives in a caravan. Alex reckons Pauline has 'a face like a camel's arse' (though I'd say it's more like a warthog's face, what with her bulging eyes and jutting lower teeth). Apart from Pauline's one-off victory, what really rankles the Woods is that she supposedly shouts 'It's a fix!' when Anne wins. For her part, Pauline has told me that she has no ill feelings toward Anne. 'Her and I are the best of friends now . . . I *think*,' Pauline says, denying that she's ever claimed the competition is rigged.

Still, she wouldn't be the first out-of-towner to argue that Egremothians have a hometown advantage. 'Every time. *Every* time,' says Roy Millington, a 'foreigner' from Derbyshire. 'That cup's on an elastic band, and it stays up 'ere. I don't say it's fixed, but I don't think it goes out of this county. It cannot go outta this county.'

*

Egremothians have gurning in their genes, a knack that may come from living next to the home of the world's first major nuclear accident (and the second worst, after Chernobyl). Sellafield, Britain's most controversial nuclear plant, stands five miles from Egremont, situated incongruously between the Irish Sea and the Lake District. Which raises a question: why build a nuclear plant near one of Britain's national treasures? For Egremothians, the answer is simple. 'Because we're the little *blip*,' grumbles Alan Read. 'West Cumberland 'as never been a place of any consequence with Labour or Conservative governments for, ay, seventy years. If anything happened, it just meant that West Cumbria would have cracked off, floated into the Irish Sea and disappeared.'

Originally called Windscale, Sellafield has its roots in the A-bomb race after World War Two. Given that atom splitting was in its infancy, a lot of guesswork was built into Piles No. 1 and 2. Nevertheless, Windscale's reactors eventually came up with the glow-in-the-dark goods, and Britain exploded its first plutonium bomb in 1952. Having ensured its A-list status, the UK then focused on producing nuclear power, hailed by Winston Churchill as 'a perennial fountain of world prosperity'. In 1956, Queen Elizabeth visited Windscale to flick the switch on the world's first full-scale nuclear power station. 'It may well prove to have been the greatest of our contributions to human welfare that we led the way in demonstrating the peaceful uses of this new source of power,' she said.

As it turned out, Britain led the way in demonstrating how dangerous the new technology could be. A year later, in October 1957, a routine test at Windscale Pile No. 1 overheated the graphite core, triggering a full-blown nuclear fire within the reactor. Rather than a hellish inferno, the blaze was insidiously cosy, like a coalfire full of embers – only the embers were 2,000 tons of glowing carbon burning at more than 1,200 degrees Celsius. Sellafield manager Bill Rooney, then an eighteen-year-old apprentice, remembers something strange about one of the massive chimneys that morning. 'We noticed there was smoke coming out of the top of it, and thought it was a bit . . . *unusual*.'

To say the least. He and others were immediately drafted in to fight the fire, shunting thousands of radioactive fuel cartridges out of the reactor's core, just as you might use a poker to knock embers out of a coalfire. In this case, though, the pokers were scaffolding poles scrounged from the site. The crews rammed them into holes in the seven-foot-thick wall of reinforced concrete, the only barrier between them and the radioactive core. 'The official version of events is that these volunteers were all fitted out with respirators and protective clothing . . . but the official version is still disputed by some who were there,' writes Harold Bolter in *Inside Sellafield*, the only in-depth history of the plant. The former Sellafield executive cites stories of men removing red-hot rods dripping with molten metal. However, Rooney disputes this, arguing that the rods would have been lethal. He also says health officials gauged each man's radiation exposure, and no one worked at the face of the fire for more than ten minutes. 'I don't see it's done me any harm, do you?' he jokes, surveying his fulsome belly.

After two days of trying to put out the fire, Windscale's scientists risked a desperate last attempt to prevent meltdown: they decided to pour water on it. At the time, even the men who made the decision knew it was extremely dangerous. The combination of water and burning graphite and uranium could have created an explosive hydrogen-fuelled fireball that would have spewed radiation into the air, just as Chernobyl did thirty years later. 'The hydrogen released could have exploded the whole shebang,' Rooney says. Even so, the eggheads took the risk, calculating that if enough water were pumped in fast enough, the fire would be extinguished.

Fortunately, it worked – but not before two bursts of radioactivity spewed into the air, sending invisible clouds of contamination across England and the rest of Europe. Incredibly, West Cumbrians weren't warned about the fire until it had been put out, and the media didn't report on the top-secret accident until after the fact. During the two days the fire contaminated the environment, there were no public warnings to stay indoors. The locals didn't know that their lives were being put at risk by scientists attempting a seemingly simpleminded solution – *Let's pour water on it!* 'Evacuation might have been as dangerous as the fire itself if there had been mass panic,' Bolter argues. Whereas the US required nuclear power plants to be linked to four-lane highways, the only way out of this corner of West Cumbria was a narrow two-lane road (still the main route today).

According to official accounts, no one was killed in the fire itself. However, as world-class nuclear accidents go, Windscale ranks a solid second: worse than Three Mile Island in 1979, but far less serious than Chernobyl in 1986. Coincidentally, in the long term, Chernobyl's fallout is expected to kill as many as 100 people in Britain – the same number of cancer deaths caused across the UK by the Windscale Fire. Just seven years after they opened, Windscale's reactors were sealed, never to be used again. Nearly half a century later, they've yet to be dismantled. With their narrow chimneys and rectangular bases, the piles loom over the landscape like massive dynamite plungers. Sellafield's scientists have racked their brains to figure out how to tear down the buildings safely, but they still haven't worked out how to prevent the fifteen tons of uranium in the core from reigniting during decommissioning, potentially triggering a repeat of the first Windscale Fire.

Bizarrely, Sellafield now has its very own Visitors' Centre, which ranks as one of the top tourist sites in West Cumbria, second only to Carlisle Cathedral among freebie attractions. More than 100,000 people visit Sellafield Visitors' Centre every year, compared with 2,000 for Egremont's forlorn Florence Mine. The reason for the nuclear plant's popularity is simple: 'They let you in for nowt,' a pensioner says, praising The Sellafield Experience. What's more, the company effectively *pays* for people to visit. Sellafield buses in school kids free of charge.

Rather than a reality waiting to be satirised, the centre is satire already realised, and well ahead of its time, too. An old episode of *The Simpsons* features a parody of a public information film fronted by Smilin' Joe Fission, an atomic cartoon cowboy that talks down to kids on school trips. Sure enough, Sellafield has its own cartoon mascot named Mighty Atom, a cheery sundot with a smiling yellow nucleus for a face that's ringed by red electrons. The mascot's trust-me, tyke-o'-the-north accent makes him perfect for the light entertainment bits, while a female narrator weighs in for the serious science. Her cool, calming tones are reminiscent of HAL, the psychotic computer in *2001: A Space Odyssey* and the movie's theme of technology overpowering humans.

Incidentally, Sellafield has its own lurking menace called HAL: the hot radioactive waste, or 'highly-active liquor', that's been building up at the plant since the 1950s. Sellafield's HAL tanks contain 2,100 kilos of highly radioactive caesium, the same stuff released by Chernobyl. And here's the scary bit: the Ukrainian disaster managed to contaminate Europe by spewing only 27 kilos of caesium into the atmosphere. Sellafield's stockpile could produce a far worse catastrophe, particularly if terrorists copied the 9/11 attacks on New York and Washington. According to some experts, a direct hit on the plant with an airliner full of fuel could discharge as much as half the HAL into the air, producing a cataclysm at least forty-four times worse than Chernobyl and contaminating Britain, Ireland and much of the Continent.

On your way into the centre, you can actually see the runner-up to Chernobyl: the tall, narrow chimneys of Windscale less than half a mile away – but if kids from Chernobyl can enjoy The Sellafield Experience, who am I to grumble? Every year a charity called the Friends of Chernobyl's Children sponsors a dozen kids to come to Cumbria for a month, to help build up their immune systems. At the very least, it seems bizarre to deliver victims of the world's worst nuclear mishap to the site of its rival 1,500 miles away, unless it's part of some morbid package holiday (*next stop – Three Mile Island!*). Joking aside, though, the kids come from a factory-choked city in Belarus, where most of the fallout from Chernobyl landed. Operations for thyroid cancer are so common there that the scars are known as a Belorussian Necklace. Compared with their home-town, the Cumbrian countryside must seem hazard-free, nuclear plant or not. 'It's quite ironic,' the charity's organiser admits, 'one of the best days out that the children ever had was to the visitors' centre at Sellafield.'

*

The World Gurning Championships cap a week of events so thoroughly wholesome, so wilfully old-fashioned, that they verge on the perverse in this postmodern age. While drugs, fetish clubs and 'alternative' lifestyles are well on their way to becoming the norm in London and other trend-setting capitals, Egremont and its clean-cut Crab Fair could end up as the counterculture of the future. You can imagine a time, say a century from now, when few would blink at the idea of a prime minister whose pastime is 'pleasuring himself' while bound in a body bag – *That's his choice, and I respect it.* But gurning? Wheelbarrow racing? *What kinda sicko are you?*

The main festivities start on Saturday with two events that hark back to the hard-knock days of yore – the Greasy Pole and the Parade of the Apple Cart. Around 8 a.m., the organisers hoist a lard-smeared pole in the centre of town with a leg of lamb on top as bait. The Greasy Pole used to be a big hit with kids back in the days when a broken neck must have seemed like a small price to pay for putting meat on the table. Nowadays, despite some half-hearted attempts to shinny up the thirty-foot pole, kids don't feel the need to risk their necks for a few pounds of lamb. The meat usually ends up languishing on the pole until the organisers take it down.

The subsequent Parade of the Apple Cart isn't so much a parade as an all-out assault, while the cart is actually a flat-bedded truck trundling down Main Street. The organisers stand on the back and laugh as they chuck hundreds of apples at people. Instead of running away, the throngs crowd the street. Every time a volley of red-and-green apples fills the air, a dozen arms shoot out to catch the flying fruit. A middle-aged woman with a child on her shoulders manages to snatch an airborne apple. 'YES! YES! YES!' she squeals, jumping up and down. Men muscle each other out of the way so they can pluck a piece of fruit from the air. The youngsters scamper after the truck, begging to have an apple thrown at them. From their excitement, you'd think the treats were sweets or chocolate bars, not apples the size of tennis balls.

A flying apple nails a boy on the head. He starts to howl, but that doesn't happen as often as you'd think in this rough-and-tumble town; most of the kids don't cry when they get hit. 'It almost knocked me out!' a girl laughs, rubbing her budding concussion.

After the Attack of the Apple Truck, the fair moves to the outskirts of town. An anonymous cow pasture has been converted into a Sports Field for the day, hosting dog shows, bicycle racing and daredevil stuntmen. Young mums push babies over the cow-patted minefield as the voice on the loudspeaker mutters strange requests: 'Can we have the under-23-inch rough bitch in the bottom lurcher ring, please?' Meanwhile, the chimneys of Sellafield loom in the distance, giving added encouragement to donate generously to the leukaemia foundation at the entrance.

In the centre of the field, men are grappling against each other in Cumberland Wrestling, a unique style thought to date from the Viking invasions a thousand years ago. To wrestle Cumberland-style, you first have to 'tek hod', or take hold, by locking your hands behind your opponent's back. The object is to throw him flat on his back without breaking his hostile hug. Oddly enough, clergymen used to excel at this sport, and Egremont lays claim to one of its great innovators. Abraham Brown, born around 1750, was a local curate and wrestling champ credited with adding the throw known as 'buttocking' to the sport's repertoire. Now, I've never been 'buttocked' myself, but from what I gather, the move essentially involves throwing your opponent on his backside. Over the years, variations have evolved, ranging from the 'full buttock' to the 'cross-buttock' and what must be the worst fall of all, the dreaded 'leg-up buttock'.

Apart from its strange terminology, Cumberland Wrestling has one of the most unique uniforms in the history of sport. The wrestlers – all muscular, even macho men – wear white long johns with tank tops, complemented by velvet underpants worn on the outside of their uniform and dark socks pulled up over their ankles. What's more, the entire get-up is *embroidered* with colourful birds and flowers. One young man has a bouquet of needlepoint flowers blooming from his groin, while a little boy has a small wreath stitched on his bottom. Come to think of it, Cumberland's wrestlers, with their fancy dress and hard-man muscles, may be the closest modern equivalent to the enlightened athletes envisioned by the ancient Greeks – hugging and 'buttocking' each other by day and embroidering flowers on their underpants by night.

Reeee-Reeeee-Reeeee!

Gai-guh, gai-guh, gai-guh, gai-guh!!!!

Over on the other side of the field, the hound-trailing races have reached their crazed climax. Men, women and children are waiting for the trained dogs to bound into view after following a ten-mile aniseed-scented trail around the fells. A dozen grizzled farmers stand next to a clapped-out car that's been converted into a makeshift betting shop. They're wearing tweed jackets and flat caps from the Kangol factory down the road in Cleator, the unlikely home of global hip-hop accessories. Armed with binoculars and walking sticks, they gather next to the hedgerow to spot the first dogs leaping across the field. The dogs' owners seem to have superhuman vision: as soon as their hounds appear – small white dots bouncing against the green landscape – the trainers start barking, shrieking, warbling and whistling in a cacophony of hoarse encouragement.

Jack-ay, Jack-ay, Jack-ay, Jack-ay!

Go-oooooooooonnnnnnnnnnnnnnnnnnn!!!!!!!!!!

Ick-bod, ick-bod, ick bod, ick-bod!!!

Ai-ya! Ai-ya! Ai-ya!

This unholy howling echoes across the fields until the hounds scatter a flock of sheep and finally leap over a fence to reach their bucketful of reward at the end.

As if that weren't exciting enough, the fair also includes a Chip Pan Fire Demonstration. A pot of fat burns ominously on a stovetop in a small hut as an old fireman addresses the crowd. Careless fathers have been known to come home from the pub, turn on the kitchen deep-fat fryer for a late-night snack, and fall asleep – *never to wake up again*. The point of the pyrotechnics is to warn potato-eaters that they should never dowse a grease fire with water (instead, you should smother it with a damp rag).

'Andy's now goin' to demonstrate what happens when you put water on a chip pan fire,' the veteran narrates in meat-and-two-veg tones.

A can-do fireman in full protective gear meekly opens the door of the hut. While the audience watches eagerly, he pours a long ladleful of water on the fire and jumps back. A splattering *BOOM*, and an orange fireball fills the hut like a miniature mushroom cloud. The crowd is hushed into awestruck silence. A little girl starts to cry.

'So, dads, if you're goin' out to the pub, stop off at the takeaway and sleep safely,' the narrator concludes grimly.

If that's not entertainment, I don't know what is.

Brrrrrrrrrrrrrrrriiiiiiiiiiiiiiiiiiiiiiinnnnnnnnnnnnnnnnnnnnggggggggggggg!!!!!!!!!

My God, it's hot in here. So hot the fire alarm's ringing – but there's no fire. It's just the combined body heat of hundreds of spectators crammed into Egremont's market hall. The small all-purpose auditorium has the pine-strip floor of a gymnasium and the striped pink-and-green wallpaper of a provincial dinner theatre. It's the kind of place that hosts a fitness class one night and a tea dance the next. Tonight, it's standing room only at the back, and the lobby is brimming with latecomers anxiously awaiting Egremont's main attraction – the World Gurning Championships.

The festivities started calmly enough hours ago, with a brass band and a junior talent contest, featuring an Ode to the Apple Cart, a kiddie impersonation of Elvis and a boy who could turn his tummy into an elephant's face. However, the night quickly turned noxious with the old-fashioned pipe-smoking contest. The rules for the smoke-off are simple – the first to finish a small pipeful wins. But the 'bacca' is hard-packed, and the old-fashioned pipes are made of clay, so the harder the contestants suck, the hotter the pipe gets, burning their lips and hands. Dull-eyed and drooling, the men and women smoke themselves into a haze, sending great, billowing clouds of queasy smoke drifting over the children beneath the stage. The kids were trapped between the pipe smokers in front of them and the cigarette-puffing spectators behind, but they didn't seem to mind; they're blissed out on the Coke, candy and crisps being fed to them by adults on the sidelines.

Brrrrrrrrrrrrrrrriiiiiiiiiiiiiiiiiiiiiiinnnnnnnnnnnnnnnnnnnnggggggggggggg!!!!!!!!!!

Somebody's finally opened the side doors, but you wouldn't

know it. The air's so thick you could snorkel through it, a humid mixture of sweat, smoke and booze. Huge drops of perspiration are going to come splashing down from the ceiling any second now. Still, these farmers, odd-jobbers and nuclear plant workers wouldn't mind. They've withstood the heat with sturdy determination, sipping their pints and fluttering makeshift fans. After four hours of endurance, including at least three repetitions of the theme to *Titanic* – 'My Heart Will Go On' and on, and on – they're not about to give in now. They'll get through this if it kills them.

Only half a dozen women volunteer for the Ladies' Gurning, and Anne Woods hangs back to make sure she's the last onstage. In her pink Crab Fair T-shirt and orange trainers, she's happy and relaxed. She's got her dentures out, and she's ready to gurn. As her husband and daughter cheer in the audience, she sticks her head through the leather horse collar and pulls her knockout face, the Invisible Cartoon Punch that looks as if an unseen fist has been rammed down her throat.

When the crowd sees that mug – those drooping eyes, those swallowed lips, that collapsed face – they turn manic. They shout and holler and whistle in a hometown hurrah that could be heard miles away, while all Anne's thinking is *I hope I win I hope I win*. In the end, she does – for the twenty-first time. She accepts the trophy with a beatific smile and misty eyes. That's right, she's *crying*, as if she's just won a beauty pageant, not a contest for the ugliest mug in creation.

However, the women's face-off is just a warm-up for the high-light of the Crab Fair, the World Gurning Championship. The burning question for all proud Egremothians is this – will Peter Jackman win the title again for his hometown?

Peeeeeeeeetuh-errrrrrrrrrrrrrrr! Peeeeeeeeeeeeetuh-errrrrrrrrrrrrrrrrr!

That's Paul, the nephew who got him into gurning in the first place. He's leading the cheers while his uncle makes his way to the stage. As the audience roars, Peter jogs on the spot and pumps his fists in the air like a boxer waiting to go into the ring. The spotlights burn through the haze of cigarette and pipe smoke onstage.

Peter's challengers – mostly out-of-towners – grunt, growl and grimace through the horse collar, with one of the organisers holding them from behind so they don't go lunging off the stage. Gordon Blacklock, five times world champion, turns his mouth into a hyena's snout, whiskers and all. Another gurner looks like his head's been put in a vice, his mouth completely caved in and his lips swallowed; other contestants do variations of the same, only with their lips puckered and lopsided. One of the more disturbing gurners scrunches up his eyes and sticks out his tongue, convulsing as if the demon-possessed fillet were choking him.

As it is, most gurners don't have to work too hard at being ugly. Many are fat and bald to begin with – the ugly mugs just complete the picture. Tommy Mattinson, however, is an exception. A former champ whose dad holds the world record for the number of titles won, Tommy's at least ten years younger than the other gurners, and he's got the dark good looks of a mustachioed lady-killer. On any other night, with those tanned, lean muscles and that carefully coiffed hair, he'd probably win a Mr Bit of Rough contest. But when he gurns, he becomes Mr Constipated. Grunting and growling like he is, you'd think he was trying to pass a bus through his bottom. That doesn't make him any less popular with the women, though. 'I want him to win,' a female photographer purrs on the sidelines. 'He's cute.' Trouble is, Tommy's an out-of-towner. And ever since the Great Gurning Fiasco, 'foreigners' face a tough fight against homegrown favourites.

To gurn, Tommy sticks his tongue up under his lip to form a vertical ridge, scrunching his mouth and nose together like the radiator grille on a classic car. At the same time, he fans out his neck muscles, crosses his eyes and tilts his head from side to side, transmogrifying into a creepy, snuffling extraterrestrial. 'To me, it's like, *totally alien*,' he says, 'or like *An American Werewolf in London*.'

The crowd rewards Mattinson's Alien Werewolf with loud applause, but that's nothing compared to the response for Peter, who is Egremont to the very core of the crab apple on his Crab Fair T-shirt. He pumps his fists and waves his arms to stir up the crowd and get his adrenaline going – *C'mon! C'mon!* Once he's whipped them into a frenzy, he turns his back to get into character. Then he spins around, sticks his head through the collar and lunges at them, his pupils rolled up under his eyelids and his dentures shoved under his lips. He snarls like a maniac, the adrenaline buzzing and his eyes stinging from the sweat off his scalp. The only things he sees are blurs – lights everywhere, hands reaching up at him – but right now, all he's thinking about is that face. *I am Bela Lugosi* – eyes rolled back, snarling, attacking, vicious. He's hunched over, lunging at the crowd and flailing his arms like some kind of goateed demon running amok.

Pe-ter! Pe-ter! Pe-ter! Pe-ter! Pe-ter! Pe-ter!

The crowd roars, baying for him to be as ugly as he can be. Suddenly, they're a stadium of football fans cheering England to victory . . . a throng hailing a new king . . . or a mob that will lynch the judges if Peter doesn't win.

There's a break as the judges mark their scores. The heat has cut the numbers in the kiddies' den to two dozen from nearly a hundred an hour ago. The youngest are clinging like babies to their mums, coming down from their sugar highs, surrounded by the twisted paraphernalia of their sweet-toothed habit. It'll be the old folks next, keeling over in their chairs, clutching a ciggie in one hand and a pint of Jennings Bitter in the other, muttering 'I'm not leavin' 'til I found out who's won it.'

The results are tallied, and the winner is –

Brrrrrrrrrrrrrrrrrrrrrrriiiiiiiiiiiiiiiiiiiiiiiiiiiiiiiiiiiiiiiiiinnngggg!!!

The fire alarm jangles to life, interrupting the emcee and milking one last drop of suspense – and perspiration – from the audience.

When the winner is finally announced, it's no real surprise – Peter Jackman wins for the third time, beating Tommy Mattinson by just one point.

Peter's scalp glistens in the hazy spotlights, and his T-shirt is drenched with sweat as he takes the stage one last time. After mugging for the cameras, he does one last thirty-second gurn, giving his all for the crowd. They respond with a hometown hurrah, pumping their arms and whistling and cheering.

'Audience! Thank you! Great support – thank you!' Peter croaks. His two kids run onstage and give him sweaty embraces.

'We knew you could do it, dad!' his teenage daughter gushes. Her dad has just won a contest for acting like the village idiot, but to her, he's a hero.

PART TWO:
BELA RAISES THE STAKES

Sadly, Bela's appeal faded the following year. In the same way that the public spurned the real Lugosi's gurning for the gorier thrills of modern horror flicks, Peter's beloved Bela lost out to Tommy's grotesque Alien Werewolf. Before his defeat, though, Egremont's gurner had let me in on a secret: 'I've got a new face comin' next year,' he enthused, showing off a new Crab Fair tattoo before dropping his bombshell. 'I'm gettin' all me teeth out this year. I can't *wait* to see the options.'

Yes, Peter was going to have his eight remaining teeth ripped out . . . all for the love of gurning. 'Times are changin', and to keep to the top of the gurnin' profession, I can't carry on winnin' with just one face,' he explained, his clear, blue-grey eyes unwavering. 'So I'm gettin' me teeth out, and then I'll 'ave at least three or four different faces. I wanna try and give what the people want.'

Returning to Egremont this year, I've been keen to see the results of Peter's tooth pulling. Surprisingly, though, for tonight's rematch with the Alien Werewolf, he has decided to fall back on Bela. 'The old face is a Championship Face, and these ones aren't ready yet,' he tells me. However, he denies feeling any disappointment. 'Oh, *nooooo*. No, no, no, no. No, no, I'm not disappointed,' he stresses backstage, his consonants slushy after a dozen or so pints. 'Because I know that you can't just pull a face one year, and that's it. I would like to think I've got a couple of surprises under me shirt, or arm, or whatever in the future years. I want to last. I don't wanna be a one-hit wonder. I wanna *last*. I want people to know that *Gurnin' is Peter Jackman*.'

For now, though, the drastic dental work has convinced him of something he suspected all along – Bela might just be the best gurn he'll ever pull. 'Bela's the one. I've tried all sorts, but Bela is the one.' As Lugosi himself could have told you, unless you're willing to use prosthetics (like that accursed Boris Karloff), your gurning options are physically limited: you only have one face. Sure, you could make modifications, even have your teeth pulled, but the basic facial structure remains the same, and most gurners rely on variations of the traditional Popeye gurn. However, the new generation is taking it to a new level. Having mastered the old art, men like Peter and Tommy Mattinson are developing new styles. They're the Picassos of Face-Pulling, gurning's *avant garde*. By raising the stakes to new, tooth-wrenching heights, Peter has tried to break the bonds that restrict ordinary gurners. He's betting that his dentist's handiwork will pay off, saving him the ignominious fate of his gurning namesake. *Alas, poor Bela!* 'What I've gotta think of now is a – how can I say – a *career*. A *career* in gurnin' – that's what I always wanted to do,' Peter explains, his breath full of beer, 'and a career in gurnin' is not just one face; it's a coupla faces. That's why I took me teeth out – to 'ave more faces. But you can't just say, "Right. 'Ere's your new face." They'll think, "That's not Bela. That's not Peter Jackman." So I've gotta go around the pubs, y'know, before the World Championships, and let them see. And go on television programmes, and let the *country* see. And 'opefully get on to the dotcom, so the *world* will see that I am tryin' to adjust and 'ave new faces for the future.'

By happy coincidence, Peter has a perfect platform to begin his consensus building tonight. A scout is in town casting for an American beer commercial, part of a long-running campaign aimed at young men who want to drink alcohol without being able to taste it. The American lager is supposed to be exceptionally smooth, devoid of the dry hoppy flavour that produces 'Bitter Beer Face'.

Love 'em or hate 'em, most Americans know the 'Bitter Beer Face' ads: a guy's at a party, *look-in' goooood*, but then he takes a swig of beer and turns into Quasimodo (*Whoaaaa! Bitter Beer Face!*). Apparently, the commercials have depleted America's gurning reserves, so the admen have decided to tap Britain, where beer is actually called bitter, to find the ultimate Bitter Beer Face. Genius! 'We looked all over America for someone who could do this, but we couldn't find anybody,' says the collegiate girl sent over to snap headshots of Britain's best gurners.

Peter has just graced her with his most promising new gurn, a real treat, considering only a select few have been allowed to see his latest work in progress. For his new gurn, Peter rolls his eyes way back in his head, just like Bela, but now that he doesn't have any teeth, he's able to pucker his lips, practically turning them inside out to form a kind of fleshy duck's bill. During the shoot, he alternated between puckering his lips and sticking out his tongue – a sliver of quivering flesh – though that may have been purely to impress the pretty American.

In any event, she picked his new gurn over Bela for the head-shot. 'So *she* must like me second one. So, it's coomin'. It's coomin',' Peter says, like a vintner waiting for a particularly promising vintage to mature.

'I ask you,' he adds, his eyes as earnest as ever. 'You saw me second one, what do ya think?'

'Uhhhhhhh. . . Bela's scarier.'

'Bela's better,' he declares.

'Bela's scarier.' That's my story, and I'm sticking to it.

'But what about the second one?'

'I thought it's got a lot of Bela in the eyes,' I say, surprising myself with something that sounds authoritative. Come to think of it, though, I'm practically a gurning connoisseur. After three years, I know enough to realise that Peter's new face is a transitional work. You might say it retains classic elements of his Bela Period, while breaking important new ground. I'd call it *When Bela Met Daffy: The Demonic Duck*.

As with any art form, gurning has its connoisseurs. Last year a couple of aficionados were down in the audience providing a running commentary. The loudest one wore a trim goatee and wire-rimmed glasses, fitting the stereotype of art critics the world over; only instead of sipping white wine, he and his sidekick were swigging beer. And rather than lofty London accents, their critiques came in down-to-earth northern tones. 'Ee's just pissed!' they shouted as a novice pulled a mediocre face. A visiting southerner received a similarly brutal putdown: 'They just don't understand, do they?'

But the veteran gurners got rave reviews:

'Oh, well 'orrible! *God* that's 'orrible!'

'Excellent style. Artistic expression, 9.9.'

'A class act, that.'

'I think it's the eyes that make it.'

'Yes! Yes! *Oogly!*' they both applauded.

So it's no wonder that Peter is nervous about unveiling a new gurn. 'I don't think I'm gonna introduce it in the World Championship.'

The choice of judges this year seems to tip the contest in Peter's favour. Then again, maybe not. Surprisingly, John Evans has been asked to judge the contest again, despite his role in the Great Gurning Fiasco. Evans, you'll recall, was the strongman who could balance things on his head but didn't have much of a head for figures.

In fact, Evans doesn't have the traditional figure of a strongman, either – at least not the inverted triangle physique. The widest part of him is his belly, a broad expanse of a stomach supported by two thinnish legs. More Humpty Dumpty than Schwarzenegger, he stands six feet tall, having shrunk two inches over the years due to age and, well, using his noggin as a balancing beam. His head is shunted into his torso, and what passes for his neck measures twenty-four inches around, disguised by a double chin on one side and a fleshy hump on the other. Instead of a strongman who can carry 225 beers on his head, he looks like a sofa jockey who could hold all that beer in his belly.

John didn't become a strongman until he was forty-four, when he saw a muscleman wowing the crowds in his village. That got him thinking about his days working on construction sites as a 'nobber' – balancing bricks on his head while climbing up and down ladders. Years later, John decided to see if he still had his knack for nobbing, and after some practice, he managed thirty-six bricks without using his hands, enough to attract TV and newspaper coverage. He soon started experimenting with milk crates, catalogues, beer kegs, burning oil drums – even people! TV presenters, weathermen, girls on bikes, audience members – he has balanced them all. At fifty-three, he's a world-record-making machine, churning out achievements in a freakish field particularly suited to milestone setting. 'The World's Biggest Nobber' now claims at least twenty-five records in eleven categories, having balanced 95 milk crates, 101 house bricks, 152 index catalogues, 11 empty beer kegs, 428 cans of Coke and 548 footballs. He even set a record for balancing 62 copies of the *Guinness Book of Records* on his head! But the death-defying feat that's won him appearances on TV programmes in thirty-eight countries – including *The Tonight Show with Jay Leno* – is balancing a Mini Cooper on his head. 'I thought, I'm *sure* I'm gonna be noticed if I balance a car on me 'ead and be famous. And I am,' he chuckles, sporting a dingy, tent-sized T-shirt exclaiming WOW! JOHN EVANS, INTERNATIONAL STRONGMAN.

'I thought I was very lucky to get invited back,' he continues, referring to his role in the Great Gurning Fiasco. 'But tonight we're gonna be real careful that the numbers are right and the names are right.'

And getting it right can mean only one thing. Even a man who carries cars on his head must be smart enough to know that if he wants to make it out of Egremont alive, he'll pick the hometown favourite.

For a while, though, it looks as if Peter's going to recapture the crown by default. A story's circulating that Tommy Mattinson is seriously ill and will have to forfeit. When I break the news to Peter backstage, all he can say is, 'I wish they would've told me,' over and over, having just found out he's spent the past few weeks worrying for nothing. Then he recovers. 'I suppose you could say it's a good thing, because he came first last year, and I came second, but I suppose you could say it's a bad thing because I wish they would've told me. We want a good competition. I hope he's okay.'

Unfortunately, Tommy is anything but. However, nothing could stop the reigning champ from travelling to the World Gurning Championship. 'There he is! There he is!' a girl whispers as he makes his way toward the stage. Gurning aficionados feel a frisson of excitement: *the rematch is on!*

Dressed in black, Tommy's as well groomed as ever, his goatee trimmed within a millimetre of perfection, his short hair shiny with gel and his biceps and triceps toned and tanned. However, you can tell from his stilted gait and the shadows under his eyes that he isn't well. Instead of the fast-talking charmer from the previous year, he looks worn and haggard, like a man who's had a glimpse of death. Doped up on painkillers, Tommy's still recovering from the surgery he had only five days ago. His sleeveless black T-shirt conceals a seventeen-stitch wound along his collarbone, the Cumbrian equivalent of Chernobyl's 'Belorussian Necklace'. 'I've gotta go back and 'ave another operation – on me thyroid. A big operation,' he emphasises. He speaks haltingly, averting his eyes every so often to keep from choking up. 'I don't really – it's as big an operation as you can 'ave, really, if you know what I mean. It isn't good news – which I just got, y'know, two days ago.'

At thirty-eight, the father of two has just been diagnosed with thyroid cancer, a disease that seems to mushroom around nuclear reactors. Though no link has ever been proven, Tommy has worked at Sellafield hundreds of times over the years as a building contractor. However, the past is the last thing on his mind. His family – particularly his father – are so distraught they couldn't bring themselves to attend the championships. In fact, Tommy himself decided to come only after his best friend convinced him. 'I am the world champion at the moment, so – who knows. I'm gonna make the best of it tonight. I don't know if I'll go in, because' – he clears his throat – 'I don't know. See, I can't' – his throat again – 'I can't really put maximum effort into it.'

Nevertheless, he manages to put on a brave Alien face for the American beer tryout. 'Oh my God,' the girl with the video camera gasps as he turns himself into a humanoid praying mantis. 'If that's not your best, I can't imagine what is.'

That's all the encouragement needed to revive the wheeler-dealer in Tommy. Temporarily forgetting his life-threatening illness, he starts asking about the overseas gurning market. While he was on vacation in the US last year, *The Tonight Show* had been calling him every day to coax him out to the West Coast for an appearance. He couldn't make it, but he's eager to go back again. 'I'd like to go over to America,' he says, ever-ambitious, 'because I think I could do more, y'know?'

By now, the opening ceremonies for the World Gurning Championships are as familiar as Anne Woods's punch-faced gurn: the tootling town band . . . the tots singing pop tunes . . . the pipe smoking, horn blowing and hunting-song singing – it's all here, the same as last year and the year before it, cloaked in the smoky funk of this dual-purpose Tea Dance/Fitness Class market hall, where the humid mix of booze, sweat and cigarettes muscles out any clean air.

Anne Woods wins the women's title again, for the twenty-third time. Then six men do their thing onstage, snarling and growling and lunging around, some of them thrashing like it's a Demented Dancing contest, drawing smatterings of praise from the men at the back of the hall, in the form of a sporadic, sing-song chant: *Oh-you-ugly-bas-tard!* or *Oh-you-ugly-gyp-syyyyy!*

But it's Peter who gets the biggest cheer. He's second to last, and the crowd's behind him as he strides toward the platform. There's a high-pitched teenybopper chant at the foot of the stage – *Pe-ter! Pe-ter! Pe-ter!* – and a baritone howl from the standing-room-only section at the back of the hall: *Peeeeeeeeetuh-errrrrrrrrrrrrrrrrr! Peeeeeeeeeeeetuh-errrrrrrrrrrrrrrrrr!*

The three-time world champion dons the horse collar and turns his back to the audience. He hunkers down, taking a long time to roll his pupils up into the back of his head and make sure his upper denture plate is in the perfect position. When he spins around, with that demented gargoyle look, stamping and lurching and lunging around the stage, pumping his arms like some lunatic let off the leash, the crowd bursts into a cacophony of whistles, boos and applause.

The organisers then call for the reigning World Champion to take the stage. After a few seconds of uncertainty, Tommy appears, slowly wading through the crowd, his steps unsteady, like a man who has no business being on his feet. When he puts on the braffin, though, he's transformed. For ten seconds, it's as if nothing's wrong, even though the organisers have to hang the horse collar on his head rather than his neck to keep it from rubbing the gash on his chest. Despite his efforts, he's not the hometown favourite. The crowd responds with tepid applause, then reverts to chanting Peter's name.

While the judges tally their results, the two rivals wait back-stage in the shadows without speaking, the other gurners scattered around them. Peter's sitting behind the stage curtain in a plastic chair positioned at a right angle to Tommy, so that neither man has to make eye contact. Peter smokes nervously, uncertain of victory. He thinks the crowd has cheered louder for him, but he's not sure. The reigning champion, accompanied by his minder, looks haggard and worn, leaning against the white panelled wall and staring forlornly at the dirty beige diamond pattern in the carpet. Tommy's depression and Peter's nervousness cast an uneasy silence over the other gurners. From the way the two men are fretting, you'd think they were awaiting execution.

Finally, Peter breaks the tension.

'You wanna sit down, son?' he says, offering Tommy his chair.

'No, I'm all right.'

Alan Clements comes round the curtain and tells the men that the top six gurners need to strut their stuff again. He glances uncertainly at Tommy.

'I'm all right,' the champ mouths. 'I'm all right.'

The other gurners do their faces to cool applause. The cheering ignites only when Peter spins around and grimaces at the crowd.

It's Tommy's turn again, his last gurn of the evening, and he puts everything into it. 'Go on, Tommy! Go on, Tommy lad!' his mate bellows from the sidelines, virtually the sole voice of support. The rest of the audience is indifferent.

Tommy staggers offstage and huddles on the steps, wincing as his friend checks the wound on his chest. But by the time Alan Clements starts announcing the winners, he's back on his feet again, clinching hands with Peter, who's telling him he's glad he came, he's been a great champion, and he's sorry about his illness.

Alex Woods comes in fourth place, Gordon Blacklock third, and –

Tommy wins second, losing to Peter by just one point. He accepts his award sheepishly, as if he knew all along he couldn't win. A couple of reporters swoop on him backstage: Will he come back next year?

'Yeah,' he mumbles, offering a weak handshake as he quietly slips away.

For Peter, commiseration quickly gives way to exhilaration. When the emcee proclaims him World Gurning Champion, Jackman doubles over and buries his head in his hands, his face crumpling. He strides onstage, eyes red with sweat and tears, pumping his fist in the air as, somewhere down below, Tommy makes his way through the crowd to the exit.

Peter gives the audience one last championship-winning gurn, then turns round to recover, bracing himself against a desk and wincing from the sweat in his eyes. Immediately, the cameras and reporters surround him, but he asks for a few minutes to celebrate with his daughter.

'Is this good? Is this good? Is this good?' he keeps asking her.

'World Champion! We knew you would!'

Then come the hugs, the handshakes, the claps on the shoulders, the kisses on the cheeks, the Beauty-and-the-Beast poses with the Crab Fair Queen, and the bombardment of reporters' questions, a hundred ways of asking *How does it feel?*

'To win again, it just feels –' Peter shivers with delight '– *wonderful*. I was 'ungry tonight. I was 'ungry for it. I knew Bela would do it! I knew it!' His bald dome glistens in the camera lights. 'Bela is The One.'

At the foot of the stage, a grey-headed man grabs Peter's attention. He happens to be wearing a sleeveless black T-shirt, just like the one Tommy had on. Peter crouches to receive a slap on the back from his friend.

'It's come 'ome! It's come 'ome!' the man shouts, voicing the jubilation of all Egremont tonight. 'The World Championship has come 'ome!'

R.I.P. BELA

Tommy Mattinson has since recovered from his bout with cancer and reclaimed the world gurning title. Tragically, though, Peter Jackman was killed when an embankment he was walking on collapsed during a recent holiday in Spain with other Sellafield workers. His funeral in Egremont included a 'guard of honour' of Crab Fair organisers and a eulogy by Alan Clements. In keeping with Peter's wishes, he was cremated and his ashes scattered on the Crab Fair Field. 'We spread them by the beer tent,' Clements said. 'That's where he wanted 'em.'

CHAPTER EIGHT

ADDRESS UNKNOWN

FAGGOT CUTTING, SHERIFF PRICKING AND COIN COUNTING IN LONDON

CLEANING UP THE CAPITAL: A humble porter sweeps the street for the Worshipful Company of Vintners, who carry posies to clear the air during their annual procession.

© J.R. DAESCHNER

PART ONE:
TWENTY-FIRST-CENTURY TRICORNS

Out of touch, out to lunch and as outdated as their wigs and robes, Britain's judges invariably get a bad rap. Every so often, some old duffer, usually 'one of the finest legal minds in the country', will ask a question so obtuse you wonder if they ever let him out of his cryogenic chamber, except when he's thawing out on the bench: 'I bid thee,' one of the Men in Wigs will enquire, 'where might one sample this delicacy known as a "ham-burger"?' or 'What, pray tell, is a "sex pistol"?'

However, when you set foot in Britain's Cathedral of Justice, you begin to understand the cloistered existence of the legal elite. The Royal Courts of Justice dominate the Strand in the heart of London, straddling the border between the City and Westminster, just across the street from a half-timbered pub and the original Twinings tea shop (est. 1706). Like Big Ben and the Houses of Parliament, the Victorians built the Royal Courts to look older than they really are. The Gothic agglomeration of towers and flying buttresses is a cathedral in all but name. The nave, or Great Hall, boasts a rose window, stained glass and a mosaic floor. The only thing missing is a graven image of Justice, with scales in one hand and a sword in the other.

Once you clear the modern security scans and leave the Great Hall, you wander into a rarefied atmosphere of long stone corridors riddled with peaked arches and Corinthian columns. The high priests of the law flap around in horsehair and silk, muttering intensely in English and Latin, while mock-Gothic lettering distinguishes the 𝕮𝖊𝖑𝖑𝖘, the 𝕭𝖊𝖆𝖗 𝕲𝖆𝖗𝖉𝖊𝖓, and the 𝕲𝖊𝖓𝖙𝖑𝖊𝖒𝖆𝖓 𝕬𝖉𝖛𝖔𝖈𝖆𝖙𝖊𝖘 𝕽𝖔𝖇𝖎𝖓𝖌 𝕽𝖔𝖔𝖒 from the other thousand rooms in the labyrinth. Up in the east wing, through another maze of corridors, you find the chambers of one of Britain's highest-ranking judges, who also happens to be the guardian of some of the country's most ancient ceremonies apart from the Coronation. As the Queen's Remembrancer, Master Robert Turner oversees the annual Quit Rents Ceremony and the Trial of the Pyx, in addition to helping Her Majesty 'prick' High Sheriffs every year. As if that weren't olde worlde enough, the Queen's Remembrancer has his own personal Writer who produces illuminated manuscripts on vellum, and he's the only judge in the land who regularly wears a hat in court – the tricorn of the Cursitor Baron on top of his full ceremonial wig. Given his impossibly quaint titles and duties, then, the last thing you expect him to say is: 'I'm expecting a videophone call from Singapore.'

In fact, the Royal Courts of Justice are possibly the last place in Britain where you would expect to see a videophone. It's surprising enough to learn that they've mastered telephones, let alone the latest technology. Master Turner has pastoral scenes of Old England on the walls, a tome on Magna Carta on his leather-topped desk and wall-to-wall bookcases full of hidebound volumes with colour-coded spines – and there, behind the outsized desk, between the various books and files, stands a futuristic black rectangle mounted on a base. It makes a mellow burble, and then an unlikely image fills the screen: a giant pot with a flower sticking out of it.

Master Turner leans over to get a better look. 'That's the court in Singapore,' he says eagerly.

It looks like a flowerpot to me, but the camera quickly swivels to reveal a clerk at a desk, asking about technical specifications for a videoconference later today. Her accent doesn't travel well halfway round the world, and Master Turner has to speak loudly and slowly to be understood, but hey – it's a videophone.

The Remembrancer clearly delights in this unlikely mix of the old and the new. 'I'm in the twenty-first century,' he smiles. 'I have a video machine, a conference machine, and, of course, a palmtop diary to keep all my appointments.' On his desk, the grey tricorn conference-call phone – the kind found in company boardrooms –

contrasts neatly with the triangular hat he's wearing in a portrait on the wall.

For ceremonies, Master Turner dons full judicial regalia – black tricorn, chest-length wig, frilly scarf and cuffs, black robe and knee breeches, plus hose and buckled shoes. Today, though, he's wearing his other hat, so to speak, as Senior Master of the Queen's Bench Division, the High Court branch that handles commercial and maritime disputes, and cases involving serious personal injury, breach of contract and professional negligence. Even in his workaday role, Master Turner is nattily turned out in a pinstriped double-breasted suit, a pale canary shirt with cufflinks, a gold signet ring and a powder-blue pocket square that complements his tie. Now in his late sixties, he spends his days juggling hearings, applications and paperwork, while ensuring that the Queen's Bench Division runs smoothly – and for a few days each year, he upholds some of the most ancient, and seemingly absurd, traditions in the land.

'*All* ceremonial functions in this country have to be performed at the highest standards and in the most rigorous manner and with dignity,' he stresses. 'That's why we're so good at it. I'm very *proud* to be Queen's Remembrancer. When you're proud of a job, you try to do it to the best of your ability.' As it happens, one of his most difficult tasks is keeping the tricorn on his wig.

I ask how he manages the feat.

'That is a secret between me and my hat,' he says, allowing himself a smile.

Of course, Britain has a surfeit of officials whose titles once described practical duties but now sound like something out of Gilbert and Sullivan: the Herb Strewer, the Cock o' the North, the Knight of the Bath, the Seigneur de Serk and the Black Rod, to name but a few. As you'd expect from a man billed as the Remembrancer of the Realm, Master Turner has a fearsome memory, though it does take a second to switch from the hectic twenty-first century to England's ancient past. Sitting in a leather-upholstered chair overlooking the inner courtyard, he rubs the side of his face as if trying to warm up his noggin and reboot his brain. At other times, he keeps his eyes closed and his palm on his face: he seems to be trotting to the back of the library of his mind, rummaging through the archives until he finds the ones marked 'Sheriff Pricking' or 'Trial of the Pyx'. As he reopens them, collateral facts come spilling out, revealing ancient details that explain why we speak and do business the way we do now, not to mention the accumulation of customs and compromises that make the UK truly unique.

The Queen's Remembrancer owes his title to a lazy beancounter who kept nodding off while counting the monarch's money. After a disastrous battle against the Vikings in AD 991, the English king, aptly known as Aethelred the Unready, bought off the Danes by jacking up taxes. The country's 'shire reeves', or sheriffs (an Anglo-Saxon invention), collected this Danegeld and delivered it to the king's treasurers. 'They, in turn, had to battle with the problem that you cannot add up, subtract, or multiply Roman numerals,' Master Turner explains. 'The concept of nought wasn't introduced into England until well after the eleventh century.' In the meantime, they relied on an ingenious system to keep track of monies received and debts owed.

To demonstrate, the Remembrancer produces something he carved earlier: two rectangular 'tally sticks'. The eight-inch strips of hazel rod have notches cut into them, with deep Vs for pounds and narrow slits for pence. One of the sticks is whole, and the other has been split down the middle like a set of disposable chopsticks. In the days when even most aristocrats were illiterate, England's treasury, or Tally Court, used these sticks to record transactions and keep both sides honest. After marking the wood, the officials would split the stick down the middle, cutting through the notches. Then they would give one piece of wood to the payer as a receipt and keep the other for their records. 'This is like a small dagger, or foil,' Master Turner says, poking the air with the pointed splinter of wood, then holds up the larger piece: 'And this is the *contre*, or counter, foil.' He pulls out a red chequebook from Coutts, the bankers to the Queen. 'And if you take a chequebook, you have the foil and the counterfoil. It all originates from this little bit of wood.' What's more, the fibre of the wood caused each tally stick to split differently, resulting in a medieval form of encryption. 'You can't forge it,' he says, running his finger along the fibrous edge of the wood. 'If you tried to forge this, it would never fit together. It is a *brilliant* bit of security, and of course, when the two pieces match up, they *tally*.' Over time, money-men began trading these bits of wood, also known as government 'stocks': the foundation of the modern stock market.

Even keen to keep a money-spinner, the Treasury continued cleaving tally sticks right up until the nineteenth century, storing old ones under the Houses of Parliament. Finally, in 1834, Westminster's mandarins decided to dispose of Parliament's centuries of 'worm-eaten, rotten old bits of wood', as Dickens ridiculed them in one of his speeches. 'It would naturally occur to any intelligent person that nothing could be easier than to allow them to be carried away for firewood by the miserable people who lived in that neighbourhood,' he said. Instead, the less-than-intelligent bureaucrats opted to burn them on site. In doing so, they overloaded the boilers, and the old Houses of Parliament burned to the ground. Their iconic mock-Gothic replacements, including Big Ben, owe their existence to this tally-stick bonfire.

Likewise, the unique name for Britain's finance ministry, or Exchequer, comes from the merger of the old English Tally Court and its French counterpart after the Conquest of 1066. The Norman *scaccarium*, or chessboard, was manned by *magistri* ('masters'), who sat at a table covered with chequered cloth. At the merged Court of the Exchequer, a clerk would put counters on one end of the chequerboard to show the amount owed and place markers on the other side to 'check' how much was paid. 'And so up the two sides of the table the counters would march, until at the end of the day, they should *tally*,' Master Turner says. All this checking and double-checking was extremely tedious – so much so that it put at least one treasurer in the 1100s to sleep. 'Aware that he was losing out because the checking was not being properly done, Henry II sent two of his best civil servants down to the Court to put the king "in remembrance" of all things owing to him.' Eventually, this post was formalised as the monarch's Remembrancer, who is now also the guardian of the Great Seal of the Exchequer, the Chancellor of the Exchequer's symbol. 'He's not allowed to keep it,' Master Turner clarifies. 'I have it, and I keep it in my safe and look after it.' That keeps disgruntled finance ministers from trying to take it with them after they leave office. To this day, whenever there's a change of Chancellor, the Remembrancer's clerk hops in a taxi and takes the Seal of the Exchequer to Number 11 Downing Street, which then delivers it to Buckingham Palace. The Queen then hands the symbol to the new Chancellor, thereby confirming his appointment, and he returns it to Number 11, where it's collected by the Remembrancer's staff and stored until the next cabinet reshuffle.

As for the chequered cloth, the only time it's still used is when the Remembrancer presides over the annual Quit Rents Ceremony in October. A feudal throwback, 'quit rents' are more common than you might think in the UK and its former colonies. These nominal payments can take the form of anything from roses to pennies to turnips and peppercorns (hence, a 'peppercorn rent'). When the tenants pay their dues, they go 'quit' of the rent (just as two people are 'quits' when they no longer owe each other anything). Usually, the principle at stake is more important than the payment: the quit rents serve as a reminder that the landowner is the ultimate boss.

In the Quit Rents Ceremony at the Royal Courts of Justice, the Corporation of London 'pays' the Crown two knives, six horseshoes and sixty-one nails for two pieces of land in Shropshire and the capital – but here's the strange bit: no one knows for sure where the properties are. The rent-paying rituals have taken place for so long – nearly 800 years – that even the Remembrancers seem to have forgotten the exact locations of the land. As near as anyone can tell, 'The Moors' in Shropshire now encompass Moor Ridding Farm near Eardington, south of Bridgnorth, while the London property known as 'The Forge' stood on what is now the site of Australia House, in an alley off St Clement Danes Church in the Strand.

The story goes that King John was hunting in Shropshire around 1211 when he lost his weapons and was attacked by a boar. A local farmer threw him a knife, thus saving the king from the boar and the country from boorish kings (John was forced to sign Magna Carta four years later). In a rare show of generosity, John granted the man a stretch of land called The Moors. The farmer was required to give the Crown two knives every year as a token payment – one blunt and the other sharp. During the modern ceremony, the knives are tested on a hazel rod measuring one cubit, as determined by the length of the Remembrancer's forearm from the tip of his middle finger to his elbow. 'That, for the record, is 19½ inches at the present time,' Master Turner says, adding that the unit could vary from 18 to 23 inches, depending on the royal representative's measurements. The rod is cut in half to form two sections the size of tally sticks. The purpose of the sharp knife is obvious enough: it was used to strip the bark and cut notches into the wood. However, the blunt knife also had a purpose. 'If you write with ink on wood, the fibrous nature of it makes it all run, but if you smooth it down with a blunt instrument, you can get a fairly smooth surface on it, and it will then take the ink,' the Remembrancer explains. 'So basically, by giving these two knives, the tenant was replacing those used throughout the year. It's a *very* utilitarian object.'

The other quit rent, for The Forge in London, dates from around 1235, when the Knights Templar had their base on the Strand, now the busy landlocked street in front of the Royal Courts of Justice, but then the very bank of the Thames. To keep in shape for the Crusades, the knights held jousting matches on their tournament field, with a farrier on hand to make sure their mounts were well shod. 'And he must have done something that distinguished him, because the king – and that would be Henry III – gave him a plot of land to the south of the field for a forge,' Master Turner says, adding that this was probably in a place called Tweezer's Alley. In fact a blacksmith's shop stood on the site up until the 1930s, used by WH Smith for shoeing the carthorses that delivered its books and newspapers. Next door, a type of jousting still takes place on the former grounds of the Knights Templar: legal champions prepare for battle in the Inns of Court known as the Inner Temple and the Middle Temple.

The annual payment for The Forge was six horseshoes and sixty-one nails to fit them. Around 1360, the land passed to a woman who asked the Court if she could exchange the horseshoes and nails for an annual rent of eighteen pence. 'And they said, "Yes – subject to you making a ceremonial set of horseshoes and nails, because this is an old English practice, we've been doing it for 126 years or so, and we can't let it go like that."' The Quit Rents Ceremony has apparently been using the same set of horseshoes and nails ever since: experts have dated the shoes from the 1300s. The fat iron crescents were designed for shire horses that carried armour-clad knights into battle. Six of the shoes would have shod three warhorses: they wore them only on their front two feet. 'The horse was taught that, in order to protect its belly from foot soldiers who might try to stab it, it should raise its front feet up and hammer them down on the infantrymen. Hence the size of the whole bloody thing.' Unlike the knives for The Moors, the current payment for The Forge uses the same set of shoes and nails, stored in the Remembrancer's safe. 'Each year, I hand them to the Corporation of London, who solemnly hand them back' – he smiles at the absurdity – '*after* they have counted them out, and I am satisfied that it is a good number.'

The City of London took over the payment of both quit rents in the 1500s, after a debacle caused by a pigheaded official (and ancestor of the Royal Family). Sir Martin Bowes was a goldsmith who ended up becoming Lord Mayor of London, Knight of the Bath and Treasurer of the Royal Mint. However, back when he was just an arrogant alderman, he insisted on meddling in the Quit Rents Ceremony. 'He asked if he could cut the hazel rod instead of the tenant. And he failed. As a result, the poor old tenant was fined ten shillings. Thereafter, it seems, the Corporation of London said, "We're not going to have this happen again. We will do it properly."' From then on, a man from the Corporation (now the City Solicitor) has wielded the knives and counted the horseshoes.

Over the past two centuries, the Quit Rents ceremony has gone from pomp to pennypinching to somewhere in between. An etching outside Master Turner's chambers shows a large court in 1813 crammed with men in Napoleonic (or 'Nelson') hats, women in Georgian bonnets and children dressed like their parents. In the middle of the room, a square table at least fifteen feet across is shrouded in black-and-white checked cloth with the horseshoes and nails on top, plus an axe and a hatchet – improper substitutes for the knives. Eighty years later, the tradition seems to have suffered a round of Victorian budget cutting. In an ink drawing called the 'Ceremony of Cutting Faggots', the event is a backroom affair attended by a dozen adults in contemporary dress, the men in beards and muttonchops, the women chindeep in their best Victorian black. There's not a wig, robe or even a scrap of chequered cloth in sight.

The modern event has reverted to the fancy dress of old, thanks partly to the presence of the two Sheriffs of London, the City leaders elected each year to assist the Lord Mayor (as opposed to the regular Mayor, who runs the capital). Besides receiving the quit rents on behalf of the Crown, the Remembrancer grants the new Sheriffs royal approval. A few weeks later, their boss also demonstrates his feudal obeisance on Lord Mayor's Day (the second Saturday in November). As a symbol of the City's loyalty to the Crown, the Lord Mayor has to take off his hat in the presence of the Queen or her representative, the Remembrancer. 'He's not Lord Mayor until I swear him in,' Master Turner says. 'Before I am prepared to swear him in – or indeed, to stand up in his presence – he must remove his hat, after which I stand up. But I don't remove my hat.'

Master Turner also plays a role in choosing the High Sheriffs from the provinces who are specially 'pricked' by the monarch each year. Rather than a euphemism for the dreaded *droit de seigneur*, the pricking refers to the archaic way the Queen selects these officials, whose post is predated only by her own. Like the monarch, the sheriffs now serve mainly as titular officials, giving speeches, attending ceremonies and hosting garden parties. Unlike Her Maj, though, the High Sheriffs are volunteers who pay their way entirely out of their own pocket. In recent years, the government has criticised the shrieval system for operating effectively as an all-white male club, but the problem is largely self-perpetuating: the outgoing sheriff nominates his successor. A list of three candidates for each county is passed to the Remembrancer, who then sends it to the Queen. She uses a silver bodkin to prick a hole in the parchment next to the name of the new sheriff.

Despite his title, the Queen's Remembrancer has very little interaction with the monarch these days. Master Turner's description of the Queen is predictably bland: 'Perfectly charming,' he says, pointing to a photo of one of the few times he has met her. The Remembrancer's appointment is confirmed by the Lord Chancellor rather than the Queen herself. And now that the government plans to abolish the Lord Chancellor (a position older than even that of Prime Minister), the Remembrancer could also face the chop amid the ongoing legal reforms. For the time being, though, Master Turner prefers to focus on the immediate impact of the changes. 'The Queen's Remembrancer becomes the oldest individual judicial office – dating from 1164,' he tells me via email. When Lord Falconer, the interim Lord Chancellor, broke with tradition by being sworn in bareheaded, wearing a business suit and tie, Master Turner was on hand to maintain standards. He recorded the event a full ceremonial regalia, complete with black tricorn and full-bottomed wig.

To the keepers of Britain's Cathedral of Justice, the grandiose Court of the Lord Chief Justice of England and Wales is known simply as Court 4, where the highest judge in the land hears appeals in cases such as the murder of TV presenter Jill Dando and the execution of James Hanratty, one of the last men to be hanged in Britain. However, for one hour every year, Court 4 adjourns its grim caseload to host the Quit Rents Ceremony.

The courtroom itself is a vision of fusty majesty, full of chocolatey oak and red velvet trappings, lit by lamps and chandeliers, with carved rosettes and Gothic arches decorating the walls and colour-coded tomes lining the bookshelves. A distinctive feature of Court 4 is its Royal Coat of Arms, which takes pride of place behind the bench declaring the sovereign's authority from on high: *DIEU ET MON DROIT* – GOD AND MY RIGHT. In the average courtroom, the monarch's motif is painted in bright, gaudy colours, but in the lair of the Lord Chief Justice, the crowned lion and unicorn are carved in rich, dark oak to match their tasteful surroundings.

From up here in the public gallery, though, the most striking feature is the thick coat of dust running around the room at eye level. The court's wood panelling stops halfway up the walls forming eave-like overhangs just beneath the gallery. Whereas the lower half of the room is dressed in warm, sumptuous wood, the upper half consists of naked grey stone rising all the way to the oak ceiling. Downstairs, the seats normally reserved for barristers and solicitors are occupied by various dignitaries from the City, as proud of their official badges as their wives are of their new hats. Upstairs, in the Gallery of the Great Unwashed, the seating is restricted to three rows of unforgiving pews: if you lean back, all you can see is the judges' bench below. To get a good look, you have to crane over the balcony or crouch in your seat.

Even so, at least fifty people have turned out to watch the ceremony, some queuing for nearly an hour to make sure they got a seat. Most are day-tripping pensioners in fleeces and raincoats, with a few teens and twentysomethings making up the difference. I've come with Doc Rowe, who is keen to add the Quit Rents Ceremony to the long list of annual customs he's documented. On my other side are a mother and her two boys. She's originally from Cheltenham, near the Royal Forest of Dean, where the Queen's Remembrancer visits each year to oversee the planting of new trees. Greyheaded and matronly, with dangly earrings and a West Country accent, she explains that this is a field trip of sorts for them. She's an advocate of home schooling, and whenever she can, she takes her boys to events as living history lessons. 'It's important to give them a sense of where we came from. Because although a lot of these events are fun and ceremonial, there's also a broader historical context.'

I certainly don't envy her the task of teaching her precocious offspring. Both boys are well-fed and well-mothered, with reddish hair, pink cheeks and round faces. The younger has his nose stuck in a Harry Potter book – 'I'm rereading it' – while the elder, who's fourteen, baffles me with a litany of obscure facts about the capital. He's not showing off (well, maybe a little) mostly, he's just fascinated.

'Every year, the City of London stops traffic by holding a red silk across Temple Bar – because they can,' he smiles triumphantly.

'Yes, but those are our *rights*,' his mother interjects.

'And the Lord Mayor has *six* Shire horses pull his coach through the City for the Lord Mayor's Show – because he can.'

'But those are our *rights*.'

She tries hard to keep up with her son, explaining that these seemingly absurd practices are part of a bigger picture. If you did away with traditions, you'd be in danger of undermining the principles they're meant to reinforce. Unlike civil law on the Continent, which is based on absolute theories of Right and Wrong, England's common law has evolved over the centuries to reflect the practices of the people.

Which brings to mind a controversy in the papers today. The Austrian owner of a *bierkeller* in Worcester (of all places) has been banned from selling beer in traditional litre-sized steins. Under British law, beer from a pump has to be sold in pints or half-pints. Surprisingly, the landlady has won backing from Britain's 'Metric Martyrs'. At first, it was a mystery to me why a group fighting to keep imperial measures would support an Austrian battling to sell beer in Britain by the litre, but of course, it's the principle at stake: custom versus diktat, practice over theory. 'The customer should be given the right to decide whether he buys Austrian beer by the litre or bananas by the pound,' a Metric Martyr said, echoing what the mother has been trying to explain to her sons up here in the gallery: *Those are our rights.*

'Silence!' The usher downstairs orders the court to rise. Two footmen in scarlet coats, tan breeches and white stockings lead in the Common Serjeant – a judge in a long horsehair wig and black robe – and the two new City Sheriffs, who have arrived at the courts by boat from Tower Pier, a custom harking back to the days when it was quicker, and safer, to travel by the Thames rather than the streets. The sheriffs, potential Lord Mayors of London, wear scarlet robes trimmed with ermine and carry black tricorns and foppish white gloves. After we've sat down, we're told to rise again, this time for Her Majesty's representative, the Queen's Remembrancer. Master Turner strides purposefully into the room in his black robe and frilly cuffs, his tricorn 'hat' – in reality, a triangle turned up at the edges – floating as if by magic on top of his full-bottomed wig.

When he nods toward the officials, though, the hat tips forward precariously, and he quickly has to clamp it into place.

'Pray, be seated.'

Rather than the exalted throne of the Lord Chief Justice, the Queen's Remembrancer makes do with the humble table below, usually reserved for clerks. The chequered cloth in front of him, all white squares and black borders, covers half of the table – a mere slip compared with the massive expanse of fabric used in the Georgian era. Several thick horseshoes are lined up on the table, as well as a length of hazel rod, a couple of large gold seals and some illuminated manuscripts.

Peering over his spectacles, the Remembrancer welcomes the sheriffs by saying he hopes they had 'calm seas and a prosperous voyage' from Tower Pier. 'These are trying days for the shrievalty,' he adds. 'Its very *raison d'être* has been called into question in some parts. Reformers should acknowledge our shared traditions and the evolutionary nature of our institutions. I am confident, though, that a *modus vivendi* will be achieved.' His choice of words reflects this evolution: 'shrievalty' comes from Old English, *raison d'être* from French and *modus vivendi* from Latin. Rounding out a brief history of the 'shire reeves', he concludes that they have served the monarch for more than a thousand years, ever since AD 991: 'an unbroken chain of service unequalled in any other office under the Crown'.

Having established the ceremony's serious purpose, Master Turner is quick to acknowledge its idiosyncrasies. For instance, he recently had to explain to the Queen that the City always uses the same half-dozen horseshoes to pay for the property in London. 'She did acknowledge my embarrassment if I were to render to her the 700-year-old horseshoes, which are conveniently re-presented each year by the City,' he says, adding: 'They are obviously leaders in the modern world of recycling.' As with the horseshoes, the knives and nails are checked each year. 'This court leaves nothing to chance,' he quips. 'The City Comptroller will use *all* the numerical skills which mark the City's leadership for financial services by *endeavouring* to count up to six for the horseshoes and sixty-one for their accompanying nails.'

This year's event is unique in that the current occupants of what are thought to be The Moors are actually present. Mr and Mrs Bill Williamson own Moor Ridding Farm, 'a delightful fourteenth-century house' in the heart of Shropshire. The Remembrancer notes that people often ask what would happen if the knives in the ceremony weren't sharp enough to pass muster. 'One of my more legalistic colleagues has assured me that failure to cut the hazel rod *could* be deemed to be failure to pay rent, which of course *would* lead to the forfeiture of the land to the Crown – and the provision of a blessed retirement home for worn-out Remembrancers,' he adds, getting a big laugh from the crowd. 'But I will resist that temptation: I frankly could not face the early-morning milking sessions.' In any event, he's confident that today won't repeat the 'disastrous' ceremony of 1556, when the farmer ended up being fined ten shillings.

The Queen's Remembrancer wishes the sheriffs a successful year and cedes the floor to the Common Serjeant, a top judge at the Old Bailey with a fine baritone voice and an equally dry sense of humour. Addressing the bench in his long wig and black robe, he prefaces his introduction of the City Sheriffs by thanking the officials of the Inner and Middle Temples – the cloistered Inns of Court next to the Thames – 'for ensuring our safe passage through that potentially unruly maze'.

The audience thinks he's kidding, but he's not: 'Indeed, we remind ourselves that as recently as 1756, as the City party made its apprehensive way to the Court of the Exchequer, it was both abused and assaulted by students as it passed through the Inns of Court.' He pauses. 'It is said history repeats itself – *lawyers* certainly do – and we are grateful to be protected from any repetition of such behaviour.'

The Common Serjeant then introduces the City of London's new sheriffs by presenting them as the Ultimate Old Boys: born into respectable families, educated at Oxbridge or overseas, married to musical wives and veterans of blue-chip insurance or accounting firms, having advanced British interests abroad while always remembering their allegiance to London. Both have been Masters of the Worshipful Company of Merchant Tailors and currently serve as churchwardens at one of the capital's more oddly named sanctuaries, St Lawrence Jewry, which stands next to the Guildhall, making it the official church of the Corporation of London.

Duly impressed, the Remembrancer rewards the men with their illuminated approbations before returning to the main business of the day the paying of the quit rents.

The sharp-nosed woman sitting at his right hand rises. 'Tenants and occupiers of a piece of waste ground called The Moors in the County of Shropshire, come forth and do your service.'

The City Comptroller approaches the bench, a tall, middle-aged man with a brush cut and broad shoulders. The Remembrancer's sidekick takes the blunt knife from him and holds it against the chequered cloth, its dull edge facing up. With a playful flap of his elbows, the proxy tenant takes hold of the hazel rod as if it were a Herculean task.

After testing the bark against the dull blade, he confidently moves to the sharp one. As the woman braces the knife against the table, the Comptroller presses down on the hazel rod, and – nothing happens. The stripling bends without breaking. The audience guffaws, but he's not laughing. *A man's farm could be at stake!* Frowning, he puts some English into it, bearing down on the rod with his upper body. The knife wobbles from the force, until finally some assistance from his thumbs produces the requisite *crack!*

'Good service,' Master Turner says, suppressing a smile.

The hard part over, the Comptroller can relax a little while doing the honours for the rent covering a 'certain tenement called The Forge in the parish of St Clement Danes in Greater London'.

The official sets a black leather bag on the table, along with the sixth horseshoe.

The Comptroller starts to count in a loud voice: 'One, two, three, four, five' – he pauses – 'and six.'

'How many have you?'

'Six, my lord.'

'Good number.'

The proxy tenant then does the same with the nails. His back to the audience, he makes a big show of digging in his pockets, revealing the final nail from his trousers like a magician pulling a rabbit out of a hat.

'How many have you?'

'Sixty-one, m'lord.'

'Good number.'

Summing up, the Remembrancer can't resist a joke: 'There was a moment when I did think that I might *benefit* property wise.'

To round out the event, a guest speaker usually gives a talk on a historical subject such as Chaucer's 600th anniversary or, this year, the City's livery companies, those ancient trade associations that seem as outdated and mysterious as their medieval job titles: Loriners, Tallow Chandlers, Cordwainers and the like. The Clerk of the Mercers Company – daringly underdressed in a business suit – informs us that the members of these early trade unions were identified by their clothing, or livery. No one was allowed to work in the City as, say, a fletcher, without having first worked his way up in the arrowmakers' guild. What's more, anyone who flouted this code would have to go as far as Coventry to escape the long arm of London law: hence the expression 'being sent to Coventry'. From the Saxon era to Tudor times, the livery companies had real power. 'But since then,' the clerk admits, 'they have become rather quaint and charming institutions closer to the fringes of City life.'

Even so, the City has an ever-growing list of more than a hundred livery companies, ranging from the Great Twelve of the Middle Ages – Drapers, Fishmongers, Goldsmiths, etc. – to the modern Worshipful Companies of Actuaries, Environmental Cleaners . . . and Information Technologists. Other groups like Management Consultants have yet to be made up, but it's only a matter of time. The companies take part in the Lord Mayor's Show in November, which is partly why the parade is three miles long – nearly twice the length of the route to the Royal Courts of Justice. The companies used to fight over their order in the procession. In 1484, the Lord Mayor tried to put an end to their feud by ordering the Merchant Tailors and the Skinners to alternate between the sixth and seventh places – as good an explanation as any for the term 'being at sixes and sevens'.

It so happens that the official who leads the Lord Mayor into Court 4 for November's swearing-in is the same man who escorts us out after the Quit Rents Ceremony. The Tipstaff's uniform is as contemporary as it gets in the Royal Courts. The brimmed pillbox hat, braided gold trimming and white bow tie and gloves are modelled after a Victorian police inspector's uniform; apparently, the moustache also comes standard-issue. Arm outstretched, the Tipstaff holds his twelve-inch wand of office upright as he leads the Queen's Remembrancer, the Sheriffs, the Common Serjeant and the other officials out of the courtroom, through the mock-Gothic corridors and on to the Strand, where bobbies block traffic so the procession can cross the street for a private reception in Middle Temple Hall. Black cabs, red double-deckers and white minivans idle impatiently as the menagerie passes by: judges in horsehair, women in hats and sheriffs in gold and fur, all following a Victorian police inspector and his magical marching baton. They get some odd looks, but not half as many as you'd think. After all, this is London.

PART TWO:
ECCENTRIC CITY

Like capitalinos everywhere, many Londoners imagine themselves a cut above the provincial hoi polloi, far too busy and sophisticated to waste time or money on Olde Worlde traditions. Loudly proclaiming their love of multiculturalism, they're often quick to sneer at their own country's diversity, particularly when it takes the form of odd pastimes practised by Little Englanders, Weird Welshmen and Crazed Scots. However, London itself is teeming with traditions as strange and fascinating as anything you'll find in the provinces.

Most of these events take place in the very heart of the capital, in that bastion of twenty-first-century banking, a rival to Wall Street – the City of London. There, between William the Conqueror's Tower and the all-conquering skyscrapers, right under the noses of the Masters of the Universe, thrives an alternate universe of gold and ermine, choirboys and boundary beatings, boat races and blessings. In common with their country cousins, many City-dwellers have a hard time explaining why they uphold these seemingly nonsensical customs: maybe it's simply because they're Londoners.

Then again, who needs flu jabs when the Blessing of the Throats is just around the corner? In early February, office workers flock to Britain's oldest Catholic church, St Etheldreda's in Holborn, to have a priest hold two candles over their necks in the sign of the Cross to honour St Blaise (the patron of throats). Every Good Friday, a sailor adds a hot cross bun to the mouldy collection hanging in the Widow's Son pub in Bow, each one a reminder of a son lost at sea many Easters ago. In April, the church of St Andrew Undershaft hosts a memorial service for John Stow, the Elizabethan writer hailed as 'London's first historian'; afterwards, the Lord Mayor replaces the quill in the hand of Stow's effigy on the wall. Also in spring, several churches mark Ascension Day with the Beating of the Bounds – whacking the boundaries of their parishes with sticks. At All Hallows By The Tower, the officials hold a schoolboy upside down over the Thames to the accompaniment of the 'Beating Hymn' sung by the congregation on shore; every three years, they also stage a mock standoff with the Beefeaters from next door, commemorating a blood feud from more than 300 years ago. In June, All Hallows presents a freshly cut rose to the Lord Mayor as a quit rent for a building code violation by Sir Robert Knollys in 1346, even though the disputed property on Seething Lane has long since disappeared under an office block. The following month, after electing its new Master, the Worshipful Company of Vintners processes in full livery to St James Garlickhythe, carrying posies to clear the air while a top-hatted porter sweeps the street. A few days later, the Vintners join the Dyers Company and Her Majesty's Swan Marker for Swan Upping, a weeklong jolly up the Thames to count the number of cygnets on the river. Back in London, traffic on the Thames briefly comes to a stop for the world's oldest rowing race, the Doggett's Coat and Badge. Founded in 1715 by an Irish comedian, the course runs from London Bridge to Chelsea. After rowing hard for four miles and five furlongs, the winner receives a bright red coat with a big silver badge on the sleeve.

These are just a few of the dozens of customs based in the City (not to mention the hundreds in Greater London). In fact, the City is an eccentric institution in its own right. London is the only major capital to have two mayoral posts: the recently restored Mayor of London and the ancient Lord Mayor of the City of London. Whereas the former is a career politician paid to run Greater London (or not), the Lord Mayor is usually an unpaid professional who promotes the City as a cutting-edge centre of capitalism by dressing up in medieval robes and chains. Like Dick Whittington before him, the Lord Mayor heads up the Corporation of London, Britain's richest local authority and the UK's oldest governing body. The Corporation boasts that Parliament itself was based on its Court of Common Council, making it the Grandmother of Parliaments. This assembly oversees the Square Mile and has strong links to the City's livery companies. Many of these old guilds now function as charities and training groups, while others have reinvented themselves to survive. For instance, the Worshipful Company of Coach Makers and Coach Harness Makers now covers the auto and aerospace industries, while the Horners – who used to make drinking flasks from horn – represent the plastics industry. Meanwhile, some of the oldest trades are still gainfully employed. Among the oldest Great Twelve companies, the Fishmongers visit Billingsgate Market daily to inspect the plaice, while the Goldsmiths house the London Assay Office in their hall, stamping their mark of approval on quality metal (hence the term 'hallmark').

The Goldsmiths' Hall also hosts the annual Trial of the Pyx, a tradition dating from at least 1282 that has inspired imitations in the Commonwealth, the United States and even Japan. Presided over by the Queen's Remembrancer, the ceremony is a bona fide jury trial held every year to check the coinage of the realm. Back when coins were made from precious metal, the trial was an effective way of keeping moneymakers honest, particularly since the country's mints were in private hands. By cutting the gold or silver content with base metals, a crooked coin maker could pocket a fat profit – provided he still had the use of both hands. In 1124, King Henry I discovered that the country's moneymakers had been short-changing him by cutting their silver pennies with tin. So at Christmas he invited all the moneyers to his court in Winchester, where naughty mint masters had their right hands chopped off. The pennies' quality quickly improved.

Subsequent monarchs developed other ways of preventing moneymakers from getting out of hand. Juries of laymen and goldsmiths would test coins in London, and the government issued standardised metal plates, or *assaia*, representing one pound of sterling, to the various mints around the country. These trial plates had their own in-built security system, similar to tally sticks. Cut into distinctive shapes, they were divided between the mints, the government and the Goldsmiths, so that they fitted together like a puzzle, with the Exchequer keeping the key piece. The plates would be clipped and the coins tested, or assayed, against their purity by weighing or melting them. In the thirteenth century, 240 silver pennies weighed precisely one troy pound of sterling (the £ sign comes from the Latin for 'pound', *libra*, while the 'd' used to denote pennies up until 1971 stood for *denarius*). Mints were required to pick a penny at random from each pound produced and store them in a locked box, or *pyx* in Latin. At the Trial of the Pyx in London, the jury would open the boxes and put the mint masters' handiwork to the test.

Eventually, the Crown took over the production of coins and housed the Royal Mint at the Tower of London (where it remained until 1975 before moving to Wales). The Trial of the Pyx allowed the Master of the Mint a margin of error. So long as he stayed within the 'remedy' of the law, he could keep any shortfalls in gold or silver, a prospect that excites statisticians to this day. A professor at the University of California in Los Angeles has calculated that an honest Master of the Mint was almost certain to pass the trial, while a dishonest moneymaker had a better than one in two (58%) chance of surviving, provided that he didn't get too greedy, and that the trial plate was up to snuff. In 1710, Sir Isaac Newton stood accused of trying to line his pockets by producing substandard gold guineas as Master of the Mint. However, the great hit-and-miss scientist managed to prove that the trial plate the coins were assayed against had been made too fine. He survived with his reputation, and person, intact.

Given the technological advances since Sir Isaac's day and the lack of precious metal in everyday coins, the Trial of the Pyx might seem as archaic as, well, gold guineas and silver pennies. Oddly enough, the only country outside the Commonwealth to continue the tradition is Japan, which imported it along with the machinery for its mint around 1872. The fledgling US government also copied the concept from Britain but gave it a different name. The US Assay Commission was abolished in 1980 after nearly two centuries. Meanwhile, Britain's original Trial of the Pyx continues to take place every February, with minor adjustments to keep it up-to-date. Although the Trial used to check the coinage of Canada and Australia, these days the only Commonwealth country to put its currency to the test regularly is New Zealand.

The Queen's Remembrancer defends the Trial of the Pyx in the same manner as the Quit Rents Ceremony. 'Although these ceremonies appear in some respects to have archaic features, they serve very real modern functions – the Trial of the Pyx is the largest quality-control testing by an independent jury of the coinage of the realm, and some of that coinage is extremely valuable, such as the £20 bullion Britannia coins. So all these features of these ancient ceremonies are in fact very modern. The government gets a full quality check on the coinage, for nothing. So they're jolly lucky.'

The Goldsmiths Company began picking up the tab around 1871 after the Chancellor of the Exchequer baulked at paying to feed the jurors. 'But the Treasury officials are always very happy to accept the invitation to lunch,' the Remembrancer notes. As the titular Master of the Mint, the Chancellor himself is on trial during the ceremony, albeit in absentia. In recent decades, Tory finance ministers seem to have better attendance records than their Labour counterparts. Kenneth Clarke put in an appearance, as did Norman 'Black Wednesday' Lamont. There's even a photo of Lamont grinning during the 1991 ceremony – a year before the pound crashed out of the ERM (so much for maintaining the value of the currency). Master Turner says the current Chancellor has yet to attend the Trial of the Pyx. However, he refuses to speculate on whether his absence has to do with the alleged disdain that Labour and its 'Scottish MacMafia' have for old English traditions. 'I make no comment,' the Remembrancer says, adding only that the Chancellor usually sends his Economic Secretary in his place.

'Would the trial continue if the UK adopted the –'

'No problem,' he says, anticipating my question. 'The euros would become part of the coinage of the realm, and the Trial of the Pyx would continue.'

As it is, the Royal Mint produces coins for some 100 countries – including euros – 'But we don't say too much about that,' he smiles. This mix of pragmatism and principle often frustrates reformers and traditionalists (and completely baffles foreigners). The fact that the UK would seek to profit from minting the euro while refusing to adopt it might seem contradictory at least and even hypocritical. However, it also reflects the great ability of the British – in particular the English – to find a middle path between the old and the new. Although this *via media* can lead to mediocrity and 'muddling through', it has also produced institutions flexible enough to be adopted around the world, ranging from common law to parliamentary democracy and the English language itself. In their wariness towards change, the British seem to be instinctively conscious that traditions, like civilisation itself, take centuries to build but can be all too easily destroyed. In fact, one of the City's most colourful (and surreal) traditions was killed off on the cusp of the twenty-first century. According to legend, Freemen of the City had the right to drive sheep across London Bridge as a way of dodging taxes and turnpikes. In 2000, the Lord Mayor and the Freemen donned ermine robes over their pinstriped suits and led fifteen woolly mammals across the Thames for the last time:

although it raised £40,000 for charity, killjoys put an end to the traffic-jamming tradition.

In truth, the Freemen's 'right' to shepherd sheep across London Bridge was probably based on myth rather than reality. Even so, it reflected the hard-fought origins of the liberties we take for granted today. Unlike serfs in the country, London's Freemen weren't bound to feudal lords. They were 'free' to make money and own property under the protection of the City. In an editorial, 'The Baa of History', *The Times* mourned the custom's demise by arguing that the City's traditions 'hark back romantically to a past in which the British can take pride, for it is upon this old culture that new ones take root.' The Queen's Remembrancer echoes this sentiment. 'They do provide continuity with the past, and they make people appreciative of what has gone on before. I'm always sorry when I see the loss of colourful traditions which give a great deal of pleasure to a great deal of people and make our lives that much brighter than they would otherwise be.'

Goldsmiths' Hall may back on to Gutter Lane, but there's nothing of the gutter about it. Hemmed in by narrow streets next to St Paul's, the Italianate façade is impressive enough in its own right, with unicorns, cornucopia and trumpets parading across six Corinthian columns. However, like so many buildings in the City, the grey stone exterior barely hints at the grandeur within. The Goldsmiths have been based on the same site off Cheapside for nearly seven centuries, but the third version of their hall opened in 1835, anticipating the gilded rule of Victorian design: 'When in doubt, gob some gold on it.' The domed entrance hall boasts so many mixed media it makes modern interdisciplinary artists seem colour-blind by comparison: patterned carpeting, period oil paintings and oak doorways, not to mention a silk banner, a blazing chandelier, a mahogany clock, gold and silver artefacts, a bronze head of Elizabeth II and a gilded wooden effigy of St Dunstan, all surrounded by columns, walls, statues, arches, staircases and floor tiles carved from marble in ten different colours. Granted, High Victorian Ostentation isn't every-one's cup of tea, but the golden hues of rose, emerald and blue immerse you in a warm bath of wealth. Flushed with vicarious power and riches, you feel like firing up a cigar, knocking back some cognac and clapping an old boy on the back. After all, this *is* the Goldsmiths' Hall; it would be disappointing if it were anything but a temple to imperial splendour.

Upstairs, the Livery Hall keeps the Midas vibe going. A chamber of wall-to-wall, top-to-bottom gilding, carving, painting and panelling, the hall must be at least forty feet high – so high, in fact, that the six outsized chandeliers are hanging closer to the floor than the ceiling so they can light the room. Lit electrically nowadays, they also hold forty-eight candles each, just in case. Way up at the front of the room is an altar-like alcove with red velvet swagging to show off the Goldsmiths' gleaming ceremonial plates and goblets. Around the hall, Corinthian columns in rose-coloured marble and gilded wood support the walls, which are decorated with portraits of the young Queen Victoria and her consort on one side and stained-glass panels on the other, displaying the arms of W. Gladstone and other famous names from the past. Mix in the dense patterns overhead and underfoot, the tall mirrors topped off with frolicking cherubs, plus the all-encompassing peacock colour scheme, and you've got the perfect setting for today's costume drama, the Trial of the Pyx.

Our host this morning is a charming gent in a blue suit cut to taper at his waist and flare just so over his backside. What we're about to witness, he informs us, is 'one of the oldest forms of consumer protection'. 'It may seem like a bit of Gilbert and Sullivan, but it is a *formal* ceremony,' he stresses, pointing out that the trial is an actual court of law, presided over by the Queen's Remembrancer. The modern pyxes are stacked in the far corner of the hall, pale wooden crates holding 81,000 coins with a face value of £45,000, including 4,500 two-pound coins, 13,000 one-pound coins and 24,000 twenty-pence pieces. The most expensive specimen on trial is the £100 Britannia coin made of bullion, while this year features another rare mintage: gold Maundy money. Monarchs of old used to dole out gifts and apparently even wash the feet of the poor on the day before Good Friday, in emulation of

Christ's command (or *mandatum*) at the Last Supper to love one another. Apart from Fergie, though, the current royals don't do feet. Instead, the Queen hands out pocket change at the Royal Maundy Service held each year at a different cathedral around the country. In a tradition that dates from at least AD 600 in England, Beefeaters carry silver trays full of leather pouches on the flat tops of their hats. The Queen doles out one white purse and one red purse to a number of pensioners determined by her age: in 2003, for instance, 77 men and 77 women received Maundy money with a face value of 77p (though the coins are worth much more as collectors' items). Usually made from sterling silver, the golden batch marks Elizabeth's half century on the throne. Incidentally, her very first public engagement as Queen was the Royal Maundy Service.

After his introduction, our host takes a question from the hundred or so middle-aged men and women sitting at the back of the hall, including a few guides from Westminster Abbey, where the sample coins used to be locked in the Pyx Chamber.

'Have you ever had any that weren't up to standard?' a woman asks.

'*Noooo*, of course not,' he joshes. 'The biggest problem we have is making sure all the coins are here.' The worst thing that can happen is when one of the coins is missing. 'All hell breaks loose. We have to turn you upside down and put you all through a metal detector.' Another laugh from the audience. 'The last time it happened the missing 20p coin was in the turn-up of a juryman's trousers.'

The banqueting table where the jury sits is so long the Queen's Remembrancer has to use a microphone to make himself heard. The four wardens of the Goldsmiths' Company, in their fur-trimmed scarlet robes, sit along the crossbar at the top, counting gold coins, while the chief executive of the Royal Mint and a government official sit at the bottom of the mile-long table, no doubt feeling very small indeed. On the sidelines are the dark, stocky men from the Mint in Llantrisant, wearing matching blue jumpers and badges like a Welsh choir. You half expect them to burst into 'Land of My Fathers'.

Three sharp raps of a gavel, and the Queen's Remembrancer strides into the room. He swears in the jury by rattling off the list of 'gold, silver, gold-plated silver, cupro-nickel, nickel-brass and bi-nickel' UK coins to be counted, including 'aluminium-nickel-bronze' for New Zealand's coinage.

To remind them of the ceremony's ancient roots, the Remembrancer recalls that King Alfred's grandson was issuing decrees on the currency 'as recently' as AD 928, while one of Magna Carta's lesser-known demands called for a standard set of measures throughout the kingdom. 'You, ladies and gentlemen, are the guardians of those standards, both ancient and modern.' By way of explanation, he conjures up the son of a Saxon farmer in Gloucestershire and a goldsmith's apprentice in London. The farmer cut a hazel rod long enough to drive his six-strong team of oxen. The rod measured 16½ feet, and four of its lengths (66 feet) marked the baseline of the section of field to be ploughed in one day. His oxen could plough a furrow ten times that distance before they had to turn around, a distance that came to be known as a furlong. In Saxon times, a tenant farmer's daily work quota measured one furlong by four rods – or one acre. Meanwhile, in Cheapside, the goldsmith's apprentice also relied on society's agrarian roots in his trade, counting out 480 dried grains of barley to measure one ounce of precious metal.

In keeping with the current law of the land, though, the trial's verdict two months from now will be announced in metric terms, the Remembrancer notes. 'Now, I have to *struggle* to relate the metric metre to the length of the path travelled by light in a vacuum, during a time interval of *approximately* one two-and-a-half millionth of a second,' he says. 'I *also* have to struggle to recognise the weight of one kilogram as being equal to the mass of international prototypes made of platinum and uranium retained at the Bureau of Weights and Measures in Paris.' He pauses. 'But somehow I suspect that the successors of the farmer's son, or the goldsmith's apprentice – *your grandchildren* – will find those standards as rooted in the technological soil of the twenty-first century as did their Saxon forebears.'

As he exits, the men and women of the jury get down to the tedious task of counting change. In the meantime, a portly man carries around a silver tray with samples of the coins laid out like after-dinner mints. He holds it over the scarlet cordon so that the public can look but not touch. The Maundy pence are so tiny you'd have to dab them with your finger to pick them up.

'Are there any free samples?' a man asks.

'No, unfortunately.'

On my way out of Goldsmiths' Hall, I notice some guidebooks in the foyer marked 'For Display Only' with a list of prices, but none to buy. I glance over at the security desk about ten feet away. The lumpen face behind the counter has been watching the coin-counting on CCTV, a job that must rank somewhere between watching grass grow and paint dry. Having learned the hard way about jobsworths, I instinctively frame my question in the negative, as if to say, *I know it probably isn't your job, but* – 'You wouldn't happen to have any of those guides for sale, would you?'

'Which ones?'

'The ones on the table. I think they're five pounds.'

'They're two pound.'

'Even better. Do you have any?'

'Yeah,' she grunts. '*If* you got the right change.'

The verdict of the trial comes a couple of months later, on ANZAC Day this year, or 25 April, when Australians and New Zealanders honour their war dead. The Kiwi High Commissioner is on hand to find out whether his country's coins are up to scratch, and the Queen's Remembrancer welcomes him with a special mention of Aotearoa and Maui-tiki-tiki-a-Taranga. 'I hope he'll excuse my Maori pronunciation; it is a first for the Trial of the Pyx.' This may also be the first time that a black man has represented the British government at the trial. Chief Treasury Secretary Paul Boateng, the UK's first black cabinet minister, is filling in for the Chancellor at the Goldsmiths' Hall.

I can also claim an exclusive of sorts in being allowed to witness the verdict. The ceremony is closed to the public, partly to keep costs down (there's a lavish lunch afterwards) but mainly because most people would be bored stiff. Apart from the Remembrancer's performance, the actual reading of the verdict is monotonous in the extreme. An official in a black robe gives a blow-by-blow account of how the UK and Kiwi coinage was weighed and assayed. Finally, after reading virtually the same checklist for each denomination, he gives the results: 'It was found that all coins mentioned in this verdict were within permitted variations.'

The ten-minute tedium allows plenty of time to take in the Drawing Room, a smallish chamber decorated in gilded cream. Dressed in full eighteenth-century attire, the Remembrancer is sitting at a gold curlicue table facing the jury members, the Goldsmiths, and the strange Flemish tapestry above their heads. From what I can work out, Cleopatra is about to straddle Antony's lap, her bare leg dangling over his thigh. The thing is, the leg in question is a sickly pink, apparently a botched attempt by the Victorians to dye her carnal flesh the same colour as Antony's robe.

As always, the Remembrancer tries to liven things up, this time by decrying a case of 'brazen impertinence' in his own 'bailiwick' in Sussex. 'Three pound coins were passed over the bar counter of one of our local pubs, *each* a gross forgery, of which this is one,' he says, flinging a coin on the glass-topped table. 'But for the difficulty in identifying the culprit in a somewhat dark and smoky snug bar, I would have brought this offender before you for defrauding your Remembrancer of *three whole pounds*.' He also tells how Britannia, 'that defender of our shores', first appeared on Roman coins in London in AD 119 under Hadrian and more recently graced the country's pennies. 'In these troubled times, it is fitting that Britannia's striking image now appears on our gold bullion coins, a reminder that our currency has a *heritage* stretching back over two millennia and maintained to the right old standard of England,' he concludes. 'We all remain citizens of no mean city, where the maintenance of standards, as you have ensured by your verdict, is on a par with the City's promise: that its word is its bond.'

CHAPTER NINE

HEAVEN FOR HELL-RAISERS

BURNING THE POPE
IN LEWES

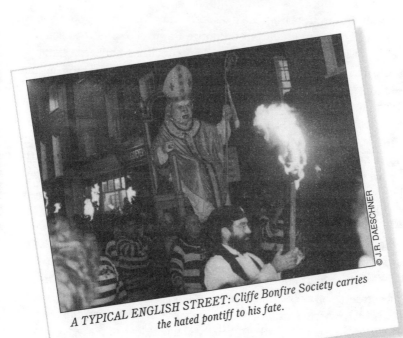

A TYPICAL ENGLISH STREET: Cliffe Bonfire Society carries the hated pontiff to his fate.

© J.R. DAESCHNER

PART ONE:
POPERY AND APOSTASY

Ah, November the Fifth in England! Bonfires scent the countryside, fireworks light the skies, and down in the Deep South, barely an hour from London, young men's fancies turn to drinking, dressing up . . . and burning the Pope in effigy.

Bonfire Night is England's de facto national day, and the Sussex town of Lewes is its de facto Bonfire Capital. Across the country, revellers gather on Guy Fawkes Night to light bonfires, shoot off fireworks and torch the Catholic who plotted to blow up King and Parliament four centuries ago. In most places, the event's anti-Catholic roots have long been forgotten; the dummy on the bonfire is just some 'guy'. In Lewes, however, Bonfire stalwarts continue a Protestant tradition that was once widespread in England: not only do they burn Guy Fawkes; they also torch the Pope himself – the Vicar of Christ, Successor of St Peter, and Supreme Pontiff of a billion believers around the world.

For one night every year, this model English town transforms itself into a bastion of Catholic-bashing. Torch-bearing men, women and children disguised as Vikings, smugglers and black-faced Zulus chant 'Bonfire Prayers' calling for the Pope's destruction, while police in riot gear control the crowd. Blazing crosses march through the streets, banners proclaim NO POPERY and the crisp air reverberates with bloodthirsty cries to *Burrrrrrrrrrrrrrrrrrrrrrrrrnnnnnnn the Pope!!!* The most heartfelt Pope-bashing takes place at a chapel owned by none other than the Reverend Ian Paisley, the Calvinist politico from Northern Ireland, creating a truly combustive combination: a little bit of Ulster, right in London's backyard. And for anyone who protests against Pope burning, Lewes's Bonfire Boys

262

have an ominous response: they burn them in effigy, as Enemies of Bonfire.

The Pope has never commented publicly on his annual immolation, although the Archbishop of Westminster did venture some criticism back when he was bishop of the area. During a flare-up in Northern Ireland's Troubles, an Irish MP lambasted the event in Parliament, outraged by an unseemly (and thus short-lived) link between the Prince of Wales and Pope burning. More recently, Rome's man on the ground, the local priest, has repeatedly denounced it, and been burnt in effigy for his troubles.

In their defence, the Bonfire Boys stress that the pontiff in question is not the incumbent at St Peter's, but Paul V, the Pope at the time of the Gunpowder Plot in 1605. What's more, not all of Lewes's five rival bonfire societies burn the Pope, past or present. However, critics see the historical link – tacked on in recent decades – as a smokescreen for overt anti-Catholicism. Strangely, Paisley's ultra-Protestants aren't that keen on Bonfire Night itself. Although they happily host a seventeenth-century Bonfire Service, thanking God for saving Britain from Catholicism, they frown on the celebration's drunkenness and sexual innuendoes. 'There's so much *apostasy* around here,' rues a black-hatted woman in Paisley's historic chapel.

Apostasy? Now there's a word you don't hear every day. But it's just one of many sulphur-and-brimstone terms floating around Bonfire time, words that sound vaguely sinister, even if you can't remember what they mean. Kyle Paisley, Ian's preacher son, was confused when he heard about the NO POPERY banners. 'Over here, when people talk about "popery", sometimes it means "air freshener",' he told me, adding a novel pronunciation of 'pot pourri'. 'Y'know, pot purry?'

Apart from their perennial anti-popery, the Bonfire Boys are remarkably even-handed in their hate figures. Alongside the Pope and Guy Fawkes, they've burned Paisley himself (for handing out pamphlets on Bonfire Night), many Archbishops of Canterbury (for cosying up to Rome), practically every Prime Minister and a slew of local politicians, policemen and foreigners. This ritual mayhem takes place in a veritable microcosm of Britain, a country where the national anthem is an abridged ditty against Romish rebels and where Catholics to this day are barred from the throne. In fact, Lewes has links to all the major religious and political events that shaped the UK: this is supposedly where England's last pagans tried to kill the Pope's emissaries in AD 666 (aptly enough), where William the Conqueror's right-hand man had his ancestral seat, where the Battle of Lewes gave birth to the Mother of Parliaments, where Henry VIII destroyed a Catholic priory, where his 'Bloody' Catholic daughter burned seventeen Protestants at the stake and where the Age of Reason (and Nonconformity) subsequently took root.

Although up to 60,000 people swarm into town on November the Fifth, Lewes's Pope burning remains relatively unknown to the world at large. Even when the Bonfire Boys do make the headlines – say, for burning a US president or a Muslim leader – the media rarely mention the controversial tradition of torching of the Pope year-in, year-out. And the Bonfire Boys want to keep it that way. Having been burnt in the past, so to speak, they're reluctant to talk to outsiders. Some still carp about a 1950s headline: BIGOTS AROUND THE BONFIRE. What's more, modern safety regulations have threatened the event's very existence. 'We don't want people to come and see Bonfire Night,' a Bonfire official told me when I asked for an interview. 'We'd rather there was no people on the streets, 'cause we do it for ourselves – for Lewes people.'

So I wasn't expecting a warm welcome. As idyllic England goes, Lewes has it all: a hilltop castle built by William the Conqueror's closest ally (and the richest Brit in history); the voluptuous South Downs and the chalk cliffs of the English Channel; the River Ouse moseying through town, flanked by waterfront houses and fishing boats; and a winding high street for a backbone, with ancient alleyways known as 'twittens' running like cobbled ribs down the hillside. For urban refugees, Lewes is close to London but off the radar of the desperate hipsters who flock to Brighton. Neither too big nor too small, Lewes offers small-town intimacy and big-city anonymity, an extremely liveable mix of the rustic and the modern, ranging from an old-fashioned pub where you can engage in dwyle flunking to a trendy eatery serving muffuletta sandwiches and mochaccinos. Lewes also boasts the county's last independent brewery, producing a harsh beer whose purgative side effects are known by some as 'Harveys Guts'. And most importantly, for my purposes, the town has a colourful local tradition.

Of course, all this can mean only one thing: *The Americans will love it.* And I do. In fact, I'd live in Lewes if I could, but I may have a problem. As the local priest put it when introducing me to a parishioner, 'This man is looking for trouble, digging up Bonfire lore. He may very well be the first American to be burnt.'

The more digging you do, the more you realise that for all its surface gentility, there's something not . . . quite . . . right . . . about Lewes. Opponents from both sides of the Bonfire divide attest to the town's strange vibe. Some local history buffs believe the mysterious mounds around Lewes are remnants of an ancient necropolis, or City of the Dead: the Old English root of the town's name (*hlaew*) meant 'burial ground' as well as 'hill', and the museum has a stone head of a spooky, bug-eyed Celtic goddess, the Guardian of the Dead – billed as the only one ever found in England. To this day, self-styled spiritual types claim they can detect pockets of light and dark energy while walking around town, swirling around them like warm and cool undercurrents in the sea. Others compare the town to one great big dysfunctional family, wary of outsiders for fear that they'll be forced to change their strange ways. Some see Bonfire as a manifestation of the town's ancient divisions, re-enacted for eternity. 'A lot of people 'ave said they can feel that something has gone on in this town,' one Old Bonfire Boy confided, 'because there's a lot of history – y'know, since before the Romans – and all those people, especially with the funny little streets, and you think of 'em all creepin' up there.' Not a model of articulacy, but you get the idea: if you're not careful, Lewes can give you the heebie-jeebies.

Of course, many locals adamantly deny this. Bonfire has nothing to do with religion nowadays, they claim. Now that religious relativism has long since given way to irrelevantism, they argue that the tradition is nothing more than a chance to party and take a pop at the authorities. However, there's no denying that Lewes does have a remarkably long history of division and strife. Cut off from the rest of England for most of its existence, Lewes itself is actually two towns, physically divided by water and wedded together shotgun-style barely a century ago. Ancient Lewes, the town on the hill, was a key stronghold by the time the Normans won at nearby Hastings in 1066. The new lord forced the vanquished Saxons to build him a castle, just as his boss, William the Conqueror, did with the Tower of London. Over the years, the Norman overlords pushed the Saxon underdogs off the hill, out of town and across the river, where they built their medieval dwellings on a flood plain. This riverfront area, known as Cliffe, is now home to many old Lewesians, as well as Pope-burning Bonfire Boys and Ian Paisley's ultra-Protestant chapel. Meanwhile, the gentrified enclave around the castle continues to attract affluent newcomers (and is also home to the Catholic church). Nearly a thousand years after William the Conqueror, some Old Lewesians in Cliffe can still be heard referring to the outsiders on the hill as 'those ruddy Normans'. As further evidence that Lewes is Schism Central, consider this: the Greenwich Meridian runs through town, dividing the globe into the East and West hemispheres.

Whether it's due to these earth-splitting divisions or pure coincidence, Lewes has always been a haven for hellraisers. Many have been political agitators, such as Simon de Montfort, whose rebellion at the Battle of Lewes in 1264 split England's government between the king and parliament, and Tom Paine, whose radical ideas about *The Rights of Man* helped inspire the Americans to break away from Britain (and the French to separate their king's head from his body). To this day, Lewes is a bastion of the Green Ink Brigade, producing what must be the most letters-to-the-editor per capita in the country.

However, most of Lewes's rabble-rousers have been religious types. In fact, virtually every spiritual ruction that has shaped Britain has been played out in local terms, particularly the Reformation. Henry VIII's break with Rome was one of the most important events in defining English national identity as something separate and unique from (Catholic) Europe – a sentiment reflected in many Bonfire Boys' opposition to the European Union. Afterwards, practically every Protestant splinter group opened a franchise in Lewes: Presbyterians, Congregationalists, Unitarians, Quakers, Calvinistic Independents, Baptists – both 'General' and 'Particular' – as well as 'Wesleyan' and 'Primitive' Methodists. The Church of Rome was officially reinstated in England in 1850, but it took two decades before a Catholic sanctuary opened in Lewes – and when it did, drunken Bonfire Boys gatecrashed the service. Nowadays, the Church of England is represented in all its High, Broad and Happy-Clappy incarnations in Lewes, while the surrounding area has a surplus of rarefied religious factions, from Mormons and Bahá'ís to Scientologists and Anthroposophists, not to mention a plethora of neopagans and the odd Satanist to boot.

During one of our conversations over the years, the local Catholic priest mentioned *The Wicker Man*, the cult classic that turned a generation of teenage boys on to paganism (*If all pagans look like Britt Ekland, where do I join?*).

'A frightening film,' he said. 'It could happen in Lewes.'

Maybe. Until the *auto da fé* comes back into fashion, though, Lewesians will have to content themselves with burning their enemies in effigy on their night of ritualised misrule, a time when all the divisions and strife that shaped Lewes – and the rest of Britain – explode into the open: Bonfire Night.

For most fair-minded people, the idea that anyone would burn the Pope in effigy is outrageous. But for me, there's something all too familiar about the Catholic-bashing in Lewes come Bonfire time. Depending on which part of the planet you're from, mine was a very conventional – or unconventional – upbringing. I grew up in mid-America in the 1970s, a time when every God-fearing, Communist-hating American had a patriotic duty to be 'born again'; even the president was a born-again Christian. Televangelists with confectionery hair would praise God and plead for Mammon while their wives wept Rivers of Jordan to wash the mascara from their eyes.

Speaking in tongues and 'laying on hands' were de facto rites of passage for young evangelicals (though most drew the line at snake handling). Churches sponsored fellowship meetings with unfortunate names like 'lock-ins' and 'lay missions'. Assorted 'ark-aeologists', including an astronaut, claimed they'd found Noah's Ark and the Ark of the Covenant (raiding that particular goldmine long before Steven Spielberg). And Satan was believed to be lurking beneath every beanbag, easing kids into devil worship with that old pagan festival, Halloween, and later brainwashing them via backward masking, a fiendish process that involved embedding rock music with blasphemous messages that could be heard only when records were played in reverse.

The driving force for all this pre-millennial fervour was the conviction that the End of the World was Nigh. Evangelicals shifted millions of books on the End Times, while mainstream denominations hosted what were effectively Apocalypse Film Nights, with screenings of a low-budget series that dramatised the end of the world from the surprise Second Coming of Christ to the inevitable Rise and Fall of the Antichrist.

And if that didn't scare you into the arms of Jesus, most churches had stockpiles of soul-saving tracts produced by Jack Chick, an illustrator who could stand his own against any *Marvel* draftsman or Soviet propagandist. The turn-or-burn theme of these mini-comics was depicted using gruesome images of burning martyrs, shape-shifting demons, grotesque exorcisms and horribly bloodied Jesuses – just the thing to fascinate and frighten a ten-year-old. Once I'd read my way through the entire collection of tracts, I graduated to Chick's later and much more controversial work, his full-sized comics attacking the Catholic Church. You'd find these hidden away in Bible bookshops, the Christian equivalent of top-shelf material. Of course, this samizdat circulation made the comics that much more exciting. So, while most kids my age were reading about Batman, I consumed comic books like *The Big Betrayal*, which explained how Abraham Lincoln's assassination was really a Jesuit plot, among other dubious claims.

Looking back, my upbringing seems too bizarre to be believed, but for many kids of my generation, these fundamentalist influences were a normal part of growing up, as innocuous as chopper-handle bikes, the Bay City Rollers and Pop Rocks (as long as you didn't mix them with Coke). In truth, the graphic warnings about The Beast and The Priest frightened me then, and they scare the bejeezus out of me now. But I don't see that they did me any real harm – *twitch, twitch* – though I'm sure they contributed to my lifelong fear of statues and dark, empty churches.

All in all, I thought my background would make me well prepared to delve into the Protestant v. Catholic conflict at the core of Bonfire Night. Even so, I wasn't expecting to be confronted with it the moment I set foot in Jireh Chapel.

'Have ya been born again?' the pastor asked after some welcoming chitchat.

Born again? I haven't heard that in years. I mumble something in the affirmative – even if it *was* a long time ago – partly out of a deep-rooted fear of hellfire, but also out of experience. In theory, places like Jireh Chapel are open to saints and sinners. In reality, though, you wouldn't want to admit to being anything but a Bible-believing Christian for fear of being offered up as a sacrifice on the communion table. The regulars – all in their old-fashioned Sunday best – seem genuinely startled to see a stranger, and they go out of their way to be friendly. But you can imagine the pitying looks you'd get if you admitted to being, say, an agnostic or – even worse – an Anglican (which can, of course, be one and the same thing).

Jireh's pastor, Noel Shields, never wanted to come to Lewes – or England, for that matter. As an evangelist, Noel worked in Northern Ireland before building up Ian Paisley's Free Presbyterian Church in Australia. That's when the call first came: rather than returning to Ulster, he heard that he might be sent to England. Like many Ulstermen, though, he thought the English were snobs. 'I said there was no way I was goin' to England – no way.' But after much inner turmoil, he finally got down on his knees and prayed: 'Lord, I'd go anywhere for you – even England.'

Miraculously, nothing came of the rumours . . . until five years later. By then, Noel and his wife were settled in Northern Ireland, having added an extension to their home for their four children. The England scare seemed to have been a test of faith, just as Jehovah ordered Abraham to sacrifice his son before granting him a reprieve. 'I thought I was gettin' out of it,' Noel recalls, 'But then the Lord told me to come' – and not to just any part of England, either; to the south-east, the homeland of the urbane English, centred around the decadent metropolis. The Free Presbyterians had recently acquired Jireh Chapel in Lewes, built in 1805 by the followers of a famous self-taught evangelist, making it the historic gem in Paisley's church and one of its southernmost sites on the mainland. Given Noel's missionary experience, Paisley had decided that he should be the first evangelist at his Lewes outpost.

At first, Noel's wife, Joan, found it difficult. 'People in Lewes are more stand-offish,' she says. 'Not in any disrespect, but I think because they've heard so much about us comin' over – "Free Presbyterians, bigots, real hard-line Loyalists" and what have you, comin' from Northern Ireland. I think people are just wary of us – and fair play to them, y'know, ya have to win people as friends first.'

Even now, some of Noel's parishioners still have a hard time understanding his strong Ulster accent. 'More so I found it at the start. I felt totally a stranger – well, I was a stranger – but we're settled here now, and we like the work, and the Lord has brought more families in.' Before he arrived, Jireh's weekly attendance had sunk into single digits, but that figure has multiplied to as many as forty. Even so, he has a long way to go to fill the chapel's thousand-odd capacity.

Although you'd think Ulstermen would feel right at home in Lewes on Bonfire Night, Noel says the Fifth isn't an orange-letter date in Northern Ireland. 'We wouldn't make a big night of it. Maybe when we were children – y'know, "Penny for the guy" – but apart from that, it wasn't a big issue at home.' Fireworks were outlawed in the province until 1996, and even now, Roman candles and firecrackers must seem tame alternatives for a populace weaned on Semtex and Molotov cocktails. Lewes's Bonfire processions are similar to Orange marches in spirit, if not detail, Noel says. However, even for Ulstermen, burning the Pope in effigy would be almost beyond the pale.

'So what did you think when you first saw it?'

'Great!' he laughs, slapping his knee. 'No problems at all. The NO POPERY aspect was great – but there were some immoral things.' By which he means the Bonfire Boys' drinking and lewdness. Of course, many 'Enemies of Bonfire' argue that the event itself is immoral, but Noel shrugs off that criticism. 'It's the same thing that people say at home in Northern Ireland, that you shouldn't be in the Orange parades. But we're bein' honest and we're tellin' people that we're Protestants, and we're not ashamed. So it's who we are, it's our culture.

'Y'know what the problem is,' he continues, cocking an eyebrow. 'Rome doesn't like to be reminded in this town what they did. Lewes probably suffered more than anywhere else – seventeen martyrs in this town alone. Rome wants to wipe out the memory, but I don't think we should let them. There are no Catholic houses burnt in this town, and no Catholics are touched, and here's the joke – there are a lot of Catholics in the Cliffe Bonfire Society. That wouldn't happen in Ireland. That happens here, because the people do it more for tradition.'

In contrast, Noel claims that his Pope-bashing is purely theological. 'We all believe the Pope is *our* Antichrist. The system of Romanism is the Antichrist system that is referred to in Revelations.' Then he recounts some old chestnuts of Protestant propaganda: 'The Pope says he's a Vicar of Christ. The word vicar means "anti" – so he really stands up there and says "I am the Antichrist". And if you take the – y'know, the thing he wears on his head – and you take the name of it, and you break it down into Roman numbers, and you add it up, the number comes to 666.'

And here's me thinking it's just a funny hat.

Noel imparts these revelations with wide-eyed sincerity, looking for all the world like someone who claims to have been abducted by aliens. But from his point of view, he's merely telling God's Truth, as unpalatable as it may be.

Protestants have been arguing the Pope-as-Antichrist thesis

since before the Reformation, when critics attacked Catholic doctrines that seemed to have little if any basis in the Bible: praying to saints, venerating the Virgin Mary and dishing out indulgences, to name but a few. To this day, Noel and other like-minded Protestants believe Catholicism blasphemes God's Word and takes the focus away from Jesus's supreme sacrifice: 'The Mass is sacrificing Christ all over again, repeating what Christ did on the Cross.' As a result, the Catholic system is ultimately acting against Christianity; hence, it is antichristian.

It's no wonder, then, that Noel views the global trend toward unity between Protestants and Catholics as nothing less than fraternising with the Devil. The ecumenical movement is 'the number one public enemy', he says. 'The problem today is that there's been a departure from the faith . . . If you look around us, at the traditional churches, they're all goin' to Rome.' Which is synonymous with 'going to hell', in Free Presbyterian parlance. As with the Devil, the real or imagined threat of 'Romanism' is never far from the minds of hard-line Protestants like Noel. It's as if he's fighting a battle that ended centuries ago, when Britain converted to Protestantism. Back home in Ulster, Pope-bashing may have some relevance, but here in the Home Counties, it seems anachronistic and gratuitous.

'Don't you think your ministry would be more effective if you didn't attack Catholicism so vehemently?' I ask him.

'I don't go up the street and shout NO POPERY,' he counters. 'I don't carry the Pope up around the streets. I go and talk to people and tell 'em about Jesus Christ, but I certainly don't compromise with popery.'

Like his opposite number, Lewes's new priest wasn't looking for a fight when he arrived in town a week before Bonfire. Father Eric Flood was an educated man with four decades of service behind him. Originally from London, he spoke with a fine, English-oak accent, even though he had always considered himself more Irish than Anglo. Being half-Irish and a Catholic to boot automatically made him something of an outsider in England. 'Not a foreigner, but certainly belonging to a still persecuted minority. You have to remember that the restoration of the [Catholic] Church in England was only a hundred or so years ago.' His own theological leanings were 'neo-Vatican II', meaning that he counted himself among the reformers who were currently out of favour within the church. He often wore socks and sandals with his priestly finery during Mass, and his pewter hair had the styling of a man who'd hit his prime in the late 1960s; now, as he neared retirement, he had the world-weariness of a man in his early sixties.

Father Flood tried to keep an open mind about Lewes's Bonfire tradition – at least, as open a mind as a priest could have about the ritual immolation of the Pope. He'd seen many November the Fifth celebrations during his years serving in Sussex, where the burning season began as early as August and culminated on November the Fifth. In any event, Bonfire Night looked to be the least of his worries in the town; church attendance had nearly halved over the past twenty years, while Lewes's reputation as a year-round haven for occultists had grown. A few months earlier, a young man had fallen to his death from the white cliffs outside town, convinced that he had been cursed by a Catholic-cum-Satanist. So Father Flood had plenty to do without getting involved in Bonfire. 'If it was the current Pope being burnt, I would be very troubled,' he told the *Daily Telegraph* beforehand, 'but it is Pope Paul V, and I must admit we had some bad Popes hundreds of years ago. I don't see it as more than tradition and a bit of fun for the town.'

However, his views quickly changed once he witnessed the spectacle. 'I was not happy,' he says with deliberate understatement, making it clear that he was fit-to-be-tied furious. 'It was the roughest and the crudest and probably the most expensive bonfire blow-off of all of them.' He and the local prison chaplain had followed the processions in mufti – minus their dog collars. 'We saw the whole lot – the bonfire display, heard all the anti-papal ranting, and then of course, the inciting of the crowd to shout "Burn the Pope". I mean, have you ever heard a mob? Especially the children getting involved – I don't like to hear kids shouting "Burn the Pope! Burn the Pope!" – because this is how they carry on their primitive tradition.'

Outraged, he fired off a letter to the local paper. The following year, the main Bonfire society responded by declaring him an Enemy of Bonfire, toting a papier-mâché mould of his head around town on a pole before blowing it to smithereens. 'They burned my head, with a big notice: FLOOD OF BIGOTRY,' he says, brimming with indignation. He keeps a snapshot of his effigy on his mantelpiece: a rough likeness with grey hair, a longish nose, thick glasses and a priest's collar. Next to his disembodied head is another Enemy of Bonfire, TV DOCUMENTARIES, and the placard of a group marching in the procession: the SUSSEX STORMTROOPERS, with the 'S's drawn like lightning bolts. The comparison isn't lost on Father Flood, who blasts the display as a 'Nazi-style procession'. 'Many local people seem to boycott it. They don't go out that night because they feel it's a kind of yobs' rule. I liken it to the Nazi party. It's very much the same – fire, darkness, marching, machoism – it's not what I would call a very nice spectacle.'

A few years ago, shortly after Father Flood arrived, the Bonfire celebrations were almost washed out by the worst storms in living memory. 'The press asked me had I prayed for rain,' he chuckles. For the record, he hadn't. 'But I will remember to do it next time,' he jokes.

'You see, the town has not got a particularly good reputation for being on God's side. They're very superstitious, I think. It's a place associated with sorcery, magic and witchcraft, and I find that unhealthy too,' he adds, referring to a string of strange goings-on that culminated in a newspaper headline not long before he arrived – SATANISM, SORCERY AND SEX: IS THIS LEWES? He points out that Lewes and the land of the South Saxons (Sussex) was one of the last parts of Britain to convert to Christianity, largely because the hills and forests cut them off from the rest of the country. 'Lewes went its own dark way for a long time before it was converted.' And just as the Saxons were becoming dyed-in-the-wool Christians, the Normans came and kicked them out of power. 'The Norman Conquest was French Catholicism pushing its way into pretty primitive territory,' he explains, arguing that not much has changed since.

'I wouldn't call Lewes a very open-minded place in many ways.

It's a place in which ignorance can survive, bigotry can survive.' Father Flood recounts a conversation he once had with a thirtysomething man in Sussex who had never been to London, even though the capital is just over an hour away. 'All he would say is, "Lunnun is evil. Lunnun is evil",' he adds, mimicking the man's thick country accent. 'So I said, "Well, have you been –?" "No, oi don't wanna foind out," he says. "Oi don't loike that."'

When Father Flood puts it like that, Sussex sounds like the setting for *Ye Olde Deliverance*; only instead of evil hillbillies playing 'Duelling Banjos', this film would feature Catholic-burning bigots dancing to 'Duelling Accordions'. But the priest does his best to present a balanced view. 'I would hate to give the impression that Lewes was a town of bigots,' he adds. 'I think, as everywhere, you have a few bigots, and they exercise an influence out of all proportion to their intelligence.' Flood singles out the biggest bonfire society, Cliffe, for stubbornly continuing to burn the Pope even as other groups have stopped. 'The ordinary bonfire societies are pretty harmless. There's no real religious feeling there. It's only the Cliffe that uses the old Bonfire Prayers, and they express a very bad streak of bigotry and stupidity in the Protestant mind.'

These days, Father Flood avoids the bonfire celebrations, staying indoors to cat-sit and 'stop the church from being burned or something'. Stones have been thrown at the church windows on the night of the Fifth, but the priest blames that on kids rather than Bonfire Boys. Last year, Father Flood skipped town altogether. 'Did a good thing on November 4th. Left town,' he wrote in St Pancras's newsletter, denying a newspaper report that he left to 'flee' Bonfire Night. 'I see no reason for being present. Because for me, although most societies will provide you with a carnival atmosphere, somehow the Cliffe's feeling spoils the town's celebrations.'

Undeterred, he plans to continue his protests. 'I think treating Bonfire – or the wilder aspects of it – with a dignified silence doesn't actually do enough,' he says, though he acknowledges that the more the Cliffe are attacked, 'the more they like it'. In his most recent letter to the paper, he outlined his vision for the community. If the priest had his way, Bonfire Night would focus on family fun and fundraising for charity, with a service of reconciliation to erase its anti-Catholic bias. 'If we should burn any effigies, they should be to Ignorance, Prejudice and Bigotry,' he argues.

However, Flood's dreamy epistle has failed to inspire Cliffe's members. 'It was a load of gobbledegook as far as I was concerned,' one of the more intellectual Bonfire Boys tells me. 'I didn't quite get what he was gettin' at.'

No one knows exactly why Pope burning has survived in Lewes, but several elements seem to have combined to make the town a crucible of anti-Catholicism: the wildfire growth of Protestantism in the south-east during the Reformation . . . Henry VIII's destruction of Lewes's French Catholic priory . . . the burning of the Lewes Seventeen by 'Bloody' Queen Mary . . . the town's anti-authoritarian roots, stemming from the pre-Christian era to the Battle of Lewes and later Nonconformist offshoots . . . and Lewes's relative isolation versus more fashionable towns like Brighton, where money-minded burghers doused Bonfire for fear of frightening away their royal clientele.

Like the rest of the country, Lewes has probably commemorated November the Fifth since the failed Gunpowder Plot of 1605. However, its celebrations didn't take their present, organised form until the mid-1800s, after the Catholic Church was reinstated in England for the first time since the Reformation. Across the country, Bonfire Night became a protest against the return of the Church of Rome and the push for Irish independence ('Home Rule Equals Rome Rule'). In Lewes, the Bonfire Boys rioted for a month in 1847 after the authorities called in the new London Metropolitan Police to try to stop the Protestant hell-raising.

Whereas some people might be embarrassed to have a rioter as an ancestor, for old Lewesians, it's a source of pride. Ken and Norman Funnell belong to one of the few Bonfire families that can trace their involvement in the tradition back to its anarchic origins. Both in their seventies, the brothers are Life Members of Cliffe Bonfire Society, the group that has steadfastly kept the Pope fires burning despite opposition from rivals and outsiders. Their great-grandfather took part in the notorious riots of 1847, and their father helped create some of the Cliffe's most controversial tableaux in the early 1900s. He passed his know-how on to them, and they took over the making of the Pope and Guy Fawkes effigies. This tradition of defiance now spans six generations: their grandchildren march in the Cliffe's procession, and one has even followed in their footsteps by designing the effigies and becoming Pope Burner in Chief.

Like many great comic duos, the brothers are physical opposites, with Norman the straight man to Ken's practical joker. Their squarish glasses are the only things the men have in common. Norman is balding, clean-shaven and thin, whereas his older brother has a full head of hair, moustache and big belly. If they were fireworks, Norman would be a standard-issue rocket that explodes with a bang, while Ken would be a whirligig that spins on the ground, showering sparks before zooming into the air. Telling an anecdote, Ken will jump up from his chair and act out scenes, rolling his eyes and waving his arms and laughing so hard he runs out of breath. Norman, in contrast, prefers to sit back and laugh at his brother as he flops around and recoils with laughter. When they really get going, the Funnell brothers adopt a tag-team style of conversation that's capable of cajoling – or cudgelling – any opponent into submission.

The Funnells were in charge of making fireworks back in the days when men risked life and limb for Bonfire Night. Stringing bangers together on a fuse was straightforward enough; the tricky bit came when you wanted multiple explosions timed off each other. That meant you had to make a circuit by running the fuse *through* the middle of a firecracker already packed with gunpowder. If you knew a firework took a full minute to burn, for instance, and you wanted to use it to trigger another sequence after thirty seconds, you drilled into it halfway down, *while* it was filled with explosives. 'It got a bit dodgy, that,' Ken admits. Hearts thumping, he and his brother would bore holes in the bangers' paper casings with a metal drill – very carefully, or the friction could make the firecracker blow up in their faces. To judge whether they had penetrated the casing, the boys would take the drill bit outside and set a match to it. If it sparked, they knew they had gone far enough.

The Funnells used to make the effigies of the Pope and Guy out of sacking stuffed with wood shavings. The younger generation may joke that their Pope looked like an out-of-work baker, but the Funnells remember feeling pride and even affection for the hate figure after hours and hours of working on the effigy. In those days, the Cliffe didn't bother trying to justify Pope burning by arguing that it was a historical pontiff. 'We never used to put a name on him or a number, we just used to burn the Pope,' Ken says nonchalantly. 'I mean now, they seem to have fixed on Pope Paul the Fifth, don't they? So that's fair enough – it's a Pope isn't it?' He winks and roars with great wheezy guffaws.

I ask him why Cliffe has continued to burn the Pope even though most of the town's other bonfire societies have stopped.

'Well, they know what they're about. That is what's different with the Cliffe – absolutely different.' In recent decades, he notes, some rival groups have revived Pope burning after seeing Cliffe's stalwarts grow to become Lewes's biggest bonfire society. 'But the thing is, it's no good bringing things back, because that's nonsense. What we're about is rememberin'. That is why we're on top, the fact that we don't give an inch.'

The Funnells can recall countless confrontations over the years between the Cliffe and its enemies. Like the controversy that barred the society from inviting military bands to accompany its procession. At the time, in 1980, the old Odeon on Cliffe High Street had closed down, and somebody had scrawled SHAME across it to protest the loss of the local cinema. Next door, the Cliffe's NO POPERY banner hung across the street, providing a perfect photo opportunity when the guest military band marched underneath. Given that the conflict in Northern Ireland had flared up again, any military link with NO POPERY was explosive. And this wasn't just any military band; it was the Prince of Wales's Own Regiment of Yorkshire band. 'The press got hold of this, and take a picture, and have the NO POPERY banner, and they've got SHAME up there, and they worked it all in together,' Norman says ruefully.

'And of course the Catholic press in southern Ireland, they really raised the roof, didn't they, over it,' Ken chuckles. 'It got back to Parliament –'

'It ended up gettin' an Irish MP at 10 o'clock at night [in Parliament], and he said there shouldn't be any military bands playin' at a religious ceremony.'

'Well, no – not to be partisan. Anyway, that blew us off the map for military bands,' Ken concludes.

Around the same time, the Cliffe also torched THE ARCHTRAITOR OF CANTERBURY, Robert Runcie, for his push toward ecumenism.

Likewise Father Flood for trying to water down their tradition.

'He's only been 'ere for five minutes, hasn't he?' Norman says.

'We 'ad 'im on a pole – anybody who's made it in the town 'as been on a pole,' the older brother chuckles. 'They really think they've made it – they do indeed.'

Despite these scraps, Ken and Norman insist that Bonfire Night has everything to do with the remembrance of Lewes's martyrs and little if anything with modern religious antagonism. 'Don't stress the popery bit too much,' Ken says, 'because it's not about that. It's about remembrance.'

That may be, but Bonfire Boys tend to have a hard time keeping their story straight, partly because the Fifth is a mishmash of commemoration. They'll tell you that Cliffe's 'No Popery' paraphernalia remembers the Gunpowder Plot's failure, the deaths of the seventeen Protestant martyrs, and even William of Orange's triumphant arrival in England on November the Fifth, 1688. In the same breath, though, they'll let slip remarks that certainly sound anti-Catholic, despite their strong denials.

'If you look at Lewes, the martyrs were burnt right outside our town hall. Yes, it was done, and all we do is remember it, y'know?' Ken argues. 'And we don't want to forget it either, because –'

'We're celebratin' our freedom,' Norman says. 'We've all got freedom of worship in this country, and if you want to be a Catholic, you can be one –'

'But at the same time, we don't want the Pope interferin' with England – never did. And that's it – y'know, religious tolerance, yes, but don't push it too far, sorta thing,' Ken laughs. 'And unfortunately, perhaps we're a dying breed, really. Now they don't even teach 'em history, do they? They got no background.'

' "*Cool* Britannia",' Norman sniffs.

'Yeah – we want "Rule Britannia". We don't want any "Cool Britannia",' his brother adds. 'People have lost their heritage.'

It doesn't help having all these outsiders from London and elsewhere settling in Lewes, either. 'This is a Protestant county – it always was,' Ken continues. 'Now, because we're in a lovely part of England, everybody wants to flock down 'ere, don't they? You 'ave to look now to find a Lewesian, y'know? We keep dyin' off. But we got university types and they all come, "*Ohhhhh*, what a *won*derful town! *Wonderful*!" ' he coos. 'In three years, they want to change it all, don't they! And now that there's more of them in the town, you get more of this controversy rearin' up.'

'So do you think your opponents will eventually win?'

They groan in unison. 'I don't know, but we've got some hard and fast Bonfire Boys,' Ken ventures. 'It's a democratic society, obviously, y'know, and we vote, but I think before I leave we'll 'ave to 'ave a Bill of Rights: *that* [the No Popery element] is what it's about. You can change everything else, but not that!'

The afternoon of the Fifth, Lewes looks like it's bracing itself for a full-scale invasion. 'We've stopped serving,' says the hostess at a high street restaurant, turning me away at one in the afternoon. 'We have to board up the windows.'

Board up the windows?! There's going to be chaos tonight! Anarchy!

Within hours, most of the restaurant's neighbours follow suit, transforming the hillside street into a patchwork of lumber-clad shopfronts. Even the tourist office boards up its windows, as if looters are going to skip the electronics shops to steal reams of brochures. Isolated bangs and pops punctuate the afternoon, with most of the noise coming from down in Cliffe, where banners are strung across the high street, including the one proclaiming NO POPERY in bold letters flanked by Cliffe's skull-and-crossbones emblem and the head of the Pope. Around the corner, Bonfire Boys in black-and-white jumpers indulge in some pre-revelry drinking in the Dorset Arms, across the road from Jireh Chapel.

As daylight fades to dusk, Lewes's population turns into a surreal mix of characters from a hundred different period films: Viking Chiefs, Tudor and Edwardian Ladies, Victorian Suffragettes, Wild West Cowboys, Zulu Warriors, Boer Soldiers, Aztec Sun Gods and even Samurais. Most of their costumes are impressively – even obsessively – detailed, reflecting months, if not years, of hard work, such as the Saxons' long fur robes and the American Indians' floor-length feather headdresses. Each bonfire society also has hundreds of roving 'smugglers' dressed in striped jumpers, with matching red kerchiefs and smart white trousers.

By six o'clock, eager crowds are gathering on the narrow pavements, held back by metal barricades. The processions kick off with Commercial Square Bonfire Society and its unlikely blend of Americana. Hundreds of torch-bearing Red Indians, Union Soldiers, Johnny Rebs and Southern Belles solemnly march to the top of Lewes's high street to lay a wreath at the war memorial, which also marks the site where the seventeen Protestant martyrs were burnt. The acrid smell of smoke and paraffin permeates the town, and the torches send sparks and grey ash fluttering over bystanders. An Indian squaw is pushing a pram with one hand and holding a torch with the other, directly over her baby. He doesn't even notice; he's crashed out, oblivious to the fireball and booming fireworks overhead.

One by one, the other societies parade up the high street to pay their respects, accompanied by the oompah of brass bands. Tongues of flame stretch down the narrow street, the marching torches glinting against shop windows and lighting the faces of onlookers. The illuminated obelisk of the Martyrs' Memorial hangs in the sky over Cliffe, flanked by a brilliant full moon and intermittent explosions of red and green fireworks. For all their riotous history, though, most of the bonfire societies consist of well-behaved citizens in over-the-top costumes carrying torches in an orderly fashion through town. The atmosphere is carnival-like – not in the Catholic-

Latin sense of sin, sex and samba, but in an infinitely more eccentric Anglo-Protestant way, what with all the pseudo-Zulus, pale-faced Red Indians and wannabe Home County Cowboys on display. For the most part, the processions are one big blur of fire and fancy dress. Once you've seen one Sussex Zulu, you've seen 'em all.

But then there's the Cliffe.

Lewes's biggest bonfire society stands out from its rivals in every respect. For the thousand-strong Cliffe, the night starts with a couple of races – men and women in smugglers' costumes drag blazing half-barrels up and down the high street. A vanguard of Vikings then leads a procession through the neighbourhood, the fearsome warriors marching three across, clad in fur cloaks and boots, as well as shiny metal breastplates and horned helmets that cover their faces. These Cliffe 'Pioneers' carry the skull-and-crossbones symbols with NO POPERY emblazoned underneath. A contingent of Cavaliers follows, bearing banners commemorating the Lewes Martyrs, the Discovery of 'Guido' Fawkes's Gunpowder Plot and the Glorious Revolution of William III. (Never mind that many Cavaliers were crypto-Catholics.) Then there's an assortment of Scottish Highlanders and various other groups such as a gaggle of nuns and angels.

Leave it to 'Good Ole Cliffe' to inject jazz – and even sex – into the oh-so-traditional proceedings. Besides the customary marching band, Cliffe's musical accompaniment includes a feel-good ragtime group as well as half a dozen conga vamps dressed in black fetish-wear dancing to the beat of bare-chested male drummers, voguing their way through the streets to the furious jungle beat like extras from a production called *S&M: The Musical* by Andrew Lloyd Webber.

The entire assortment of Vikings and Cavaliers, Nuns and Smugglers, Kiddies and Conga Vamps comes to a halt at the corner of Cliffe Church, where a mock archbishop rails against the society's enemies. Then he leads the first of several recitations of the Bonfire Prayers during the night, including the controversial last verse that other societies have either done away with or toned down. In the torchlit darkness, a thousand men, women and children chant in rollicking, rhythmic unison:

A penny loaf to feed the Pope.
A farthing o' cheese to choke him.
A pint of beer to rinse it down.
A faggot of sticks to burn him!

The *burrrrrrn* bit really gets them going:

Burrrrrrn him in a tub of tar.
Burrrrrrn him like a blazing star.
Burrrrrrn his body from his head.
Then we'll say old Pope is dead!
Hip, hip hoorrrayyyy!
Hip, hip hoorrayyyyyyyyy!

The Bonfire Boys and Girls continue through the streets of Cliffe before starting the long slog up School Hill to the war memorial. The sheer size of Cliffe's procession dwarfs all the others: hundreds, if not thousands of torches stretching from Cliffe Bridge all the way up to the memorial, a third of a mile away. These aren't just any torches, either; they're big, fat, burn-Frankenstein-burn fireballs that make other societies' torches look like candles. What's more, there's an endless supply of these monsters, ensuring that Cliffe's Bonfire Boys are armed with new torches every step of the way. The blazing balls of paraffin-soaked sacking fill the air with eye-stinging smoke, turning the high street hazy. Most other societies make at least a token effort to keep from singeing the crowd with their torches, but Cliffe's Bonfire Boys are happy to tilt theirs toward the pavement, ensuring that bystanders make way for them.

And God forbid the procession should get held up. When it does, the Bonfire Boys get bored, so they liven things up by lighting bangers – six-foot strings of nerve-shattering firecrackers. They also fire a mini cannon with window-rattling regularity. The narrowness of the street – it's barely twenty feet across in some places – amplifies the sonic blasts as they reverberate off the buildings. Some onlookers shield their ears, but most cheer wildly, hooting and hollering after each deafening bang. The Bonfire Boys

283

laugh as they kick and throw bangers, trying to catch each other off-guard. The ones at the front take advantage of the hill's incline to roll firecrackers at their cohorts below. The Boys are careful to keep from tossing firecrackers into the crowd, but if a banger happens to roll into the gutter, right next to that weedy bloke who's standing unaware with his girlfriend, well . . . *that's all part of the fun, innit?*

The most impressive spectacle by far comes when Cliffe returns from the war memorial. Six Bonfire Boys race down the hill with flame-filled barrels, careening from kerb to kerb and blazing a trail for Cliffe's Pioneers. Three columns of Vikings carry seventeen huge burning crosses, one for each of Lewes's martyrs. The crosses stand at least twenty feet high – the men have to hold them at an angle against their bodies so they can wind their way down the incline. Meanwhile, the smugglers light hissing fuchsia flares that illuminate the street, throwing off billowing smoke that turns orange as the crosses pass through it. A replica of the Martyrs' Memorial explodes on Cliffe Bridge with seventeen bangs. As the band plays 'Land of Hope and Glory', the giant crosses disappear into the pastel haze.

Buuuurrrrrrrrrrrrrnnnnn the Poooooopppe!

The shrill cry cuts through the catcalls and hisses. The boy can't be more than ten years old, but there he is, at the front of the crowd, baying for the Pope's destruction. By the time Cliffe marches on to the muddy field, the dimpled imp has progressed to the cutting-edge of sacrilege, cupping his hands over his mouth:

Buuuuuuurrrrrrrrrrrrrrrrrn the fucking *Poooooopppe!*

The hate figure is seated on a throne a hundred yards away, across a ditch framed by barren trees and the coast's magnificent chalk cliffs. From this safety-regulated distance, the papal effigy looks like a little doll, recognisable only by his mitre and robe. In the other far corner of the field stands Guy Fawkes tied to a stake, dressed in a dark vest and a blowsy shirt, his head bowed and his sleeves fluttering in the wind as he awaits his fate.

Hundreds of people have squelched their way to the edge of town to witness the finale of Bonfire Night, many of them trying to fend off the cold with beer cans, hip flasks and even full-sized whisky bottles. On the other side of the cordon, half a dozen of Cliffe's mock judges, in their long red robes and horsehair wigs, are swigging beer and Southern Comfort, tending to a gigantic bonfire. The massive mound of lumber is at least twenty feet high and forty feet across. It starts out as a smouldering heap, but soon lights up the field, warming the crowd with face-broiling heat. Flames leap up and sparks take flight, the fire casting an orange tint on the white cliffs in the background while the full moon shimmers overhead.

The Vikings, Cavaliers and smugglers straggle in, throwing their torches on the bonfire before lining up along the ditch, their backs to the crowd. They plant the heads of the two Enemies of Bonfire next to the NO POPERY sign, and wheel the main tableau to the back of the field. The Cliffe's mock archbishop and his cohorts – a priest and two past-it choirboys – parade across the pasture, bowing to boos and cheers.

'That's not the real Pope!' a woman whines, the pedantic cry of someone in danger of having her head kicked in. Technically, of course, she's right – the man in canonicals is meant to be an Anglican 'Archbishop', a High Church buffoon. But who reads the programme? And the mock cleric certainly does look like a Pope, or at least a popish official, what with his gold-embroidered turquoise robe, cleft headgear, hooked staff and red book with a cross on it. Anyway, the crowd doesn't care who gets burnt, so long as someone does.

Besides their clerical kit, the archbishop and his entourage wear two unusual accessories – welding goggles and earplugs. The reason becomes clear once they clamber on to the raised platform directly in front of the crowd. Surrounded by four burning crosses, the mock archbishop starts haranguing the congregation about the glories of the Cliffe. Before he can even finish a sentence, though, the Bonfire Boys start peppering him with bangers – the same big firecrackers they used on the High Street. Pretty soon, the constant Boom! Blam! Boom! drowns out the archbishop's yammering, and he's trapped amid smoke and explosions, red firecracker casings littering the ground. Occasionally, a banger gets caught in the folds of a robe or the cuff of a sleeve, and the archbishop and his clerics have to shake like crazy to keep it from blowing off their arms. They're standing up there, twitching and flinching and flapping as the Bonfire Boys double over with laughter and redouble their assault.

'That's the worst job ever!' a man laughs, but the archbishop seems to relish his role – although his sidekicks look like they're having second thoughts. They don't do anything except act as human shields against the incoming rounds. Every so often, the barrage of bangers lets up long enough for the archbishop to cue the ritual immolation of the effigies: 'What shall we do with him?!?'

'Burrrrrrrrrn himmmm!'

Guy Fawkes is the first to go. Tiered fountains of sparks slowly consume him, followed by a demolishing BANG. As his body burns, rockets spurt into the air.

However, there are no slow-burn theatrics for the Enemies of Bonfire; their disembodied heads are blown to smithereens, each dispatched with a merciless BOOM!

The crowd still isn't satisfied. A chant chugs around the field, gathering speed: *Burrrrrn . . . the . . . Poooppe, burrrn the Poooppe, burrn-the-POPE, BURN-THE-POPE!*

The Pope's throne begins pulsing with lights, then explodes into sparks – spinning white haloes and red-and-green fountains. Rockets shoot out of his shoulders, snakelike tracers shriek into the sky and fireworks crackle inside his chair and torso. Soon he's nothing but a fiery shell. A sonic BOOM! blows his staff off his lap, and the flames finish him off.

'There you have it,' the archbishop declares to the cheering crowd.

A firecracker explodes against his leg.

'Ow!'

Everyone laughs while he twitches and jerks. Meanwhile, out in the crowd, a stray firecracker has landed in a woman's thick, long, man-catching mane. She's trying to panic gracefully, without losing her cool, even though sparks are shooting from her head. Her friends frantically shake her hair. The firecracker falls out just in time and hits the ground with a BANG! The woman laughs it off, but the terror in her eyes tells you she knows how close she came to needing plastic surgery.

The sky erupts into a neck-craning, chest-thumping cacophony of incandescent noise. Dozens of massive coloured camellias burst overhead, strobing the chalk cliffs with red, orange, yellow, pink, green, blue and violet. Hundreds of shrieking sodium-white snakes slither into the sky. Giant sparklers sizzle into the stratosphere, blinding white starbursts form palm trees in the firmament, boomerangs and fireballs criss-cross the air. Some of the fireworks shoot so high they seem to arc back over the crowd and explode directly overhead. The aftershocks spatter your clothing and echo through your ribcage.

The destruction of Cliffe's tableau is the night's fiery finale. The subject of the float is a mystery right up until the Fifth, and the audience typically oohs and ahhs on cue as the latest figure of ridicule is wheeled on to the field. In recent years Cliffe has consigned Bill Clinton, Tony Blair, Osama Bin Laden and George W. Bush to the flames. The tableau's demise begins gradually and ends with an all-consuming fire flash – the same pyrotechnic effect that film crews use for car explosions. The crowd cheers, its appetite for destruction sated for another year.

Leaving the bonfire site, everyone stinks of smoke, as if we've been in a packed pub rather than the open air. Then I realise – like that girl with the firecracker in her hair, I've had a near miss of my own. While I was scribbling away, some joker slipped a banger into my coat pocket. Fortunately, the four-year-old firecracker was a dud – *Fabricado en España*, not unlike 'Guido' Fawkes himself.

The Bonfire Boys make one last procession through Lewes to their neighbourhood, reaching the corner of Cliffe Church around midnight. They then throw their torches into a pile four feet wide and stumble, jump and stride through the flames in pairs, many of them swaying dangerously. The rest of the crowd huddles around and sings slurred verses of 'Rule Britannia', 'Land of Hope and Glory', 'God Save the Queen' and 'Auld Lang Syne'.

Finally, they recite the Bonfire Prayers again. A father in the crowd holds his son in his arms. The boy is dressed in a pith helmet and full colonial gear, with a NO POPERY pin on his chest. His dad prompts him to repeat the rollicking rhyme:

> A penny loaf to feed the Pope.
> A farthing o' cheese to choke him.
> *Burrrrrrn* him in a tub of tar.
> *Burrrrrrn* him like a blazing star.
> *Burrrrrrn* his body from his head.
> Then we'll say old Pope is dead!

And then the boy joins the crowd's cheering: *Hip hip hoorrayyyyyyyyy!*

PART TWO:
THE BEAST AND THE PRIEST

By the time Bonfire Night rolls around again, Father Flood has recovered from the depression he suffered earlier in the year. I had visited Lewes in the spring to see the town out-of-season, and in between Palm Sunday services, the priest told me he felt besieged. He had been savaged in the local press over Bonfire Night, and vandals had broken into the church twice and smashed windows in his car and the Priest's House – not because they were anti-Catholic; just petty criminals. 'There's general *loutishness*,' he said. 'And y'know, you're meant to be propagating Christianity, and you realise you're in a louts' town. It's like the Beast sleeping . . . I feel undermined.'

Today, though – the Sunday before November the Fifth – he tells me he has a surprise in store. The Bonfire Boys are due to hold their ultra-Protestant Thanksgiving Service this afternoon at Jireh Chapel, and Father Flood is planning a first in Lewes's history – he's going to attend. His decision to gatecrash the Pope-bashing is a testament to the pulling power of the guest speaker. This year, the organisers of the Bonfire Service have landed a Very Important Preacher indeed: Kyle Paisley, son of the Big Man Himself. 'They say he's worse than his father,' the priest says, showing me a neatly clipped article on his desk. 'Oh well, if I'm ejected, it will be . . . "Good for the Lord".'

Despite the fearsome build-up he's been given, 32-year-old Kyle Paisley turns out to be less of a hardliner than his father. Then again, it's hard to imagine anyone being more of a hardliner than Ian Paisley. Kyle has his father's stout build and jowly jaw line, as well as the harsh accent of a good Ul*sh*terman, complete with mushy 'S's, hard 'R's, and 'I's that sound like 'E's, turning 'Britain' into 'Breton'. Crucially, though, he doesn't have his da's bullyboy bearing. His fraternal twin, Ian, looks more like Ian Senior, whereas Kyle takes after their mother. Nevertheless, Ulster's Big Man raised both boys in his own image, dividing his name – Ian Richard Kyle Paisley – between them. 'So it's like "My Ego",' an opponent jokes: '"You look after my church; you look after my political party."' And one way or another, that's what happened. Ian Junior has become a budding politician in Northern Ireland, while Kyle Junior has taken over his father's preaching mantle, currently serving at the Free Presbyterians' first purpose-built chapel on the British mainland, at Oulton Broad in Suffolk.

Sitting on a hard pine pew in Jireh Chapel before the Bonfire Service, Kyle comes across as a gentler version of his father, his brown eyes softening his countenance. This Paisley is more contemplative than combative, even though his views are much the same. In fact, he can't think of any doctrinal differences he has with his da. 'I wouldn't believe something just 'cause he believes it, although perhaps I may not have believed it unless he'd taught it to begin with,' he admits.

The younger Paisley first heard about Lewes's Pope burning a few years ago. 'I said, what's the harm in burnin' the Pope?'

he laughs. 'I don't think it's necessarily a manifestation of religious bigotry. I think it's just, to most people, a matter of culture and history. And why not?' he shrugs and smiles, his arms spread wide across the back of the pew. 'It's not a real individual, and if you'd ask everybody that attended that parade, "Would you like to get the real Pope on the bonfire?" they'd probably say no. It's only a tradition. There's no harm in celebrating past history.'

However, he does concede that it may offend Catholics. 'Just as perhaps their commemoration of their martyrs may cause offence to Protestants. But you've got to learn to accept both points of view. Both Protestants and Catholics have a civil right to celebrate their history if they still want to. It's civil and religious liberty – for everybody. If they want to commemorate their martyrs, let them go ahead and do it. I wouldn't stop them.'

Likewise, he says, his father shouldn't have been stopped from protesting at the Pope's visit to the European Parliament in 1988. 'It was one of those fluorescent posters, and it just said JOHN PAUL II ANTICHRIST,' Kyle recalls.

Nothing too offensive, then.

'He believes personally that the papacy as a system headed by the individual, the Pope, is the Antichrist that is spoken of in the Bible, and I'd hold the same point of view,' he says, giving a taste of things to come. 'There's no more prominent usurper in the religious world than the Pope.'

Father Flood knows he's in for a hard time the moment he steps into Jireh Chapel. The first person he runs into is Jim North, the church's tall, po-faced former pastor, who is handing out programmes for the Bonfire Service.

'Hello, Mr Flood,' he says tersely.

Mister? The Father can't remember the last time he was called 'Mister'.

But North will quite literally be damned before he calls a priest 'Father'. 'Nice to see you,' he continues, offering his hand without smiling.

'Thank you.' Flood takes one of the programmes. The crude, black-and-white engraving on the front shows the dastardly Guy Fawkes shining his lantern into the bowels of Parliament, which is crowned with the decapitated heads of two traitors. The credit on the back explains that the illustration comes from 'an anti-Catholic booklet' printed in 1630.

And that's just the beginning. The master of ceremonies is a bona fide Orangeman – a chaplain, no less, complete with gold-fringed crimson sash and intractable Protestant views. A short, podgy man with a puff of bristly hair and the standard-issue three-piece suit of an evangelical preacher, Mark Kateley seems to take himself as seriously as his religion. Jim North introduced him to me earlier as 'the secretary of the local Orange Lodge'.

'*Master*,' Mark corrected him. Master of the South Downs Loyal Orange Order No. 398, which has adopted an even snappier moniker: the Lewes Martyrs Memorial Southdown Loyal Orange Lodge No. 398. As if that weren't impressive enough, Mark's also Chaplain of the Metropolitan Provincial Orange Order, which covers south-east England, including London.

Now, having lived in England for nearly a decade, it comes as a surprise to me to learn that the Orange Order still has followers on the mainland, much less in London. Mark seems to be a decent enough man who just happens to be the leader of an Orange lodge. Born in Lancashire, he spent most of his formative years in Northern Ireland, and he admits that the movement has seen better days. His group in Lewes has only about a dozen members, while a fellow society in Brighton has shut down, along with its affiliated Ladies' Lodge. Even as groups fold, though, new ones form. Not surprisingly, the annual Bonfire Service is a high point in the local Orange calendar. 'It is largely a secular event, but it's a good opportunity to preach the Gospel.'

The group that's gathered to hear the Gospel According to Orangemen is very diverse indeed. Representatives of virtually every 'ism' imaginable are scattered around the chapel, herded into the old-fashioned box pews, which have gates at the end like corrals. Not only is there an official Son of Rome in attendance for the first time, there's also a Son of Paisley. Despite their spiritual differences, they both have identical dog collars. Father Flood is joined in his pew by Jeremy Goring, an ally in spirit, if not theology: Lewes's former Unitarian minister comes from an old Sussex family, but he also happens to be the European representative of a Nigerian sect called the Brotherhood of the Cross and Star, led by a man named Olumba Olumba Obu. A couple of pews over is a gay humanist with a Hare-Krishna-style haircut who's wearing a spiffy linen suit for the occasion. Although he suffers from gout, Simenon Honoré is planning to lead a unity march on the Fifth, encircling Lewes with love and light using a barely altered rainbow banner from Brighton's Gay Pride movement. His religious dabblings range from Judaism to French Catholicism, Buddhism, reincarnation and the Silent Blessings of Mother Meera. Rounding out the menagerie are a Quaker schoolteacher, some black-hatted Jireh regulars, a couple of Orangemen in fringed sashes, a few leather-clad biker types, little old ladies galore, and more children than you might imagine. One of the few Bonfire Boys in attendance is Ken Funnell (Norman couldn't make it).

Father Flood notes the sparse attendance with satisfaction. From where he's sitting – the fifth pew from the front – it looks like just twenty-eight souls have shown up, though the organisers' tally of nearly a hundred is probably more accurate. Either way, the visitors could each have a hard, pine pew to themselves and still have room to spare.

Mark Kateley takes his place in the goblet-shaped 'flying pulpit' that sweeps up over the audience's heads, forming the chapel's commanding focal point. A lectern down below has been draped with the Union Jack, a tiny red-and-gold crown adorning the Bible on top. Up above, the chapel's perennial orange Scripture signs flank the Orangeman in the pulpit, his identity made clear by the swirly embroidery on his gold-fringed purple sash: *Chaplain*. With Noel and Kyle riding shotgun in the balcony behind him, Kateley welcomes the audience to this annual commemoration of the Failure of the Gunpowder Plot and King William III's Landing in England.

Then the singing kicks in. The first hymn starts off innocuously enough: 'In the name of God, as Father . . .' But by the fifth line, it's blasting 'slaves in priestly thraldom' and 'priestly absolution'. By now, word has gone round that there's a real live priest in the house. Noel Shields and Father Flood have tangled with each other in the press, but they've never met before. From the balcony, Noel and Kyle have ringside seats to watch Father Flood's misery below: as they sing, they're sneaking peeks at him – and each other – holding the hymn sheet between them and sniggering like schoolboys. It's all they can do to keep from laughing out loud as they triumphantly sing verse after verse of anti-Catholic abuse:

> Shall a cruel superstition
> Undermine the Reformation
> And debase this mighty Nation
> Rob it of its strength? . . .

Father Flood is hunched over in his coat, leafing bemusedly through the programme as the hymn grinds to an end. There's a brief reading from the Bible, but that's followed by a recitation of the seventeenth-century Prayer of Thanksgiving, the one decreed after the Gunpowder Plot, complete with 'thees' and 'thys' and a reference to 'our gracious Sovereign King James'. There's also a swipe at the 'Popish treachery' that tried to kill the country's rulers 'as sheep to the slaughter, in a most barbarous and savage manner'. Then there's a similarly dated corollary thanking God for 'bringing His Majesty King William, upon this day, for the deliverance of our Church and Nation from Popish tyranny and arbitrary power'.

And so it goes on. The priest baiting is relentless – practically every verse of every hymn brings a new insult, or rather, the same insult phrased in a different way. Father Flood stands with his head bowed, gently beating time on the pew in front of him – then again, maybe that's just his way of controlling his temper.

After the last bombastic chord, Mark welcomes the crowd again, this time stressing that the service is *not* a celebration of bigotry but rather of religious freedom. 'Yes, this service is unabashedly Protestant,' the Orange chaplain declares, denouncing the 'wicked philosophy' of attacking those who are different. 'I do welcome you from whatever background you come, from whatever race or religion. This service is *not*, and never has been, an occasion for stirring up hatred against any people or any religion.'

Given that this is coming from a sash-wearing Orangeman flanked by two bright orange posters in a chapel run by Ian Paisley, this statement seems disingenuous at the very least. After all, it's only because of an organisational glitch that Cliffe hasn't erected its NO POPERY banner in here this year.

Kyle Paisley ascends to the pulpit after the solemn roll call of the seventeen 'Lewes Protestant Martyrs' burned at the stake in the 1500s. 'Why is it that the Sussex Martyrs died?' he asks. 'They died because they believed what God said in contradiction to what the Pope said.'

Behind him in the balcony, Noel has his hand on his chin to partly cover his face. His eyes are twinkling, and he's rubbing his lip so hard you'd think he's broken out in a rash. Down below, Father Flood still has his coat on. Eyes closed and arms crossed, he's decided to simply suspend belief. For him, the service is a panto-mime, like a recording of John Calvin from 450 years ago. Kyle Paisley seems a nice chap, but he's preaching pure Calvinism expressed in archaic language. Like *Romanism* – nobody uses that these days! Catholics don't even say 'Roman Catholic'; it's just 'Catholic'. And those hymns – *papists' cunning plots* and all that stuff. Surely not even the Bonfire Boys believe that God changed the winds to blow the Spanish enemy on to the rocks – what a load of *crap*. The priest would laugh if he didn't feel like crying.

As Kyle's sermon nears its conclusion, a baby's cry reverberates through the chapel, briefly reviving the dozens of nodding heads and flagging eyelids in the congregation. An old dear with bird's-nest hair and a chunky jumper sleeps balled up in a pew, her face sunk down in her flour-sack bosoms. For many people, the service will be more than enough church to last them for another year. Even for Noel, the novelty seems to have worn off. The sun is streaming in through the plain glass windows, so much so that Jireh's Jim North has to shield his face from the light.

The hour-and-a-half-long service ends with one last pop at popery, courtesy of the second verse of 'God Save the Queen' (the one about 'poli*tics*' and 'knavish *tricks*' – a dig at Catho*lics*). Father Flood heads toward the door. 'I can't take these long services any more,' he grumbles, but he perks up on his way out, shaking hands with frosty North ('Goodbye, Mr Flood'), and then Noel and Kyle, wishing them all the best.

'Perhaps we could have a meal together – or maybe a drink,' he suggests, clinching Noel's hand in the doorway of the chapel.

'Well, we'll see,' the pastor replies, a polite smile frozen on his face.

'So we'll have a meal.'

'We'll see.'

In other words, *Hell will freeze over before I sup with Sir Priest.*

As Flood turns his charm on Kyle, his attendance is hot gossip among Jireh's faithful inside the chapel. Noel is wide-eyed and excited. 'Did ya see the big priest, then?' he asks the leader of the Sussex Martyrs Memorial Society.

The stooped old man shakes his head.

'The priest – Flood – he came to the service!'

'*Did ee?!*'

'Yeah, he offered me a *drink*! He wanted to take me out for a drink!'

For his part, Kyle seems surprised to find that the Spawn of Satan could be so personable. 'I've had Jews and Catholics in the congregation before, but never a priest,' he says. However, it doesn't take long for suspicion to kick in, an emotional reflex. 'He may come just to prove his bravery,' he ventures, theorising that the priest may be doing research for another letter to the local paper. 'There's no reason why he shouldn't be saved,' Kyle adds, pointing out that the main push for the Reformation came from ex-Catholics – 'from a man as dark as he is', he says, nodding in the direction of the departing priest.

PART THREE:
UNTO CLIFFE, A FLOOD

To: Cliffe's Bonfire Boys (cc: Jireh Chapel)
From: God
Message: Never mess with a priest named Flood.

A year after Father Flood's roasting in Jireh Chapel, Lewes has been ravaged by a near-biblical disaster. Weeks before Bonfire Night, the worst flood in living memory has cut the town in half, providing a graphic reminder of the ancient divisions between Cliffe and the rest of Lewes. The River Ouse drowned Cliffe in up to five feet of murky brown water, transforming the area into a canal district separated from the lofty hilltop dwellings of gentrified Lewes. Some 400 families had to leave their homes, and more than a hundred shops and listed buildings have been flooded, including Cliffe's head-quarters, their bonfire site and . . . Jireh Chapel. Although you might expect the Bonfire Service to be held come hell or high water, the flood has cancelled it for the first time in years. 'I don't feel good about it,' Orangeman Mark Kateley confesses. 'The Bonfire Service has its enemies, and in one sense, they've got what they wanted this year by default.'

Perhaps the Orangemen should have turned to their enemies in their time of need. Lewes's Catholic church, located on high ground on the other side of town, has been spared any damage. 'I would have liked it if they'd asked to have the Bonfire Service here,' Father Flood deadpans. Of all the Enemies of Bonfire, he is probably the most entitled to *schadenfreude*. However, he's quick to point out that the flood has caused suffering for Protestants and Catholics alike. 'I never saw that in any way as . . . retribution,' he says, deriding an evangelical who wrote a letter to the paper claiming that the tragedy was God's judgement on the town. 'It was a damned silly thing to say.'

Father Flood and Pastor Shields never did have that meal together, but they have met again since their first encounter. Noel and a couple of evangelicals were ministering door-to-door one wet night when they realised they were near the Catholic church on Irelands Lane. So they paid a visit to the Priest's House next door. Noel tells me he started off by assuring the priest that they weren't singling him out. 'I'm visitin' every home around here with the Gospel, and that includes yours.'

Flood invited them into the sitting room of the presbytery, which has surprisingly little 'Papist trash' on display, apart from the icon of the Virgin and Child on one of the many bookshelves.

'Well, Noel,' Flood began, sitting in one of the lounge's plush velvet chairs. 'Why is it you won't have anything to do with us?'

'Well, I'm glad ya asked me . . .' And Shields told him how he disagreed with Catholic teachings and how the Bible says Christ is the only way to salvation.

'And I told 'im all this, and he had no answer for me, quotin' the Bible. Because, of course, Rome has no answer when you bring the Word of God into the argument,' Noel recalls. 'He did not argue from the Scriptures at all – because he couldn't. In the argument, he was nearly sayin' that all the Muslims and all was gonna go to heaven. There was things like that, there's a universal God, a God of all love, that loves everybody. But that's not the teachin's of the Bible.'

For his part, Father Flood says one of Noel's companions kept quoting the Bible, until he told him: 'Stop doing that. I know the Bible at least as well as you do.' For Catholics, he tried to explain, the Bible is only one source of tradition.

'Their body language was incredible, in that they can't believe you believe as you do,' Flood says. 'I said the Bible's not the sole rule of faith – *Ahck!*' – he chokes, flailing his arms – 'they look as if they were going to have a heart attack. I said, "Are you aware the Catholic Church put the Bible *together*?" *Ahck!* Another heart attack,' he chuckles. 'It's very strange, because they sort of believe the Bible came from *heaven* – pre-packaged, cheap version, all there, all translated and everything. The Bible took *centuries* to put together, and they have no idea.'

Flood is interrupted by a phone call. 'Yes . . . yes . . . *yes* . . .' he says wearily, answering each question posed by the caller.

'That was someone from the parish,' he explains, rolling his eyes. 'They wanted to know whether Guy Fawkes was a Catholic.'

Somewhere in Lewes, someone has just lost an argument.

Most Bonfire Nights, Pastor Shields takes advantage of the massive turnout to distribute Gospel tracts, but this year a foot operation has prevented him from making a stand, so to speak. Nevertheless, a handful of Jireh's faithful have braved the cold to spread God's word. Flanked by her tall son and short husband, Marlene Turrell is doing her best to hand out leaflets on Cliffe High Street during the processions. However, the trio's Bible placards and earnest appearance seem to scare people off, even on a night renowned for frightening banners and costumes.

Everything about Marlene says 'mild-mannered Sunday school teacher': from her trademark dark hat to her long hair (chopped severely in front), wire-framed glasses (the better to read God's Word with), and even her name (pronounced 'Marleen', without any Dietrich-style sex appeal). When the meek inherit the earth, she stands to make a killing. In the meantime, it takes real guts for her and her family to subject themselves to the scorn of strangers. Thankfully, the abuse has never turned physical in Lewes – though on Bonfire Night, anything could happen. She's always felt that it's a very peculiar evening, with a mobbing-looting-pillaging spirit abroad.

The Turrells are handing out their godly propaganda from the Georgian doorway of one of Lewes's oldest law firms – Wynne, Baxter and Godfree. For those who refuse a leaflet, their fluorescent-yellow placard bears a stark message: 'The wages of sin is death . . .' The sign carried by the teenage son is equally uncompromising: 'Jesus said, I am the Way, the Truth, and the Life . . .' In keeping with the occasion, the Turrells have also propped up another poster in the doorway. 'CELEBRATE THE GLORIOUS FIFTH: Thank God for Deliverance of this Nation from Popish Plots,' it declares, listing the key dates in the anti-Catholic calendar – 1588, 1605 and 1688 – to show Jireh's allegiance to Cliffe's cause.

Which is why it's such a surprise to see Cliffe's main Enemy of Bonfire effigy coming toward them. Marlene has to squint to make out the decapitated hate figure – the balding head, the arched eyebrows, the sharp nose and moustache . . .

It's Noel! Cliffe has condemned Jireh's pastor to the flames! In the reddish light of the torches, surrounded by smoke and darkness, Noel looks like Satan himself. Two twisted sheets of paper are tacked to the sides of his papier-mâché head, a sign underneath proclaiming him LEAFLET-EARS. 'That just shows they do it out of ignorance,' Marlene frowns. 'He's not anti-Bonfire at all. In fact, he's all for burning the Pope,' she adds, unable to fathom why Pope burners would want to torch the host of their Bonfire Service, a God-fearing Protestant.

The reason becomes clear as she reads the fine print on the effigy's ears:

JIREH NEWS
WOT NO PHALLICISM
CLIFFE BANNED

And then she remembers: Noel had written to Cliffe a while back protesting about its lewd tableaux. The first year he saw Bonfire Night, for instance, Cliffe had satirised the Monica Lewinsky scandal by casting Bill Clinton as Captain Viagra, with an exploding missile for a penis and the motto IN GOB WE THRUST. In his letter, Noel had asked Cliffe's Bonfire Boys to assure him they would not have any immoral effigies in future processions. If they agreed, they could continue to store their bonfire paraphernalia on Jireh's forecourt, as they had done for years; if they refused, they would have to put their stuff elsewhere. Blowing up the Pope was fine, but joking about presidential blowjobs . . . well, that was immoral. Predictably, the Bonfire Boys responded by telling him they were fiercely independent and would parade as they pleased – so Jireh's pastor locked them out of the chapel's forecourt. That may be why I happened to see a Cliffe Cavalier peeing, well, cavalierly on the chapel's grounds last year (not for nothing is Paisley's church called the 'Free P'). In historical terms, the act was accurate enough – the Royalists hated the Puritans – but the urinary disdain also symbolised just how royally pissed off Cliffe was at Jireh.

True to form, Cliffe's tableau this year is as risqué as ever, depicting two Labour politicos in an S&M scene. In their caricature of Noel, the Bonfire Boys have not only avenged themselves in the chapel dispute, they've also taken a swipe at the Ulsterman's street ministry, particularly his co-opting of Bonfire Night to hand out Gospel tracts. Nearly twenty years ago, Cliffe declared Ian Paisley an Enemy of Bonfire for the same offence, and now it's his disciple's turn at the stake.

Trouble is, Noel's not here, so his followers end up taking the heat. Flanked by the columns of Wynne, Baxter and Godfree, the godly trio face the godfree masses, hopelessly outnumbered by a thousand torch-bearing Bonfire Boys. Even worse, the procession gets held up, so the effigy of LEAFLET-EARS and its escort of mock clergy stop just fifteen feet away from the real-life leafleteers. The Bonfire Boys turn the caricature to face the Turrells so they can get a good look at what happens to Enemies of Bonfire.

Marlene and her family stand frozen to the spot, rictus-faced but stoic, turning their Bible placards in the direction of their hecklers. With the mock clergy glaring at them, suddenly it's as if they're reliving events from the town's past. *Surely they won't actually attack us!* Marlene thinks, but for a second, it's as if the clergy are the real thing, and they want to tie her family to the stake while shouting BURN THE PROTESTANTS! BURN THE PROTESTANTS!

The 'archbishop' glances at their placards, then admires Cliffe's effigy. 'Ours is bigger than theirs,' he sneers. 'The likeness is quite amazing, isn't it?'

'Is that 'im?' a gangly, pinch-nosed boy bishop asks, relishing the chance to bully someone else for a change.

'No. That's *them*.'

Fortunately, the procession begins to move again, and the Enemies of Bonfire make their way up the high street. As they cross the intersection, though, Noel's wife and four children are turning the corner to see the parade. From where she is, about forty feet up from the Turrells, Joan Shields gets only a glimpse of the back of the effigy and the leaflets coming out of the ears, but she knows straight away who it is.

'That was your daddy,' she tells her oldest son, twelve-year-old William.

'No it wasn't. It couldn'ta been daddy.'

'It *was* your daddy.'

Then it dawns on her – the cryptic remark the day before from a friend, a primary school teacher with Cliffe connections. The woman had mentioned something about her brother being an old Enemy of Bonfire, and how he had just laughed it off. Joan didn't think anything of it at the time, but now, looking back on it, she was probably trying to soften the blow.

Unfortunately, that trick doesn't work so well on eight-year-olds. Her youngest daughter immediately recognises her father as the Cliffe procession returns, the decapitated head glowing pink in the flares.

'That's my daddy,' she says, her eyes filling up.

'Don't worry, those people can't harm daddy,' her mother tries to calm her. 'It's only an image of daddy. They can't harm him.'

'Well, *why* did they do it?'

'They've had a dispute, but they cannot harm daddy. It's just for a laugh.'

The older children do try to laugh it off, but they can't help wondering why hundreds of people want to see their dad's head on a pole.

'Every year they have to have enemies,' Joan explains, 'and sooner or later, no doubt your daddy was gonna be one of them.'

The next morning at church, Noel's head is intact and his ears unscathed despite last night's ritual immolation. Good-naturedly, he informs the nineteen souls gathered in Jireh's temporary sanctuary

– the gym of the local primary school – that Cliffe has burned him as an Enemy of Bonfire. A woman gasps, but Noel remains defiant. Like Cliffe, he thrives on opposition; it convinces him he's doing the Lord's work: 'We will not bend, and we will not budge, and we will not burn.'

Even so, after the service, he confesses to some confusion about why he was blown to smithereens alongside the Pope. 'It's very strange that they burned me as an Enemy of Bonfire, the only boy in this town who preaches against popery and who takes a stand – Paddy Irishmen probably wouldn't do such a stupid thing!'

Joan Shields also insists that she doesn't feel intimidated by the incident. 'We're thick-skinned,' she jokes. For her and her husband, burning someone in effigy must seem terribly quaint – genteel, even. Back home, if they don't like you, they kill you or cripple you in that fine old Ulster tradition known as kneecapping. By comparison, effigy burning is laughable. *D'ya call that a threat?! I* laugh *at your threat!* 'I honestly laughed at their stupidity,' she smiles. 'I had to admire them because it was a really good likeness. It was funny, but stupid of them at the same time.'

However, her steely mirth isn't entirely convincing. The more she gets talking about it, the less amused she seems. 'Y'know, I feel sorry for those people, because while they can laugh at us, and take the mickey out of us and have fun at our expense, they're the ones who's gonna spend a lost eternity in hell if they don't come and repent. They can put Noel in the bonfire, and that's as much harm as they'll ever do, 'cause we're protected by the Lord Jesus Christ. Ya have to feel for those people,' she says earnestly. 'Unless they put their faith and trust in God, one day all the mockery and all the fun that they've had at our expense will be turned on them, which is very sad. And I wouldn't like to see them lost for eternity.'

Likewise, the Turrells try to see the humour in the situation, though they can't help feeling a twinge of hurt and even righteous anger. 'You wanted to get hold of people and explain to them that "You don't realise what you're doing. You've got the wrong bloke",' Marlene says ruefully. 'But y'know – we're the Lord's people, aren't we? We're so few against so many.'

*

In the end, after years of battling the Cliffe and the Calvinists, Father Flood has had a conversion of sorts, though not exactly as some might have hoped. He's surprised to hear that his Calvinist counterpart has joined him as an Enemy of Bonfire. He cackles dryly, without any real malice. 'They burnt their own man. He's their chaplain, and they burnt him. It's rather sad, really.'

During the morning service, he makes a shocking announcement. 'Y'know, I had a real change of heart last night watching the procession outside on the street,' he ruminates, leaning on his lectern. 'Why aren't we in it?' He pauses before dropping his bombshell: 'I think I'm going to join the Cliffe.'

The congregation titters. Surely he's joking.

But then he goes on to explain how the Church has always worked best from the inside, like yeast in bread. Afterwards, he expands on the theme further, while shaking hands with his parishioners outside. He tries to convince one elderly man that Cliffe Bonfire Society should have a strong Catholic contingent.

'Now that's where I would have to part company with you,' the man says, wagging his head.

However, Father Flood insists he's serious. 'I need a day off tomorrow, especially after the conversion experience,' he muses drolly. 'They probably won't let me in, but at least I can try. The Church should be in there, working from within.' He points to the spot on the street where his heart had been strangely warmed the night before. 'It's a far more realistic position,' he adds, turning to go into the Priest's House, 'and I'll get far more free drink.'

CHAPTER TEN

OF 'COLOUREDS' AND CORNISHMEN

BLACKING UP
IN PADSTOW

WOULD YOU BAN IT? The photo that caused a furore.

© SUNDAY INDEPENDENT

PART ONE:
'A DARK DAY FOR TRADITION'

Now, don't get the wrong idea – most people in Padstow will tell you they're *not* racist, at least no more than anyone else in this great country. 'Coloureds' are welcome to stroll along the harbour or dine in Rick Stein's restaurant or stay in the Metropole overlooking the Caribbean-blue waters and golden beaches where the rich and royal come to play. The Cornish wouldn't treat them any differently to any other outsiders. And anyway, how can you be racist if there aren't any blacks around to be racist against? Except for one, of course – good ole Ziggy, a West Indian who has lived here for years (or did he move away?). At any rate, it never bothered him. And the former mayor, why, she used to march in London to Free Mandela, and she never thought twice about the pot calling the kettle black, so to speak. All of which goes to show why on Boxing Day and New Year's Day – when there aren't too many emmets about – Old Padstonians see nothing wrong in dressing up like blackface minstrels, parading through town and singing about 'niggers'.

At first, they seem to come out of nowhere, like the tradition itself. The drums, accordions and voices pulse through 'Padsta' like a heartbeat, permeating the air as they make their way down the hill from the social club. The rough music – an infectious noise – resonates through the winding lanes, but it's hard to tell where it's coming from. Just when you think you're close to the source, it seems to fade away. Then you turn the corner, and – there they are! Two dozen men, women and children done up as surreal stereotypes: Cornish approximations of Aunt Jemimas, Jim Crows, Uncle Toms, Sambos, Mammies, Pickaninnies and Rastafarians, all with burnt cork or greasepaint smudged onto their ruddy white faces. The men sport bow ties and sequined vests, plus top hats and bowlers festooned with tinsel and flowers. A couple of jokers wear black crazy-curl wigs, the kind you see at football matches, while an elderly woman gads around in sunglasses and a Rasta Novelty Tam, her fake dreadlocks decorated with blue and gold Christmas balls. The rest of the women favour the Mammy chimneysweep look, as typified by a little girl with a smudged face, headscarf, gaudy earrings, long floral skirt and red apron hanging down to her knees.

No fewer than eight accordions lead the group, followed by a handful of drums, rattling collection boxes, bone castanets and a couple of 'lagerphones' – long staffs studded with bottlecaps, so that when they beat the ground, they ching-ching in time to the music. The movable hootenanny struts through town singing snatches of 'Polly Wolly Doodle', 'Oh! Susanna' and 'Uncle Ned', shocking outsiders and serenading friends and relatives, before getting down to the serious business of drinking. At each of Padstow's half a dozen pubs, the merrymakers burst in singing and hollering, fill their boxes for charity and then stop for a pint (or three). More laughter and singing, then it's off to another pub along the crescent-shaped quay. As they roll out into the blinding winter sunshine, chatting and laughing, the music swells. One drummer, his double chin as pink as his face is black, throws back his head to belt out the climax of 'Uncle Ned', the bit where Al Jolson would have dropped to one knee and brayed:

> There's no more work for the poor old *maaaaaaaan* –
> Heeeeeee's gone where the good niggerrrs go, aye oh
> He's gone where the good niggerrrs go.

*   *   *

WOULD YOU BAN IT? shrieked the front page of the *Sunday Independent* a couple of weeks after Darkie Day. The Plymouth tabloid specialised in shouty headlines, announcing everything in bold-faced capitals that made even the most innocuous news look alarming. Its front-page 'exclusive' about Darkie Day featured a photo of Padstow men, women and children in blackface. Posing with their drums and accordions, the whole dark-faced gang was cheesing for the camera, blissfully unaware of the national controversy about to be set in motion.

'To a West Country community it's a bit of harmless fun,' the article began. 'But to race watchdogs it's evil – and they want it banned NOW.' 'I'm not black and it offends me,' huffed Eileen Bortey, the 'chairperson' of Cornwall's new Race Equality Council. 'Padstow is a beautiful place. It's a great pity it is being defiled in this way. If we need to kick up a stink, we will. It has to be condemned.'

Compared with the offended white woman, one of Britain's best-known black politicians was initially a model of restraint. 'I thought the days when white people dressed up as black people were well behind us,' London MP Bernie Grant said. After a token defence from 'Ziggy', Padstow's lone black resident – he called Darkie Day 'great fun' – the report ended with locals vowing to continue the tradition, while the police warned that it could be banned if it stirred up trouble. *What do YOU think?* the paper enquired, sensing it was on to a sure thing. *'Write to Race Row, Sunday Independent . . .'*

And so, in just sixteen paragraphs, a local tabloid took an obscure tradition – so back-of-beyond, in fact, that hardly anyone in Cornwall had ever heard of it – and transformed it into a national scandal. Within days, follow-ups appeared in national papers ranging from the *Guardian* to the *Daily Mail*. 'A dark day for tradition as the race police sail into port,' rued the *Mail*, alongside a photo of Ziggy posing on the pier. On national radio, a shock jock branded Padstonians 'racist rednecks' and urged listeners to boycott the town. Rumours circulated that previously unheard-of groups like the Cornwall Race Equality Council were threatening to bus black protesters into Padstow with 'lighted up' faces, and soon enough, Bernie Grant cranked up the rhetoric with a veiled warning to Padstonians: 'If they want their nice idyllic little town to turn into a minefield, that's up to them.'

The debate soon turned into a Town versus Country clash with a Cornish twist, pitting critics from 'up-country' against the salt-of-the-earth 'Westcountry', 'politically correct zealots in the big cities' versus 'two or three dozen Padstow people', and the 'London media' versus local papers that were 'Flying the Flag for Cornwall' (the motto of the *Sunday Independent*). Most importantly, the uproar seemed to reflect the ancient conflict between the English, the offspring of Anglo-Saxon invaders, and the Cornish, who regarded themselves as the country's true natives. Whereas callers to a radio chat show in London loudly condemned Darkie Day, most letters to newspapers in Cornwall supported the tradition. For natives, Darkie Day became a symbol of their dying culture.

In their defence of Darkie Day, the Cornish kept coming out with statements of shock and dismay that were just too innocent to be believed – at least from an urban perspective. 'It is an old Cornish custom, and they are not taking the mickey out of coloured people,' a woman from Plymouth said. 'They just go round singing and dancing dressed up with their faces darkened,' Padstow's mayor said. 'Although the word nigger in several songs could be seen as inflammatory nowadays, it is not meant in that way,' another Padstonian explained. One local said that as a girl, she didn't know the day after Christmas was called Boxing Day; she knew it only as Darkie Day. The *Western Morning News* blamed the uproar on 'an increasingly censorious urban attitude': 'To brand the people of a small Westcountry fishing port redneck racists who deserve to have their town turned into a minefield is a disgraceful slur and entirely counterproductive to genuine racial harmony.' By the end of the article, the paper had turned things around, somehow arguing that the condemnation had been 'so offensive and bigoted' that it was effectively a 'racist attack' in its own right – on the Cornish!

Against this 'racist attack', Padstow found an unlikely defender in a big-city black journalist. 'You can make yourself see racism anywhere, if you look hard enough – even in a Cornish town on the day they celebrate the abolition of slavery,' wrote Darcus Howe in the *New Statesman*. The pundit and broadcaster had first visited Cornwall back in the 1960s and returned many times since. Chiding Grant, the MP for Tottenham – 'not exactly a Cornish constituency' – he added: 'May I offer a little local history lesson for our metropolitan radicals?' Then he regurgitated an unlikely tale about the event's origins: 'Slave ships used to anchor in Padstow to avoid storms. The slaves would disembark and entertain themselves and the local people in a song-and-dance routine,' he said. Citing a 'local expert', Howe concluded that Darkie Day was an anti-slavery celebration: 'The critics maintain that Darkie Day is some time-warped throwback to the bad old days of *The Black and White Minstrel Show*. The reality is the opposite; but the politically correct brigade never stopped for long enough to find that out.'

Two weeks after its 'scoop', the *Sunday Independent* reported that the National Front was planning to fight an election in Cornwall for the first time in nineteen years under the banner of 'Keep Cornwall White'. 'NF supporters believe they can pull in a large slice of the votes – especially following the Darkie Day race row,' it said, quoting an NF spokesman as saying: 'We fully support the rights of white people in Padstow to celebrate Darkie Day. As for Bernie Grant and his ilk, they would be far from these shores, back in the Caribbean and Africa, under the National Front's humane repatriation and resettlement programme and no longer able to interfere in our country's internal affairs.' Padstow's Darkies were horrified. 'Whatever the National Front are saying is not what the people of Padstow believe. They are not welcome,' one declared.

Nevertheless, many observers predicted that Padstow's Darkie Day would soon come to an end. 'And we can only hope it's not a violent one,' lamented the *Western Morning News*. The only other Cornish village known to have a similar tradition quickly white-washed its Darkies to avoid a similar controversy. Calstock, an hour from Padstow, had revived its 'ancient' blackface tradition in 1983. Locals claimed that singing Cornish Christmas carols and collecting money had nothing to do with blacks or slavery; its roots were in the medieval traditions of 'guising' and mumming, when people would darken their faces and entertain the crowds for food and money. In a canny move, the Calstock Darkies officially rebranded themselves the Calstock Guisers (pronounced 'geezers') and painted white crosses over their black faces, forming the Cornish flag of St Piran.

Padstow's Darkies also agreed to alterations after meeting with the police and the local branch of the Commission for Racial Equality in the run-up to Christmas. 'But we refused, point-blank, not to go out,' one local said. 'The police didn't want us to dark our faces up or anything – I mean, that would've made a mockery of it.' So they compromised. Like their countrymen in Calstock, the Padstow Darkies officially became known as the Padstow Mummers, with black faces but no minstrel-style white make-up around their eyes or mouths. Most importantly, they agreed to substitute 'mummers' for the word 'niggers' in their songs.

Even so, a national broadsheet revived the controversy the following year with an article threatening that the National Front might march in Padstow. Throughout the furore, though, few (if any) of the journalists, politicians or other outsiders who commented on Darkie Day ever actually saw it. After all, who in their right mind would want to spend Christmas or New Year with a bunch of 'racist rednecks' in Cornwall?

When I first read about Darkie Day, I was astounded. *What kinda local yokels would black up and sing racist songs in this day and age?! And why in Britain, of all places?!* Not even the most country-fried, Confederate-flag-loving hillbillies in the Deep South would do something like that!

Then again, who was I to throw stones? My grandfather was a member of the KKK. As far as I can tell, though – and as absurd as it sounds – he wasn't a cross-burner or even a racist. His father, a German immigrant to the Midwest in the 1850s, had joined the Republicans at a time when they were the upstart anti-slavery party led by Abe Lincoln. At just seventeen, my great-grandfather volunteered for the Civil War, sneaking off in the middle of the night to fight for the Union. It seems unlikely that a man who had voluntarily risked his life to fight slavery would then indoctrinate his children with racist teachings. It is possible that his son rebelled by joining the redneck group founded by Confederates at the end of the war, but from what I can gather, my grandfather wasn't the type: he was a gentle soul, more henpecked than hellraiser. He certainly wasn't overtly racist, and he taught his children to treat blacks as equals. Without trying to defend the indefensible, I think he joined the KKK for one simple reason: everybody else was doing it. In its heyday, the Klan was very much a mainstream organisation (which arguably made it more sinister than its current incarnation on the lunatic fringe). Although its rhetoric was undoubtedly bigoted, its rank-and-file members didn't hide behind hoods, and they didn't go around burning crosses or lynching people – at least not in Kansas. The secret history of the KKK seems to be that outside the South, it functioned like any 'respectable' social club, hosting picnics, baseball games and fundraisers.

For what it's worth, I was brought up to view people of all races as equals. Not that there were many minorities in the middle of Kansas: no blacks, only one family of Mexicans/Catholics and just one Asian – my Vietnamese foster brother. When I entered my teens, we moved to Lexington, Kentucky, a city that prides itself on being part of the Progressive South. This may sound like a contradiction in terms, but it's true: they don't lynch people any more; capital punishment is strictly by electrocution. Bordering the North and South, Kentucky used to be a slave state, though its sons fought on both sides of the Civil War. One of Kentucky's most famous adopted sons was Stephen Foster, America's first great songwriter, who made his name writing minstrel songs. Two ended up becoming the official anthems of Southern states: 'Swanee River' for Florida (which he never visited) and 'My Old Kentucky Home' (which he did). As in Padstow, both songs had to be modified because they contained the word 'darkies'. Kentucky changed the offending word to 'people' in 1986 after a group of Japanese students serenaded the General Assembly with 'My Old Kentucky Home'.

For most of my youth, my best friend – and later best man – was black, from the deepest backwoods of *Kin*tuckee: Hazard, to be precise. (TV's *Dukes of Hazzard* wasn't actually set there, but it could've been.) Through him and other friends, I learned what it was like to be a member of a minority, albeit in a very limited sense. Blondish and blue-eyed, I was often the only white in black churches, talent shows and neighbourhoods. My girlfriend and I were the only mixed couple at the prom, and I reciprocated at her predominantly black school. I left Kentucky to study international relations at a university in Washington, D.C. (aka 'Chocolate City' among blacks). During summer breaks, I worked for a newspaper in Indianapolis, where I covered migrant farm workers and the Miss Black America Pageant (the same event where Mike Tyson later earned his rape conviction). After university, I lived in Peru at the height of a terrorist insurgency, travelling to shantytowns and villages where I was at least a head taller than the locals; an easy target for any would-be *yanqui*-killers. Instead, I met my wife.

I mention all this knowing that veteran race-baiters will dismiss it as just a longwinded version of the old *cri de coeur* of a closet racist: 'Some of my best friends are black!' All I can say is: judge for yourself. In my experience, race relations are never black and white. Just when you think you've worked out people's differences, along comes an exception to contradict everything you've ever thought. So it's with real trepidation that I write about race in the UK . . .

Despite all the hype about 'multicultural Britain', modern Albion remains overwhelmingly white. Living in London or any sizeable city, it's easy to forget just how racially homogenous England is, not to mention Scotland, Wales and Northern Ireland. Although roughly one out of every four people in Greater London is black or Asian, for the UK as a whole – including the capital – that ratio plunges to 8 per cent, most of whom are Asians. Afro-Caribbeans number just one million out of the country's total population of 59 million – around 2 per cent. In north Cornwall, minorities make up 1 per cent of the inhabitants, though barely one person in 1000 is of African descent – just 0.1 per cent of all locals.

I arrived in Padstow with my family a few days before New Year's Day. At first, I'd had my doubts about taking them to see Darkie Day. My Latin wife is often mistaken for being Asian; our daughter is decidedly mixed, a cross between a German-Swedish-American and a Spanish-Italian-Inca. However, I happened to know a couple of people who had seen Darkie Day, and they assured me there wouldn't be a problem. We'd also visited Padstow the previous summer, and the locals couldn't have been more welcoming. Small towns are often portrayed as bigoted back-waters, but in my experience, that ain't necessarily so. Having lived in Smalltown USA as well as half a dozen world capitals, I've found that city-dwellers can be just as bigoted as villagers, if not more so.

As for the term 'darkie', well, it's like something out of the nineteenth century. You never hear it nowadays – unless you go to Padstow. Then, boy do you hear it: the Cornish give Rs their full value and then some, so when they say 'darrrkie', 'colourrred' or 'niggerrr', it's all the more *jarrrring*. For many Padstonians, 'coloured' seems to be an accepted synonym for 'black', while 'Negro' also occasionally pops into conversation; 'nigger' is only ever used in the context of the Darkie Day songs (at least that I've heard). The first time I witnessed the tradition – not long after the media storm – I interviewed only one local. 'Because of this – this word, niggerrr, I'm sensitive even talkin' to you about it,' he said. 'Any stranger who asks questions will be viewed with a little bit of suspicion. For all they know, you're writing for the *Black Power Journal*.' Padstow's merrymakers were also wary of me, but that was only natural – I was a stranger with a camera. 'Have ya paid for them photos?' an ersatz Aunt Jemima asked me. Once I put some money in the collection box, though, no one seemed to mind me tagging along.

I decided to return during the summer, when people might be more forthcoming. Even so, I felt self-conscious asking about the event. I tended to mumble the offensive words or bury them under my breath, so that Darkie Day became (Darkie) Day. However, the locals had no such hang-ups, rattling off the lyrics about 'niggers' as if they were just any old words, as innocuous and nonsensical as 'polly wolly doodle'. You could view this openness as proof that they don't mean to cause offence; on the other hand, you could argue that they don't care who they offend.

Time and again, Padstonians protest their innocence: 'How can we be racist if we don't have any blacks around to be racist against?' This is the racial equivalent of the chicken-and-egg conundrum – which came first: blacks or bigots? Race-baiters cut their teeth on this question, tearing into it like lions mauling an easy kill. 'This is almost the same as saying that racism only exists where there are significant numbers of black people present, i.e., before "they" came, "we" didn't have a problem,' wrote the head of the Devon and Exeter Racial Equality Council during the Darkie Day uproar. 'Racism is usually (not always) about white people's attitudes, and that is essentially the problem.' This emphasis on whites' attitudes takes the debate into the realm of Orwellian wrongthink; if you're reckless enough to speak your mind, you might as well stick your face in a cage full of rats. Of course, it is possible for people living in an all-white society to be racist, but just because they live in an all-white society doesn't necessarily make them racist. To my mind, the true test of whether someone is racist is how he or she treats people of other races when meeting them face-to-face.

'I'd *never* thought of Darkie Day as being offensive – just because it was part of something that had always gone on in Padstow,' says former mayor Keltie Seaber, although she admits: 'If it would've gone on in *London*, we would've said, "Ooh, isn't that terrible?"' And she would have been among the first to protest. It wasn't until outsiders objected to Darkie Day that her eyes were opened. 'I had this discussion with mum, when we both decided that – "God how thick were *we*",' she laughs. 'There we were, liberal, educated people, we thought, politically *very* correct – not a racist bone in our bodies – and I said, "*Why* didn't it occur to us that blacking our faces up and dressing as negresses, *why* didn't it even cross our consciousness that it might be considered racist?"' Keltie reckoned it was because Darkie Day had always been there. Although she had never taken part in it, she knew most of the people who did. And knowing Padstow people, they were very . . . *non-racist* somehow; very inclusive towards people who were down on their luck.

'Down here, race isn't really an issue because we don't have black families,' she emphasises. 'If you had a *black* area in the town, with twenty black families, and went round their streets singing these songs, I think it would have dawned on me that yes, it could be construed as perhaps insensitive and intolerant and *racist* – but they were singing these Darkie Day songs – when there was no race issue in Padstow. It wasn't done to wind anybody up, because there was nobody to wind up. Darkie Day has never *ever* been malicious, or had any motive, apart from the fact of just going out and having a sing. They do it because they do it.'

In trying to explain Darkie Day, I don't know which is stranger: the locals' story about dancing slaves, or the fact that many journalists – including defenders like Darcus Howe – swallowed the fishy tale hook, line and sinker. To my mind, commemorating slaves' suffering by blacking up and singing about 'niggers' would seem like more of a sick joke than an honest *hommage*. So far as the historical record shows, though, slave ships never docked at Padstow – and even if they had stopped, it's unlikely the captive men, women and children on board would have been in any condition to sing and dance.

The true roots of Darkie Day lie in the nineteenth-century 'nigger minstrel' craze that swept both sides of the Atlantic, popularised by a couple of Yankees. Thomas Dartmouth Rice and George Washington Dixon developed the two black stereotypes that dominated the stage for more than a century: the sympathetic Southern plantation slave (Rice's 'Jim Crow' character), and the uppity Northern dandy (Dixon's 'Zip Coon') – who also inspired the golliwog, another transatlantic creation. These New World minstrels combined the music, masking and drama of Old World traditions such as 'guising' and mumming. Between Christmas and New Year, folks around Britain – including Cornwall – would 'disguise' themselves by blacking their faces and singing, dancing and performing for food or money during the holidays. Inevitably, European and African customs intermingled on the plantations of the British West Indies and the American South. Slaves were allowed time off over Christmas, and they celebrated with processions centred on the towering figure of 'John Canoe' or 'Jonkonnu' – a man in a tall mask and outlandish clothes. John Canoe's followers would dress in rags and animal skins, or sometimes poke fun at their masters by wearing fancy European dress – and white make-up with pink Caucasian features. Jonkonnu extravaganzas still take place in Jamaica and the Bahamas around Christmas and New Year, though they died out in America after the Civil War. As it happens, Kwanzaa, the US holiday invented during the Black Power movement of the 1960s, runs from 26 December until 1 January, coinciding with Jonkonnu and, ironically, Padstow's Darkie Days.

After Jim Crow's transatlantic tours, minstrelsy quickly became commercialised. Stephen Foster made his name writing minstrel songs and became the first composer to receive royalties for hits like 'Oh! Susanna' and 'Camptown Races'. One-man blackface performances turned into blockbuster Minstrel Shows, arguably the first bona fide 'show business' – and a big influence on American vaudeville and British music hall traditions. 'Nigger minstrel' troupes also made the rounds in Britain. The Gowongo Minstrels performed in Padstow just after Boxing Day in 1899, and the first known photo of Padstow's Darkies dates from around the same time. Nine men and boys pose in front of a stone cottage with accordions, tambourines and drums, dressed like dandified Negroes, sporting top hats, frilly collars, oversized buttons, crazy-colour formalwear – and, of course, tar-black faces. At least one man in the picture is a forebear of a current Darkie.

Professional minstrel shows had all but died out in America by the time Al Jolson bawled for his 'Mammy' in 1930, while in Britain, minstrels remained incredibly popular right up until only a few decades ago. Unbelievably, *The Black and White Minstrel Show* didn't cakewalk off the air until 1978. In hindsight, it's clear that all minstrelsy played on outdated and even repugnant black stereotypes. As in the early days of the genre, though, I think Darkie Day in Padstow was literally a way of adding some colour to people's plain-vanilla lives. The burnt cork on their faces acted as a mask that freed them from their daily routine, allowing them to sing, dance and cavort during the holidays without any malice intended toward blacks. And before rushing to judge Darkie Day or indeed blackface performers of the past, it's worth keeping in mind that future generations may look back on our era and view white stars ranging from Elvis and the Beatles to 'blue-eyed soul' singers, white rappers and any number of boy bands as little more than minstrels without the make-up: singers and songwriters who copied black American slang, diction, dress and singing styles to produce the most commercial music of our time. Eminem boasted as much in his Number 1 single 'Without Me', bragging that he and Elvis had enriched themselves by exploiting black music. Although modern pop like *The Eminem Show* may not mock blacks in the same way as old minstrel shows, the deeper issue of exploitation remains.

In its own unique way, Darkie Day represents a variety of traditions come full circle: Old World customs were exported to the New World and mixed with plantation-style music to create black-face minstrelsy, which was then exported to Britain at the same time as blacks developed white-face counterparts in the British West Indies. A similar phenomenon occurred in South Africa, where to this day 'Coloureds' imitate old-time American minstrel performers during their annual New Year's celebrations in Cape Town. The mixed-race revellers, many wearing black-and-white minstrel make-up, have stubbornly resisted attempts to rebrand their hootenanny as the Cape Minstrels Carnival. Instead, they call it by its old-fashioned name – the Coon Carnival.

Likewise, Darkie Day clings to its controversial roots. The event starts with the lyrics 'Oh, I just come out before you/To sing you a darkie song', then samples snippets of half a dozen ditties, such as 'Polly Wolly Doodle'. One of the most contentious verses comes from an international hit by Stephen Foster, 'Uncle Ned':

> On a cold and frosty morning my Uncle Neddy died,
> And he died many years ago.
> He had no woolly on the toppy of his head
> In the place where the woolly ought to go.
> Up with the shovel and a ee-aye-oh
> And down with the shovel and the hoe.
> There's no more work for the poor old man
> He's gone where the good niggers go, aye oh
> He's gone where the good niggers go.

As outrageous as those lyrics seem now, the reality wasn't so black and white back in Foster's day. The famous black American abolitionist (and former slave), Frederick Douglass, cited songs like

'Uncle Ned' and 'My Old Kentucky Home' as 'allies' in the fight against slavery: 'They awaken the sympathies for the slave, in which anti-slavery principles take root and flourish.' In Britain, 'Uncle Ned' was a standard in school songbooks well into the twentieth century. One Padstonian told me that the Darkie Day songs were taught at the local primary school in the seventies, and possibly even as late as the eighties, including a tune called 'Little Nigger'. Seeing that I wasn't familiar with the song, he recited the words, penned by an anonymous author:

> I 'ad a little nigger
> He wouldn't grow no bigger
> So I put 'im in the wilebeest show.

What? Surely I'd misheard him. 'Wilebeest? Like "wild beast"?'

'Yeah,' he shrugged. 'Of course, there's all different verses. We don't sing the *whole* song. 'Cause ya know we 'ad problems. So wherever we've got the word "nigger" we now change it to "mummer".' He grinned. 'So then we're politically correct.'

'So what do you make of that?'

'Welllll . . . when you're drunk, who can tell what you're singing?'

As Padstow's Berthing Master, Malcolm McCarthy keeps vigil in the modern Harbour Office on the edge of the quay, a stone's throw from the sixteenth-century Court House where Sir Walter Raleigh lived and worked as Warden of Cornwall. Through the wide windows of the corner office, he can see the assorted boats gleaming in the small harbour, the seagulls cawing overhead, and the last rays of sunlight rippling towards Rock, on the other side of the estuary. Failing that, he can always admire his own photos of Padstow. The screensaver on his laptop flashes photos of him and his family taking part in Padstow's May Day celebrations, and if you ask, he'll also show you digital images of Darkie Day. 'There's me,' he chuckles. 'With me boys.' They're nine and twelve, both in blackface, one in a top hat with a collecting tin, and the other in a bowler with a tambourine.

Malcolm's own bowler is fringed with tinsel, and his face is smudged with make-up. 'When I was younger, say when I was at school, I didn't take part in Darrrkie Day,' he says, leaning hard on his Rs. 'But since I've been older, and realised it's an old tradition that's got to be kept up, I've made sure that I take part and my kids take part.'

Malcolm swivels in his chair, one leg folded across the other, a man in his element with nothing to hide. His red hair comes from his father – an Irish Londoner – but the rest of him is 'proper Padstow'. At forty-five, he has a pub bloke's build, with a stout Cornish accent and picaresque eyebrows that rise and fall according to the conversation: protesting his innocence, they fly at full mast; for jokes and asides, they furl down around his eyeballs. And if that doesn't win you over, he'll start working his head and hands, nodding this way and that, or rolling his wrists and showing his palms to explain Darkie Day: 'It's just an excuse to 'ave a *drink* – it is, really!'

In other words, Malcolm comes across as the Cornish equivalent of a Good Ole Boy. He may say some outrageous things, but he's got just enough charm to get away with it. Of course, you could take offence and argue with him, but you're not going to change his worldview. He prides himself on speaking his mind, in calling a spade a – um . . . spade. At least with him, you know where he stands; not like these damnfool foreigners who come round asking about Darkie Day so they can write about it.

Apart from his rogue Irishness, Malcolm is practically Padstow aristocracy. One branch of his family can be traced back to at least the 1580s, the time of Sir Walter Raleigh and the construction of Padstow's manor house, still owned by the Prideaux-Brune clan. 'I think you gotta 'ave about three graves up in the cemetery before you're local,' he says. Unlike many born-and-bred Padstonians, though, Malcolm has spent time living abroad – in England. In fact, he used to be a policeman in London during some of the worst racial violence the capital has ever seen. While training, he was drafted in to serve on the front line during the Brick Lane protests by Asians in 1978, and three years later, he was in one of the first cars to arrive on the scene of the Brixton riots.

PCs are notoriously some of the least PC people you could meet, but Malcolm claims race was never an issue for him before moving to London. 'I must say, I went up to London, and in all honesty, I thought that between the white person and the coloured person, there was no difference. They were just the different colour. But I learnt that that wasn't necessarily the case. If I stopped a black person, they would say that I'm stoppin' 'em because they're black. Which wasn't the case!' His voice and eyebrows rise in unison. 'I mean, they might have one headlight on a car, you're lookin' at the car, and all you can see is the headlight in the dark, you can't see who's in the car or what colour they are until they get out. So they get out, and "you've stopped 'em because they're black"! You're on the defensive straight away. And I found that there were some coloured people I got on with, but with the *majority* of coloured people, there was conflict. I used to travel on the Underground in my white shirt and black trousers – they knew I was a policeman – and they would look at you, and stare at you – looking for trouble. Whereas with the ordinary white person, I didn't *get* that.'

I suggest that it's a vicious circle, but he doesn't buy that. 'I wouldn't say that being a policeman affected how I looked at *them*. Being a policeman affected how they looked at *me*. And how they treated me affected how I dealt with them.'

Not like back home. Malcolm claims that Ziggy, Padstow's lone black man, was always accepted. 'Never any problem at all. We're not racist people down here,' he concludes, relaxed and smiling.

'But I found' – returning to life in the big city – 'I was totally not racist in any way at all when I went to London, *but* I would say that I *am* racist now, because of the way I was treated by the coloureds. *Not* by the way I've been brought up, or influenced in the town, but just in the way my experiences have led me, dealing with those people.'

And immediately, he realises: *I just said I'm a racist!*

'Same as you could be "anti-drug-addict" because that's how you've been treated by them,' he adds quickly. 'I mean, I've just said I was a racist, but . . . if a coloured person came in here now, I wouldn't treat 'im *any different* than how I've treated you – *unless* he was aggressive towards me.'

For what it's worth, I believe Malcolm when he says he wouldn't treat blacks differently from whites, and I think 'racist' is too strong a word for him. 'Prejudiced' is probably more accurate; then again, most people prejudge others from time to time, whether they realise it or not: whites prejudge blacks prejudge Jews prejudge Arabs, men prejudge women prejudge blondes prejudge brunettes, and so on. Few – if any – humans are entirely prejudice-free; those who say otherwise are either deluding themselves or lying. The difference is whether you act on your prejudices or try to overcome them.

Malcolm's depiction of Smalltown, Cornwall, as a haven of racial tolerance also may sound too good to be true, but it's substantiated by Darcus Howe, the black pundit who defended Darkie Day. He described the Truro of the late sixties as 'a civilisation away from south London, where natives spat racial abuse from foul mouths'. When African students at the local mining college got into arguments with racist South Africans, the Cornish would side with the former. 'The locals, reared on Home Rule for Cornwall, imbued with a sense of their local differentness from their English rulers, embraced the Africans – nationalists to the bone – against white African racial superiority,' Howe wrote. As for the present situation, I would give Malcolm the benefit of the doubt, although his qualifier – '*unless* he was aggressive' – obviously reflects the old stereotype of the Angry Negro. That said, I think Malcolm – or any black person, for that matter – would react the same way towards an aggressive white.

Having struggled to explain himself, Malcolm brings us round to the subject at hand: 'But Darkie Day has got *nothing* to do *at all* with bein' a racist,' he smiles, relieved to be back on course. 'Y'know . . . everybody . . . it's just –' he sighs: *how to explain it to outsiders?* '– it's a bit of fun. It's a tradition – that's what I would say.'

After our talk, Malcolm and I walk out on the harbour wall to shut the port for the evening. Before the wall was built in 1988, only small boats could stay overnight. The pond-sized harbour used to dry out at low tide, and the silt would stink – so much so that nobody wanted to live on the waterfront. Once the wall was in place, though, the buildings next to the harbour became prime property, completing Padstow's transformation from a closed community into a popular port of call for outsiders. As the sun sinks over the hill, a couple of dozen boats crowd the harbour – rubber dinghies, luxury yachts and a few big fishing boats, including one named *Defiant Padstow*. I mention to Malcolm that I'm planning to come back for Darkie Day next year.

'Oh, you mean *Mummer's* Day,' he smiles.

'I'll have to remember to call it that.'

'Well, gotta keep up the pretences.'

Initially when I tried to find Padstow's only black man, Siegfried 'Ziggy' Holder, people would shrug and say they hadn't seen him for a while; he may have even moved away. Eventually, I found out where he lived and made a cold call in person, half expecting him to slam the door in my face. Ziggy had been widely quoted during the Darkie Day controversy, and he might not want to risk re-igniting the issue by speaking to a strange American. However, the elderly man who opened the door greeted me with a smile partly overgrown by a wiry, black-and-white beard. I still wasn't accustomed to using the word 'darkie' – but Ziggy didn't seem at all fazed by my mention of Darkie Day. After some preliminary chitchat, though, he suddenly mentioned the (latest) case of an American cop caught on video assaulting a black man. 'I thought it wasn't *real!*' he said, cocking his head to one side, the glint in his eyes turning to indignation. 'But no, it was real. And I felt sick. I felt all the anger, all the frustration, all the disillusionment – all the emotions known to man welling up inside me. I still haven't got over it.' He shook his head. 'It seems some people never learn.'

Whether this was simply a coincidence or his way of warning me against judging Padstow too harshly, I couldn't tell. At the very least, it showed that Ziggy wasn't a pushover on the subject of race. It also reflected the ironies of race issues on both sides of the Atlantic. Ziggy was entirely right to voice his disgust; even so, he was doing it from a place where twice a year, the locals black up like Uncle Toms and Aunt Jemimas and sing publicly about 'niggers' – something that would be unheard of in the States.

Although he's lived in Britain for nearly half a century, and in Padstow since the late seventies, Ziggy still has a Trinidadian accent, the Caribbean cadences placing an unexpected *emphasis* on nearly every other *word*. When he tells a story, you know a joke is never far around the corner – like how he used cricket to overcome prejudice when he came to Britain in 1955. 'There's a saying that anybody who understands cricket is a decent guy,' he starts out. Given that cricket is practically a religion in the West Indies, Ziggy was able to use his Talmudic knowledge of the sport to bond with the British. During a job interview, for instance, he could tell that he wasn't welcome, but he managed to work cricket into the conversation, and the boss ended up inviting him to the pub. 'I got the job,' he laughs.

'Maybe I'm one of the lucky ones, but I've always been lucky to run into decent people,' Ziggy continues. Especially in Padstow. 'I give them a lot of hell,' he chuckles. 'I say "I'm the only one you've got – you've got to take care of me!"' Even so, he can recall a couple of negative encounters. 'There were certain people down here that don't entirely approve of, well' – this cracks him up – 'of visitors overstaying their – their welcome. A certain number of people were quite friendly at first. But it was a different kettle of fish when they found out that I was' – he starts laughing again – 'that I was coming to stay. They changed *completely*.'

Race was definitely a factor, but the main reason may have been that Ziggy was an outsider. 'That was more important than the fact that he could be yellow, green, or whatever,' Keltie Seaber had told me. 'There's all these things that you don't think about with Padstow because it's pretty and idyllic, but it has a port mentality. It's not a quaint fishing village; it's a *port*. So it has everything that's inherent with a port – the threat from the outside. When I was a young girl, the local lads didn't like the trawlermen coming in because our girls would see new *talent*. So there were all these *fights* – and usually over the women. Because they were threatened, y'know, that they would be taken away.'

Ziggy agrees. 'Oh, boy, did I get stick, man! Oh, yes, because I am the only um . . . man of colour in the *town*.' Then he picks up

Keltie's point. 'The whole truth of it is that as long as people don't feel *threatened* . . . You must understand that as soon as they get to know you and see you and well, observe you from afar, that finally would determine their attitude toward you.' He reckons a few diehards still object to his presence, but his involvement in community groups such as the Padstow Lions has broken down barriers over the years. One night in the pub, a guy with 'the *reddest* hair' told Ziggy that if he ever had any trouble, he would sort it out, and when the Darkies used to sing about niggers, they would come up to him and say, 'We don't mean you!'

'They're people straight from the community, man,' he says, adding that most of the Darkies are friends and acquaintances. 'When they come by the pub, I've got to make sure that they don't come kissin' me, or rubbin' off the black. That was my greatest fear, man. They get you in a corner, and you're just *covered* in black soot.' One year, he made the mistake of going into town in a white jumper and trousers on Darkie Day. 'I was *covered* with black lipstick and burnt cork!'

For Ziggy, Padstow's celebrations seem to connect the West Country with the Caribbean. 'There's a helluva lot of ties,' he says, explaining that when he first came to Cornwall, 'I listened to people talking on the streets, and I could hear bits of Jamaica, I could hear bits of Trinidad.' Something similar happened when he first saw Padstow's May Day celebrations back in 1969. As the drums thundered in front of him, the strangest thing happened – he started crying uncontrollably. 'I couldn't work out where I'd heard this music before . . . Not to be pretentious, but it must be something in the race memory. It sounds like something from Africa – West Africa . . .'

'So is that where your ancestors were from?'

'No, they came from East Africa!'

As for Darkie Day, Ziggy's quibbles have to do with his taste in music rather than the songs themselves. He prefers Wagner, Strauss and Mahler – 'all heavy stuff'. When he was a young man, Ziggy once gave a one-man concert in Hampstead, north London, playing Stephen Foster's music on a steel drum and using the lyrics to talk about slavery. 'It's the only music that I could actually play and make that connection,' he says. 'Some of them have got the most beautiful, haunting melodies.' Nowadays, though, nobody would dare sing songs like 'Old Black Joe'. 'They think that would give offence,' Ziggy laughs. 'I *don't*! That is why I may sound like a bunch of contradictions. Because I want to make sure I know what I feel angry about, and what I don't: what I think encouraged racism, and what I wouldn't give a second thought to. This is the sort of balance you have to maintain in *any* sort of discussion about racism.'

PART TWO:
RUTTING AND SMUTTING ON MAY DAY

Call me a racist, but you can't deny that they *are* a very musical people, always singing and dancing, joking and flashing their teeth, usually after a drink or two – and God knows they *do* like a drink! No matter how poor or exploited or downtrodden they've been throughout history, slaving away for their various masters around the world, forced to live as second-class citizens in their own land, their language and culture uprooted and left to die – despite all that suffering, somehow they've managed to retain their sense of pride, and humour, and innate musicality.

I'm talking about the Cornish, of course. And Padstonians in particular. Music unites the town's traditions, and the biggest and loudest hootenanny of them all takes place on the First of May, or May*Day*, as the locals pronounce it. The mark of true Padstonians is whether they return home for May Day – and in the rarefied world of Britain's folk scene, Padstow May Day is a rite of passage. You can let your body hair grow, wear jumpers year-round, change your name to Dave and learn the melodeon, but until you've made a pilgrimage to Padstow, well, you're just a folkie wannabe. While Darkie Day remains little known even within Cornwall, Padstow's May Day celebration regularly attracts thousands of spectators – its famous Òbby Oss, or Hobby Horse, has even been copied in America (but don't tell the locals that).

Despite – or perhaps because of – all the ecstatic recommendations from folkie anoraks, I have to admit I wasn't particularly interested in seeing May Day in Padstow. All that talk about folk songs and wheezing accordions, crepe paper and flowers, hobby horses and adults prancing around a maypole . . . it sounded like a twee Victorian interpretation of Merrie England, as practised by hirsute earth-mother pachamamas and pub bores with real ale dribbling down their beards. Inevitably, May Day does attract folkies, but rather than a fossilised relic, it's a living tradition that's fiercely guarded by locals. What's more, it's the counterpoint to Darkie Day. Whereas one consists of a couple of dozen locals blacking up in the depths of winter, the other involves hundreds of Padstonians dressing up in white shirts and trousers to celebrate the coming of summer, accompanied by bands of drums and accordions. Instead of Christmas lights and illuminations on the harbour, colourful streamers, flowery hoops and multicoloured flags adorn the maypole in the market place, along with sycamore branches on every street corner.

For all their black-and-white contrasts, though, Darkie Day and May Day are merely different manifestations of the same community spirit. 'Scratch the Darkies, and May Day's underneath, and vice versa,' says John Buckingham, an Old Padstonian who helps run the town museum. Both events share the same people, the same instruments and similar traditions. Back when the Obby Oss was made of blackened sailcloth, the locals used to smear the tar on each other's faces for good luck. To this day, the Darkies also practise 'smutting' as a way of marking their friends and family and showing membership in the community. Likewise, both traditions involve the locals taking control of the streets and reclaiming 'their' territory. 'May Day is our day,' the locals will tell you, the unspoken corollary being 'and Padstow is our town.' Up until recent decades, the

Second of May used to be known as Darkie Day by some old-timers because they would dress up in costumes and sing a few minstrel songs for charity. Nowadays, the Second has become an extension of May Day itself. After the tourists leave and the iconic Obby Oss has been locked up for the year, the locals parade through the streets with a cardboard mock-up. Inevitably, their path takes them to Rick Stein's restaurant, where few locals can afford to eat. One year, the Oss party decided to enter the restaurant. After the staff tried to stop the Oss, the patrons sided with the locals, and the revellers were allowed to parade through the dining room, exiting via the kitchen. Along the way, the Oss party claimed a number of souvenirs: cutlery, saltshakers and kitchen smocks – *May Day is our day (and Padstow is our town).*

For the record, Padstow actually has two official Obby Osses, neither of which looks anything like a horse. What's more, nobody rides the Osses; their followers take turns incarnating them, becoming 'No Longer Man But Beast', to quote a poem written by Malcolm McCarthy. Folklorists have documented dozens of Hobby Horses around the world (supposedly as many as 150), including a rival May Day tradition up the coast at Minehead in Somerset. The Padstow breed looks like a large round tabletop covered with a shiny black tarp, or skirt. The man inside the Oss sticks his head through a hole in the middle and wears a tall, conical mask. The face has pointy white teeth, a floppy red tongue, and a fluffy white beard and eyebrows, its features painted in bold red-and-white lines on a black background. The mask is topped off with a tuft of black horsehair and a red-white-and-blue ribbon streaming from its tip. With a pointy mask for a head and a black cylinder for a body – plus a token pair of snapping jaws and a tail sticking out either end – the Oss could be a one-man miniature parade float. Instead of gliding sedately through the crowds, though, he lurches around like he's having a fit, pitching and weaving and bucking and whirling, his tail occasionally whacking bystanders as he marks out his territory. A man or woman dances in front of him waving a padded club in the air, but the 'Teazer' has little if any control over the Oss. Occasionally, the beast will charge into the crowd and trap a woman under his skirt. When the music dies down, he sinks to the ground, springing to life once the beat picks up. His white-clad acolytes shout 'Oss Oss!' and the crowd thunders 'Wee Oss!'

When the first outsiders came to see this spectacle, the locals told them strange tales about how they built the Oss to stand guard on the cliffs overlooking the estuary, fending off a French invasion in the fourteenth, eighteenth or nineteenth centuries – the date was sketchy, but then again, Britain and France were always fighting. The townspeople beat drums and made such a ruckus that the foreigners were convinced the black beast staring down at them was the Evil One himself; in a proto-feminist twist, the women of Padstow supposedly manned the cliffs while their menfolk were off besieging Calais in 1347; the would-be invaders saw an army in red cloaks led by a devil and quickly decided to save their souls by sailing away. For Britain's vanguard of professional folklorists, though, this 'aetiological myth' just wasn't good enough. Keen to find relics of the romantic past, they took one look at the Oss's mask, the maypole and the apparent symbols of sex, death and rebirth, and quickly jumped to the conclusion that Padstow's May Day celebration was nothing less than an ancient pagan fertility rite. Over the past century, these outsiders have hailed the Oss as 'Padstow's spring daemon' and lauded Padstow May Day with flowery (and often embarrassing) tributes that reveal more about them than the tradition itself. Thanks to their adulation, an obscure country tradition has been pumped up into 'Cornwall's oldest pagan festival', 'the only European pagan festival which has survived unchristianised', and 'a fierce celebration of the sexual instinct' that's supposedly anywhere from 800 to 4,000 years old.

Of course, Padstow's Obby Oss celebration is so unique – so *exotic* – that some outsiders have concluded it couldn't possibly come from boring old Britain – after all, everybody knows white men can't dance. The famous American anthropologist Margaret Mead compared it to the ritual dancing she studied in the Asia-Pacific, while others have noted similarities between the Oss's mask and those found in Malaysia, New Guinea and even the so-called Dark Continent – providing a neat parallel with Darkie Day.

Padstonians start celebrating May Day on May Eve, preferably in the pub. The home of the original Red Oss is the Golden Lion in the heart of town, a cosy establishment with a low ceiling that comes in handy in case you drink too much. 'You can press the top of your head against it, and that way you know which way is up,' an old-timer tells me. Judging by his West Country comedy nose – the varicose veins turn redder with each drink – I reckon he knows what hc's talking about. With great noise and commotion, a band of men in white march into the pub, armed with accordions, drums and castanets made from rib bones. As the drinks flow towards them, they set up in a corner and start belting out songs, the livelier and louder the better, everything from Cornwall's anthem ('Trelawney') to a sea shanty ('South Australia'), an Irish singalong ('The Wild Rover') and a gospel song ('Old Time Religion' with a Cornish twist), interspersing them with Padstow's very own 'May Song'.

Now, not many tunes can withstand such repetition without driving both singers and listeners insane. Fortunately, the 'May Song' is a happy contagion. Wherever you go on May Day, you can hear the tune echoing across the town. The main reason that Padstow's signature song holds up so well under repetition is that there are two versions, known simply as the 'Night Song' and – wait for it – the 'Day Song'. Both manage to sound simultaneously joyous and solemn, carefree and poignant. Whether by coincidence or not, their refrain echoes Cornwall's motto, *Onen hag Oll* – 'One and All':

> Unite and unite and let us all unite
> For summer is acome unto day
> And whither we are going we all will unite,
> In the merry morning of May.

'The merry morning' actually starts with the Night Singing on May Eve, right after a rowdy procession to the maypole. At midnight, the accordions and drums stop their racket, and the masses quietly retrace their steps through the narrow streets to the Golden Lion. There, amid much shushing and the occasional 'Shut up!', the revellers begin singing a cappella as the landlord and his wife lean out of their window overhead. Although it has the same melody as the jaunty 'Day Song', the nocturnal version is sung more softly, slowly and, crucially, without accompaniment – making it seem more reverential and magical than any of the music that's gone before. For both versions, the lyrics are adapted according to the audience. For instance, when addressing the Golden Lion's landlord (who was also mayor during the Darkie Day controversy), the crowd sings:

> Arise up Mr Rickard, and gold be your ring . . .
> And give to us a cup of ale and the merrier we shall sing
> In the merry morning of May.

This continues well into the wee hours, sometimes as late as five a.m. as the Night Singers go from house to house (and drink to drink), serenading friends and families around Padstow.

May Day proper begins a few hours later, just after daylight. My landlady presents me with a May Day posy, a red-white-and-blue arrangement of a tulip, cowslips and bluebells. Depending on their Oss party affiliation, the locals usually add a red or blue ribbon; as an outsider, I'm advised to stay neutral. 'And you should wear your sprig upside down – after all, you're in Cornwall.'

Upside down? I wonder if maybe they take this pagan stuff more seriously than I thought, but the landlady assures me that the boutonniere is inverted simply to keep it from flopping over as it wilts. At least, that's what she tells me . . .

True to its God-fearing, upstanding origins, the Blue, or 'Temperance', Oss is the earliest to rise, bounding out of the Village Institute at 10 a.m. The Old (Red) Oss doesn't come out for another hour; as the most popular of the two, it can afford to take its time. Men and women in white and red scarves form a ring around the door of the Golden Lion – the same place where they stood for the Night Singing – only this time they're repeating the upbeat 'Day Song' as if to awaken the Old Oss from its slumber. After several minutes, the accordionists emerge from the small pub, ducking under the lintel one by one in a seemingly endless line, pumping up the excitement with their jaunty accompaniment. Next come the drummers, sauntering into the sunshine, their driving rhythms adding yet more urgency. The anticipation builds with each layer of the music – the voices, the accordions, the drums and finally – the Oss! The black beast charges out from the doorway, bucking and lurching and whirling and rolling in the narrow lane as the crowd sings and cheers. The Teazer prances around in front of him, high-stepping and flailing his arms, beating the air with his club. The Oss's followers are belting out the 'May Song', some of them joining arms as they hippety-hop in time to the music. This raucous cavalcade continues up the lane, the Oss occasionally charging into the crowd, the Teazer restraining him as best he can, accompanied by accordions and drums and followed by men, women and children, all dancing and singing through town on this merry morning of May.

In London, 6,000 police are on the streets bracing for yet another May Day riot – a nascent tradition in its own right – yet there are few signs of violence in Padstow, despite the crowds. That's not to say there aren't any fights; after all, festivals traditionally functioned as safety valves. 'May Day is when everything comes out,' a woman explains. 'They'll harbour grudges all year – and I do mean *all year* – but on May Day, they settle it, usually with their fists.' As Rick Stein apparently found out a few years ago at the end of the evening. The story goes that the celebrity chef had finished filming a TV segment and was congratulating the Old Oss party outside the Golden Lion when a drunken reveller punched him in the face, flooring him. 'That was my mate,' brags a Padstonian with a Cornish flag dyed into his hair. 'He told Rick Stein, "Fuck off, this is our day."' Perhaps wisely, Stein prefers not to discuss the alleged incident, 'I really don't think we'd want to comment,' his spokeswoman tells me. So far, I haven't seen any fistfights – or floored chefs – barely able to stay upright – even the followers of the Temperance Oss have fallen off the wagon.

Around six o'clock, the two Osses meet at the maypole and try to outdance each other, their supporters exchanging barbs before setting off again for their final perambulations around town. The evening ends around sunset, with the Osses returning to their stables.

After the final rounds of the 'May Song', the Oss sinks for the last time and the man inside throws it to the ground. Exhausted, emotional – and usually the worse for wear – the Oss's followers gather around the lifeless corpse for the farewell song, a wartime Edwardian ballad designed to wring every last drop of moisture from your eyes:

No more will I behold thee,
Nor in my arms enfold thee . . .
Farewell, farewell, my own true love.

By the end of the warbling chorus, everybody's bawling in one great big weepy hug. The women are crying, the kids are crying, the men are crying – even I'm tearing up – and none of us quite knows why.

As the sun sets on May Day and the Old Oss returns to the pub, the crowds fade away outside the Golden Lion. Down the street, a couple of twentysomethings are hugging and holding hands outside the Chinese takeaway: young love in the springtime. His white clothes and blond hair contrast with her ebony skin and shoulder-length braids: a vision of tolerant, multiracial Britain . . . in the home of Darkie Day.

PART THREE:
THE TWIST

The following Darkie Day, a blacked-up Aunt Jemima bustles through the Golden Lion, joking and singing with the regulars. Every so often, she produces a wedge-shaped make-up sponge stained with greasepaint and smears it across someone's cheek. When she gets to me, though, she takes one look, realises I'm not a local, and quickly moves on, not wanting to risk a confrontation.

The rest of the Darkies are in the front bar, mixing rounds of music and drink, a fitting finale to last night's New Year's Eve celebrations. All the joy of Padstow had been packed into its pubs, with everyone from teenagers to pensioners singing, dancing and having fun. Most had dressed especially for the occasion, masquerading as tramps, GIs or French maids. The landlord of the Old Ship served up pints as Henry VIII, while youngsters frolicked in coordinated costumes as condoms, lager cans and Alice in Wonderland and the Mad Hatter. One group themed itself after London Tube stations: Bond Street did his best to look like 007, while Baker Street wore a chef's smock, a broken baguette and a sign reading: FRANK 'N' STEIN OBE – a dig at the Queen's New Year honour for Padstow's celebrity chef.

Malcolm McCarthy is standing in the doorway, a ginger minstrel with red-and-green tinsel dangling from his bowler and a half pint in his hand. 'I've been on the whisky this morrrnin',' he grins, measuring out a four-inch shot with his fingers.

He and a friend swap stories about the infamous radio show attacking Darkie Day, and how Malcolm was suspiciously cut off just as he tried to counter the critics.

'It's quite difficult because the things you say quite openly can be . . .'

'*Misconstrued*,' they say in stereo.

'And twisted,' Malcolm adds.

If anything, the Darkie Day controversy seems to have rejuvenated the tradition, judging by the number of twenty-somethings involved this year. Last time I talked to Malcolm, he wondered whether the uproar might have hardened youngsters' attitudes. 'Before all this, it was just a *song*,' he said. 'Whether it was the word "banjo" or the word "oss" or the word "nigger", it didn't *matter*; it was just a word in a song. But with all this fuss, I would think for the younger kids, it would make them think, "Right – what's all this about?" And it makes them more aware, and perhaps more prejudiced. Perhaps they may look at it now and think, "Oh, we're takin' the mickey outta the coloured people", whereas we *weren't* – or, we *aren't*, y'know. So it's having the reverse effect, really.'

Of course, kids aren't racist at all, someone says; it's adults who twist things.

A woman listening in nods vigorously. She's wearing everyday clothes, but she has dark make-up smeared on her face. She moved to Padstow fifteen years ago from south London after marrying a native Padstonian. She has no plans to go back. 'My children have roots here, and that's something I never had,' she says. Both her little boys are taking part in Darkie Day: one on accordion, the other on tambourine. Smiling, she tells me about her younger son's reaction when he saw a black man in person for the first time. 'Mummy,' he exclaimed, 'that monkey's walking!'

'And I think he heard,' she winces. 'And I died. I just died.'

And part of me dies with her.

'He'd seen coloured people on TV,' she continues hastily, 'but he'd never seen one in real life, and to him, it was just, y'know, "This is *amazing*." And of course once you explain it to them, they're fine.'

But *still*. In twenty-first-century Britain, how is it possible that a four-year-old could mistake a black man for a monkey? *What kinda local yokels* . . . Maybe it's true what they say about white flight to the West Country; maybe I'm wrong about Padstow.

In between pubs, I slip away to join another transplanted Londoner – Ziggy Holder. Originally, he suggested meeting at noon in his local, the Ship, where I'd spent New Year's Eve. The sight of Padstow's only black man and the Darkies together promised to make an interesting scene, but secretly I was dreading it. As a foreigner interviewing him on Darkie Day, my presence would trigger all sorts of small-town suspicions. After all, I could be writing for the *Black Power Journal*, right?

Ziggy didn't show up, so I gave him a call. His explanation seemed to confirm my own paranoia: 'I am . . . *scared* to go outside, man,' he said, speaking very slowly and deliberately. 'I am . . . absolutely . . . *terrified* –'

Terrified!? Of what?

'– of falling down.'

Ziggy doesn't get out much any more – he doesn't like crowds – so I visited him in his bungalow at the top of town. Despite his health, he's in robust good humour. He tells me how, when he quit the Royal Mail and moved to Padstow in the late 1970s, he stripped off his winter uniform and threw it out of the train at Paddington station. 'Absolutely, man!' he wheezes. 'I chucked *every single thing* – my wristwatch – I haven't worn a wristwatch since then. Look at that' – he holds out a thin brown wrist – 'there's not a single mark there! My whole attitude was to get as far away from that place, and you couldn't pick a place further away than Padstow, could you, really? You couldn't!' He gazes out of the window, past the street to the green, sloping fields trimmed with hedges. 'Movin' down here, I was already home. This is about the most beautiful place you could ever live in, y'know? I go down to the pub, and bet your life, half a dozen people would come up and give me a great big cuddle and whatnot – "Where the hell have you been?" I couldn't have been more . . . welcome,' he concludes, pausing to reflect on his time in Padstow. 'I feel more welcome *here* than I would if I went back to Port of Spain.'

Even with Darkie Day?

He smiles patiently. 'There's no *intent* – that's the key word – there's no intent to be nasty. *Any* sort of offence . . . of black and white friction, has got to be guided by one element: as long as you don't feel threatened, there's no offence. I live here, I don't feel threatened. So let them dance their dance. I will dance with them also.'

ACKNOWLEDGEMENTS

When the Victorian writer Thomas Hughes asked an old-timer one too many questions about the origins of cheese chasing, the exasperated man finally snapped: 'Why can't you be satisfied with my reason? Now you must find one out for yourself.'

Fortunately, the people I interviewed were altogether more patient.

Many thanks to all the gurners, bog snorkellers, Burry Men, horn dancers and other True Brits who took the time to explain to a damn-fool foreigner why they do the things they do. I have done my utmost to get their stories straight, and any mistakes, misunderstandings or cockeyed opinions are strictly my own.

True Brits would not have been possible were it not for the talent-spotting skills of Lizzy Kremer at Ed Victor, the editorial guidance of Anna Cherrett and Lindsay 'Hatchet' Davies at Arrow, as well as the enthusiasm and support of the entire team at Random House/CHA, in particular Lizzy Kingston, Rebecca Ikin, Charlotte Bush, Sarah Pocklington, Faye Brewster and Susan Sandon.

I would also like to thank my confidant, Andrew Young, for his unerring encouragement, Tony Roddam for his spontaneous outbursts, my parents and Jeff and Julie Buck for their divine intercessions, and a host of other kind souls who helped me, often without realising it: Elena Orrego, Nancy Caceres, Matt Galimi, Mike Butti, Jonathan Birt, Edna Fernandes, Andrew Atkinson, Colin and Colette Crone, Abby Bowen, Finbar Hawkins, Will Richards, Abigail Levene, Hans de Jongh, Jean and Richard Jefferies, George and Binita McClintock, Elizabeth Haylett and Angela Wigglesworth.

I have also had some of the best mentors in the business: namely, Bob Mann, James Brooke and the late George Short, plus the all-knowing Dr D. R. (Doc) Rowe.

Of course, my most heartfelt gratitude goes to Malena, who brings new meaning to the term 'long-suffering wife' (sorry about that recurring cheese-rolling nightmare).

Finally, a word to wise readers. Traditions don't just happen: they're easily lost, yet hard to maintain. The extraordinary events in *True Brits* have survived down the centuries purely because of the hard work and sacrifice of their local guardians. To support them directly or indirectly, please see *www.truebrits.tv* for details.

J.R. Daeschner
London